The urban and cultural climate of Rotterdam changed radically between 1970 and 2000. Opinions differ about what the most important changes were, and when they occurred. *Imagine a Metropolis* shows that it was first and foremost a new perspective on Rotterdam that stimulated the development of the city during this period. If the Rotterdam of 1970 was still a city with an identity crisis that wanted to be small rather than large and cosy rather than commercial, by 2000 Rotterdam had the image of the most metropolitan of all Dutch cities. Artists and other cultural practitioners – a group these days termed the 'creative class' – were the first to advance this metropolitan vision, thereby paving the way for the New Rotterdam that would begin to take concrete shape at the end of the 1980s. *Imagine a Metropolis* goes on to show that this New Rotterdam is returning to its nineteenth-century identity and the developments of the inter-war years and the period of post-war reconstruction.

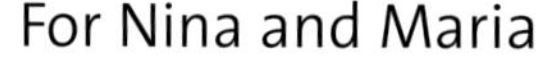

For Nina and Maria

IMAGINE A METROPOLIS ROTTERDAM'S CREATIVE CLASS, 1970-2000

PATRICIA VAN ULZEN

010 Publishers, Rotterdam 2007

This publication was produced in association with Stichting Kunstpublicaties Rotterdam. On February 2, 2007, it was defended as a Ph.D. thesis at the Erasmus University, Rotterdam. The thesis supervisor was Prof. Dr. Marlite Halbertsma.

The research and this book were both made possible by the generous support of the Faculty of History and Arts at the Erasmus University Rotterdam, G.Ph. Verhagen-Stichting, Stichting Kunstpublicaties Rotterdam, J.E. Jurriaanse Stichting, Prins Bernhard Cultuurfonds Zuid-Holland and the Netherlands Architecture Fund.

Research and text Patricia van Ulzen
Editing and correction of the original Dutch
Els Brinkman
Translation John Kirkpatrick
Graphic design Via Vermeulen/ Rick Vermeulen
Printed by Die Keure, Brugge

Picture credits
Gemeentearchief Rotterdam pp. 46, 52, 54, 65, 69, 74, 113, 132, 156, 176, 196-197; Hotel New York pp. 206; Joris Ivens Archief, ESJI, Nijmegen/Estate Germaine Krull, Museum Folkwang, Essen pp. 51; Ted Langenbach pp. 141, 203; Viktor Mani pp. 142, 145, 152; Paul Martens pp. 12, 14, 15; Men At Work TV Produkties pp. 26; Nederlands Fotomuseum pp. 113; Neon Film-TV pp. 80; Hans Oldewarris pp. 108, 120, 127, 135, 136, 138-139, 141, 145, 146-147, 150, 152, 175; Hajo Piebenga pp. 96-97, 190; Hal 4 pp. 102, 123, 124, 125, 141; Bas van der Ree pp. 21; Chiel van der Stelt pp. 150; Patricia van Ulzen pp. 6, 9, 10, 24, 26, 65, 68, 120, 176, 180, 192; Rick Vermeulen pp. 32, 61, 62-63, 86, 87, 89, 90-91, 92, 118, 152, 162; Louis Verschoor pp. 115, 118, 119, 127; Hans Werlemann pp. 145; Hans Wilschut pp. 214

ISBN 978-90-6450-621-5

The Dutch edition has been published as *Dromen van een metropool. De creatieve klasse van Rotterdam 1970-2000* (ISBN 978-90-6450-620-8)

Table of Contents

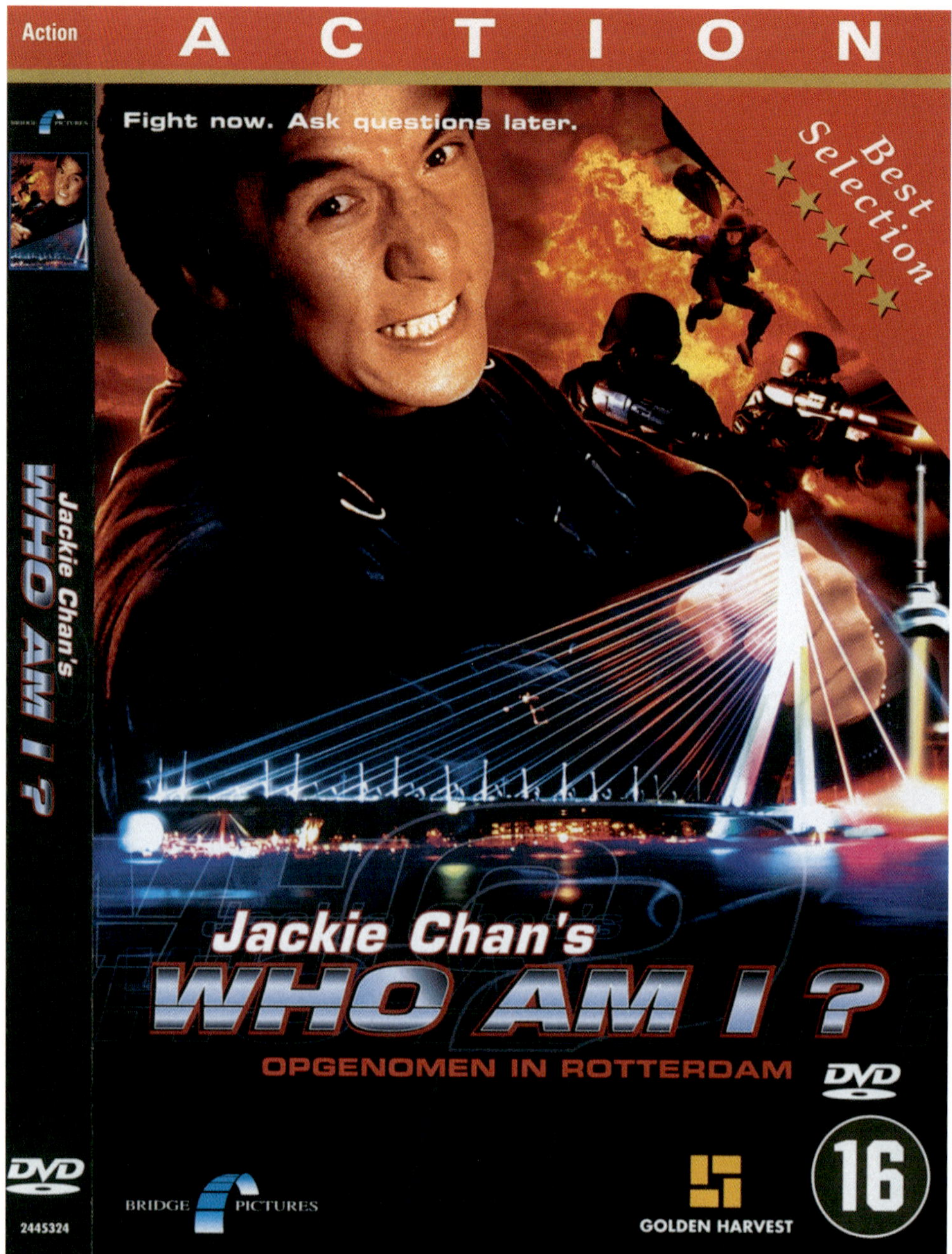

DVD cover of the Jackie Chan film *Who Am I?*, first shown in 1998.

'When everything proves an illusion, illusion is the thing that remains'

(lines by Jan Koonings printed on dustcarts in Rotterdam)

When I embarked on the research that ultimately produced this book, my working title for it translated as 'Rotterdam Cultural City 1970–2001'. My study was to dovetail into Paul van de Laar's recent standard work on the history of Rotterdam in the 19th and 20th centuries, *Stad van formaat*.[1] It was to pick up where his book (whose title translates as 'City of stature') leaves off, that is, at the year 1975, but above all it was to resolve the issues stated at the close of his introduction: 'Has Rotterdam shaken off its image of a city of work? Will Rotterdammers of the 21st century witness a shift in their city's image from city of work to city of culture?'[2] Broadly speaking, I envisaged a study on Rotterdam's cultural development since 1970 that would end with a provisional peak: its nomination as European Capital of Culture for 2001. It soon dawned in me, however, that an approach along these lines could only lead to an enumerative, defensive and ultimately meaningless result. Perhaps I should explain.

How was I to try to convince my readers that Rotterdam had made impressive advances on the cultural front during the period in question? By showing how many cultural activities and organizations have been added during those 30 years, and by drawing attention to the high quality of the culture on offer at the end as compared to the beginning. In other words, by enumerating and defending.

This was an undertaking I was not exactly looking forward to, and I suspected I would not be doing my readers any favours by pursuing it. Besides, what would it prove? Rotterdam would still be a dwarf in cultural terms in comparison with New York, London, Paris or even Amsterdam. Well-meaning readers might feel respect for the achievements of those Rotterdammers who have stimulated culture in their city. Others might find the enumeration not merely irritating but pedantic as well. And in the meantime that book would have seen me exchange scholarship for a new career in city marketing. Altogether not the most appetizing prospect!

And yet. Friend and foe are agreed that something of Rotterdam changed dramatically in the years 1970–2000. But opinions vary as to what the most important changes were, and when they took place. I decided to choose an aspect that showed the change better than any other, namely the city's representation in about 2000 as compared with that in 1970. If Rotterdam in 1970 was still a city with an identity crisis, a city that wanted to be small instead of big and cosy instead of rational, at century's end it was presented as the most metropolitan of all Dutch cities. This is an aspect of Rotterdam only latently present in the literature. It is a phenomenon that has never been seriously explored, though it is familiar to everyone. How is Rotterdam presented as a metropolis in words and images as the third millennium dawns?

Rotterdam the metropolis

Rotterdam has the reputation of being a metropolis, an image that has become stronger than ever at the turn of the 21st century. Whenever Rotterdam gets mentioned in the mass media, it is almost always accompanied by the term world city (*wereldstad*) or metropolis, sometimes in passing, sometimes with emphasis. This holds as much for the independent media as for the city's promotional material.[3] Even authors who feel that Rotterdam is *not* a world city draw attention to its metropolitan image – and then ridicule it.[4] The term *wereldstad* seems to have become synonymous with Rotterdam, along with its derivatives international city, world port city (*wereldhavenstad*), modern city, real city, bustling city, cosmopolitan city... These metropolitan words have metropolitan images to go with them. Rotterdam looks like a major metropolis whenever the skyline on the banks of the river is brought into view, its tall modern buildings conjuring up the expression 'Manhattan on the Maas'. The image obtained by photographing Rotterdam from a plane or the top of a tall building, preferably in a broad, panoramic format, is of a modern high-rise city extending to the horizon on all sides.

The *Rotterdam City Map* of 2001 is a clear example of such a deliberately metropolitan image. Aimed at tourists, this street map of Rotterdam is published and distributed free of charge by Rotterdam Marketing & Promotion. What is remarkable about the 2001 edition is first of all its emphasis on high-rise and on modern architecture. In its folded state it shows three tall, colourfully illuminated

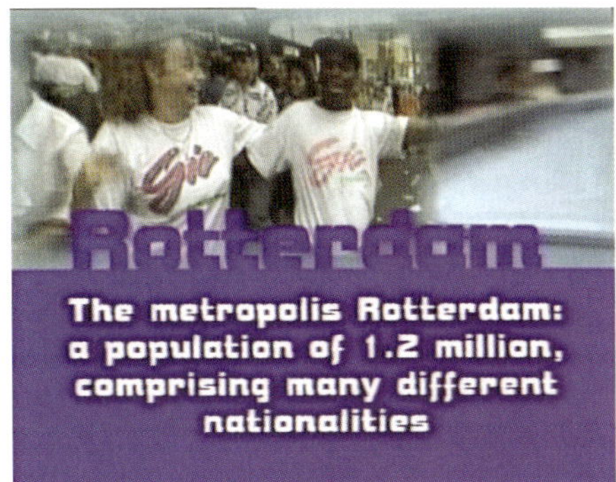

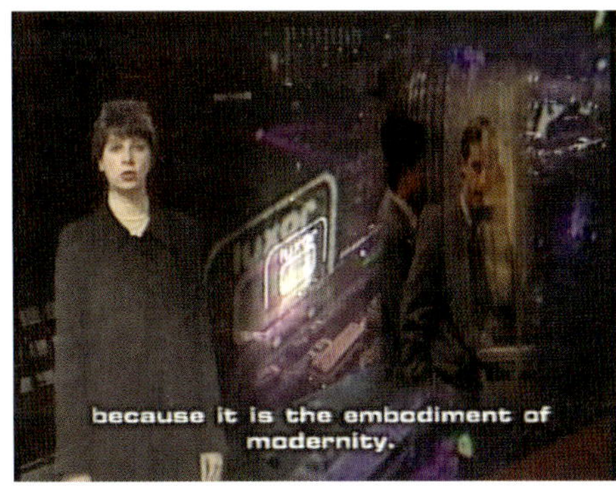

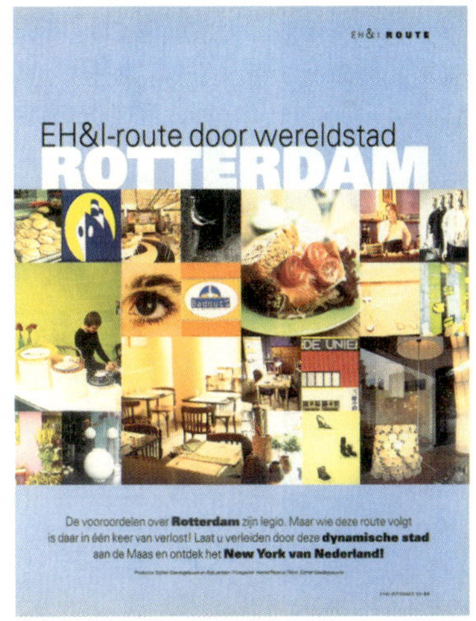

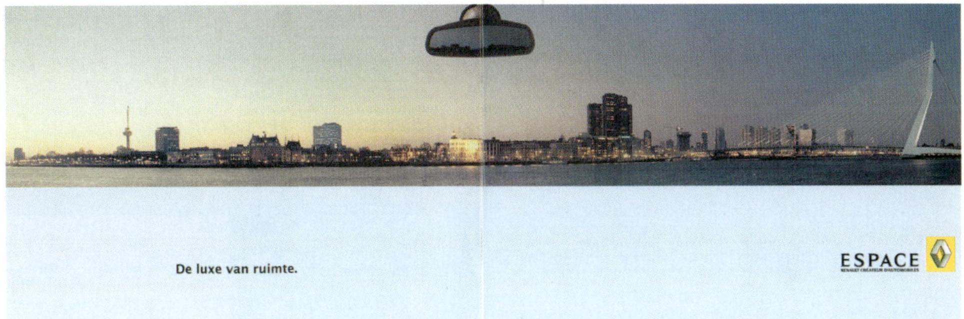

Top stills from the promotional video *Rotterdam Cultural Capital of Europe*, Neon Film/TV, 1997. This film was shot by Bob Visser at the behest of the council to get the city designated European Capital of Cultural 2001. In it, Rotterdam is described as a 'metropolis' and made to seem bigger than it really is, not least by regarding everyone in the region as a Rotterdammer. The metropolitan image is strengthened by verbally and visually referring to Rotterdam's internationality and modernity. It introduces another stereotypical characteristic of a metropolis: the city lights at night.

Middle first page of a supplement on Rotterdam in the home design magazine *Eigen Huis & Interieur*, September 1999. Rotterdam is eulogized as 'a world city' and 'the New York of the Netherlands'.

Bottom example of the Rotterdam skyline used for commercial ends, published in *M Magazine*, May 2006.

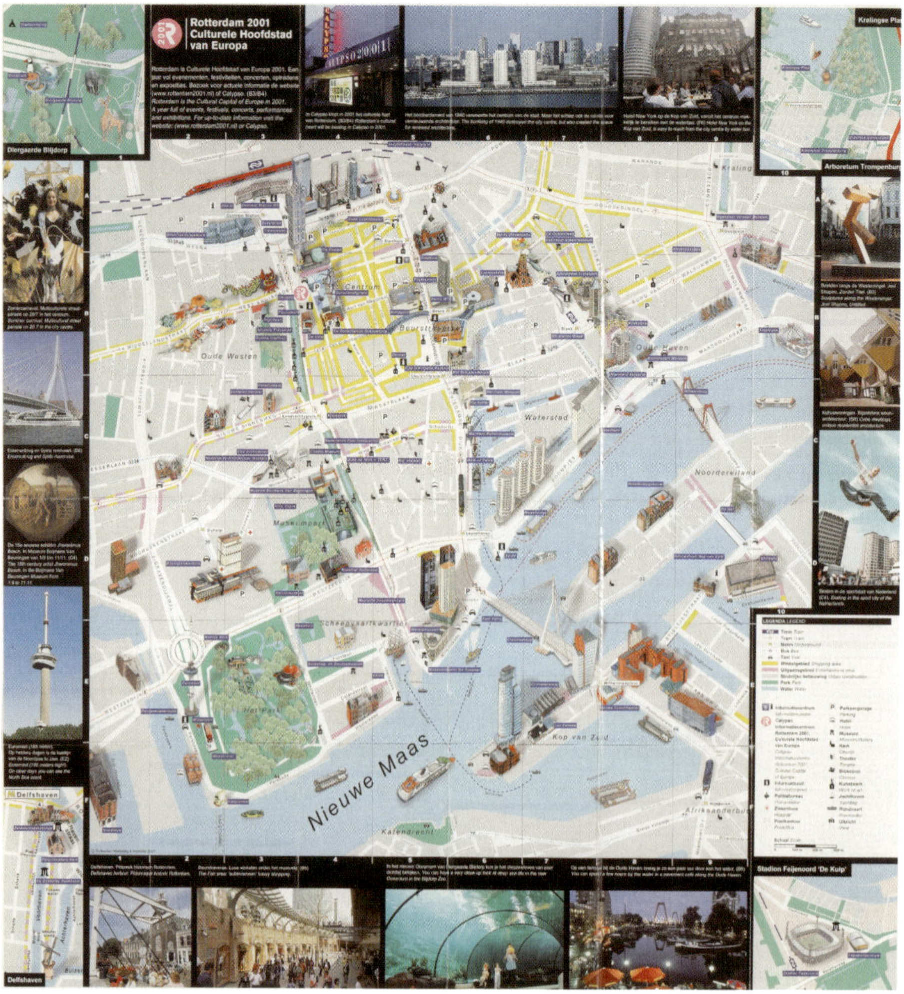

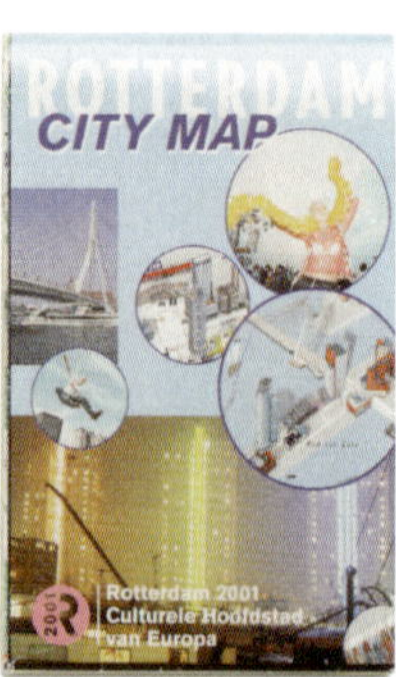

Rotterdam City Map 2001. A clear example of a constructed metropolitan image of the city. In its folded state the map shows two stereotypical characteristics of a metropolis: high-rise and city lights.

buildings at twilight and details from the map inside with tall buildings drawn onto them. Open it up and you have an illustrated map of the centre of Rotterdam in which the positions of buildings and attractions of note are indicated with perspective drawings. All sides of the map are lined with photographs and accompanying texts giving extra weight to certain aspects of the city. The hypermodern, high-rise development at Kop van Zuid and on the banks of the river Maas is drawn bigger than the buildings more to the north, suggesting an aerial view of Rotterdam from the south. This emphasis on high-rise is driven home by the inclusion at the far left of the map of a tall building of no tourist interest whatsoever and located some way from the centre, namely the former electricity company building on Rochussen-straat. Its only distinguishing feature is that it is one of Rotterdam's oldest 'sky-scrapers'. Modern high-rise is likewise given emphasis in the photographs framing the map, featuring in no less than seven of the fourteen shots. The caption to the second photograph clockwise at the top, a prospect of high-rise on the north bank of the Maas, brings Rotterdam's profile as a city of modern architecture into sharper relief: 'The bombing of 1940 destroyed the city centre, but also created the space for renewed architecture.' The photograph itself suggests a much larger city than Rotterdam is in reality. This metropolitan image is underpinned by shots of subjects traditionally associated with a metropolis. The photo at top left of a non-Western looking woman illustrates Rotterdam's international ambience. The caption explains: 'Summer carnival. Multicultural street parade on 28.7 in the city centre'. Rotterdam's multicultural life spills over onto the map itself, notably at its most multicultural street, West-Kruiskade, which is illustrated with drawings of a Chinese dragon and all kinds of exotic vegetables and fruits. Further, various photographs illustrate the city's street life and entertainment in such a way as to give the impression of a vibrant urban climate. The dazzle of night-time lighting is a proven means of visualizing Rotterdam as a bustling city that 'never sleeps' and this map draws on this aspect. And lastly, a shot of a skater in action symbolizes Rotterdam as a modern, dynamic city with provision for youth culture.

Whether one takes these metropolitan words and images as gospel or not, it cannot be denied that Rotterdam does keep up metropolitan appearances. I have taken those appearances as the stepping-off point for my research. The working title of 'Rotterdam Cultural City' accordingly changed to 'Imagine a Metropolis'. In this book the question of whether Rotterdam is a metropolis is not asked, let alone answered. Instead it proceeds from the fact that Rotterdam the metropolis is an illusion that is deceptively real and cherished by millions of people. The illusion is kept going by words and images that reach a wide audience. In most cases there is no question of deliberate city marketing: producers of metropolitan images operating in the free market or the makers of television productions react specifically to the demands of their clients. This is evident from the success of, say, Paul Martens' photographs.

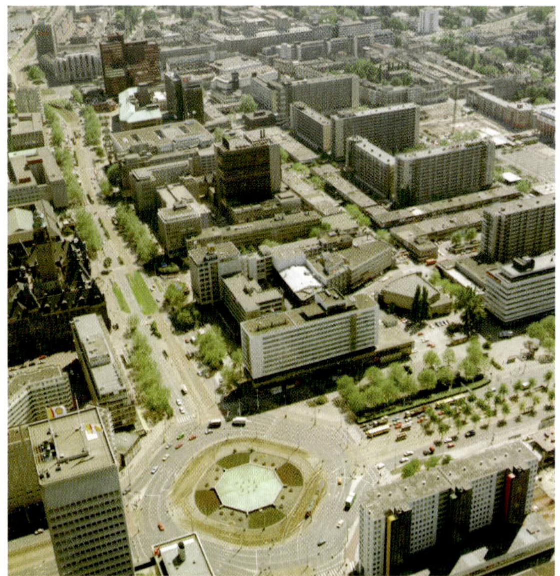

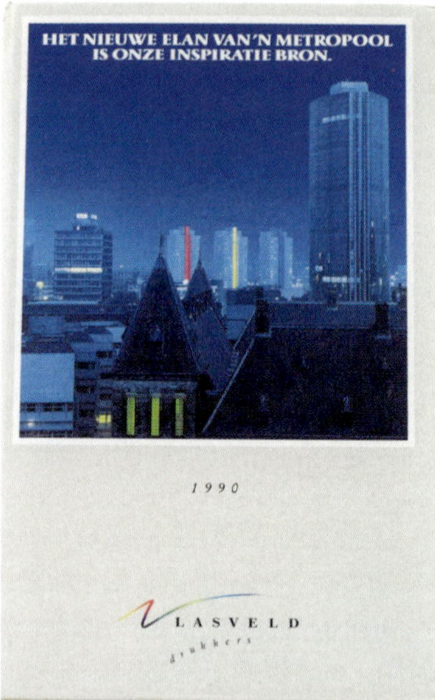

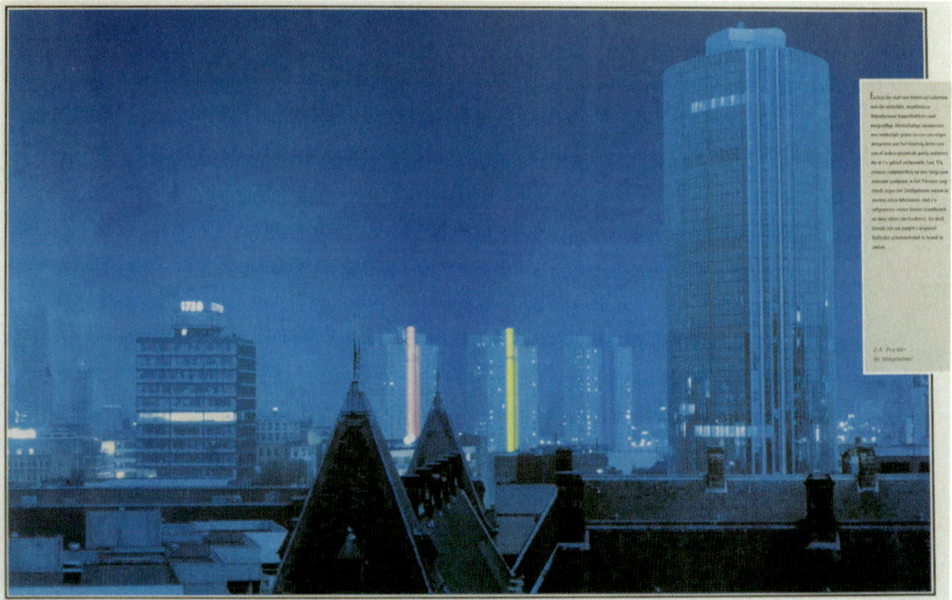

Top left Paul Martens, aerial view of Rotterdam, 1985.

Top right calendar for Vlasveld printing house, 1990, photo by Paul Martens.

Bottom page from calendar for Vlasveld, 1989, photo by Paul Martens, text by Jules Deelder.

A perfect dream reality: the photographs of Paul Martens

If we proceed from the panoramic colour shots of Rotterdam taken by the photographer Paul Martens, Rotterdam is a city that can easily hold its own with such metropolises as New York or Tokyo. Martens manages to capture the city's image in such a way that Rotterdam seems prodigiously vast with a skyline that is in no way inferior to those of the major American cities, and holds the promise of an urban life that is not only dynamic during the day but perpetuated at night. Paul Martens is not the only one to represent the city along such lines, as is evident from the above. However, there are three aspects that make his work special. First of all, Martens succeeded in capturing Rotterdam in this way in the second half of the 1980s, before the skyline was anything like as impressive as it is today – 'it still looked pretty shabby', as he himself puts it. Another aspect is that Martens was inspired in the first event not by reality but by books of examples of city panoramas which he had studied and admired during his training. He has perfected this manner of urban representation to the point that in principle he can photograph any city and make it look like an impressive metropolis. And lastly, Martens' work has a prodigious circulation, as he has postcards, posters and calendars made in high print runs and distributed at a great many generally accessible sales points.[5] We can therefore assume that his image of Rotterdam has been extremely influential and still is.

At the end of 1979 Paul Martens opened a modest photographer's shop in the Rotterdam district of Delfshaven. His work then chiefly consisted of photo reports and portraits. He began taking aerial photos of Rotterdam from a small plane purely for his own pleasure and placed them in the window of his shop. He noticed that these sold particularly well and elicited enthusiastic reactions from clients and passers-by. In 1982 he began receiving occasional commissions to photograph buildings in Rotterdam. A major commission came his way in early 1987 from Van Stijkel and Ballast Nedam, the developer and contractor, respectively, of the Willemswerf office tower. This building designed by architect Wim Quist on the Maas Boulevard was still under construction and photos were required to aid deliberation on how to proceed further. An accomplished mountaineer at the time, Martens for this commission decided to climb the 120 metre tall construction crane equipped with fall protection and steel mountaineering boots. Having arrived at the top he took the opportunity to take photographs of the city as well; these also ended up in his shop window in Delfshaven.

Van Stijkel and Ballast Nedam kept coming with the commissions and Martens' 'Rotterdam' work began to gain a reputation. This led among other things to a calendar of Rotterdam photos made by the Van Vliet advertising agency in 1989 at the behest of the Rotterdam printer Vlasveld. Each of its 12 pages featured one of Martens' photos accompanied by lines of poetry by Jules Deelder, some of which came from his nationally famous poem of 1977, *Stadsgezicht* ('Cityscape'). The photos Martens provided included views of Rotterdam in the evening and at night,

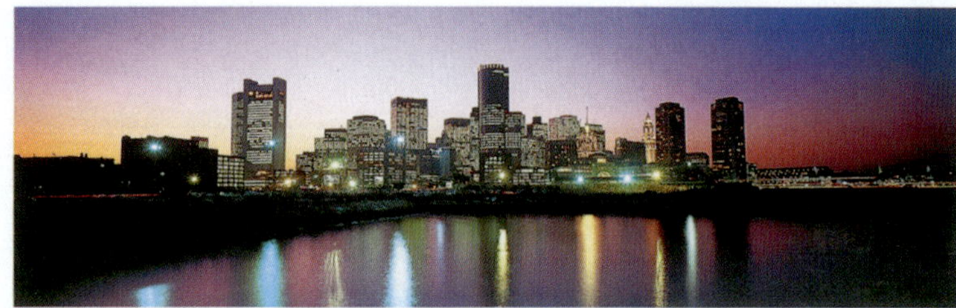

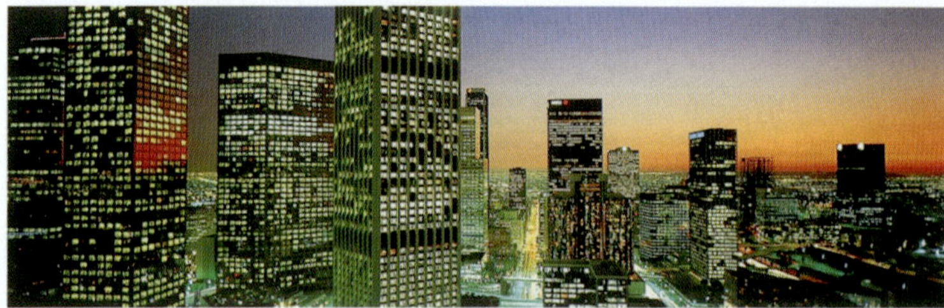

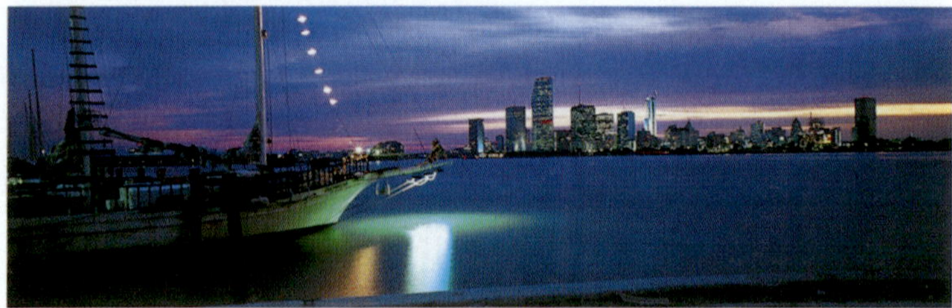

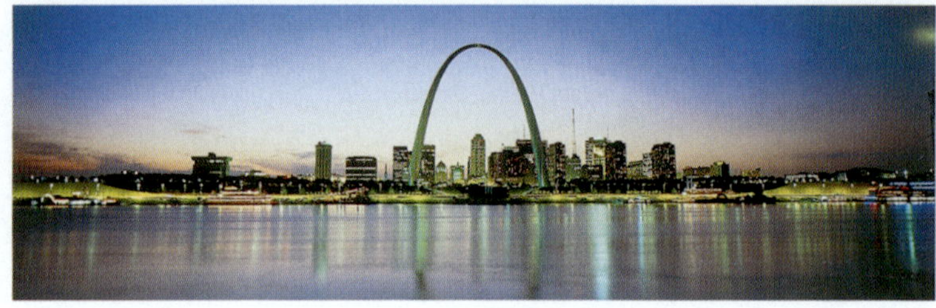

Photos from the Photothèque Mon-Trésor publication, **from top**: Boston, Los Angeles, Miami and St. Louis. The shots include a number of regular ingredients suggestive of metropolitan status.

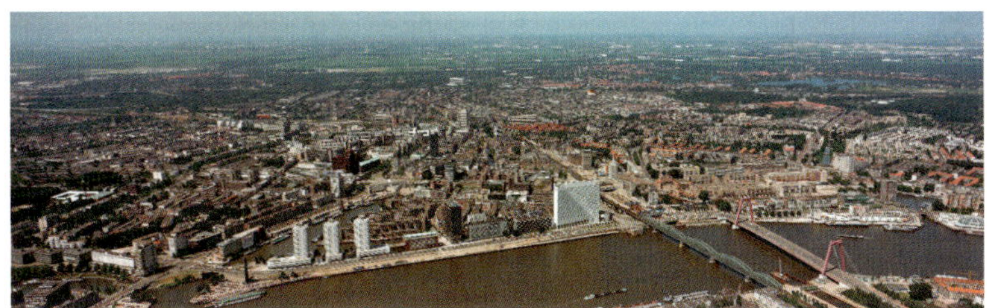

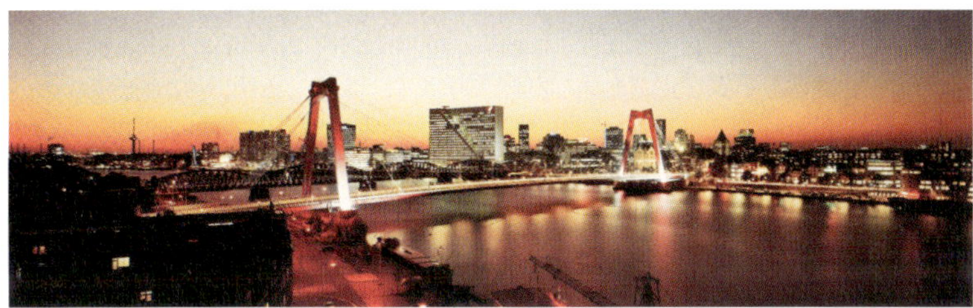

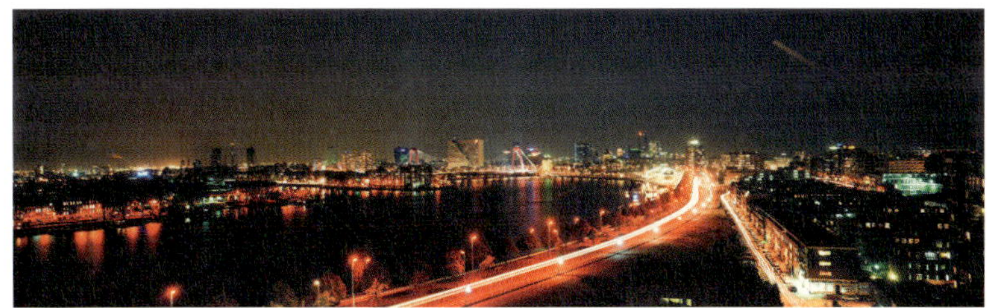

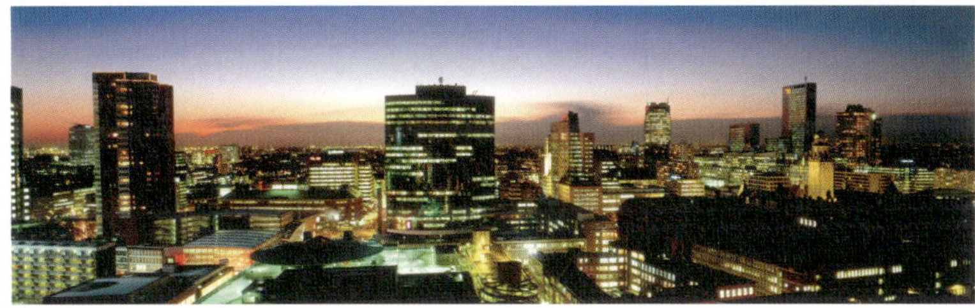

Photos by Paul Martens, **from top**: Rotterdam, 1989; Rotterdam, 1990 (Christmas card for Gemeentelijke Grondbedrijf); Rotterdam, 1990 (Christmas card); Rotterdam, 2006.

Rotterdam's Hofplein roundabout at night and a shot of a Rotterdam metro station.

Martens' work was also noticed by Gemeentelijke Grondbedrijf, the fore-runner of today's City Development Corporation (Ontwikkelingsbedrijf Rotterdam). In 1990 this local governmental organization used one of Martens' photographs for its Christmas cards for business contacts, in a print run of between 5000 and 6000. Grondbedrijf would use work by Martens for other Christmases too. It now became clear that these photos were ideal for picture postcards. Other large commissions for Christmas cards came in 1990 from a major publisher of illustrated cards. There were large print runs involved, sometimes more than 10,000 for each card.

In 1989 Martens first made use of a panorama camera for his city shots, a technique that would become his trademark. During his professional training as a photographer he had been intrigued by panoramic shots of cities and landscapes and owned magazines and books containing panoramic photos. These overviews of panoramic photographs were a key source of inspiration for Martens. A book he has made use of since the mid 1990s – the book itself is undated – is a publication by Bildagentur Bavaria exclusively of panoramic photos on order from Photothèque Mon-Trésor. Besides many photos of nature and others with a rural-picturesque theme, the book included some 56 panorama shots with a clearly urban demeanour. These photos mainly of American metropolises exhibit a number of recurring traits. First of all, they are obviously extremely broad with a ratio of about 1 (height) to 3 (breadth). This format alone suggests metropolitan status: it means that the city is too expansive to fit into the customary format. This suggestion is consolidated by the fact that often buildings, bridges or roads are cropped on the left- and right-hand sides of the photo – a sign that the image extends even further. Secondly, high-rise is invariably in evidence. Thirdly, main roads and bridges are brought out, particularly after dark, by the lines of light produced by moving vehicles using a long exposure time. Remarkably many shots are taken at dusk or in darkness. Then the big city is at its most magical, with the lights of its streets, the advertisements and the windows of buildings. There is, clearly, a more or less fixed iconography of the metropolis; the presence of a number of established characteristics are indicative of the metropolitan condition. Paul Martens has come to master this iconography perfectly, for his Rotterdam panoramas of recent years would not be out of place amidst all this metropolitan spectacle.

The metropolitan dream that Martens gave visual form to from the end of the 1980s on, certainly struck a chord with the public at large. 'Do you have any more photos of the skyline?', was at one time the question most frequently asked in the shop in Delfshaven. That question has been largely instrumental in guiding the direction of his output. Over the years he has reached more and more people by producing picture postcards, calendars and posters himself and enlisting the services of a distributor. In 1993, for the first time, he himself produced several picture postcards of Rotterdam in a print run of roughly 1000 per postcard. Since then the size of runs has been increasing steadily. These days the cards are sold at some

120 places in Rotterdam, set in their own revolving display rack emblazoned with the name of the photographer. The 44 postcards in the rack are regularly replenished. Since 1994 Martens has been making panorama calendars with views of Rotterdam, in runs that have increased in recent years to several thousands. Those of his posters vary between hundreds and thousands per item. They are usually sold out fast and are replaced every two years or so with new posters. Martens works almost exclusively in colour although he does make black-and-white prints on request. The fact that his work sells so well means that the metropolitan dream of Rotterdam is a popular one. It also means that this photographer's perspective on Rotterdam lends direction to how millions of people see that city. But how they see it is as much driven by the way Rotterdam figures on television and in films.

Rotterdam the metropolitan film set

In the 1990s Rotterdam became popular as a film location, particularly when a metropolitan environment needed suggesting. Makers of commercials as well as independent film directors often choose to shoot in Rotterdam whenever they require a metropolitan setting. It was the Hong Kong-based director and actor Jackie Chan who opened the eyes of other film-makers to Rotterdam's potentials as a film location. In 1997 Chan shot much of the film *Who Am I?* in Rotterdam, and this made such an impression that many other film-makers would follow suit.[6] People with a knowledge of Rotterdam can recognize many of the places in *Who Am I?*, even in the part that takes place in South Africa. Unquestionably, the key Rotterdam location in the film is the aforementioned Willemswerf, a tall white office slab on the north bank of the river, whose diagonal wedge in the facade is a major visual element in the Rotterdam skyline. Not only is it the office of the bad guys, it is also the location where the film's most spectacular stunt is enacted. Chan, who also plays the lead, devised this perilous feat – sliding down the steep glass slope – while standing on the building's roof looking down.

In part one of *Who Am I?*, which takes place in South Africa, locations in Rotterdam are used to suggest an anonymous modern metropolis interchangeable with any other modern city. After just under an hour, the main characters announce they are to take a plane to Rotterdam, and the second part begins with an introduction to the city. The viewer first sees an overcast Dutch sky, after which the camera sweeps down for a panoramic view of the river Maas – made to look extremely wide by the type of lens used – the red Willems Bridge and the buildings lining the two banks. A smooth transition then leads to a new shot, of the Willemswerf building, followed by a camera movement from the left that ends with a view through the windows of a café opposite Willemswerf.

In the Rotterdam segment of *Who Am I?* the city is mostly filmed from the baddies' office in Willemswerf and from the roof of the building. What we see are impressive images of a large, modern high-rise city. All Rotterdam's urban landmarks

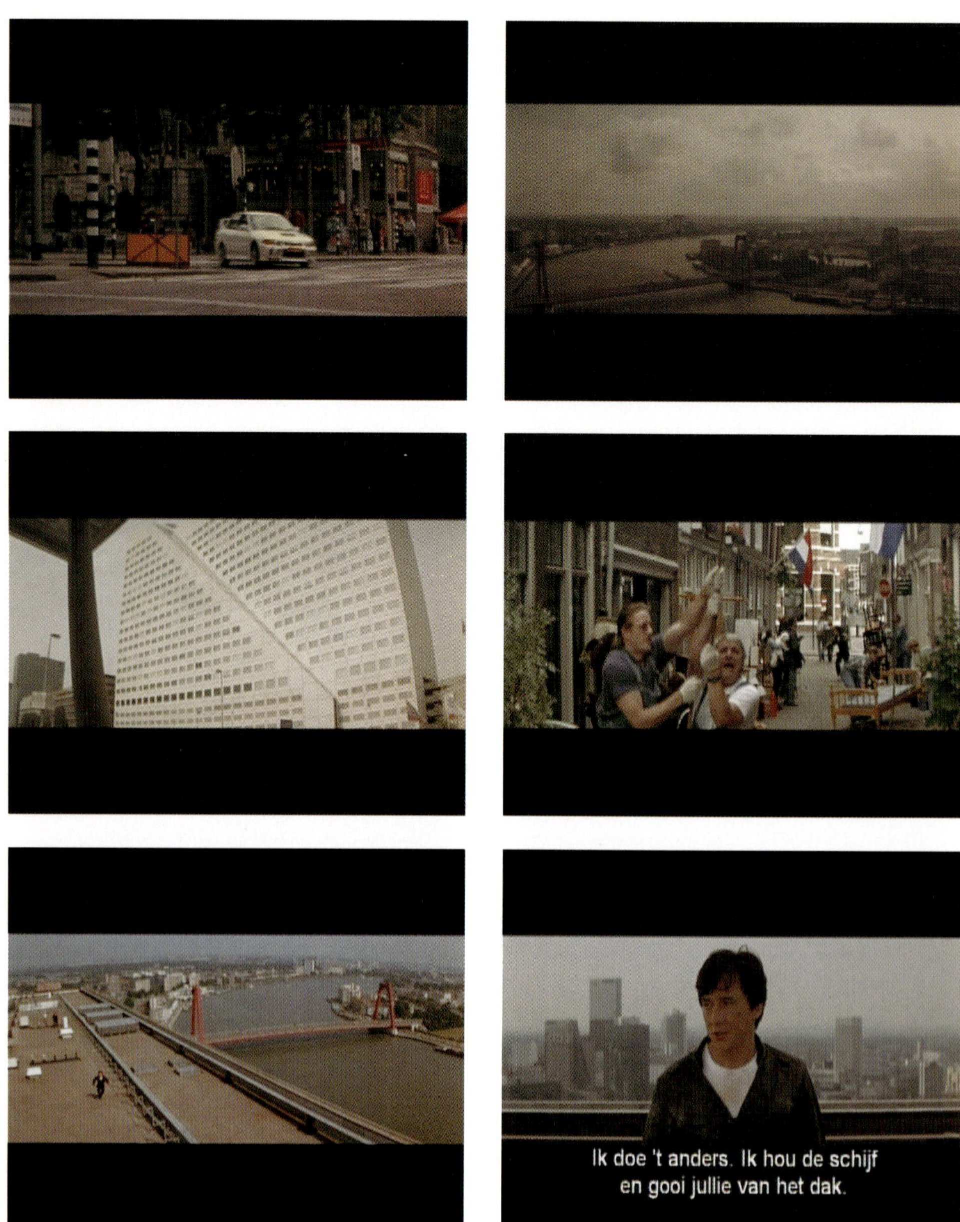

Stills from the Jackie Chan film *Who Am I?*, 1998.

Top left chase scene in an anonymous modern metropolis in South Africa, shot on Coolsingel in Rotterdam; **right** first shot of Rotterdam; **middle left** first shot of the Willemswerf building; **right** typically Dutch scene enacted in Rotterdam according to the script but shot in Dordrecht; **bottom** well-known Rotterdam buildings come into view during the fight scene on the roof of Willemswerf.

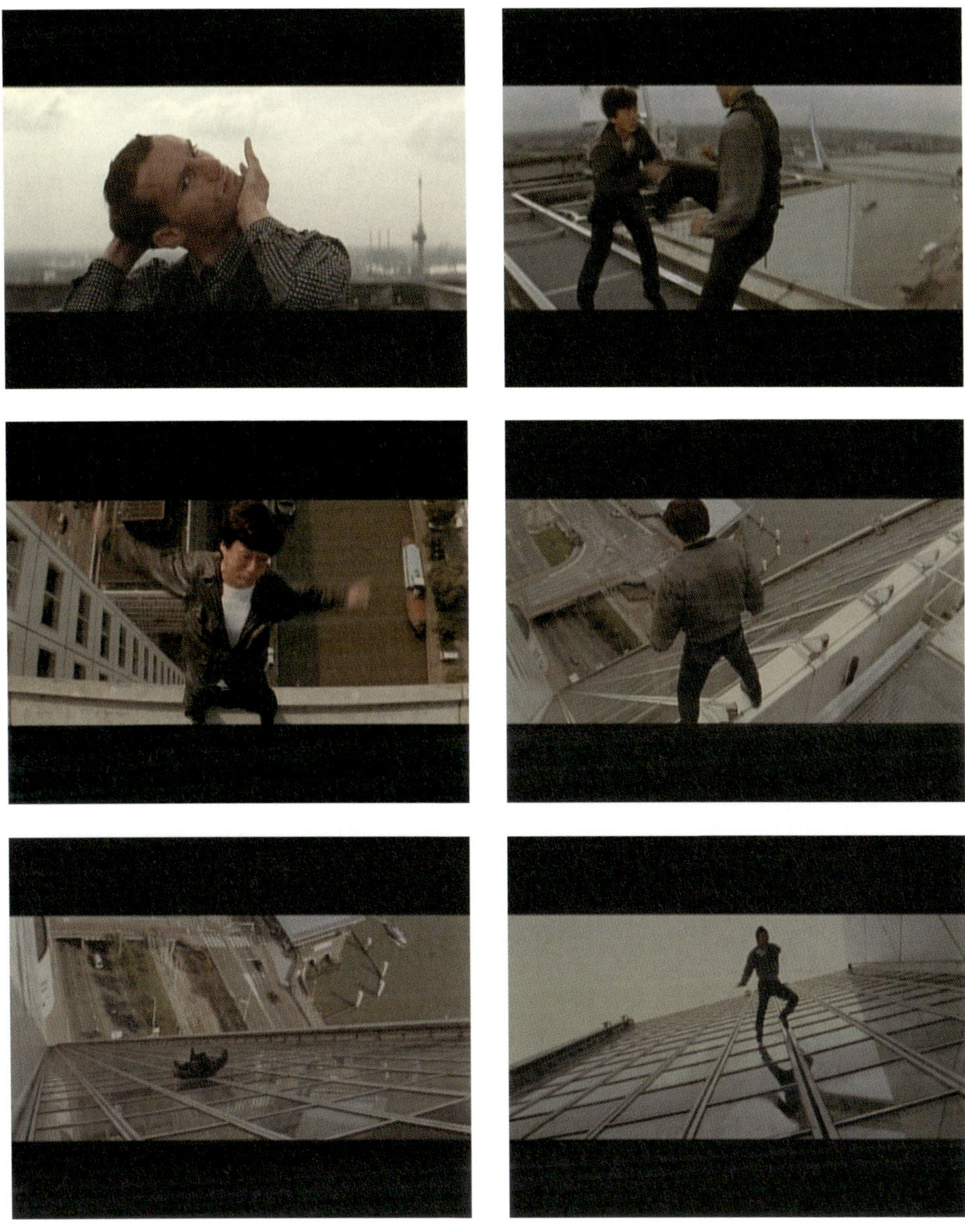

Top left in the background is the Euromast, which for years was the urban icon of Rotterdam; right fight scene on the roof of Willemswerf with today's urban icon, the Erasmus Bridge, in the background; middle and bottom four moments during the stunt on the steep glass slope of Willemswerf.

– Erasmus Bridge, Euromast, Hotel New York – are there. Willemswerf itself is shot
as a smooth, hypermodern, inaccessible, white, anonymous building. Whereas
locations in Rotterdam do duty in the South-African part, as we have seen, the
Rotterdam part features a location in Dordrecht! This was required to provide the
necessary local colour: there is an Old Dutch cobbled street graced with flower boxes
where household goods are hauled up the facades by lifting beam, there are Dutch
flags flying, there is a shot of a barrel organ and during the chase scene that unfolds
here, a colossal rack of clogs is sent flying. There is even a female extra in traditional
Dutch dress. This scene contrasts starkly with the other images of Rotterdam, un-
characteristic of the Netherlands as these are.

　　According to Bas van der Ree, who was a location scout for *Who Am I?*, more
than 213 million people have seen the film worldwide. In the Netherlands, moreover,
there was quite a lot of publicity surrounding the location shooting in Rotterdam.
The NOS news telecast on October 3, 1997 showed images of the film set on the
Erasmus Bridge. The front page of the July 30, 1997 edition of the national daily
Algemeen Dagblad featured a shot of Chan and his father fishing between takes
near that same bridge. This alerted many Dutch people who would never go to a
martial arts action film like *Who Am I?* to the fact that a major international film
production was under way in Rotterdam. The bridge had to be closed for a full two
days during the shooting. Van der Ree had the full cooperation of the council on
this matter, particularly mayor Bram Peper and aldermen Hans Kombrink and Hans
Simons, as they warmed to Van der Ree's argument that the upheaval would in fact
produce positive publicity for the city. According to Van der Ree, *Who Am I?* gave
Rotterdam 'a big push in the right direction' as a film city.

　　And indeed, as the 1990s came to a close, Rotterdam was making more
and more appearances in films, commercials and television series. This was not
entirely due to Jackie Chan, however. Back in 1996, at the city council's instigation,
the Rotterdam Film Fund had been set up with the aim of stimulating film activity
in the city. The key tool to this end was (and still is) the provision of rent-free loans on
condition that 200 per cent of the sum loaned is spent in Rotterdam's audiovisual
sector. Another condition is that the subsidized films are about Rotterdam and contribute to Rotterdam's image in the eyes of the world.[7]

　　At the bilingual website of the Rotterdam Fund for the Film and AV Media,
as they call themselves nowadays (or RFF for short), you can find a wealth of visual
material related to locations in Rotterdam as well as all kinds of practical information. Rotterdam emerges from this as a sleek, spacious, gleaming, hypermodern
world city. This, according to Bas van der Ree, is the Rotterdam that draws most
film-makers here. This is why Van der Ree would prefer it if all greenery in the city,
trees and other plantings, was got rid of: 'I don't understand this desire to lay on
masses of green in a large city. I've nothing against greenery, say in parks, but it
spoils the look of the architecture, the facades. From the end of April to September
the city is a lot less interesting to me, as all those facades are hidden from view.

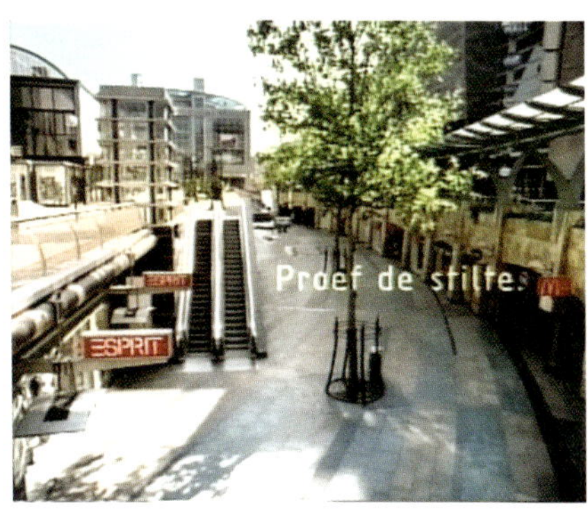

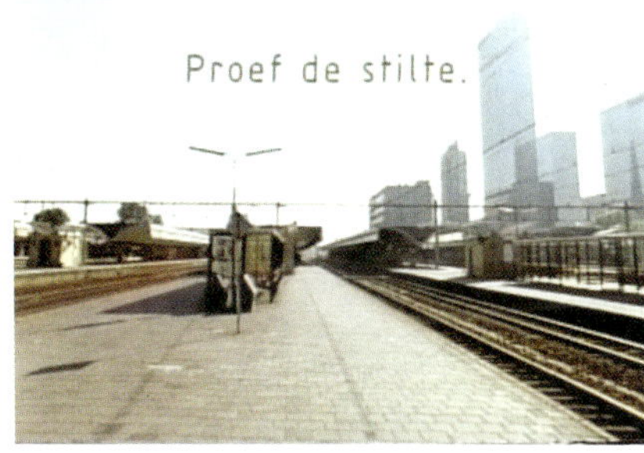

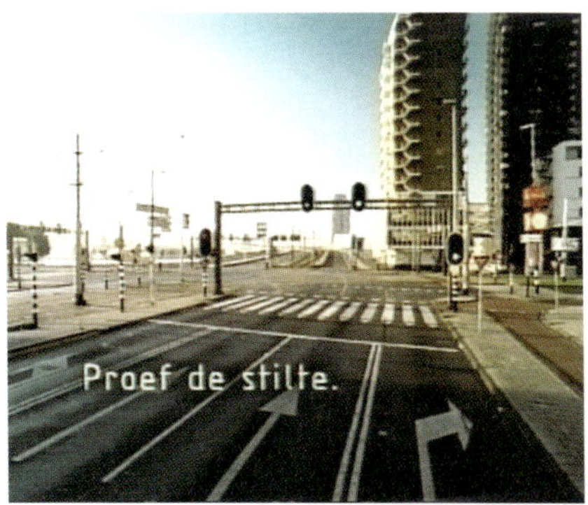

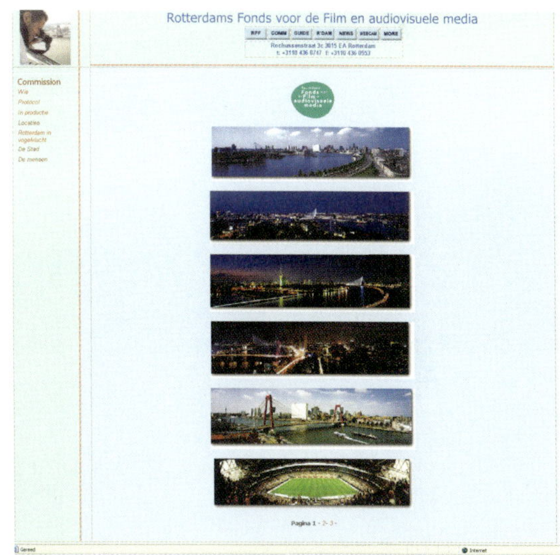

Stills from TV commercials ('Taste the silence') for La Trappe beer, 2003, showing city locations which are normally bustling as empty and noiseless. **Top left** a deserted Beurstraverse, Rotterdam's busiest and best-known shopping precinct; **middle** a deserted platform at Rotterdam Central Station with high-rise beyond; **bottom** a deserted intersection at the approach to the Erasmus Bridge.

Right photos of examples of film locations at the internet site of the Rotterdam Film Fund (RFF).

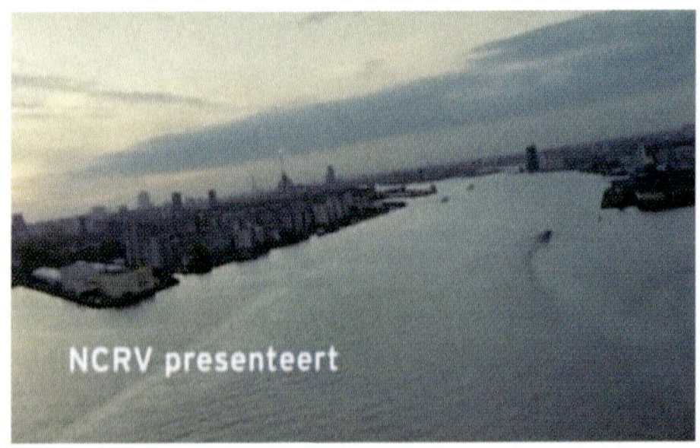

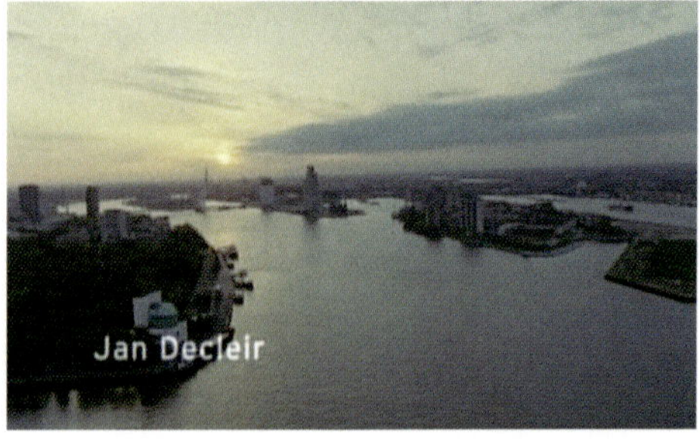

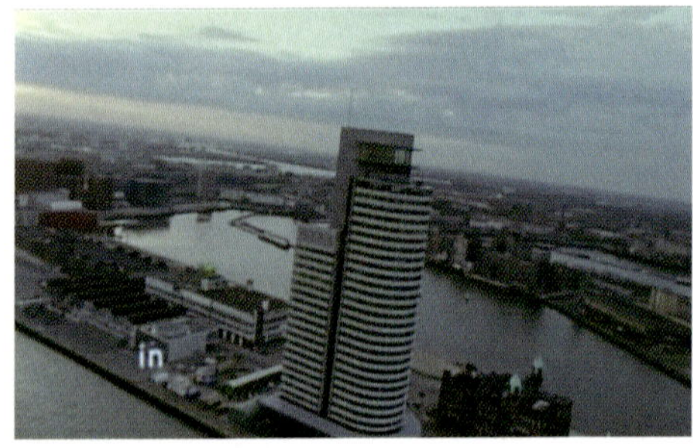

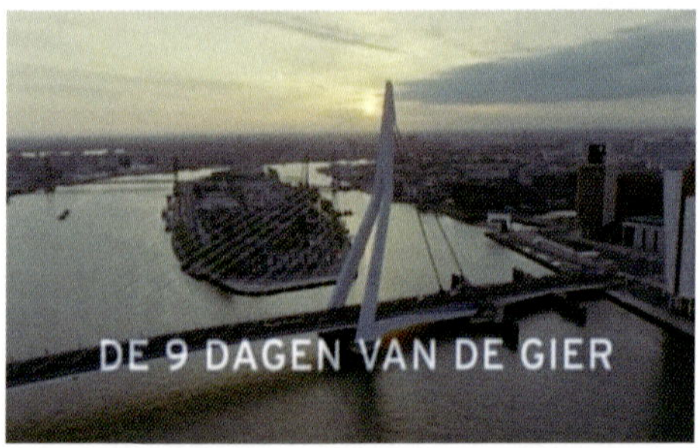

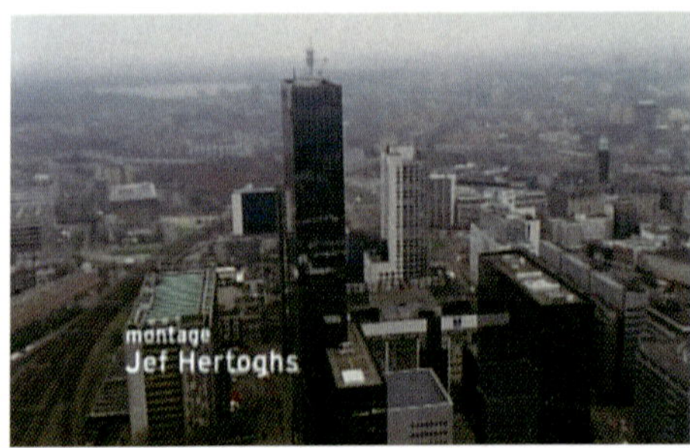

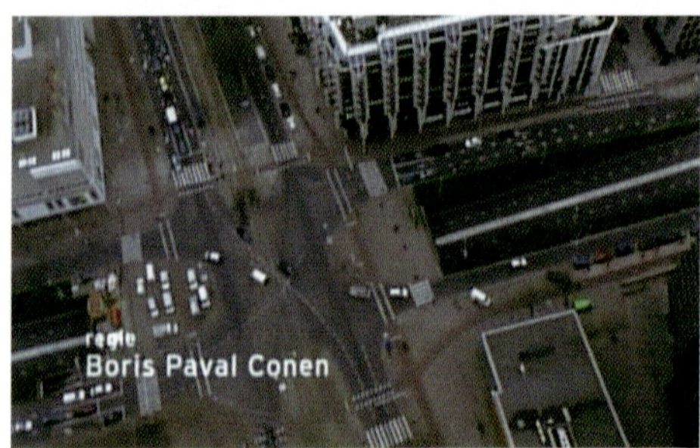

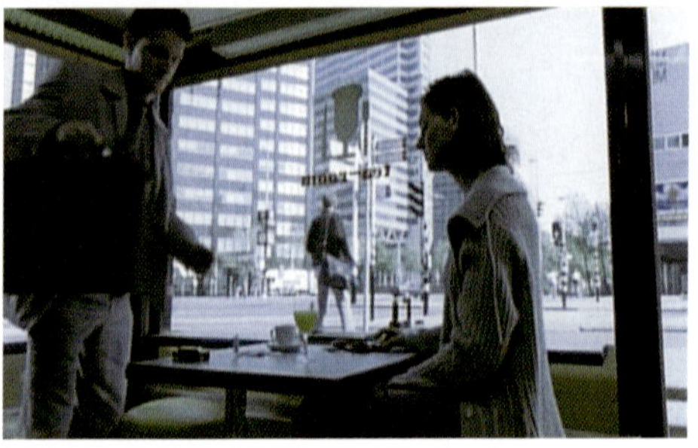

Top six stills from the intro to the NCRV-TV series *De 9 dagen van de gier*, dir. Boris Paval Conen, broadcast in 2001-2002; **bottom right** an example of a café scene from this series with a view of the street.

Whenever people plan to shoot here in August, I tell them three-quarters of the city has gone missing.'[8] One audiovisual production that has captured this sleek, spacious Rotterdam more than any other is the eight-part television series *De 9 dagen van de gier* (The nine days of the vulture) directed by Boris Paval Conen, which was telecast in 2001–2002 by the NCRV broadcasting organization. In the introduction to each instalment and in-between scenes we see Rotterdam filmed from a helicopter as an endless city whose vast reaches seem to extend to the horizon on both sides of the Maas. The entire series was shot with a filter that creates a bluish-grey effect. The landscape consequently seems much more homogeneous that it really is: older buildings which as a rule are brownish or yellowish disappear amidst the images of sky-high new-build. In this series the city is as clearly identifiable as in *Who Am I?* and the actors constantly reiterate the fact that they are in Rotterdam.

A factor that makes Rotterdam extra attractive for film-makers, according to Van der Ree, is that it is not all office buildings but has shops, cafés, restaurants, pedestrians, cyclists, cars and other signs of urban life. That makes Rotterdam a rival for office parks, which are far less alive as film locations. This is an important aspect for producers of commercials requiring a modern, urbane ambience. Many Dutch television commercials are shot in Rotterdam for that reason, such as the recent hip hop-style clips for a children's drink (Joy) which were filmed in the skate park with ramp in the city centre.[9] The commercials for the beer brand La Trappe whose slogan translates as 'Taste the silence', were deliberately shot at locations in Rotterdam that normally speaking are crowded with people but were cordoned off to make the commercials, creating an unnatural quiet and emptiness. In *De 9 dagen van de gier* many dialogue scenes take place in cafés, looking out onto life in the street and the surrounding modern buildings.

In some TV commercials, such as one for Heineken in 2000, Rotterdam is clearly recognizable. Other films exploit its ability to play the neutral modern city. A commercial for Nissan, for example, was shot in Rotterdam because of the American-looking urban environment yet not identifiable as any one American city in particular.[10]

It is remarkable how often television series and documentaries about lawlessness and the seamier side of life are expressly situated in Rotterdam, even if not all filming is done there. This can be explained by Rotterdam's reputation as a city of crime.

City of dodgy lists

There is also a downside to Rotterdam the world city: it has a reputation for criminal activity. Rotterdam stands as the Dutch city with the most problems related to a metropolis. This image is so tenacious that even the mayor was unable to sidestep it in his New Year's Address of January 3, 2000. He put it this way: 'But I can see you're thinking: how about safety on the street, the vulnerable groups in our society, the

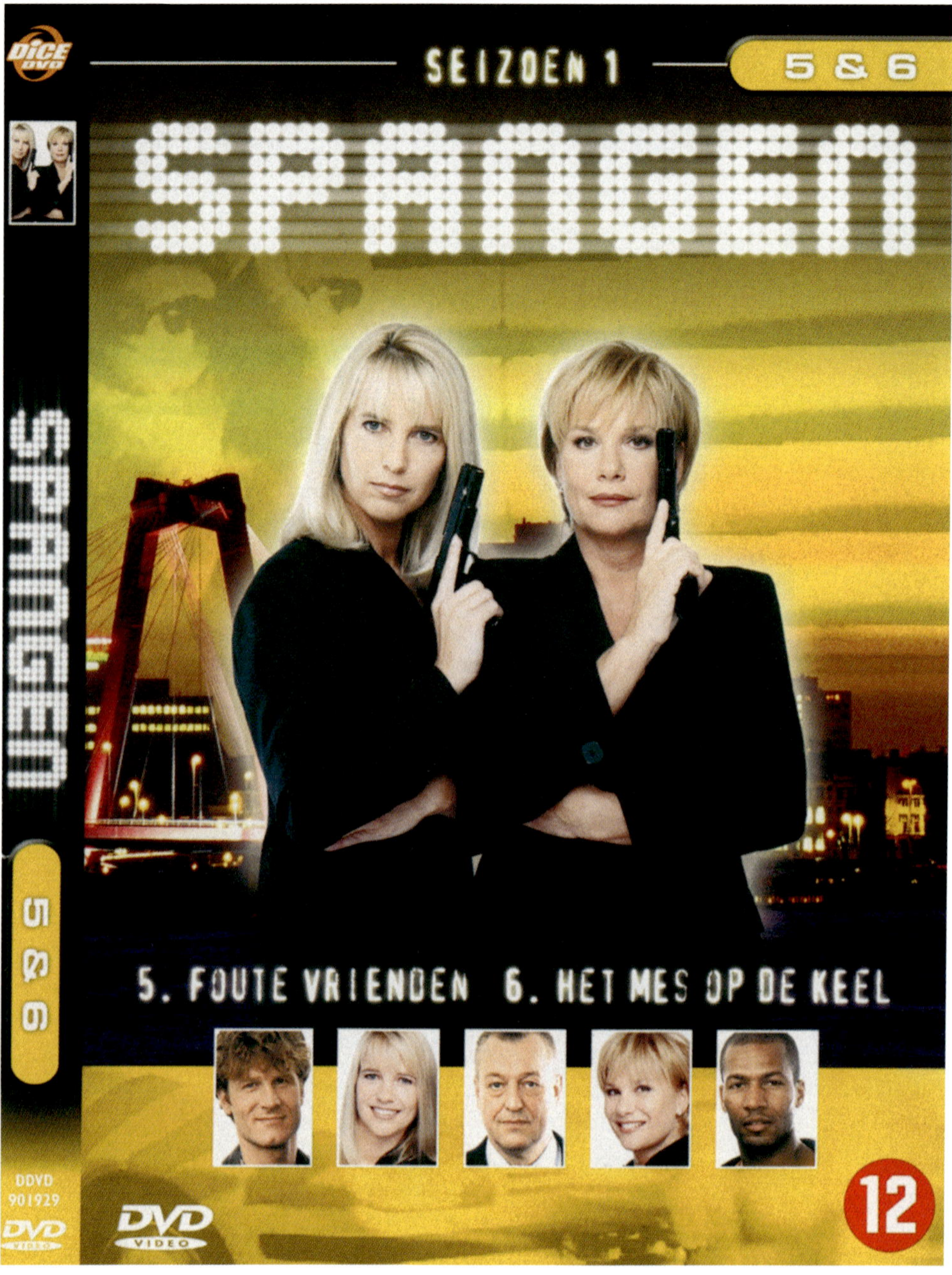

DVD cover of the TROS-TV series *Spangen*, broadcast in 1999. Spangen is a Rotterdam neighbourhood with a reputation for crime.

unemployment, the poverty? Isn't Rotterdam the city of dodgy lists? You're right: another image Rotterdam has is that it has a disproportionate share of metropolitan problems. We're quite open about it.'[11] The expression 'metropolitan problems' is in itself enough to show that this seamier side is all part of the image of a real city.[12] All the most famous metropolises – New York, Chicago, London, Paris – have a reputation when it comes to crime and social upheaval.[13] Even when they are represented in a fictional context it is striking that crime and social conflict are uppermost: London has always been the city of serial killers, and most TV police series are set in New York. Looked at in this light, the mass media's focus on the downside of Rotterdam is in no way detrimental to its reputation as a metropolis, quite the reverse in fact – in a way, it completes the picture of an exhilarating world city. One of the most powerful agents in this respect is television, and Rotterdam has begun the 21st century in fine style as a city of crime in documentaries as well as in series. Crime series set in Rotterdam are *Spangen* (1999), *Dok 12* (2001), *Luifel en Luifel* (2001) and the aforementioned *De 9 dagen van de gier* (2001–2002). Ironically, most of *Spangen*, set in the Rotterdam no-go area[14] of the same name, was filmed in Amsterdam. Amsterdam film-makers don't go to Rotterdam if they can help it.[15] The harsh reality of Rotterdam was the subject of documentaries like *Het Oude Westen* (2000, about life in this problem neighbourhood) and the ultra-confrontational *Meiden van de Keileweg* (2000, about street prostitution). In *De 9 dagen van de gier* it is the opposition thrown up between the gleaming, sleek, slightly over-illuminated images of the city seen from the air, and the part mysterious, part savage actions of the actors at street level, which are shot with an exaggerated use of contrast so that parts of what you see are entirely black.

Another attribute of a metropolis is international allure. Since the rise of the major metropolises at the end of the 19th century and the start of the 20th, the presence of cultures from all over the world is associated with metropolitan status. This is a British journalist describing New York back in 1907: 'Here, on the narrow rock which sustains the real metropolis of the United States, is room for men and women of every faith and every race. The advertisements which glitter in the windows or are plastered on the hoardings suggest that all nationalities meet with an equal and flattering acceptance.'[16] This international or multicultural aspect is indeed crucial to the way the world sees Rotterdam.

'I prefer things to be international, which is why I prefer this city'[17]
Rotterdam's reputation as an international city is largely due to its international port. From as early as the 14th century, goods as well as people from other countries and continents arrived in its harbours. It is a minor step in linguistic terms from *wereldhavenstad* (world port city) to *wereldstad* (world city). These days, Rotterdam is home to many immigrants from non-Western lands such as Suriname, the Antilles, the Cape Verde Islands, Turkey and Morocco; in 2005 36 per cent originated from

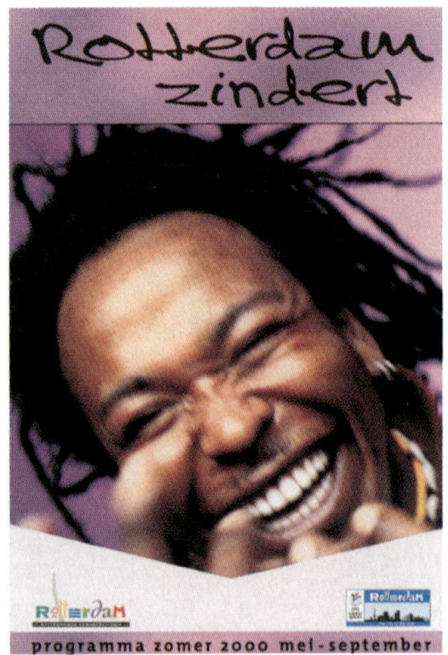

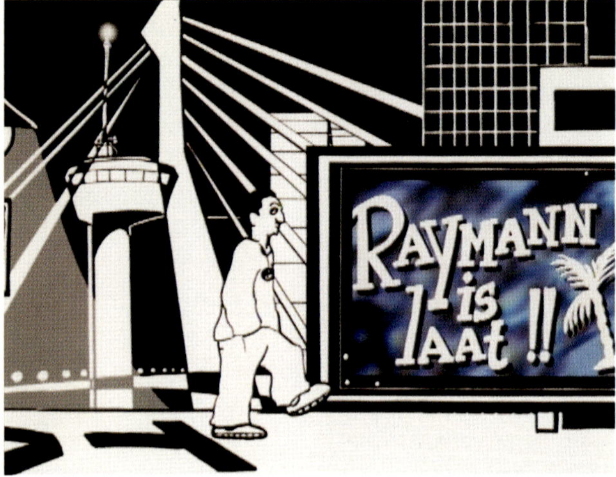

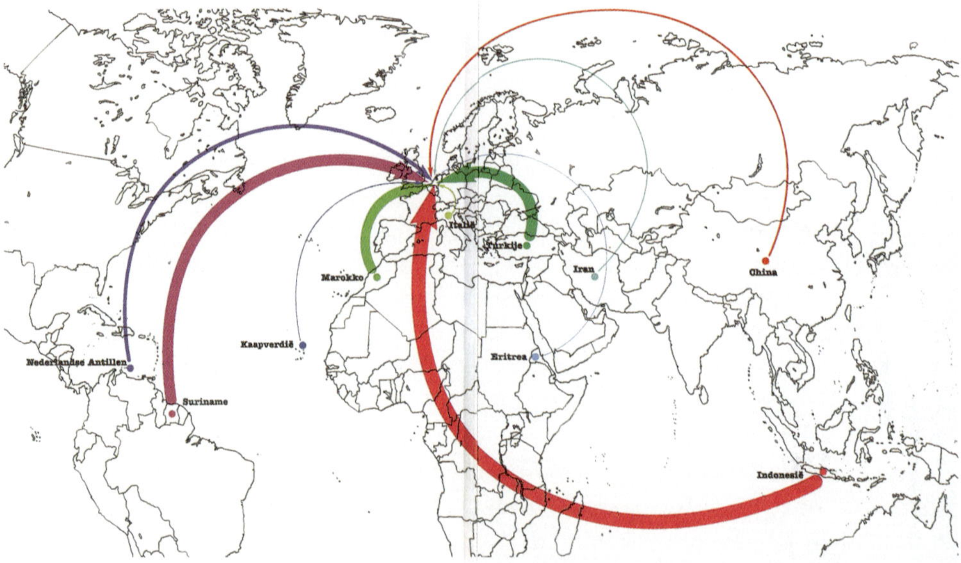

Top left front of the Rotterdam Marketing brochure for 'Rotterdam zindert' (2000), a campaign extolling the virtues of Rotterdam the cosmopolitan city.

Top right still from the intro to the NPS-TV programme *Raymann is laat*.

Bottom map of the world in *Rotterdams Kookboek*, 2004, a cookery book that stresses Rotterdam's cosmopolitan qualities.

these and other non-Western countries, and of those aged between 15 and 29 nearly
50 per cent.[18] Rotterdam additionally has a non-indigenous population from Western
countries of more than 10 per cent. Not that Rotterdam is unique in this respect:
the other three major Dutch cities (Amsterdam, The Hague and Utrecht) have high
percentages of non-Dutch residents too. But Rotterdam heads the list when it comes
to non-Western, ethnic minorities[19] and the city is often represented in the mass
media as the pre-eminent city of immigrants. There are several mutually reinforcing
reasons for this.

First of all, immigrants in Rotterdam are more visible than in the other
major cities as the often poor non-Western citizens live in the centre whereas people
with more money and a better education live on the edge of town or in the suburbs.
In the other three major cities, on the other hand, the centre is favoured by well-to-
do nationals as the place to live. The centres of Amsterdam, The Hague and Utrecht
consequently have a predominantly 'white' look population-wise whereas visitors
to the centre of Rotterdam can expect a colourful melange of peoples from all over
the world.[20] Right at the centre of Rotterdam is West-Kruiskade, a street known for
its exotic shops – as a reporter for the weekly paper *De Groene Amsterdammer* put
it, the street begins in China and ends in the Caribbean.[21] Rotterdam Marketing, the
organization set up in 1999 to sell Rotterdam as a tourist product, deployed West-
Kruiskade as a means of peddling the city as exotic and multicultural: 'This hetero-
geneous variety of West-Kruiskade is something we cherish as it gives an extra
gleam to our city-product.'[22]

In 'Rotterdam zindert' (Rotterdam sparkles), the campaign launched by
Rotterdam Marketing in 2000, Rotterdam was unmistakably presented as a 'multicultural' city. The visual nub of the campaign was a portrait of a young negroid man
with dreadlocks and earrings laughing infectiously. His face in the photo is blurred,
suggesting vibrant energy: indeed, so dynamic is the image that it seems to be
defying the camera to capture it. The annual Summer Carnival (Zomercarnaval)
is another favourite subject with which to depict Rotterdam as a multicultural
paradise. It is good for images of revelling non-whites decked out in non-Western
festive garb.

But even publicity not emanating from a city marketing agency often
lays emphasis on Rotterdam's multicultural character. *Rotterdams Kookboek*, the
Rotterdam cookery book published in 2004 as an initiative of the Madame Jeanet
Foundation, describes 'ingredients, recipes and backgrounds to 13 cultures',[23] these
being Dutch, Chinese, Indonesian, Hindu Surinamese, Afro-Surinamese, Antillean,
Cape Verdean, Eritrean, Iranian, Turkish, Moroccan, Italian and Jewish. The text on the
back of the book triumphantly reports: 'After the Hague and Amsterdam cookery
books, both standard works on traditional Dutch cuisine, there is now the Rotterdam
cookery book for *all* Netherlanders.' The first double page in the book is taken up
with a map of the world with coloured arrows leading from places all over the
planet and converging at Rotterdam. The similarity between it and depictions of

Rotterdam as a world port is striking, and the introduction indeed refers to Rotterdam's long history as a port city.[24] But the author, Linda Roodenburg, goes on to observe that the diversity of cultures in Rotterdam can be 'seen, heard and felt' all over the city. She too refers to the fact that the city centre is not 'the exclusive domain of the rich as in so many other cities'.[25]

A television programme that showcases Rotterdam as the home base of young people with a non-Western background, and which therefore appeals to very many viewers (as many as 700,000), is the weekly late-night show *Raymann is laat* ('Raymann is late') which has been on the air since 2001. Its host, Jörgen Raymann, a stand-up comedian of Surinamese origin, presents this programme from Rotterdam in front of a live audience mostly consisting of young, hip members of minority ethnic communities. The fact that this programme is recorded in Rotterdam is given emphasis in the intro, a cartoon drawn in black lines in which a comic-strip version of Raymann saunters past familiar Rotterdam locations such as the Euromast and the Erasmus Bridge. Additionally, webcam-type images of the nightlife in the street can be seen in the background during a regular segment of the programme. The principal theme in *Raymann is laat* is the multicultural society in the Netherlands, which is addressed along satirical-critical lines. There is no comparable television show that depicts the other major Dutch cities as multicultural meeting places.

Since Ted Langenbach organized the first dance parties in Rotterdam in the 1980s, a veritable dance culture has sprung up in the city with some 13 clubs, of which the most famous nationally and even internationally are Now & Wow, Off Corso, Las Palmas and Nighttown.[26] The dance scene prides itself in being able to effortlessly bridge cultural differences between young people from different countries. That outsiders also value this bridge-building function of dance organizers should be clear from the award in 2000 of the prestigious Laurenspenning to Ted Langenbach. The Laurenspenning has been awarded by the City of Rotterdam every year since 1959 to a Rotterdammer who has been of particularly great service to the urban community in the field of art and culture. One of the key arguments of the jury in granting this distinction to Langenbach on that occasion was his commitment to dance as a binding factor between young people of widely varying cultural backgrounds: 'He has made Rotterdam a "hip" city by promoting dance music as a binding agent for cultures.'[27] Or, as DJ and stylist Isis Vaandrager put it in 2001: 'Multicultural? Minority groups and that stuff. You only get a decent mixed audience in Now & Wow and Nighttown.'[28]

The structure of this book

What led to Rotterdam to be regarded as a metropolis? This is the key question in this book. There are several answers that at first sight seem to hit the nail on the head, but in my opinion none is adequate. For example, the explanation that Rotterdam's metropolitan image is simply the result of years of city marketing, I find unconvincing. I feel supported in this by experts on city promotion strategies. Hans Mommaas for one, in a book on city branding, argues that not every image can be imposed on every city. He illustrates his argument with a number of examples of successful and failed image campaigns for Dutch cities: Maastricht conforms perfectly with the image of a city given over to life's pleasures, whereas Utrecht simply refuses to become a 'city of knowledge'.[29] Dirk Noordman is another to emphasize that the image desired for a municipality should be carefully tuned to that municipality's identity.[30]

An answer that might seem even more obvious, rooted as it is in an every-day, common-sense conception of image and reality, is that construction of the Rotterdam skyline has produced the image of a metropolis. This answer fails to hold up to scrutiny either. We have already seen that photographer Paul Martens made images of Rotterdam as a metropolis when there was hardly a skyline to speak of. In chapter 2 we shall see that Rotterdam's metropolitan image is in fact much older, going back at least to the 1920s. Another fact that refutes this answer is that a Dutch city like The Hague by now has an impressive skyline yet is still not presented as a metropolis. The American geographer Harvey Molotch is intrigued by this phenomenon that cities have particular images ascribed to them that often have little to do with reality. In an essay published in 2000 he describes this phenomenon as a city's 'holistic characterizations'.[31] He and his co-authors put forward as examples the 'city of light' that is Paris and the 'broad shoulders' of Chicago. The authors suggest that social scientists are unequipped to handle this phenomenon and seek to explain it using quantitative indicators, but that these are inadequate to the purpose. Molotch *et al.* conclude that the explanation should be sought in a city's historically shaped internal structure. The ethnologist Rolf Lindner likewise contends that a city's history is a contributory factor in creating a particular urban characterization.[32]

Summing up, one can conclude that the commonsensical explanations for the coming about of Rotterdam's image as a metropolis – and for a city image in general – fall short on three counts: they overestimate the ability to craft an image for the city, they underestimate the persistence of the existing image, and they ignore that image's historical roots. To arrive at an explanation that does fit the bill, I have drawn on theories developed by others on the representation of cities. How I have used this theoretical material to arrive at an approach of my own, is the subject of chapter 1.

Chapter 2, 'From metropolitan airs to provincial ambitions', addresses the historical roots of Rotterdam's representation as a metropolis. It ends at the crisis encountered by the metropolitan image at the end of the 1960s, beginning of the '70s. The main title of chapter 3 is a quote from Jules Deelder, 'Modern times are here again'. Much of this chapter is devoted to the poet and performer Jules Deelder, or rather to his contribution to the revival of Rotterdam's metropolitan dream. Back

in 1977 Deelder together with the Rotterdam film director Bob Visser made a
documentary about Rotterdam that showcased the city's metropolitan aspects.
Chapter 4, 'Magic years', steps off from two policy documents of 1987 in which the
city council expounded on a renewal programme for Rotterdam. If the literature
regards these documents as decisive for the city's further development, in this
chapter I argue that that development was long under way when these documents
saw the light of day. Chapter 5 charts the emergence of a network of artists and
cultural entrepreneurs in Rotterdam who worked together out of a shared metropolitan perspective on the city. Chapter 6 shows why these men and women,
Rotterdam's 'creative class', unfurled their activities in Rotterdam and not in
Amsterdam, even thought Amsterdam was the largest city in the Netherlands with
the strongest cultural heritage. In chapter 7, lastly, I describe the development of
the Kop van Zuid project in the 1990s as the materializing of a dream, a dream that
Rotterdam's creative class had been nurturing since the 1970s.

1 Laar, P. van de (2000), *Stad van formaat. Geschiedenis
van Rotterdam in de negentiende en twintigste eeuw*,
Zwolle: Waanders.

2 Laar, P. van de (2000), op. cit. (note 1), p. 11.

3 Some examples chosen at random from various
media: Antoine Verbij toys with the notion that
Rotterdam 'is a true world city', Verbij, A. (1999),
'Romsterdam', *De Groene Amsterdammer*, June 30,
1999; in the council's promotion film *Rotterdam 2001,
Cultural Capital of Europe, Mirror of a New Society*,
directed by Bob Visser, 1997, Neon Film/TV, the expression 'the metropolis Rotterdam' is used consistently
throughout; in September 1999 the cover of the home
design magazine *Eigen Huis & Interieur* drew attention
to a supplement on Rotterdam with the words
'Wereldstad Rotterdam'; in the same issue Thimo te
Duits describes Rotterdam as 'a real city, the New York
of the Netherlands'; in een interview in *NL10*, 1 (20),
June 22-28, 2005, p. 7, Maurice Lenferink of Rotterdam
City Development Corporation (Ontwikkelingsbedrijf
Rotterdam) notes that 'Rotterdam is becoming more
and more an international city with the air of a genuine
metropolis.'

4 In *NRC Handelsblad* of November 26, 2002, Tijs van
den Boomen scornfully refers to 'the Netherlands'
only real city' which likes to call itself 'Manhattan on
the Maas'.

5 My information on Paul Martens comes from an
interview I had with him on June 7, 2005, except
where otherwise specified.

6 According to Jacques van Heijningen, film commis-
sioner in Rotterdam and director of the RFF
(Rotterdams Fonds voor de Film en de audiovisuele
media), in a conversation with the author on January
19, 2004, and the Rotterdam location scout Bas van
der Ree in a conversation with the author on March 5,
2004. The construction of the Erasmus Bridge in 1996
has undoubtedly influenced Rotterdam's popularity
as a film location.

7 See www.rff.rotterdam.nl, site visited November 21,
2003 and April 21, 2006.

8 Author's interview with Bas van der Ree, March 5,
2004.

9 On view at www.drinkjejoy.nl, site visited April 24,
2006.

10 Author's interview with Bas van der Ree, March 5,
2004.

11 Speech made by Rotterdam's Mayor Ivo Opstelten
on behalf of the College of Mayor and Aldermen,
January 3, 2000 in the Burgerzaal, Rotterdam City Hall,
www.nieuwsbank.nl/inp/2000/01/0103R023.htm,
site visited April 24, 2006.

12 According to Jack Burgers, professor of urban studies
at the Erasmus University in Rotterdam, it even seems

at times that 'the measure in which problems mani-
fest themselves locally is an indicator of the degree of
urbanity', in other words, the more problems a city
has, the more metropolitan it is. Burgers, J. (2002), *De
gefragmenteerde stad*, Amsterdam: Boom, p. 8.
13 For Chicago's reputation see: Boehm, L.B.K. (1999),
*Infamous City: Popular Culture and the Enduring Myth
of Chicago. Department of History*, [Bloomington]:
Indiana University.
14 According to Wikipedia, 'the free encyclopaedia',
http://nl.wikipedia.org/wiki, site visited April 24, 2006.
15 Author's interview with Bas van der Ree, March 5,
2004.
16 Sutcliffe, A. (ed.) (1984), *Metropolis 1890–1940*,
London: Mansell, p. 90.
17 Bordewijk, F. (1998 [first edition 1938]), *Karakter:
Roman van zoon en vader*, Amsterdam, p. 234.
18 Marlet, G. & C. van Woerkens (2006), *Atlas voor
gemeenten 2006*, Utrecht: Stichting Atlas voor
gemeenten, p. 187. Data obtained from Statline, the
central database of Statistics Netherlands (CBS).
Ethnic minority residents are all those with at least one
parent born abroad and/or born abroad themselves.
The non-Western category is composed of ethnic
minority residents from Turkey, Africa, Latin America
and Asia with the exception of Japan and Indonesia.
Marlet, G. & C. van Woerkens (2006), pp. 251-252.
19 Marlet, G. & C. van Woerkens (2006), op. cit. (note 18),
pp. 58-61, 82-85, 206-209, 238.
20 Lodewijk Asscher talks of a 'white wedge in the
centre and south' of Amsterdam. Asscher, L. (2005),
Nieuw Amsterdam: De ideale stad in 2020,
Amsterdam: Bert Bakker, p. 20.
21 Verbij, A. (1999), 'Romsterdam', *De Groene
Amsterdammer*, June 30, 1999.
22 Silvius, L. (1999), 'De ontdekking van Rotterdam',
Friends in Business Rotterdam, December 1999,
pp. 15-21 (p. 21).
23 Roodenburg, L. (2004), *Rotterdams Kookboek*,
Utrecht: Kosmos-Z&K, p. 13.
24 Roodenburg, L. (2004), op. cit. (note 23), p. 16.
25 ibid.
26 In May 2005, a national dance committee
(Belangenvereniging Dance) proclaimed Rotterdam
'Dance City of the Netherlands', see
http://www.antennerotterdam.nl/read/item/id/13713
/rotterdam-uitgeroepen-tot-dancestad-van-nederland-
2005, site visited May 11, 2006. See chapter 7 of this
book for more information on Langenbach's parties.
27 'Laurenspenning voor Ted "MTC"', *Rotterdams
Dagblad*, October 3, 2000.
28 Vries, F. de, 'Vreemde stad: In Rotterdam zijn de
nieuwe creatieven "lekker bezig"', *de Volkskrant*,
January 4, 2001.
29 Mommaas, H. (2002), 'City Branding: De noodzaak
van sociaal-culturele doelen/The necessity of socio-
cultural goals', in: Urban Affairs & V. Patteeuw (eds),
City Branding: Image Building & Building Images,
Rotterdam, NAi Uitgevers/Publishers, pp. 35-47 (p. 41).
30 Noordman, T.B.J. (2004), *Cultuur in de citymarketing*, 's-Gravenhage, Elsevier Overheid.
31 Molotch, H., W. Freudenburg et al. (2000), 'History
Repeats Itself, But How? City Character, Urban
Tradition, and the Accomplishment of Place', *American
Sociological Review*, 65, December, pp. 791-823.
32 Lindner, R. (2003), 'Der Habitus der Stadt – ein kultur-
geographischer Versuch', *Petermanns Geographische
Mitteilungen*, 147 (2), pp. 46-53 (p. 50).

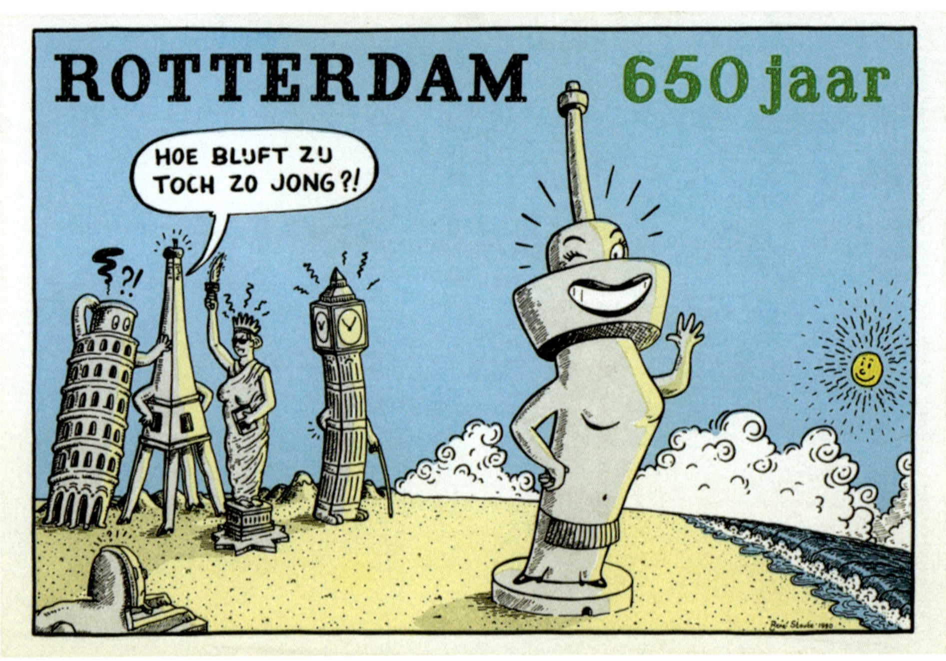

Picture postcard marking Rotterdam's first 650 years, 1990. Idea by Hugo; drawing by René Stoute. Editions Vormgeving BV Rotterdam. The Eiffel Tower is saying about the Euromast: 'What keeps her looking so young?!'

Chapter 1

'The city is, rather, a state of mind'

(Robert Ezra Park, 1925)

During the past two decades an awareness has been growing among urban researchers that how a city is represented is much less the result of that city's development than a key factor itself in that development. This awareness fits into the broader tendency within a number of disciplines that has been termed the 'cultural turn', the notion that culture is not the outcome of developments in other fields but is itself a guiding factor. The increasing interest in urban representation can be gauged from the deluge of publications and conferences on the subject.[1]

My point of departure in studying the urban-cultural climate of Rotterdam in the period 1970–2000 is locked into this general concern. I proceed from the assumption that in that period there have been trade-offs between events, the built environment and the city's image. This book regards the representation of Rotterdam as an indelible part of the recent history of that city's urban-cultural climate. It does not, however, concern itself in any way with research in the strict sense into the image built up of Rotterdam in the above period. Such an investigation would focus exclusively on the visual and verbal picture painted of the city during the period in question. This would separate representation from the events and the urban landscape, eliciting a disembodied affair with little to say about the city's history. It is by examining the interaction between *social* developments, *material* developments and developments in the *representation* of the city that the transformation of Rotterdam in the years 1970-2000 is truly brought to light.

It is uncustomary to treat the three above-mentioned aspects of the city – social, material and imaginary – as a single entity in its history. Scholars usually seize on just one of them; not just that, the activities of people in the city, the city's social history, are often divided into political, economic, demographic and cultural developments. These specialized approaches are just as evident in recent written histories of Rotterdam. There are diverse publications on the material, that is the architectural and urbanistic development of the city.[2] There are others devoted to the development of what Rotterdam has had to offer on the cultural front.[3] Broad urban historical studies such as *Stad van formaat*, Paul van de Laar's standard work on Rotterdam in the 19th and 20th centuries, as a rule treat the political, socio-economic, cultural and urbanistic histories in separate chapters. Publications on the evolution of Rotterdam's image are few and far between;[4] usually the subject is merely mentioned in passing or is confined to a discussion of targeted city promotion.[5] I assume, by contrast, a close-knit connection between the city in a social sense (politics, economics, population make-up, culture broadly speaking), in a material sense (architecture and urban design) and the imagined city, in which each of the city's three manifestations is regarded as equally decisive. Thus, for example, the image a city has may drive its urban development at times, yet conversely urban design is influential on that image. And the same mutual influence can be observed in other relations between the three aspects. For instance, the city's image is able to attract people or indeed repel them. The dynamics between these three aspects of the city are forever present in my description of the period 1970–2000 in Rotterdam.

The epistemological necessity of representation

Although interest in the image of the city fits into the wider tendency of the 'cultural turn', the question of representation in urban history is a particular problematic that thrusts itself upon us. There is a logical reason for this, although this is not mentioned in the literature on urban representation. The reasoning I wish to subscribe to is rooted in epistemology.

It is the city's great scale that requires that it be perceived through the agency of representation. Put another way: anyone in the city is able to observe only a small part of it and never oversees the whole thing. This is the basic reason why the relationship between a city and its representation is so indissoluble. A number of concrete examples will serve to illustrate this. Take the following hypothetical situation: if a person is 'dropped off' in a city without being told in advance which city it is, they will have great difficulty ascertaining which city they are in. Pointers towards identifying the city in question will include street names, advertisements and distinctive buildings, all aspects with a representative duty of their own (for example street names that refer to the city's history or logos that include the Eiffel Tower in the case of Paris) or key contributory factors to the image of the city (the buildings). It is easier to identify a city at a distance using an aerial photo or a street map – that is, using another kind of representation. It should be said in this respect that there is only a semblance of objectivity in maps and aerial photos; the viewer's gaze can be manipulated in very subtle ways by making some parts of the city more prominent than others.[6] Besides, it is debatable whether a non-Parisian would recognize Paris from a street map where the all too familiar landmarks are unclearly marked.

One of the few publications to follow virtually the same reasoning is 'Symbolic Representation and the Urban Milieu', an essay dating from 1958 by the sociologists R. Richard Wohl and Anselm L. Strauss.[7] Wohl and Strauss draw attention to the human need to take in the many impressions thrown up by the urban environment 'at a glance'. Symbolic representations of a city satisfy this psychological need. To lend weight to their reasoning Wohl and Strauss cite one of the pioneers of urban sociology, Robert Ezra Park, who in his book *The City* of 1926 wrote that the city is largely 'a state of mind': 'If, as Robert Park suggested, the city is "a state of mind", then city people must respond psychologically to their urban environment; they must, to some extent, attempt to grasp the meaning of its complexity imaginatively and symbolically as well as literally.'[8] The human condition, whether we regard it as psychological or epistemological, requires that we have a compact symbolic representation of a city.

Allied theories

The recent upsurge of interest in the image of the city originates from all manner of historical and socioscientific disciplines. Thus we see the German ethnologist Rolf Lindner working for a number of years now on an intriguing 'anthropology of the city'.[9] He is most interested in the idea of a city based on stereotypical versions of the people who live there. In an essay from 2006 entitled 'The Gestalt of the Urban Imaginary' he gives a perspective on the relationship between the imagined city and the realistic city that is closely allied to mine.[10] In this essay Lindner inveighs against the idea that the imaginary city is an entity distinct from the real city. The city as imagined, he argues, is not an escape from reality but quite specifically a means of coming into contact with that reality: '(...) the imaginary gives the real greater depth (...). In other words, the imaginary gives a place meaning, sense (...).'[11] Yet in his essay Lindner goes all out to find out how an imaginary city comes into being and how a researcher can track it down. To this end, he borrows urban researcher Gerald Suttles' concept of 'the cumulative texture of local urban culture'.[12] This texture according to Suttles can be traced by examining collective representations of the city. Lindner values in particular the sheer diversity of sites of collective representation named by Suttles, from cemeteries to telephone books, or, in Suttles' own words: 'Not just what people put in their museums, but also what they put on their car bumpers and T-shirts.'[13] According to Suttles and Lindner researching these localities will reveal that collective representations of a city exhibit a 'remarkable durability' – that is, that the nature of the imaginary city scarcely changes over a long period. This is because collective representations form a tissue to which new representation can be added that builds upon the existing tissue. Lindner compares it with intertextuality. The workings of this tissue could be illustrated by, for example, the so-called 'style musette': just a snatch of this familiar accordion music is enough to evoke an image of Paris, because it has been used so often, in combination with images and tales of Paris, as a collective presentation of that city.

These two elements in Lindner's essay, the overlapping of imaginary and real cities and an analysis of 'the cumulative texture of local urban culture', are as crucial to my own approach. Lindner and Suttles for their part fail to provide extensive historical case studies in which these theoretic departure-points are applied, indeed most writers on the representation of the city as a driving force limit themselves to erecting a theoretical framework.[14]

One felicitous exception is *The Image of Georgian Bath, 1700–2000*, Peter Borsay's exhaustive historical study dating from 2000. In it, Borsay makes clear that it is impossible to write a history of the English city of Bath without considering its representation, as some developments can only be explained from the city's prevailing image. This image may largely be the product of fiction, yet its power is such that it has had a far-reaching influence on the actual course of history. Conversely, events in turn influence the representation of the city. Thus, in Borsay's words: 'At the deepest level the imagined and the real, the cultural and the material are in perpetual interaction, part of a seamless process in which neither the substructure nor the superstructure exert primacy.'[15]

Peter Borsay's book therefore stands as a model study, although Rotterdam and Bath have little in common. In Bath today the past is ineluctably present; the city refers to its past in its built environment, its monuments, the names of its streets. Rotterdam by contrast is, as it were, a city cut off from its past by the wartime devastation and ultramodern rebuilding of its centre. And yet the two cities can still be regarded as each other's counterparts. If Bath is consistently represented with reference to its past, Rotterdam's representation as a modern metropolis invariably refers to the future. This picture of Rotterdam as the city of the future in all likelihood has its roots in the 19th century though it only really took off in the inter-war years. I shall explore this aspect at greater length in chapter 2. Borsay may have arrived at his approach through the individual case of Bath, but he signals a broader tendency in both urban and general history to attach as much importance to representation as to primary historical sources.[16]

Pinning down the imaginary Rotterdam

The following question to present itself concerns where the collective representations of Rotterdam can be found. That is, how are we to trace the cumulative texture of Rotterdam's urban culture? Or, in other more concrete terms, what should be examined, and what left aside, to construct the imaginary Rotterdam? The texture metaphor borrowed from Gerald Suttles is certainly useful for our purpose.[17] In my research I have restricted myself to texts and images (including audiovisuals) that

refer to an existing image, that embroider on an existing pattern. Strictly personal
utterances of what Rotterdam means to a particular individual have no place within the parameters of my research. The reach of the material to be examined has
been influential too; of particular interest to me are statements on Rotterdam, in
whatever form, intended for a wide audience or at least made in the public domain.
Even just the intention of making a statement in public, implies at the very least a
dialogue with the received image of the city. Public utterances (say in a newspaper)
that poke fun at the image of Rotterdam as a world city are interesting too, although
they distance themselves from the existing texture. In my search for evidence I
have steered clear of such blind strategies as going through all the volumes of a
particular newspaper throughout the years in question or watching every television
programme about Rotterdam. I have instead looked in places where I knew or suspected I would find representations of Rotterdam that refer to the received image.
My stepping-off point was the representation of Rotterdam as a metropolis. In the
introduction, I showed that this representation is resolutely present at the dawn of
the 21st century. My investigations have taken me in search of the genesis, development and guiding influence of that dominant image.

There is nothing static about the cumulative texture that shapes the
image of Rotterdam. Some aspects of that image transform over time or become
more or less emphasized. For example, the international resonance at the onset of
the 20th century was related to port activity whereas it is the multicultural population makeup that symbolizes the city's international resonance at the turn of the
millennium. The image of Rotterdam as metropolis moreover has particular nuances
not possessed by other metropolises, such as the rolled-up sleeves and get-up-and-
go attitude said to be typical of Rotterdam. These two aspects are closely linked to
the port as a visually defining feature. The characterization of Rotterdam as a locus
of energetic activity we could describe with Rolf Lindner as being anthropological,
as these are clichés about the city's inhabitants transferred to the city as a whole.[18]

The creative class

In the introduction I said that I reject the notion that city marketing is so powerful
that it can shape the image of a city at will. There are all manner of factors and
actors that contribute to the advent and development of an urban image, as this
book will show. But it transpired from my research that there is one particular group
of actors at the forefront, to wit, artists and other cultural practitioners. After a
period in which Rotterdam's image as a world city went through a crisis, roughly
the years 1965–1975, this group of creative people gave that image a new lease of
life and advanced all kinds of urban initiatives out of a metropolitan perspective on
the city. I urge that the strongest attention be paid to the activities of this group of
cultural practitioners, these days often elegantly termed the 'creative class',[19] and in
doing so reject the description of the development of Rotterdam's urban-cultural

climate as a process closely choreographed by the city council.

It is important to realize that municipal cultural policy is only one of the forces at work in an urban climate. The initiatives of individuals are often at least as important. In general, municipal policy documents are often a reaction to developments set in train by individuals. However, unlike municipal council policy these individual contributions to the urban climate are not documented and so in time their significance for the city's evolution fades from view. In the literature on the recent urban-cultural turn of events in Rotterdam little or no account is given of the role performed by these individual initiatives; I am referring in particular to the publications by Jan van Adrichem (1987), Erik Hitters (1996), Irina van Aalst (1997) and Han Meyer (1999). This is particularly surprising in Hitters' case, as his intention was specifically to describe culture in Rotterdam not just from the perspective of government policy: 'In art research the apparent certitude of Dutch cultural policy too often leads to uniform studies infused with policy thinking. This way, the art world is implicitly approached primarily as an object of government policy. This is something I seek to avoid in this study (...).'[20] Though Hitters distinguishes four dimensions in cultural urban life – finance, enterprise, organization and legitimation – of all active interest in culture taken by private individuals only the dimensions of finance and legitimation make the grade because of the book's firm commitment to professional sponsoring. In my book, the emphasis as regards private individuals lies quite specifically on the two other dimensions, namely enterprise and organization.

It is not difficult explaining why individual initiatives on the cultural front generally get less coverage in the literature than municipal cultural policy. Council policy is dutifully put on paper and archived, making it very easy for historians to reconstruct. By contrast, other urban activities, ideas and initiatives are scarcely ever documented and what does find its way onto paper is later often thrown away or poorly preserved. Whatever memories people have of what was done, thought and made is conveyed by word of mouth only. These verbal testimonies combined with incomplete documentation gives such a piecemeal picture, however, that it usually fails to attract the attention of historians planning to describe a city's development. This doesn't mean that these private initiatives are less influential than official policy. It is generally acknowledged that the input of individuals and semi-official collaborations are essential for the urban-cultural climate.[21] In order to accurately chart this input in Rotterdam in the years 1970–2000, I have interviewed a number of those involved. A list of interviewees can be found at the end of the book.

Many will counter my approach with the fact that Rotterdam's municipal policy on the cultural front has the reputation of being first-rate. Which is why I should emphatically state that it is not my intention to detract in any way from that reputation. However, I must make two qualifying remarks on that score. The first is a repetition of what was just said, namely that the trade-off with private initiatives is so rewarding; a municipal council is meaningless without an entrepreneurial creative class. The second qualification is that the successful Rotterdam municipal policy resides far less in white papers setting out a policy in the longterm than in individuals occupying municipal posts who make the right decision at the right time. Former alderman Joop Linthorst, for example, has no single policy document on culture to his name, yet is regarded by many artists and cultural entrepreneurs as an administrator who has worked wonders for the urban-cultural climate in Rotterdam.[22] His achievements include establishing the Netherlands Architecture Institute, Nighttown and the Kunsthal.[23] Ted Langenbach was able to found his now famous club Now & Wow because arts alderman Hans Kombrink saw a future in his plans, and the water taxi on the river Maas is there, according to Daan van der Have, because it had the backing of alderman Hans Simons.[24] Yet these personal merits are often left unrecorded in council documents and so fail to make the history books, as the source is regarded as hearsay and therefore unreliable.

As for the pioneering role played by the creative class in shaping the image of the city, I would like to refer to the generally acknowledged role of trailblazer attributed to artists and other creative practitioners in upgrading dilapidated districts, the process known as gentrification. Sharon Zukin was the first to describe this process in her book *Loft Living* (1982), based on the transformation of the New York district of SoHo. SoHo was a neighbourhood of small industries that had fallen somewhat into disrepair as more and more warehouses were abandoned. When artists discovered the aesthetic quality of the buildings on site in the 1960s and moved into the large, cheap, empty warehouses, the district grew in the '70s into a vibrant gathering place for artists, art devotees and gallery owners. As that decade wound down, they were joined by non-artists who also wanted a loft or large, undivided space in SoHo and from the start of the 1980s what was once a ramshackle part of town became a chic yuppie area with trendy restaurants and shops.[25] Zukin stresses that the prime mover behind this development is what she calls an aesthetic conjuncture: 'So if people found lofts attractive in the 1970s, some changes in values must have "come together" in the 1960s. There must have been an "aesthetic conjuncture".'[26]

My primary concern here is the role filled by artists and other cultural specialists in discovering the aesthetic qualities of an urban landscape. In regarding that landscape with another pair of eyes, they are in a position to alter its ambience: '(...) they interact not to build a new landscape that looks different from what went before, but to impose a new perspective on it.'[27] Rotterdam underwent a similar process after the city's image suffered a crisis in about 1970. At that time Rotterdam was felt to be too big, too spacious, too modern, too rational and, consequently, far from convivial. Artists were the first to see that the 'holistic characterizations' of Rotterdam reside precisely in its great size, its space, its modernity and rationality, in short in its modern metropolitan resonance. It is this perspective on the city that gave rise to enterprises that reattuned the image of the city to its historical roots.

Interpreting the sources

The characteristic uniting all the source material I collected for my research is that it consists of public statements that refer, as mentioned above, to the received image of Rotterdam. In terms of form and medium, however, these sources are extremely varied, ranging from publicity brochures and poems to columns in newspapers and TV commercials. My method of interpreting this wide assortment of material has an art-historical basis. I use an iconological method whose foundation was laid in the 1930s by Erwin Panofsky.[28] Panofsky applied this method exclusively to visual art of former centuries though others have adapted the principles of his method to other fields of study. Even given the recent transformation of the history of art into 'visual studies', Panofsky remains a benchmark. W.J.T. Mitchell, coiner of the term 'pictorial turn' and an influential writer on visual culture, calls Panofsky 'an inevitable model and starting point for any general account of what is now called "visual culture".'[29]

Panofsky's iconological method is one of interpretation whose aim is to get at the meaning of an art work.[30] The method says nothing about the work's aesthetic value; the artistic import of what is being interpreted is irrelevant. This means that non-artistic images can also be subjected to this manner of interpretation. In practice, the method can be used, with only the slightest modification, for describing and denoting all kinds of media including images, texts and audiovisual material.

Every iconological interpretation is grounded in a description of the image that keeps interpretation to a minimum. Next the horizon of the image to be interpreted is widened in stages, so to speak, by incorporating more and more contextual information so as to get at the image's meaning. Panofsky himself often went too far in this respect, a fact established by his critics. He sometimes related art works to texts that were much older, though his aim had been to reconstruct the work's meaning at the time it was made.[31]

Two aspects are particularly attractive about the iconological method as formulated by Panofsky. The first is the sheer wealth of material that he recommends as frame of reference for an interpretation. Texts figure prominently among it; Panofsky believes that art historians should know as much about texts as about images if they are to arrive at an interpretation that does justice to the work's significance in its day. The second aspect is the cumulative build-up, which always begins with a description. This allows the method to be applied clearly and verifiably without the interpretation being presented as an indisputable fact. This gives the reader the capacity to reject the interpretation and counter it with another.

An example of how I have applied the iconological method can be found in chapter 2 of this book. It is an interpretation of the front page of the periodical *Groot Rotterdam* of July 27, 1928, which includes a photograph of Chicago (p. 46). I begin by describing what there is to see in the photo and how the photo is positioned with regard to the heading containing the title of the periodical. Then I connect what there is to see in the photo with the caption below it and from that conclude that the photo is intended as a vision of Rotterdam in the future. Lastly I draw a broader context into the interpretation, namely the symbolic meanings attributed to the city of Chicago at that time. In this way I have set out first to describe all the material I had assembled and then step by step give it a broader relevant context. Description and interpretation merge with each other, as they do in Panofsky, who contends that interpretation is 'one organic and indivisible process'.[32]

1 Examples of conferences or specialized sessions at conferences: 'Urban Mindscapes of Europe', Faculty of Humanities, De Montfort University, Leicester, April 29, 2004; session at 'Urban images and representations in Europe and beyond during the 20th century', Seventh International Conference on Urban History, 'European City in Comparative Perspective', Panteion University of Social and Political Science, Athens, October 27-30, 2004; conference 'Art and the City', Universiteit van Amsterdam, May 11-12, 2006.
A selection of publications:
Wohl, R.R. & A.L. Strauss (1958), 'Symbolic Representation and the Urban Milieu', *The American Journal of Sociology*, 63 (5) March 1958, pp. 523-532.
Lynch, K. (1960), *The Image of the City*, Cambridge, Massachusetts/London: The MIT Press.
Suttles, G.D. (1984), 'The Cumulative Texture of Local Urban Culture', *The American Journal of Sociology*, 90 (2) September 1984, pp. 283-304.
Scherpe, K.R. (1988), *Die Unwirklichkeit der Städte. Grobstadtdarstellungen zwischen Moderne und Postmoderne*, Hamburg: Rowohlts Enzyklopädie.
Donald, J. (1992), 'Metropolis: The City as Text', in: R. Bocock & K. Thompson (eds), *Social and Cultural Forms of Modernity*, Cambridge: Polity Press in Association with The Open University, pp. 417-461.
Stieber, N. (1994), 'De representatie van de stad Groningen', in: S. Cusveller (ed.), *Stad! De stad en haar identiteit*, Hoogezand: Molior, pp. 59-80.
King, A.D. (1995), 'Re-presenting world cities: cultural theory/social practice', in: P.L. Knox & P.J. Taylor (eds), *World Cities in a World-System*, Cambridge: Cambridge University Press, pp. 215-231.
King, A.D. (ed.) (1996), *Re-Presenting the City*,

Hampshire/London: Macmillan Press Ltd.
Rodwin, L. & R.M. Hollister (eds) (1984), *Cities of the Mind: Images and Themes of the City in the Social Sciences*, New York/London: Plenum Press.
Balshaw, M. & L. Kennedy (eds) (2000), *Urban Space and Representation*, London/Sterling, Virginia: Pluto Press.
Borsay, P. (2000), *The Image of Georgian Bath, 1700–2000: Towns, Heritage and History*, Oxford: University Press.
Madsen, P. & R. Plunz (eds) (2002), *The Urban Lifeworld: Formation, Perception, Representation*, London/New York: Routledge.
Stevenson, D. (2003), *Cities and Urban Cultures*, Maidenhead / Philadelphia, Open University Press.
Lindner, R. (2006), 'The Gestalt of the Urban Imaginary', *European Studies*, 23 (2006), pp. 35-42.
2 Stadsontwikkeling Rotterdam (1981), *Stedebouw in Rotterdam: Plannen en opstellen 1940–1981*, Amsterdam: Van Gennep.
Beeren, W., P. Donker Duyvis et al., (eds) (1982), *Het Nieuwe Bouwen in Rotterdam 1920–1960*, Delft: Delft University Press.
Haan, H. de & I. Haagsma (1982), *Stadsbeeld Rotterdam 1965–1982*, Utrecht: Oosthoek's Uitgeversmaatschappij B.V.
Pinder, D. & K.E. Rosing (1988), 'Public policy and planning of the Rotterdam waterfront: a tale of two cities', in: B.S. Hoyle, D.A. Pinder & M.S. Husain (eds), *Revitalising the Waterfront: International Dimensions of Dockland Redevelopment*, London/New York: Belhaven Press, pp. 114-128.
Wagenaar, C. (1992), *Welvaartsstad in wording: De wederopbouw van Rotterdam*, Rotterdam: NAi Uitgevers.

Aarts, M. (ed.) (1995), *Vijftig jaar wederopbouw Rotterdam: Een geschiedenis van toekomstvisies*, Rotterdam: 010 Publishers.

Andela, G. & C. Wagenaar (eds) (1995), *Een stad voor het leven: Wederopbouw Rotterdam 1940–1965*, [Rotterdam:] De Hef.

Meyer, H. (1999), *City and Port: Urban Planning as a Cultural Venture in London, Barcelona, New York, and Rotterdam: Changing relations between public urban space and large-scale infrastructure*, Utrecht: International Books.

Crimson, P. Gadanho et al. (eds) (2001), *Post.Rotterdam: Architecture and City after the tabula rasa/Arquitectura e Cidade após a tabula rasa*, Rotterdam: 010 Publishers.

Rooijendijk, C. (2005), *That City is Mine! Urban Ideal Images in Public Debates and City Plans, Amsterdam & Rotterdam 1945–1995*, Faculteit der Maatschappij- en Gedragswetenschappen/Amsterdam Institute for Metropolitan and International Development Studies (AMIDSt), Amsterdam: Universiteit van Amsterdam.

Vanstiphout, W. (2005), *Maak een stad: Rotterdam en de architectuur van J.H. van den Broek*, Rotterdam: 010 Publishers.

3 Adrichem, J. van (1987), *Beeldende kunst en kunstbeleid in Rotterdam 1945–1985*, Rotterdam: Museum Boymans-van Beuningen.

Hagendijk, W. (1994), *10 jaar zomercarnaval Rotterdam*, Rotterdam: Museum van Volkenkunde/Van de Rhee.

Hulscher, L. (1994), *De menselijke stem: 25 jaar Poetry International. Sphinx Cultuurprijs voor Martin Mooij*, Zutphen: Walburg Instituut.

Gaemers, C. (1996), *Achter de schermen van de kunst: Rotterdamse Kunststichting 1945–1995*, Rotterdam.

Hitters, E. (1996), *Patronen van patronage: Mecenaat, protectoraat en markt in de kunstwereld*, Utrecht: Jan van Arkel.

Aalst, I. van (1997), *Cultuur in de stad: Over de rol van culturele voorzieningen in de ontwikkeling van stadscentra*, Utrecht.

Ulzen, P. van (ed.) (1999), *90 over 80: Tien jaar beeldende kunst in Rotterdam: De dingen, de mensen, de plekken. Rotterdam*, NAi Uitgevers/Stichting Kunstpublicaties Rotterdam.

4 Wagener, W.A. (1951), 'Rotterdam', in: C. Oorthuys et al. (eds), *Land en volk: Steden (De schoonheid van ons land*; dl. 10), Amsterdam: Contact, pp. 68-73.

Vries, J. de (1965), *Amsterdam Rotterdam: Rivaliteit in economisch-historisch perspectief*, Bussum: C.A.J. van Dishoeck.

Frijhoff, W. (1989), 'De stad en haar geheugen', *Oase: Tijdschrift voor ontwerp, onderzoek en onderwijs*, 24, pp. 14-21.

Ostendorf, W. (1990), 'Het imago van Rotterdam', *Geografisch Tijdschrift*, XXIV (3), pp. 273-277.

Laar, P.T. van de (1998), *Veranderingen in het geschiedbeeld van de koopstad Rotterdam*, Rotterdam [: the author].

Lieftinck, M. (2003), *Appeltaart zonder appels? De beeldvorming van Rotterdam van 1945 tot 1975 in Nederlandse en buitenlandse architectuurtijdschriften*, Faculteit der Historische en Kunstwetenschappen, Kunst- en Cultuurwetenschappen, Rotterdam: Erasmus Universiteit.

5 Bode, K. & S. van Beek (1988), Eenheid *in verscheidenheid, de concernmarketing van Rotterdam*, Rotterdam.

Berg, L. van den, L.H. Klaassen et al. (1990), *Strategische City-Marketing*, Schoonhoven: Academic Service.

Groenendijk, A. (1991), *Het Produkt Rotterdam: Kan het beleid van de stad Rotterdam in de periode 1945–1990, gericht op bedrijvigheid en bevolking, een city-marketing beleid genoemd worden?*, Maatschappijgeschiedenis, Rotterdam: Erasmus Universiteit.

Hajer, M.A. (1993), 'Rotterdam: redesigning the public domain', in: F. Bianchini & M. Parkinson (eds), *Cultural Policy and Urban Regeneration: The West European Experience*, Manchester/New York: Manchester University Press, pp. 48-72.

Berg, L. van den, J. van der Borg & J. van der Meer (1995), *Urban Tourism: Performance and strategies in eight European cities*, Aldershot (etc.): Avebury.

Neill, W.J.V., D.S. Fitzsimons et al. (eds) (1995), *Reimaging the Pariah City. Urban Development in Belfast & Detroit*, Aldershot (etc.): Avebury.

Bakkes, J. et al. (eds) (1996), *De stad aan de man gebracht: Vijftig jaar gemeentevoorlichting in Rotterdam*, Rotterdam: Voorlichting Bestuursdienst Rotterdam.

Cachet, E.A., M.K. Willems et al. (2003), *Eindrapport Culturele Identiteit van Nederlandse Gemeenten*, Rotterdam: ERBS (Erasmus University Centre for Contract Research and Business Support BV/Rotterdams Instituut voor Sociaal-Wetenschappelijk Beleidsonderzoek BV).
Noordman, T.B.J. (2004), *Cultuur in de citymarketing*, 's-Gravenhage: Elsevier Overheid.

6 Stieber (1994), op. cit. (note 1), pp. 59-80.

7 Wohl & Strauss (1958), op. cit. (note 1). I was led to this essay by a reference to it in Lindner (2006), op. cit. (note 1).

8 Wohl & Strauss (1957), op. cit. (note 1), p. 523. Park, R.E., E.W. Burgess et al. (1976 [first published 1925]), *The City*, Chicago/London: The University of Chicago Press, p. 1.

9 Lindner, R. (2003), 'Der Habitus der Stadt – ein kulturgeographischer Versuch', *Petermanns Geographische Mitteilungen*, 147 (2), pp. 46-53.

10 Lindner (2006), op. cit. (note 1).

11 Lindner (2006), op. cit. (note 1), p. 36.

12 Suttles (1984), op. cit. (note 1).

13 Suttles (1984), op. cit. (note 1), p. 284.

14 Lindner has published a potted case study on Berlin, but his essay is not historically grounded. Lindner, R. (2005), 'Le grand récit des crottes de chien: De la mythographie de Berlin', *Sociologie et Sociétés*, 37 (1), pp. 217-229.

15 Borsay (2000), op. cit. (note 1), p. 253.

16 Borsay (2000), op. cit. (note 1), p. 8.

17 Suttles (1984), op. cit. (note 1).

18 Lindner (2003), op. cit. (note 9); Lindner (2006), op. cit. (note 1); Lindner, (2005), op. cit. (note 14).

19 Richard Florida introduced this term in his book Florida, R. (2002), *The Rise of the Creative Class: And How It's Transforming Work, Leisure, Community and Everyday Life*, New York: Basic Books. For Florida 'creative class' embraces a much larger group of people than just artists and others with creative professions. In theory, Florida sees a creative future for every profession, as creativity yields the greatest economic value in postindustrial society. I use the restricted, common-or-garden definition of creative class, as do most Dutch journalists, policy makers and academics; that is, people with a profession in the creative or cultural sector.

20 Hitters (1996), op. cit. (note 3), p. 33.

21 On this see, for example, O'Connor, J. (1999), 'Popular Culture, Reflexivity and Urban Change', in: J. Verwijnen & P. Lehtuvuori (eds), *Creative Cities: Cultural Industries, Urban Development and the Information Society*, Helsinki: University of Art and Design Helsinki, pp. 76-101.

22 Typically, Linthorst was presented with a book at his farewell ceremony: Beijer, G. et al. (1994), *Over Rotterdam: Toekomstvisies aangeboden aan Joop Linthorst bij zijn afscheid als gemeenteraadslid en wethouder van de gemeente Rotterdam*, Rotterdam: 010 Publishers.

23 That Linthorst took up the cudgels for Nighttown is not as well known as his efforts on behalf of the architecture institute and the Kunsthal, see Burger, F. (1989), 'Town van de direktie', *Town Magazine*, February 2, 1989, p. 31.

24 Author's interviews with Daan van der Have on January 14, 2003, Ted Langenbach on November 7, 2003 and Hans Kombrink on March 29, 2004.

25 Kostelanetz, R. (2003), *SoHo: The Rise and Fall of an Artists' Colony*, New York/London: Routledge.

26 Zukin, S. (1982), *Loft Living: Culture and Capital in Urban Change*, Baltimore/London: The Johns Hopkins University Press, pp. 14-15.

27 Zukin (1982), op. cit. (note 26), quoted in: O'Connor & Wynne (eds) (1996), op. cit. (note 21), p. 53.

28 For a brief survey of the origin and development of iconology see: Falkenburg, R.L. (1993), 'Iconologie en historische antropologie: een toenadering', in: M. Halbertsma & K. Zijlmans (eds), *Gezichtspunten: Een inleiding in de methoden van de kunstgeschiedenis*, Nijmegen: SUN, pp. 139-174.

29 Mitchell, W.J.T. (1994), *Picture Theory: Essays on Verbal and Visual Representation*, Chicago/London: The University of Chicago Press, p. 16: 'The current revival of interest in Panofsky is surely a symptom of the pictorial turn. Panofsky's magisterial range, his ability to move with authority from ancient to modern art, to borrow provocative and telling insights from philosophy, optics, theology, psychology and philology, make him an inevitable model and starting point for any general account of what is now called "visual culture".'

30 Panofsky, E. (1972 [first published 1939]), *Studies in Iconology: Humanistic Themes In the Art of the Renaissance*, New York (etc.): Icon Editions, Harper & Row, pp. 3-31 ('Introductory').

31 Falkenburg (1993), op. cit. (note 28), p. 147.

32 Panofsky (1972 [first published 1939]), op. cit. (note 30), p. 31.

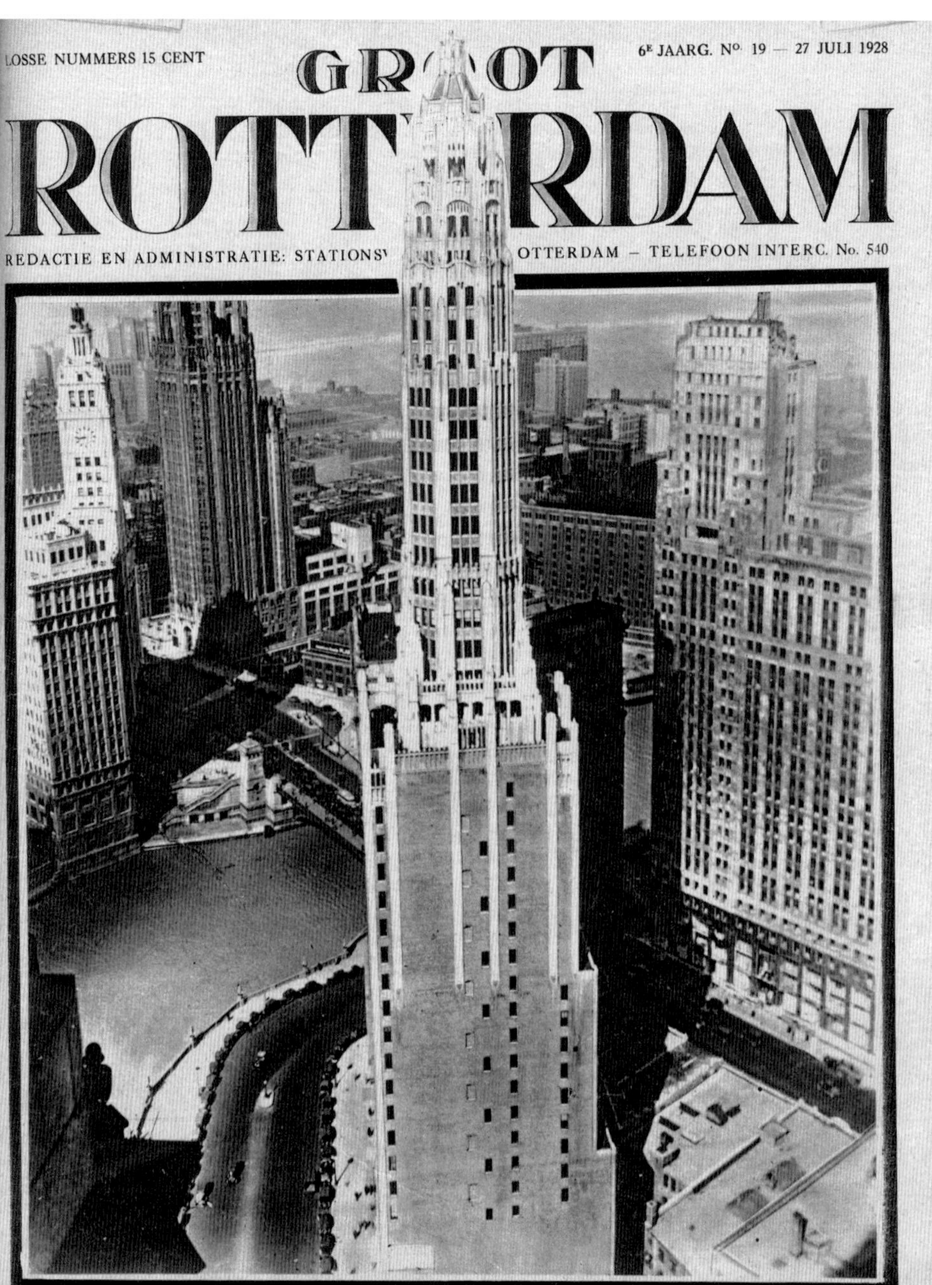

Front page of *Groot Rotterdam*, July 27, 1928, with a photo of skyscrapers in Chicago. The caption predicts: 'This is how Rotterdam will look in a few years' time'.

CHAPTER 2

From metropolitan airs to provincial ambitions

The Rotterdam of around 1900 had the reputation of being big, modern and enterprising, but not beautiful. It had grown hand over fist since 1850, synchronously with many other Dutch and foreign cities. In 1850 Rotterdam had had some 72,000 inhabitants but by 1900 this was more in the region of 300,000.[1] Expectations were that Rotterdam would overtake the country's first city, Amsterdam, in terms of size. Not only was the number of Rotterdam's inhabitants growing, the port was expanding all the time. Nieuwe Waterweg, a new, wider, deeper and shorter connection with the sea, was constructed in 1872–1885, giving a tremendous boost to port activities. The Rotterdam docks became more important than those of Amsterdam and began drawing level with the ports of London and New York.

Until 1850, Rotterdam had been known as a small, attractive mercantile town.[2] During the period of furious growth in the second half of the 19th century its visual aspect changed to that of a vast, modern, pragmatic industrial city. 'O ugly, ugly thou art. Industrial new Rotterdam' is a typical complaint from 1879 by the poet E.J. Potgieter. Rotterdam no longer satisfied the ideal image of a 17th-century Dutch mercantile town.[3] According to Paul van de Laar Rotterdam's image as a mercantile town changed in about 1880 to that of a transit city. This term refers to the function of transshipment port acquired by Rotterdam at that time. Van de Laar is none too explicit about the image a transshipment port is expected to have, yet it is clearly less favourable than that of a mercantile city. Understandably of course, if you realize that a mercantile city is both the flagship and the shop window for the wares on sale there, whereas the public realm in a transit city only needs to be functional and not necessarily attractive. According to Van de Laar, this transit city image would remain uppermost until 1940.[4] My own opinion is that the history of Rotterdam's image should be divided up differently: as I see it, the interwar years present a major hiatus. Qualities that were considered ugly at the end of the 19th century took on a positive thrust when related to the metropolitan condition. This has to do with the changing aesthetic view of modernity, which became steadily accepted during the 1920s and '30s.

The beauty of Rotterdam

The Italian Futurists in the 1910s were the first to voice their aesthetic esteem for the phenomena of the modern age as encountered particularly in the metropolis: motorized traffic, noise, a chaotic bombardment of the senses, industry, stench and engineering structures. Their ideas soon spread throughout Europe and were adopted in a milder form by many artists.[5] The ideas of the Futurists offered a framework in which to view Rotterdam, so that its recent growth could be appreciated aesthetically as well as economically.[6] This framework can, among other things, explain the appearance in 1938 of a book dedicated to the beauty of Rotterdam mainly illustrated with photographs of engineering works, shipping, traffic, city lights, modern architecture and the port – in short, the modern, technological facets of Rotterdam.[7] The book was part of the prestigious series *De schoonheid van ons land* (literally, the beauty of our country). Published between 1936 and 1962 by Contact in Amsterdam, the series consists of 18 volumes on wide-ranging aspects of Dutch and Flemish culture and nature. Each volume boasts an extensive section of excellent black-and-white photographs. The texts are of an equally high quality, and were usually written by nationally famous authors regarded as experts in their field, such as A.M. Hammacher (on sculpture) and A.J.J. Delen (on Flemish art). For the volume on Rotterdam, the prominent Rotterdam journalist and author M.J. Brusse contributed a text entitled 'Rotterdam, de wereldhaven aan de Maas'. In its rhythm, use of words and contents this text clearly contains an echo of Futurism.[8] Brusse's lyrical, poetic paean to the 'world port on the Maas' betrays the ideal of a symbiosis of technology and art, an ideal cherished by so many artists in those days:

> 'Snorting winches urge on the rhythm. The high-pitched melismas of wheeling windlasses running on and on. The metallic rattle of chains and blocks, the kettledrum thunder of ore tipped into holds, the drum rolls of trolleys across the quays, the thud of hatches and boards during loading and unloading, the thump of crates and sacks and barrels as they drop into the sling. The carts rumbling away with their stacks of freight, the throbbing of engines as the tractors squeal into action and the peal of horns:

and the clopping hooves of horses pulling long carts laden with cargo –
and the ship's whistle blasting madly through it all. And the rhythmic
chug-chug-chug of all those small craft.'[9]

Brusse goes on to mention that Rotterdam may have been long respected
for the rapid growth of port and city, but was looked down on for its outward
appearance: 'For years, Rotterdam has stood as the craftsman in the family of Dutch
cities. Toiling to earn its livelihood, it was respected for its diligence but held in
contempt for neglecting its appearance and for not taking the time to concern itself
with good manners, even with the things of refinement – let alone indulge in joyful
activity.'[10] These days, however, according to Brusse, it can be seen that Rotterdam
owes its 'significance in the world', its 'affluence and character', its 'tough and often
romantic beauty' and its 'vibrant international' central boulevard to 'the mighty
port industry'.[11] And Rotterdammers might not have the best of educations, yet they
are used to dealing with people from outside, thanks once again to the port.
Visitors to the city will be amazed, Brusse writes, at how often they get 'a candid
answer' to their questions 'in their own language'.[12] In other words, Rotterdammers
are cosmopolitans!

The photos in the book are illustrative of a new, modern aesthetic able to
show to advantage a city that shortly before had been generally branded as ugly.
Purely functional structures such as bridges, cranes, gantries, grabs and of course
ships are shot in black and white with strong contrasts that show the structure of
the objects to better effect and heighten the sense of drama. In some photographs
that dramatic effect is further strengthened by taking them from an uncustomary
viewpoint and adding a single plume of smoke or steam. Most photos in the book
are typical examples of the New Photography, a style that became famous in the
1920s and was distinguished by directness, unusual angles and a predilection for
restrained, functional, modern structures as subjects. Several illustrious representatives of the New Photography were based in Rotterdam, including Paul Schuitema
(one of whose photographs can be found in *De schoonheid van ons land*), Piet Zwart
and Jan Kamman.

That a book about these modern aspects of Rotterdam was published in
De schoonheid van ons land, a series that graced the bookcase of every Dutchman
or woman with an interest in culture, can be construed as a broad acceptance of
Rotterdam as a city of the future. This publication canonized Rotterdam's futuristic
qualities and made them part of the Dutch cultural heritage.

Weltstadtsehnsucht

De schoonheid van ons land of 1938 is only one of many examples from the 1920s
and '30s that show that the loathing once felt for Rotterdam's modern urbanity
had been replaced by admiration. Modern, large, technological Rotterdam had

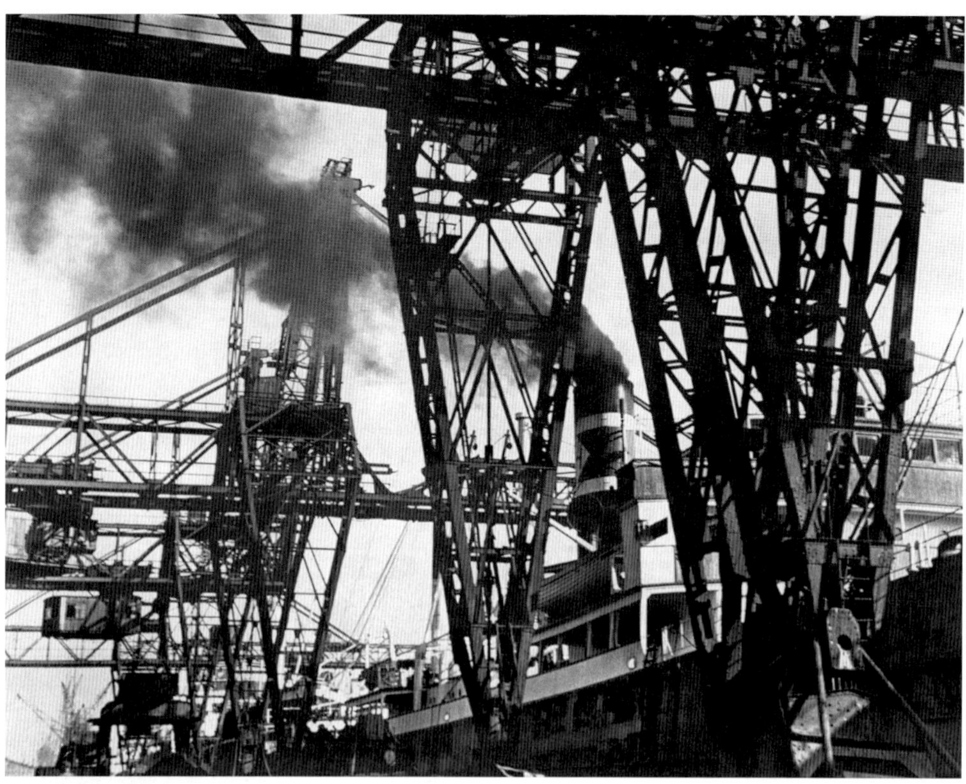

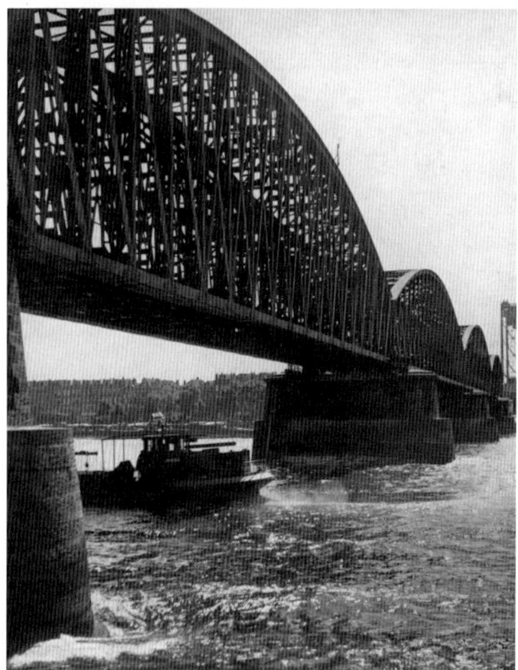

Top Jan van Maanen, 'Het daverende lied van den arbeid' [Toil's thunderous refrain], photo from M.J. Brusse, *De schoonheid van ons land, Deel VI, Rotterdam*, Amsterdam 1938.

Bottom Paul Schuitema, photo of the Maas bridge, from M.J. Brusse, *De schoonheid van ons land, Deel VI, Rotterdam*, Amsterdam 1938.

Right Germaine Krull, photo of Hefbrug, 1928.

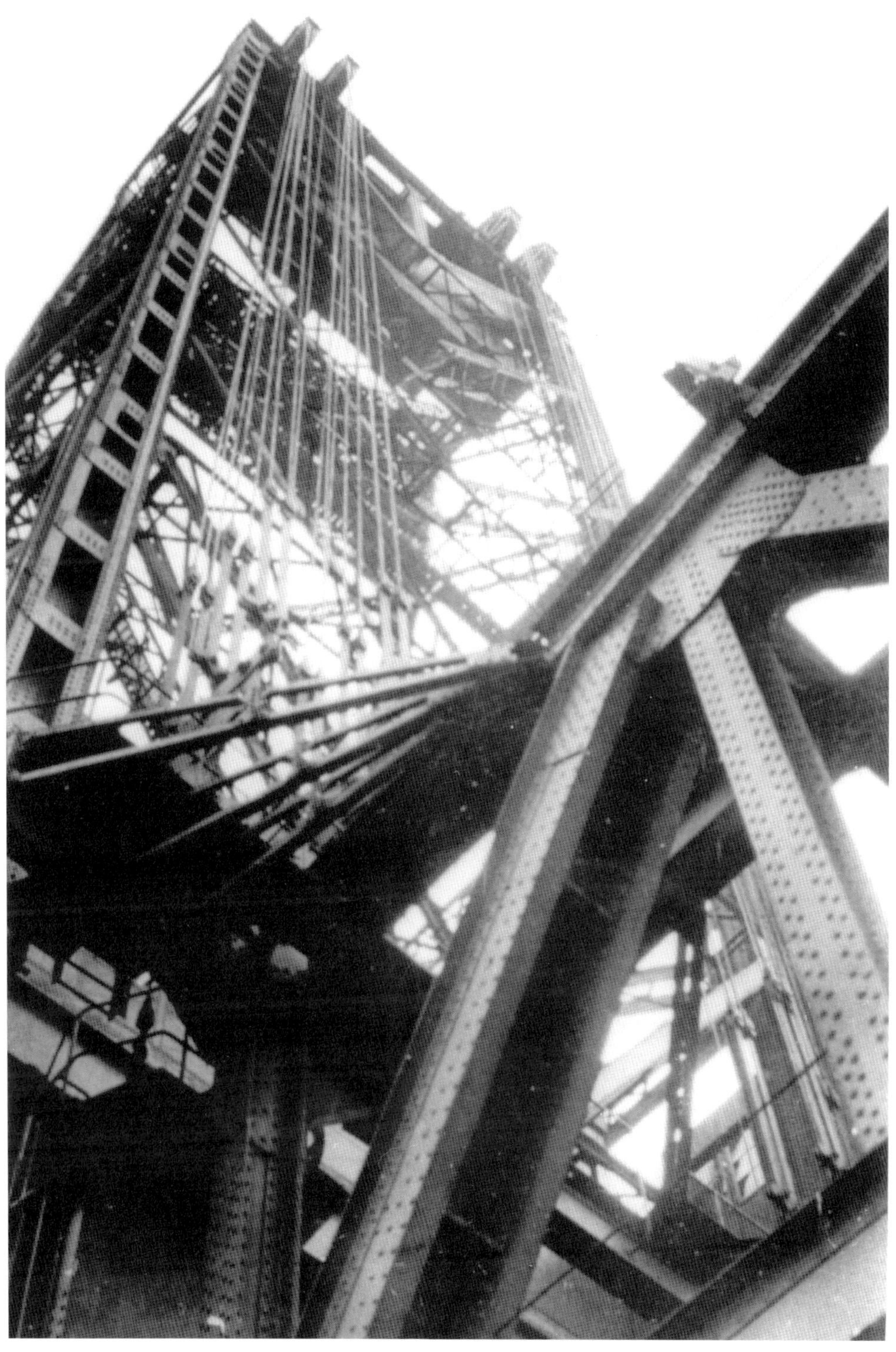

51 – From metropolitan to provincial

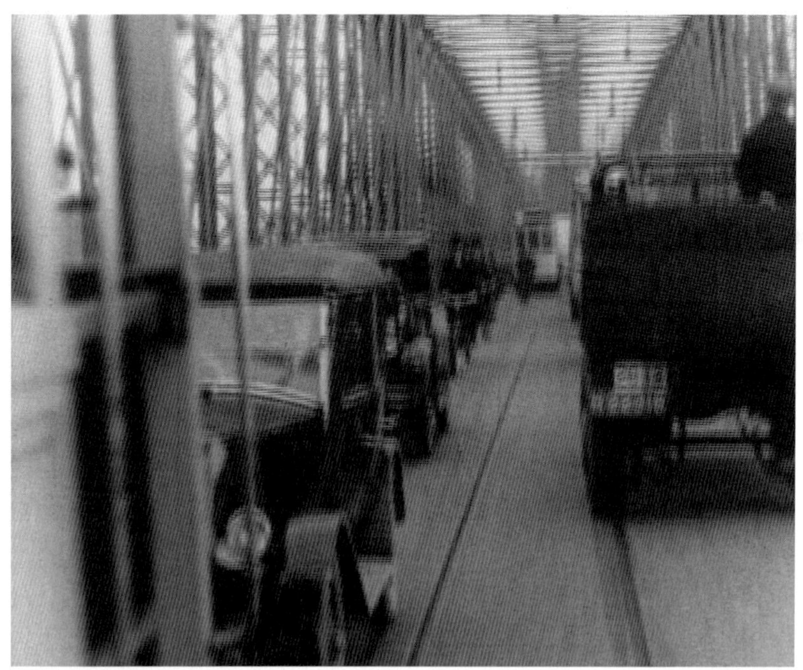

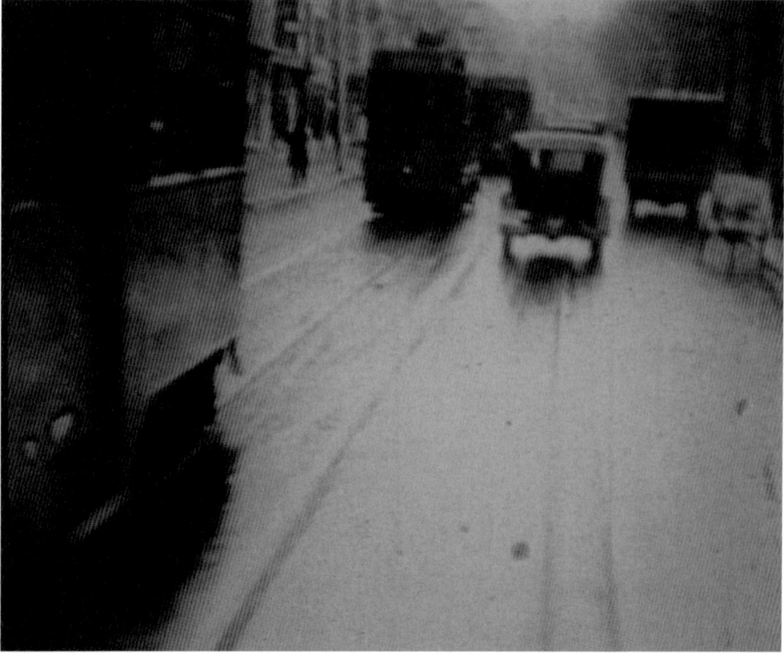

Top still of traffic from *Rotterdam de stad die nooit rust*, 1928, dir. Andor von Barsy. Traffic in the interwar years was seen as a sign of metropolitan dynamism, with no negative side as yet.

Bottom still of traffic from *De Steeg*, 1933, dir. Jan Koelinga.

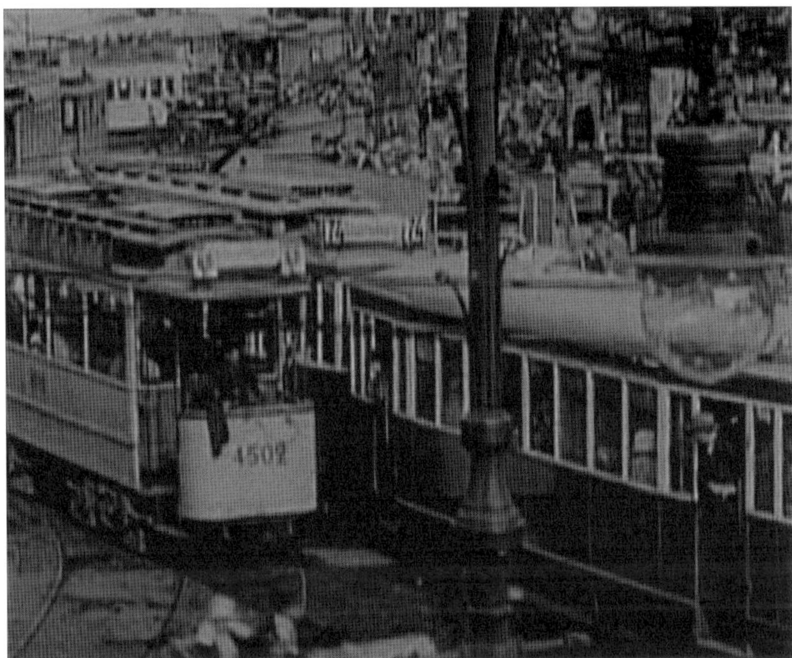

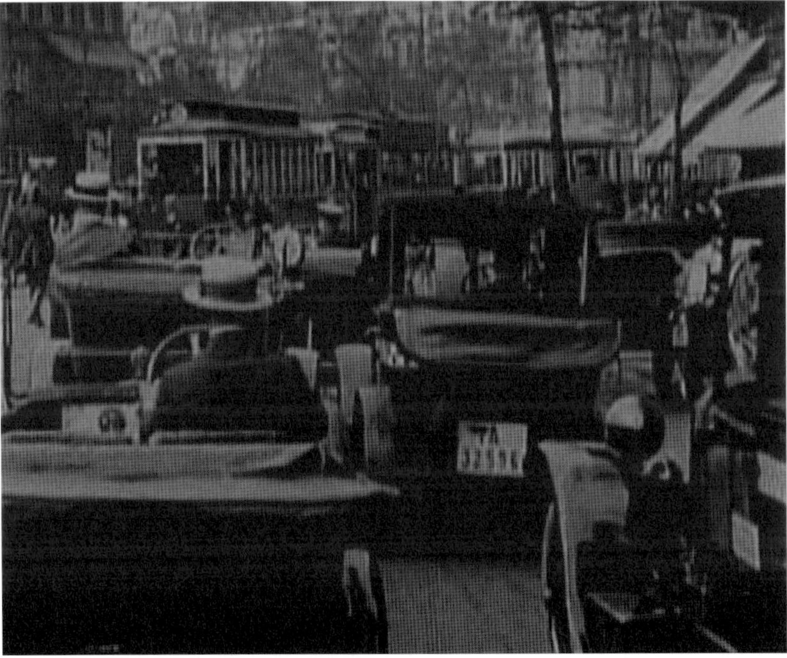

Stills from *Berlin. Die Synfonie der Großstadt*, 1927, dir. Walther Ruttmann. 'Berlin. Symphony of a Great City' was very famous in its day and inspired many film-makers. Traffic chaos in the metropolis is a key theme in this film.

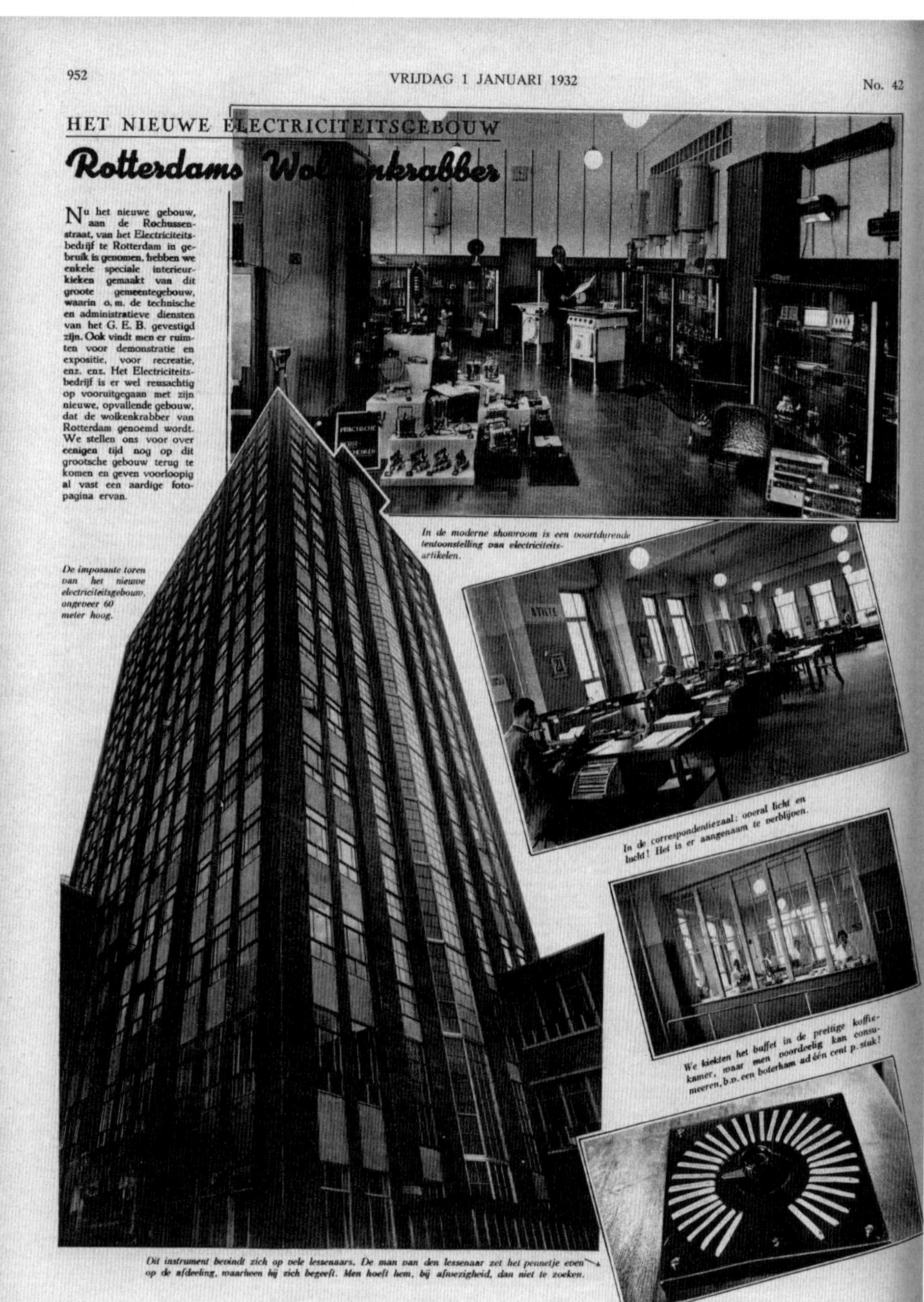

Nu het nieuwe gebouw, aan de Rochussenstraat, van het Electriciteitsbedrijf te Rotterdam in gebruik is genomen, hebben we enkele speciale interieurkieken gemaakt van dit groote gemeentegebouw, waarin o. m. de technische en administratieve diensten van het G. E. B. gevestigd zijn. Ook vindt men er ruimten voor demonstratie en expositie, voor recreatie, enz. enz. Het Electriciteitsbedrijf is er wel reusachtig op vooruitgegaan met zijn nieuwe, opvallende gebouw, dat de wolkenkrabber van Rotterdam genoemd wordt. We stellen ons voor over eenigen tijd nog op dit grootsche gebouw terug te komen en geven voorloopig al vast een aardige fotopagina ervan.

De imposante toren van het nieuwe electriciteitsgebouw, ongeveer 60 meter hoog.

In de moderne showroom is een voortdurende tentoonstelling van electriciteitsartikelen.

In de correspondentiezaal: overal licht en lucht! Het is er aangenaam te verblijven.

We kiekten het buffet in de prettige koffiekamer, waar men voordeelig kan consumeeren, b.v. een boterham ad één cent p. stuk!

Dit instrument bevindt zich op vele lessenaars. De man van den lessenaar zet het pennetje even op de afdeeling, waarheen hij zich begeeft. Men hoeft hem, bij afwezigheid, dan niet te zoeken.

'Rotterdam's Skyscraper', an article in *Groot Rotterdam*, January 1, 1932.

become enormously popular both in artistic circles and among the city's inhabitants in general. This can be deduced from the reception given the new vertical lifting bridge (Dutch: *hefbrug*) for the railway in the heart of the city, known affectionately as 'De Hef'.[13] Not only did the popular press give extensive and detailed coverage of its construction from 1925 and handover in 1927. De Hef also incited artists to experiment, most notably in Joris Ivens' almost entirely abstract film *De Brug* (The bridge) of 1928, which immediately achieved world fame. Other avant-garde artists photographed the bridge, numerous authors wrote about it and even today there are artists whose work features the De Hef, which became redundant when the train tunnel was completed in 1993.[14] One might regard it as Rotterdam's version of the Eiffel Tower. Both are engineering works that exploit their material, steel, to the maximum to achieve a soaring, airy structure. Both, too, have inspired countless artists and indeed De Hef, like its Parisian counterpart, was for many years a city landmark until the Euromast was erected in 1960.[15]

The fusion of art and machinery was a pre-eminent feature of modernist or 'functionalist' design and architecture. In the 1920s and '30s Rotterdam built up a solid reputation as a modernist city. As early as 1926 J.G. Wattjes, a well-regarded architectural historian and professor in architecture, wrote in the introduction to his book *Nieuw-Nederlandsche Bouwkunst* (New Dutch Architecture) that outside the Netherlands it was customary to distinguish between an Amsterdam strand and a Rotterdam strand in Dutch architecture.[16] Some architectural historians for this reason have advocated the introduction of the term 'Rotterdam School', by analogy with the Amsterdam and Delft Schools.[17] Indeed, the most celebrated examples of Dutch Modern Movement architecture were built in Rotterdam, for example the Van Nelle factory, Bergpolderflat, Café De Unie, the Bijenkorf department store and the Spangen and Kiefhoek housing. Many functionalist architects and designers, including J.A. Brinkman, W.H. Gispen, J.B. van Loghem, H.A. Maaskant, J.J.P. Oud, Paul Schuitema, Mart Stam, Willem van Tijen and Leendert van der Vlugt, were domiciled in Rotterdam. Oud, who was also active as a Modern Movement theorist, was City Architect to Rotterdam from 1918 to 1930. In addition, the city boasted not one but two manufacturers of tubular steel furniture and other modern interior designs; Gispen was the most famous, with D3 its less well-known rival.

Rotterdam's reputation as a city of modernism was reinforced by the image it had of a rational, modern city geared to the future. One might say that Rotterdam was also 'modern' in the broader, popular sense of the word. As such, the city was the perfect setting for modernism as a design trend. That 'modern' Rotterdam has been most convincingly portrayed in films about the city – in a medium, then, that was itself the most modern medium of the day. This portrayal of Rotterdam as a modern city extended to other media, up to and including family magazines. On each occasion the accent was on four aspects in particular: the traffic, the tall buildings, the city lights at night, particularly neon signs which were then relatively new, and lastly the docks including the river and its bridges.[18]

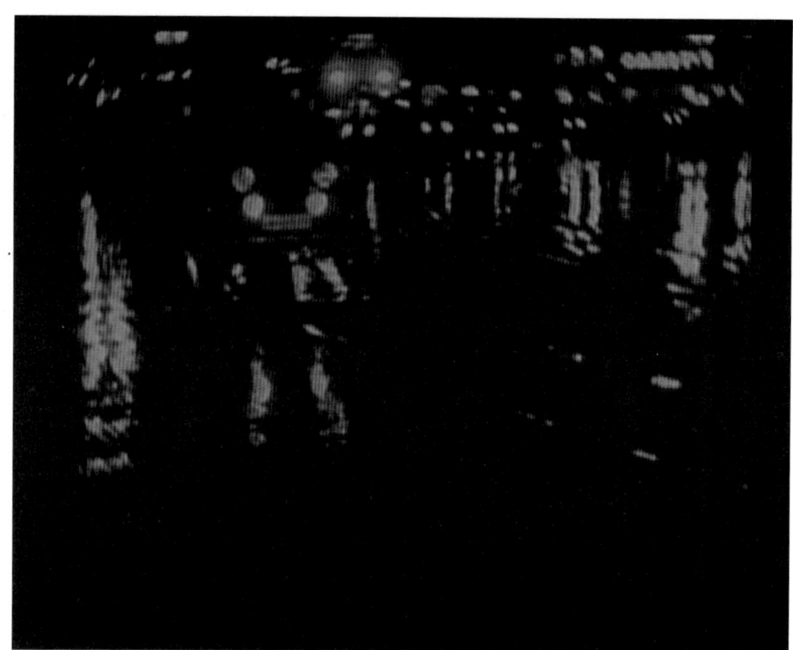

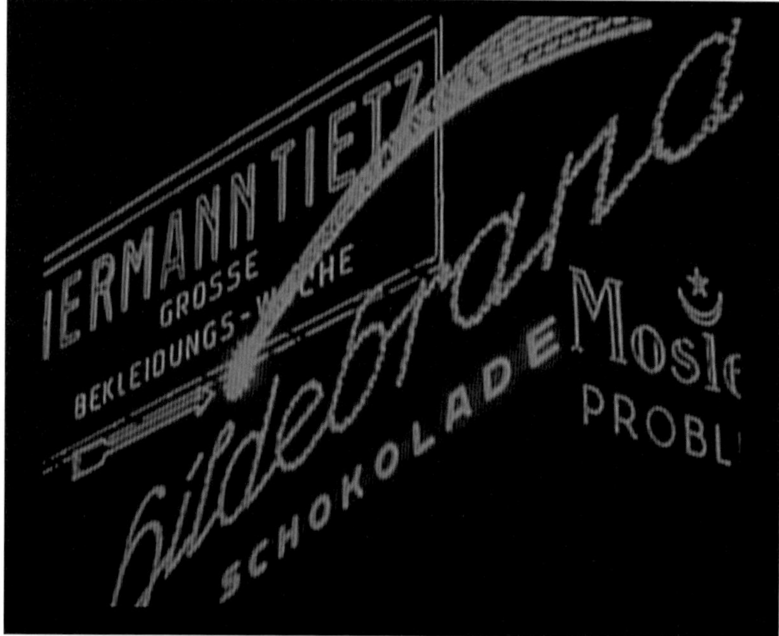

Stills from *Berlin. Die Synfonie der Großstadt*, 1927, dir. Walther Ruttmann. Street lights in the evening and neon signs were a regular feature of metropolitan iconography, as was racing traffic.

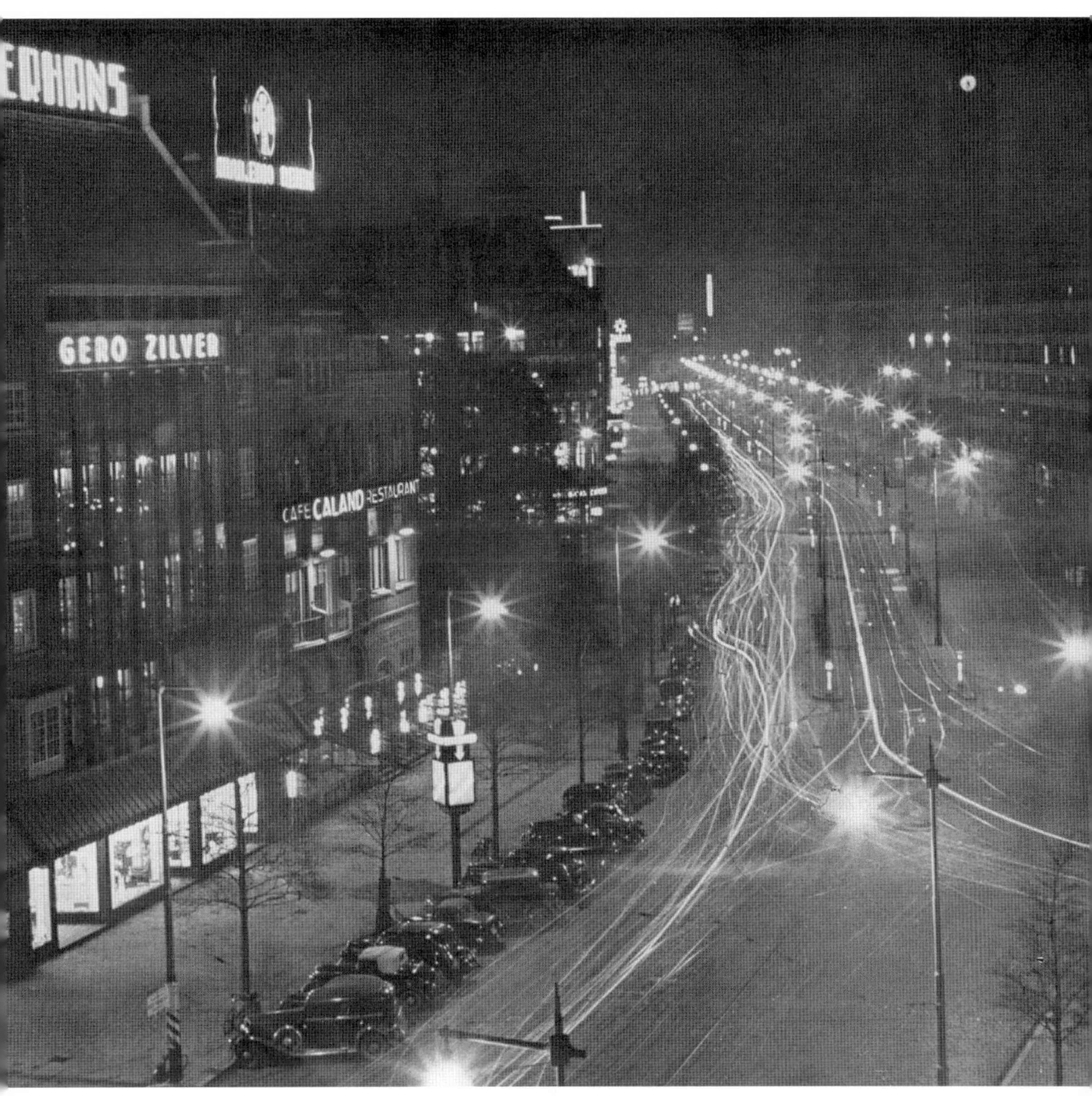

H. Schröfer-Carsten, photo from M.J. Brusse, *De schoonheid van ons land, Deel VI, Rotterdam*, Amsterdam 1938, comparing 'the narrow Hoofdsteeg and the broad modern Coolsingel by night'. So Rotterdam could be photographically portrayed as metropolitan as early as 1938.

Images of flows of traffic in those days were a popular means of suggesting a city in full swing. Motorized vehicles had yet to acquire the negative connotations they have today, quite the reverse in fact. Cars and more generally the speed of modern modes of transportation were virtually deified, as they had been by the Futurists. In a film with the revealing title of *Rotterdam. De Stad, die nooit rust* (Rotterdam, the city that never rests), made in 1928 by Andor von Barsy, a Hungarian who had emigrated to Rotterdam, we see the mad rush of traffic ploughing its way through the city.[19] Other films from those years that show Rotterdam as bustling with traffic are Jan Koelinga's *De Steeg* (The alley, 1933) and *Maasbruggen* (Maas bridges, 1937) directed by Paul Schuitema. Berlin, London and Paris were among other cities portrayed in that period with busy main roads to show just how dynamic and *metropolitan* they were.[20]

In those days the policy of Rotterdam's city council was targeted at giving motorized traffic much more room than it already had. Every urban planning intervention was given over to keeping the traffic flowing smoothly; even monuments were sacrificed to appease the traffic god, such as Plan-C, a large building containing shops overlooking the waters of Kolk. The Schielandshuis itself narrowly escaped the wrecker's ball in 1933.[21] Rotterdammers were particularly proud of the 'tunneltraverse', basically a semi-submerged extended run-up to the Maas Tunnel constructed in 1942, which allowed cars to step on the gas as early as Blijdorp well north of the river before diving into the tunnel on their way to South Rotterdam (Rotterdam-Zuid), and vice versa. The tunneltraverse was clearly made with the future in mind, at all events with regard to the growth of traffic, seeing that it still functions today in its original state. The thoroughfare has two pairs of lanes separated by a raised section and most intersections are at different levels. These are characteristics of a modern motorway that were to be found nowhere else in the Netherlands at the time. The tunneltraverse can therefore be regarded as the first Dutch motorway.

Another aspect intrinsic to the image of a modern city apart from racing traffic is high-rise. Rotterdam had few tall buildings to show in the inter-war years but was certainly proud of the fact that it had within its limits the tallest office building in the Netherlands, Het Witte Huis (the white house) dating from 1879 and 45 metres tall. For his film *Rotterdam. De Stad, die nooit rust* Von Barsy shot Het Witte Huis without the top part, so that we get the impression of a skyscraper that extends much further upwards out of view to us. Jan Koelinga filmed the Bijenkorf department store along similar lines. Similarly suggestive is the frog's-eye view published in the July 1, 1932 edition of the family magazine *Groot Rotterdam* to mark the handover of the new Electricity Building. This building was no less than 58 metres high, and so the photograph's caption proudly proclaims: 'Rotterdam's Skyscraper'. Come to that, the magazine's title alone ('great Rotterdam') is a nod to things metropolitan. The dream of ever becoming a true skyscraper city after the American model had been upheld by this magazine – and therefore by many tens of thousands of Rotterdammers[22] – for a much longer time. On the front page of the July 27, 1928 edition is a photograph of Chicago with its many skyscrapers jostling for space on the river banks. Their height is exaggerated by having one skyscraper tower continue up beyond the edge of the photo, right through the magazine's name. A broad main road and a bridge over the river, both filled with cars, are also clearly visible. The magazine does not identify the city as Chicago. The photo is made to work as a vision, a vision of Rotterdam's future to be more precise. 'This is how Rotterdam will look in a few years' time', according to the caption. And in slightly smaller letters: 'Each year the buildings in the city on the [river] Rotte are getting bigger, and taller. Once the Driehavenplan has been brought to completion, we will see the sturdy skyscrapers of world-famous Rotterdam companies rising on the banks of the Maas.'[23]

In Europe in the 1920s, modern American cities were indeed regarded as if they were a kind of solidified vision of the future.[24] And of all America's cities, Chicago stood as the most typically American.[25] According to Marco D'Eramo Chicago was regarded not an a unique city like Paris or New York, but as a typical average modern American city.[26] Berlin, a city with much in common with Rotterdam in terms of character and history, has repeatedly been compared with Chicago, first by Mark Twain in 1891 and then by many others on numerous occasions. This comparison was not prompted by indisputable resemblances between the two cities, but by Berlin's modernity, a modernity which according to Twain and company had something un-European about it. It must be said that Berlin like Rotterdam was presented as much more modern and metropolitan than it really was. Berlin suffered, as did Rotterdam, from *Weltstadtsehnsucht*, a wonderful German term that can be translated, if woodenly, as 'the yearning to be a world city'.[27] The archetype of the modern metropolis was in those days the major American city, and as said earlier, of all American cities Chicago was regarded as the most American.[28] 'Chicago stood for the march into modernity and was suitable as a metaphor for Berlin's upheaval.'[29] The comparison of Rotterdam with Chicago should be viewed in this same light. So both Berlin and Rotterdam take example from Chicago. The explanation for the 'Weltstadtsehnsucht' felt by the two cities probably resides in the fact that both Berlin and Rotterdam long enjoyed the reputation of being big but ugly.[30] Hallmarks that had first been held against them could be appreciated when looked at from a metropolitan perspective.

If anything was associated with modern city life at that time, it was the lights at night, the third aspect. Cities like London, Paris and Berlin were celebrated for their neon illuminations, and Rotterdam's streets of shops and entertainment were often portrayed in all their nocturnal glory. Boldly coloured neon signs adorned such tall buildings and structures as Het Witte Huis (an ad for Van Nelle), De Hef (Blue Band) and the then new Van Nelle factory – modernity crowned with modernity. Like the automobile, advertisements had yet to acquire the negative reputation they have today. They were seen less as misleading persuaders than as a modern

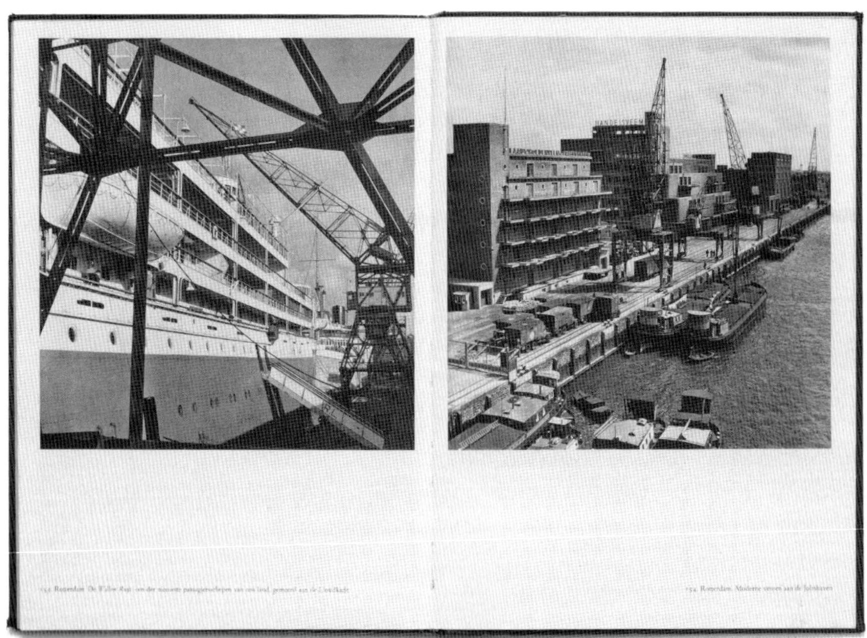

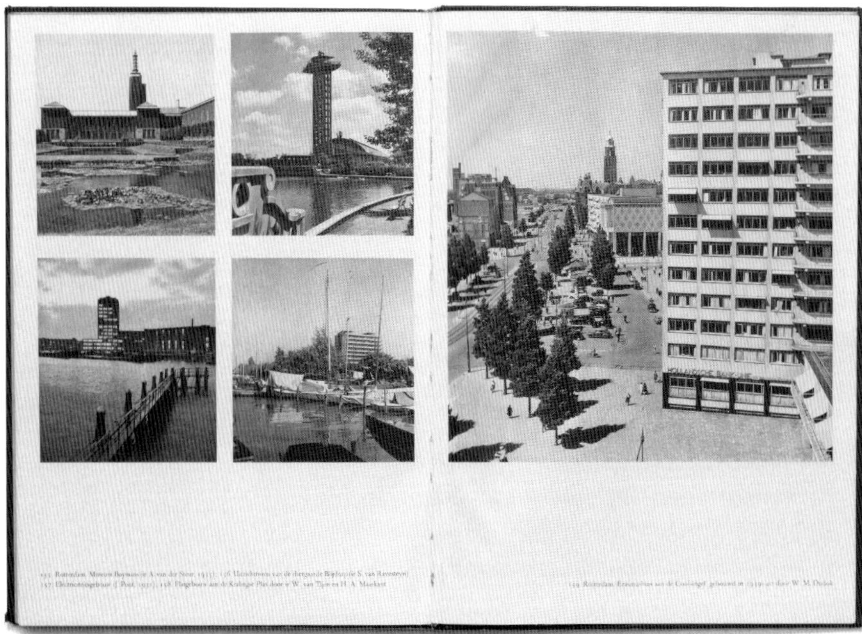

Photos by Cas Oorthuys from *De schoonheid van ons land, Land en volk, De steden*, Amsterdam/Antwerp 1951. This book was to portray the postwar Rotterdam, yet its shots are largely of prewar, modern-looking buildings.

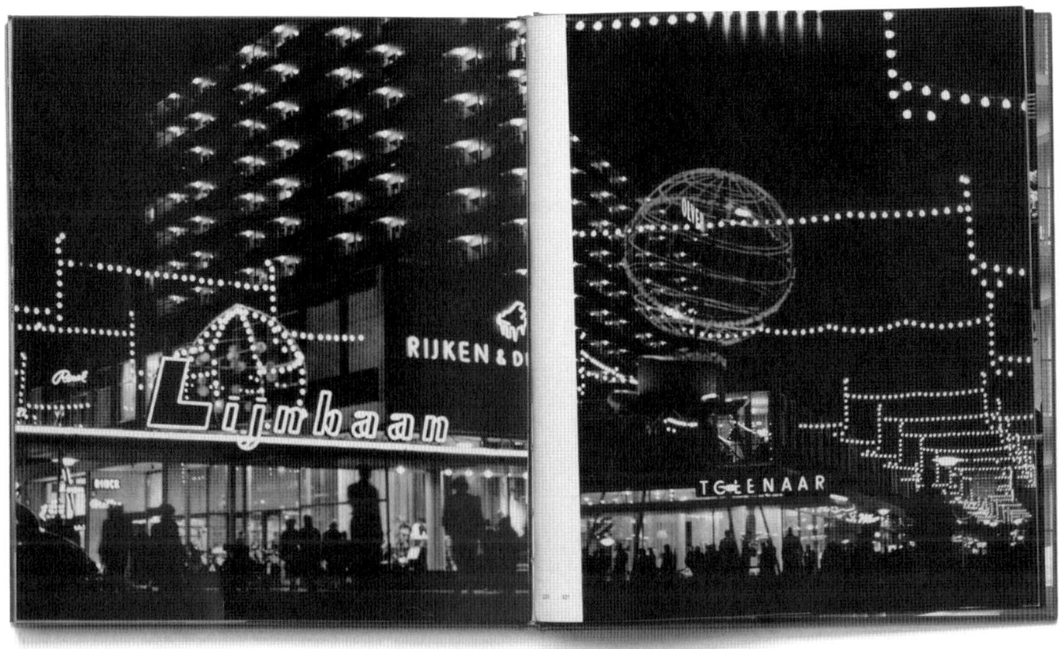

Photo by Cas Oorthuys of the entrance to Korte Lijnbaan, from J.W. de Boer, *Rotterdam dynamische stad*, Amsterdam 1959. This photobook of 236 photographs by Oorthuys was immensely popular and went through three reprints. The mood it projects is typical of the optimism of the postwar-reconstruction era, when there was still an unshakable faith in modernism. The accompanying text translates as follows: 'The lights from the rear of the surrounding flats add an element of mystery in their uncompromising regularity'.

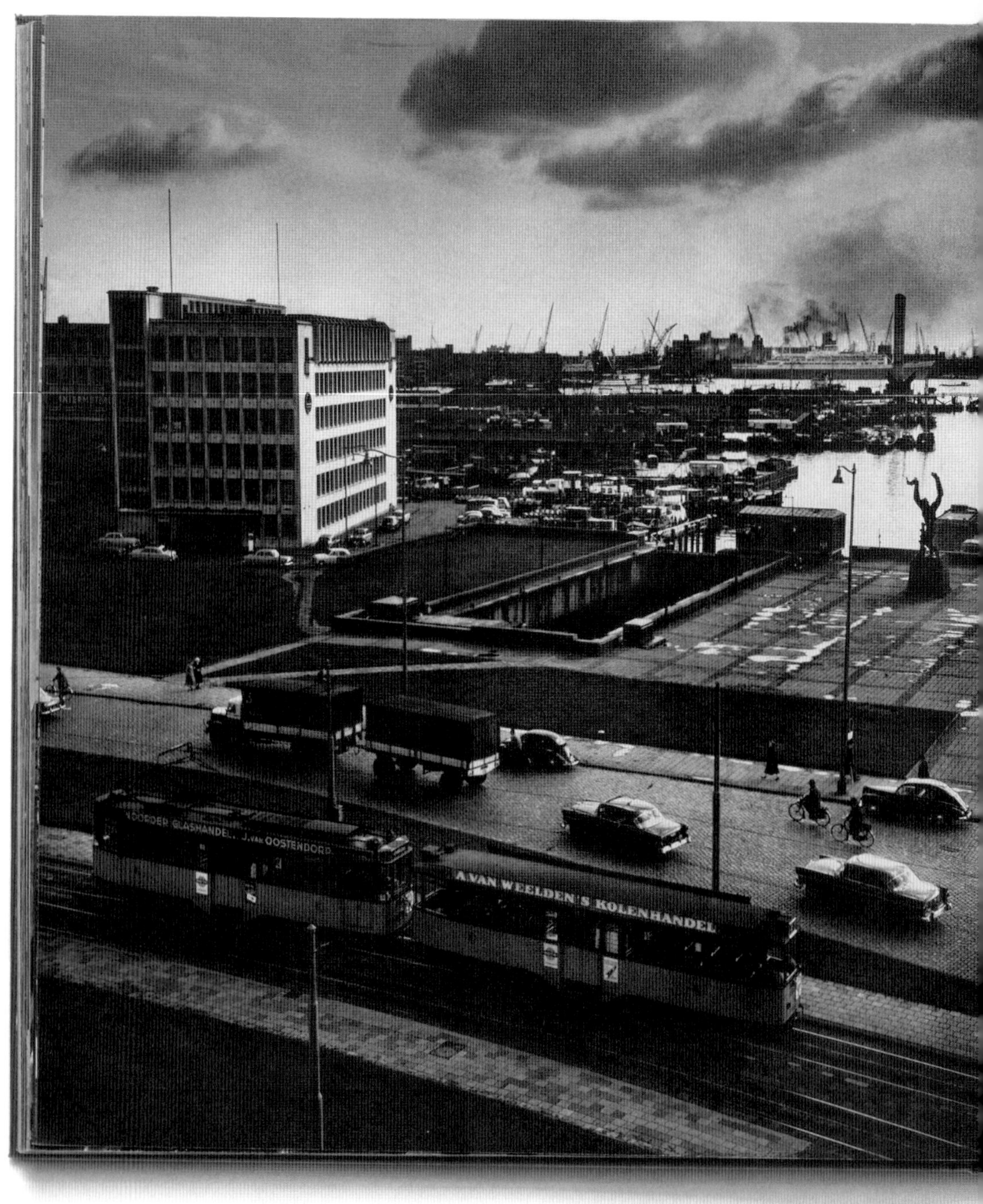

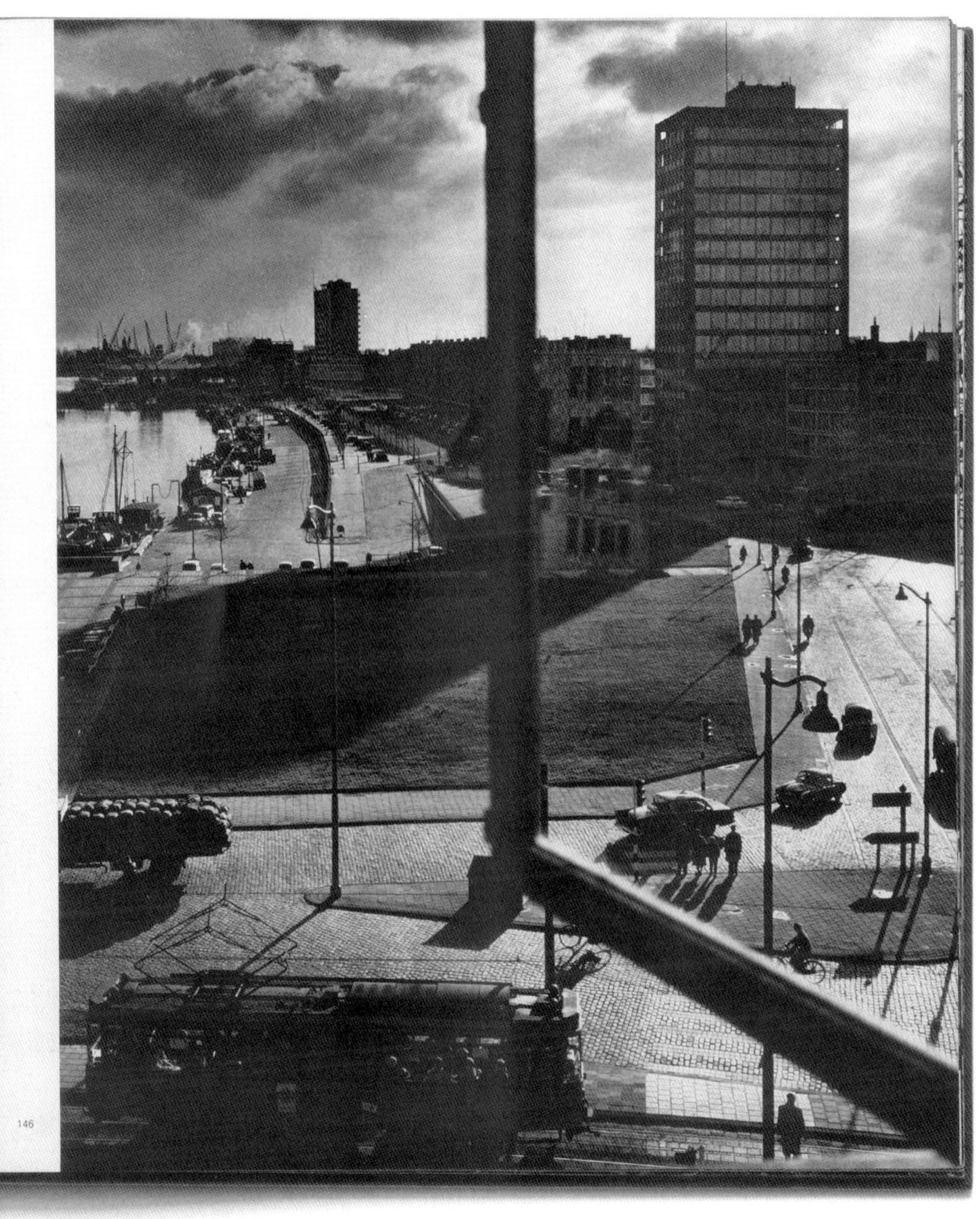

Photo by Cas Oorthuys of Leuvehaven Westzijde, from J.W. de Boer, *Rotterdam dynamische stad*, Amsterdam 1959.

means of disseminating information and in many cases as a form of art.

The docks and the river with its bridges, the fourth aspect given as evidence in the inter-war years of Rotterdam's metropolitan status, is in some respects related to the other three: the bridge, the cranes, gantries and other tall structures in the docks create a skyline that suggests a city with real skyscrapers. In other respects, the port and the river are significant in their own right in that they represent contact with the rest of the world, and consequently the cosmopolitan qualities of a metropolis.

We can conclude that representation of the metropolis is an iconographic theme recognizable from three stable elements: traffic, high-rise and city lights. In Rotterdam's case the port is an additional element that ties in with the other three.

World city under reconstruction

In those years, then, Rotterdam's status as a modern metropolis was celebrated as much by artists as by the public at large. And the sooner there were more cars, more broad thoroughfares, more tall buildings, more ships and more sounds befitting a metropolis, the better. This euphoria for the modern age gained an even more bombastic sequel during the first two decades following the Second World War. The great voids left in the city once the rubble had been cleared were seized on to once again give modernity all the room it needed. Even before and during the war work had been proceeding on a new urban plan in accordance with the latest ideas. This would result in the so-called Basisplan, which was well-received because of its metropolitan aspect. Just as before the war, the metropolitan condition was again associated with motorized traffic, tall buildings and broad streets with brightly lit shops. 'Rotterdam is expanding, it will take on the air of a world city; the rush of traffic, the broad boulevards, the tall buildings together will give an atmosphere of industry in tune with its daily life. Nothing cosy but then these days we prefer a row of gleaming automobiles to a horse-drawn carriage for elderly ladies', as the Rotterdam daily *Het Vrije Volk* boldly put it in 1952.[31]

When in 1951 Rotterdam was once again portrayed in the series *De schoonheid van ons land*, this time in a book about several Dutch cities, we see that despite the wartime devastation the description of it differs little from that in the above-mentioned book of 1938 in the same series. This time Cas Oorthuys is the photographer, and he begins by showing us the Maas bridges, then the Coolsingel boulevard with its Beurs or exchange, the HBU bank building and the Bijenkorf department store – three buildings that had survived the air raid and the ensuing conflagration – then traffic 'on and below the Maas' (below meaning the Maas tunnel), next Wilhelminakade with the offices of the Holland-America Line, then Lloydkade and Jobshaven with ships and warehouses, after that a page of examples of Rotterdam 'high-rise' (the tower on the Boymans-van Beuningen Museum, the tower in Blijdorp Zoo, the Electricity Building and the block of flats overlooking the waters of Kralingse Plas), then Coolsingel once more and lastly a detail of the facade of a new modernist

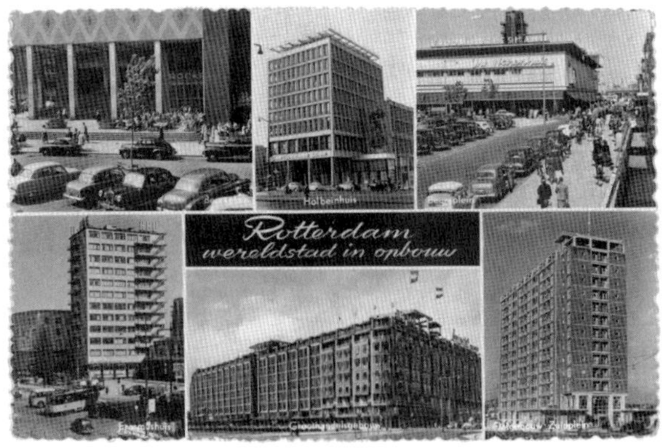

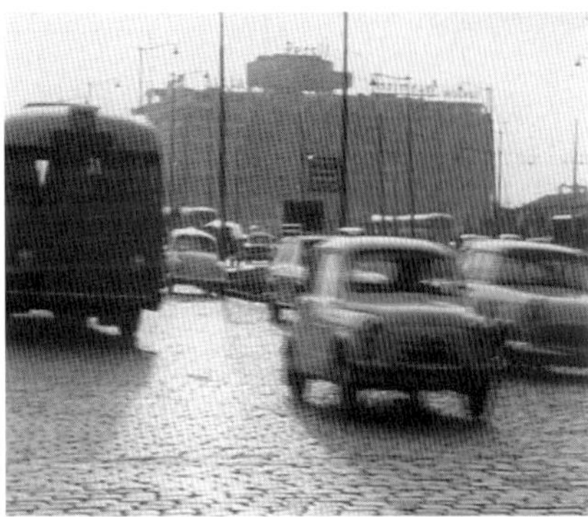

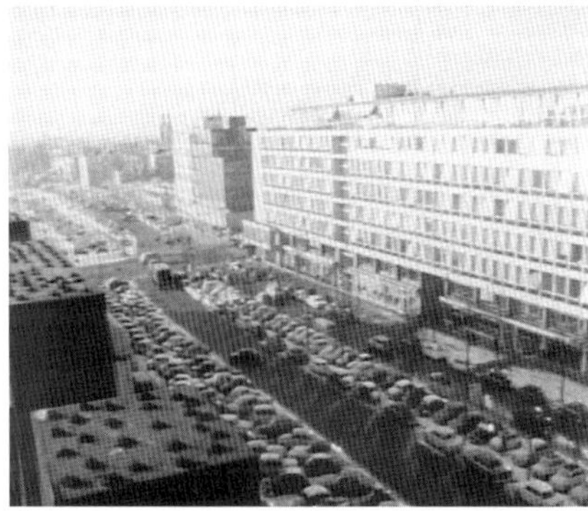

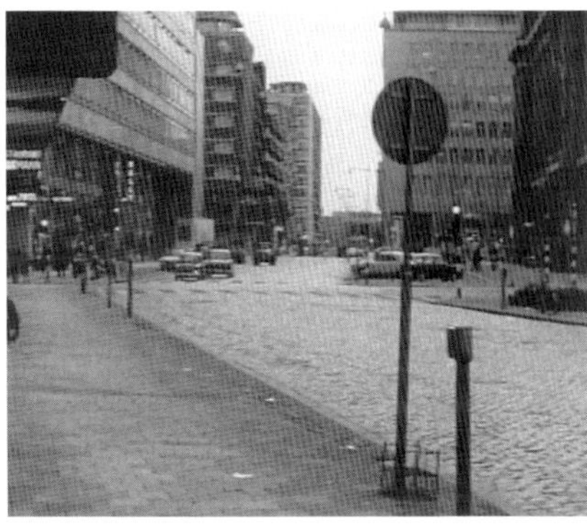

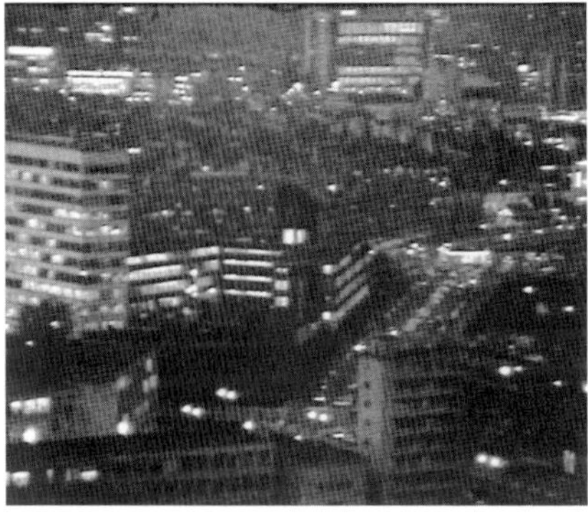

Top picture postcard entitled 'Rotterdam, world city under construction', c. 1953-1954.

Stills from *Stad zonder hart*, 1966, dir. Jan Schaper; **middle left** in this film the phenomenon of city traffic is deployed to show how rapidly the city centre empties after every working day between half-past five and half-past six; **right** here the voice-over explains: 'Instead of the other 20,000 [homes] there came offices, banks, insurance companies and, above all else, broad streets'; **bottom left** a deserted Rotterdam, described by the voice-over as 'taut facades evoking a chilly and inhospitable mood'; **right** Rotterdam in the evening, a stereotypical metropolitan image. But appearances are deceptive, according to the narrator: 'He who sees the lamps of the thousands of cars, and then turns his gaze towards the city whose lights have just gone on, then thinks: "Rotterdam is a world city". But he who arrives in the centre an hour later still sees the glittering fountain and the large buildings of business concerns, and still hears the wonderful carillon, but for him Coolsingel and Raadhuisplein will be empty, at least he will come across very few people there.'

apartment tower south of the river at Zuidplein. The photographs in the postwar publication resemble those of 1938 in terms of atmosphere in that they too stress the port activities and the city's modernity; curiously enough the resemblance is also quite literal as the photos in the 1951 book are almost exclusively of prewar buildings! And yet the postwar publication is definitely intended to showcase the new Rotterdam in the making, as witness the words of W.A. Wagener, who wrote the essay on Rotterdam: 'the new Rotterdam of the future will be a city of quite another kind of beauty, certainly as overwhelming as then [the Rotterdam of before 1800] but now for modern people'.[32] We can only conclude that the Rotterdam of the future dreamt of in 1951 was the same Rotterdam of the future that was being worked on before the war. In other words, we can observe a strong sense of continuity between the inter-war years and the period of post-war reconstruction in terms of how the city's future was envisioned. There is nothing new about this observation; for a long time it was commonplace in the literature on Rotterdam's architectural and urbanistic development to refer to 'an unbroken modern tradition in Dutch architecture and urbanism'.[33] Evidently not only architects and urbanists but also the public at large harboured this idea of a future perspective on Rotterdam living on unaffected by the war. Another book to propagate this idea of a continuity between prewar and postwar modern Rotterdam was the immensely popular *Rotterdam dynamische stad* (Rotterdam dynamic city, first edition 1959) which boasted 236 photographs by Cas Oorthuys and three reprints.

The real break in the perspective on Rotterdam came later, from the mid 1960s on. It shows through clearly if we compare two films about Rotterdam, one from the 1920s and the other from the '60s. The first is the aforementioned 'Rotterdam, the city that never rests' from 1928 by Andor von Barsy and the second *Stad zonder hart* (City without a heart, 1966) directed by Jan Schaper. We have already discussed the key ingredients of Von Barsy's film: flows of traffic, high-rise, city lights and the docks. Jan Schaper's film includes traffic sequences too, but from a negative perspective: he wants to show how the city centre empties every evening between half-past five and half-past six and is left deserted. A voice-over gives an explanation for this phenomenon: 'Some 100,000 Rotterdammers once lived in 25,000 houses in the heart of Rotterdam, before that heart was destroyed . (...) No more than 5000 of the 25,000 houses that first stood in the centre were replaced. Instead of the other 20,000 there came offices, banks, insurance companies and, above all else, broad streets'. The film shows that in those days Rotterdam's inner city indeed had very broad streets, some of them with as many as eight lanes. The average Rotterdammer was unable to summon up any further enthusiasm for this object lesson in modern city planning, to judge from the popular tone of the commentary: 'We didn't want an antiseptic, spick and span city'. The modernist buildings were summarily disposed of as 'taut facades evoking a chilly and inhospitable mood'. Rotterdam as it used to be, on the other hand, was idealized in *Stad zonder hart*. Prewar Rotterdam is presented as busy and full and the Rotterdam of 1966 as bare and empty. In Schaper's view there are no similarities whatsoever between the prewar and the postwar Rotterdam as showcased (unintentionally) in the series of books *De schoonheid van ons land*. On the contrary, the images of old and new Rotterdam are chosen in such a way that it is as if two entirely different cities are being discussed. The voice-over recites a litany of recommendations to get the city looking more like it used to look: less traffic, more stalls selling wares, more trees too, and more small entertainment facilities. Armed with images shot in one of the few such facilities of that time, Cabaret in den Twijfelaar, *Stad zonder hart* wipes the floor with the most sacred of sacred cows to Rotterdam's self-esteem: the city's dynamic character. We see and hear young people singing a song entitled *Bagger* (sludge!), whose subject is the city in its permanent state of being torn down and built up. The chorus has a derisive ring – 'Ba-ba-ba-ba-bagger' – followed by mocking lines like 'Toil away, bustle away' and 'we are full of energy'. Here, the heroic Rotterdam of the future, 'the city that never rests', is effectively laid to rest.

C70 and the small-scale ideal

In the second half of the 1960s dissatisfaction with the urban surroundings grew among residents and in the city council. To many, Rotterdam was a cold and forbidding place with little of the vibrancy of a city, and this was largely blamed on the way the inner city was being developed. This image of Rotterdam, a city whose formidable achievements on the economic front were offset by the lack of a friendly atmosphere, was pivotal to the cultural event known as C70.

C70 was the fourth large-scale festive event to be mounted by the City of Rotterdam in the postwar period. In 1950, 1955 and 1960 there had been exhibitions on a major scale with a host of other activities in tow.[34] All three had been held in Museumpark and Het Park, two neighbouring areas of greenspace separated by the Westzeedijk. The first two of these events, Ahoy' and E55, were closely related in terms of content. Both sang the praises of the rebuilt Rotterdam, its port and industry and advances in technology in general using a mix of educational and artistic presentations. The Floriade came from a slightly different angle as its core was a horticultural exhibition. But even then, it likewise embraced technology, as emerged from the (positive) attention it gave to pesticides, genetic manipulation and the latest glasshouse techniques.

C70 deviated from the earlier three events in a number of ways. For a start, there was its location: the exhibition was held not in Rotterdam's parks but in the inner city itself. It contents radiated another atmosphere entirely that clearly stemmed from the changes in mentality that had been rocking society since 1960. Technology and industry were much less prominently present and certainly not eulogized. Further, the scale of the exhibits and pavilions at C70 was much more modest in comparison. Photographs of the earlier events, particularly E55, show visitors like tiny dolls gawping at enormous, mind-numbing presentations. Typical

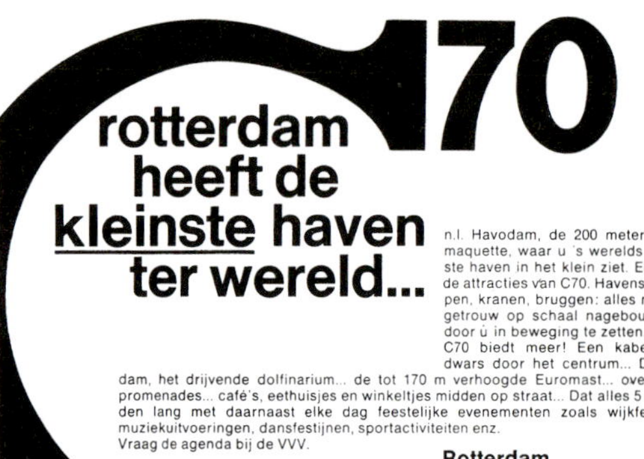

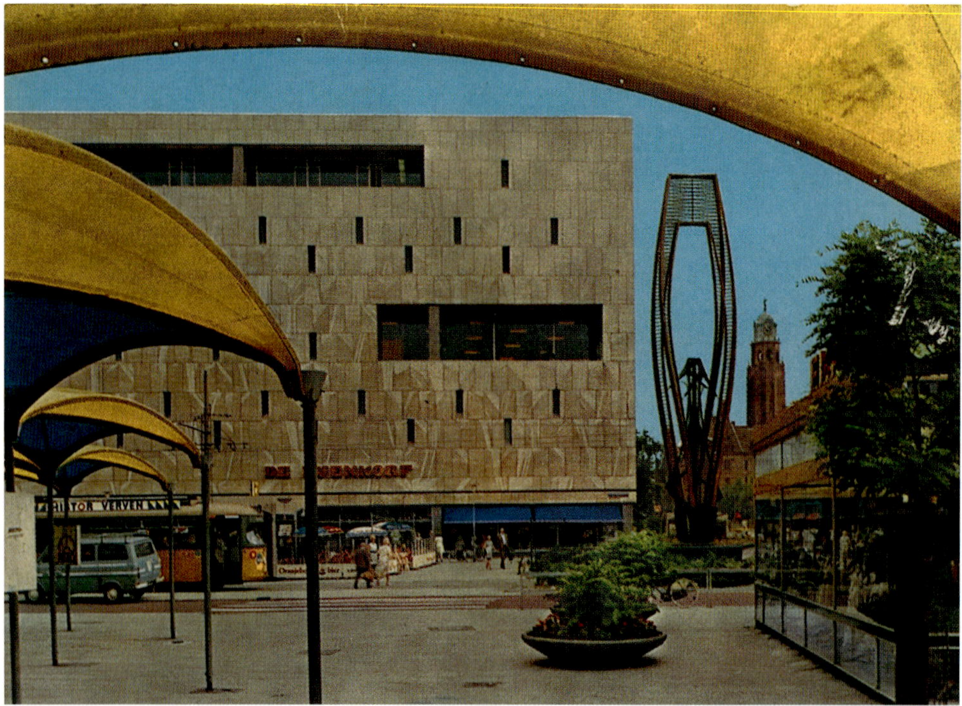

Top publicity material for a scale model of the harbour during C70. The slogan reads: 'Rotterdam has the smallest port in the world...'.

Bottom picture postcard of the coloured plastic domes during C70.

Right Coolsingel during the C70 event with the sheltered walking route, photo by Tom Kroeze.

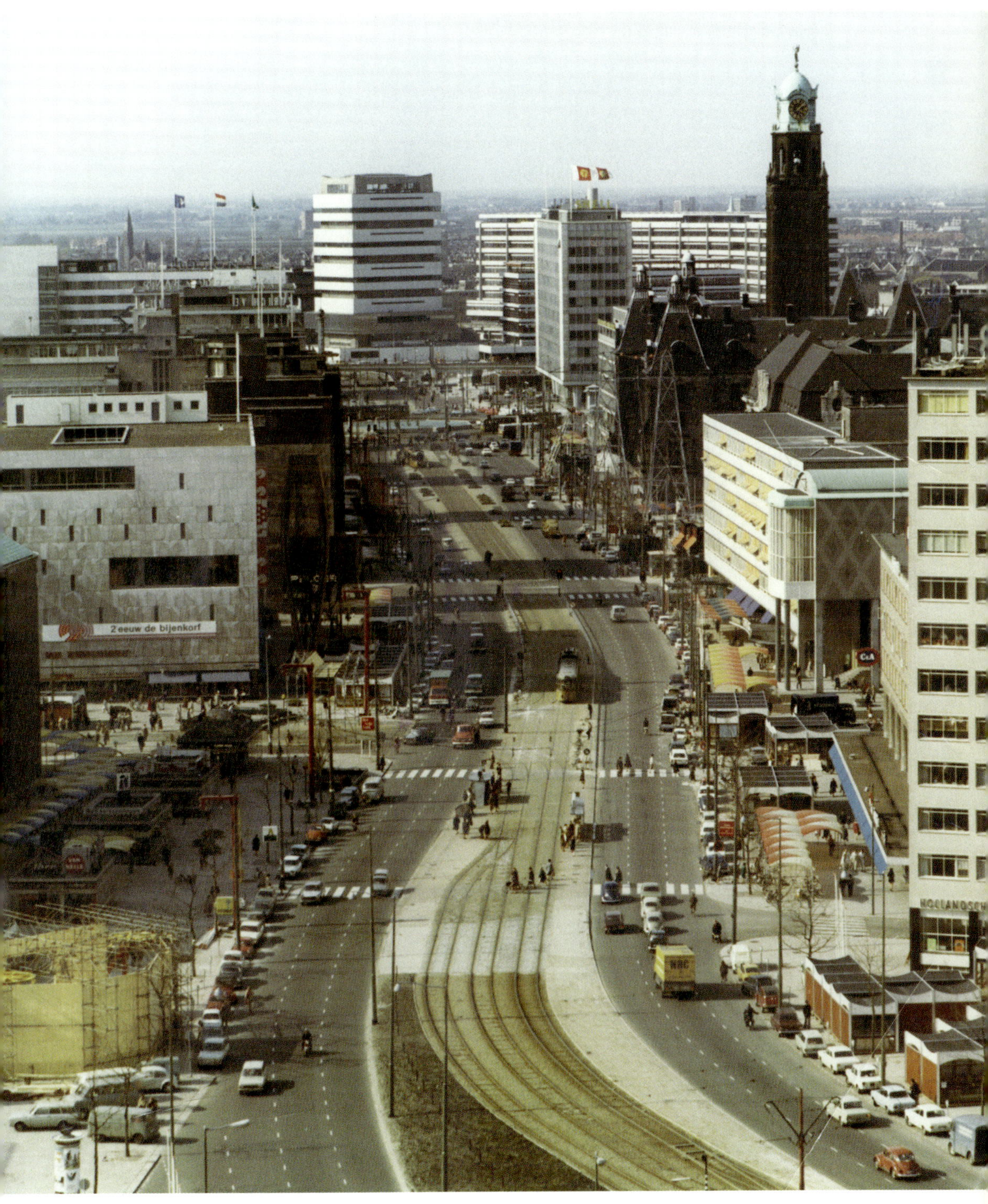

69 – From metropolitan to provincial

of C70 by contrast are the many diminutives needed to describe the various components. The exhibition was awash with 'little pavilions', 'little domes', 'little cafés',
'little stands', 'little shops' and 'little diners'.[35]

The choice of the inner city as the site for C70 and this predilection for the
small-scale were directly related. Rotterdam's centre was known for its lack of
warmth, as the promotional material for C70 and the exhibition texts made abundantly clear, and the cause of this negative quality was said to be the excessive
spaciousness of the city's social environment. The published guide to the event
puts it this way: 'The vast inner city area is said to have too a big a scale to support
a congenial atmosphere. C70 has attempted to rid Rotterdam of this none too
friendly image for a city.'[36] 'Nice and small', then, was the event's unwritten slogan,
and this is reflected in almost every part of the exhibition. First of all, there were
the little plastic domes marking out a sheltered walking route two and a half kilometres long through the city centre. Walking beneath these gaily coloured domes,
one was briefly unaware of the detested large scale of the inner city. The sheltered
route led past the outdoor exhibitions and many little pavilions, temporary structures parked in and around the Coolsingel boulevard for the duration of C70. A photograph of Coolsingel made at the time of C70 vividly shows the contrast between, on
the one hand, the little domes and little pavilions and, on the other, the permanent
buildings towering above them like giants.

Even the Port of Rotterdam, which since 1962 could rightfully call itself the
largest in the world, was playfully cut down to size in the C70 advertising slogan
'Rotterdam has the smallest port in the world...'. This was a reference to a scale
model of the port, Havodam (after Madurodam miniature city near The Hague),
one of the exhibition's top attractions. But in view of the recent criticism of the
continued expansion of the Rotterdam docks it is tempting to see the slogan as a
half-intended attempt to present the port as less of a threat. The ambivalent feelings
about the port are spelt out in the C70 guide. The tone is slightly bitter: 'Now that
advances in Rotterdam's industries have contributed to the prosperity enjoyed in
the Netherlands a quarter of a century after liberation, further industrialization is
being resisted. Understandably. (...) It is for good reason that Rotterdam is the bone
of contention in a discourse that seeks to preserve human welfare in an industrial-
ized society.'[37] If the exhibitions in 1950, 1955 and 1960 were still permeated with
Rotterdam's success story, with the port as its fulcrum, now Rotterdam was even
being described by the organizers as 'an assembly point (...) for many of today's
problems'.[38]

The negative picture painted of Rotterdam as an excessively large and
inhospitable city had been an issue two years before C70 in a scholarly study done by
a social psychologist, Professor R. Wentholt, whose title translates as 'How people
experience the inner city of Rotterdam'. Wentholt bases his study on two surveys
held among Rotterdammers about their city's centre; one was a verbal survey held
among 100 Rotterdammers chosen at random, the other a series of conversations

with 25 Rotterdam dignitaries.[39] Both brought to the fore an overwhelmingly negative
assessment of Rotterdam's inner city. The terms used to express this uneasiness are
more or less the same as in the publicity surrounding C70: 'The reasons most often
given for discontent with the centre were the lack of warmth and conviviality felt
in the inner city; it was impersonal, bare, cold, stiff, it had a rational look; there was
the appearance of the inner city as a whole, the great width of its streets, the ugliness,
its squat, ponderous buildings, the empty spaces, the lifeless places, the lack of inti-
macy.'[40] Wentholt then tries in his study to give these subjective statements about
Rotterdam an objective thrust by analysing the inner city's architecture and planning.
This analysis is on the whole scathing in its condemnation. That Wentholt's objective-
ness is doubtful, to say the least, can be deduced merely from the frequency of the
ubiquitous (and hard to translate) Dutch adjective *gezellig* and its negative, *ongezellig*.
Gezellig as applied to a city centre would mean a feeling of warmth, charm, conge-
niality, even safety. Yet to experience it depends on many more factors than a manner
of building or a particular urban design response to a situation. Besides, many of
the urban characteristics Wentholt clearly regards as negative are in effect neutral;
in another context they could even be explained as positive. The designations meant
here include 'rational', 'great width', 'empty spaces', 'openness', 'rectangular'.[41] At the
onset of the 21st century Rotterdam can still be described as rational, wide, open
and rectangular and still has large empty spaces but all these terms have now taken
on a much more positive charge.

Around 1970, however, everyone was thoroughly convinced that the sorely
missed element of *gezelligheid* could be conveyed by small-scale structures. And C70
seemed to confirm this conviction, as many Rotterdammers were of the opinion that
their city had not been so warm and congenial, so *gezellig*, in thirty years: 'After five
months of C70 comparisons are being drawn with Rotterdam prior to 1940. Older
people are saying that in all the thirty years gone by, the *gezelligheid* of before '40 has
never been as close again as in the past summer. The bare, functional inner city was
cluttered once more, not least by the crowds draped over the streets like a living
carpet.'[42] An official public survey held by the NIPO market research company con-
firmed this picture.[43] The comparison with pre-1940 Rotterdam has more to do with
nostalgia than with historical reality. Many small-scale neighbourhoods had been
demolished to build wide roads before the Germans and later the Allies bombed Rotterdam in the Second World War. It is an understandable nostalgia, and can be regarded
as part of the process of coming to terms with the loss of Rotterdam as it had been.

So, C70 was seen as a success in terms of increasing the livability[44] of the
inner city. At last Rotterdam was becoming *gezellig* again, and nothing seemed more
logical than to continue the policy of small-scale and more intensive development.
Anyone unfamiliar with the further course of Rotterdam's history would assume
that by the end of the 20th century all the wide streets and open spaces in the city
had been built up and that the modernist, rectangular mode of building had been
banished for good. Yet looking at Rotterdam at the turn of the millennium, recent

urbanistic and architectural activity is clearly closer to reconstruction-era modernism than to the small scale advocated by C70.

The inter-war years brought a new perspective on Rotterdam that placed modern urbanity in a positive light. Rotterdam's metropolitan status was given extra emphasis in representations of the city by stressing the flows of traffic, the high-rise, the city lights at night, and the docks and river. Of these four aspects the first three – traffic, high-rise and city lights – can be regarded as the basic ingredients of the metropolitan iconography that arose in those years. Berlin, Paris and the great American cities were likewise imagined with these aspects heavily emphasized.

In fact the war did nothing to disrupt the way Rotterdam was represented. The metropolitan image that arose in the inter-war years was simply resumed in the post-war reconstruction period. It was only halfway into the 1960s that Rotterdam's reputation as a world city became tarnished and around 1970 the city found itself in an identity crisis. It was still large, spacious, rational and modern yet these properties were no only appreciated. The C70 exhibition was the first in a series of attempts to give Rotterdam a smaller scale.

1 Laar, P. van de (2000), *Stad van formaat. Geschiedenis van Rotterdam in de negentiende en twintigste eeuw*, Zwolle: Waanders, p. 173.

2 Van de Laar (2000), op. cit. (note 1), p. 8.

3 Van de Laar (1998), *Veranderingen in het geschiedbeeld van de koopstad Rotterdam*, Rotterdam [: the author], p. 1.

4 Van de Laar (2000), op. cit. (note 1), p. 8.

5 On the influence of Futurism see, for example, Banham, R. (1980 (1960)), *Theory and Design in the First Machine Age*, London: The Architectural Press.

6 Koot, R. (2001), 'De Hef en het imago van de modernste stad van Nederland: Een brug tussen haven en avant-garde', in: M. Halbertsma & P. van Ulzen (eds), *Interbellum Rotterdam: Kunst en cultuur 1918–1940*, Rotterdam, NAi Uitgevers, pp. 20-44.

7 Brusse, M.J. et al. (1938), *Rotterdam* (*De schoonheid van ons land*; dl. VI). Amsterdam, Uitgeverij Contact. To be more precise, only six of the 50 photographs fail to fit one of these categories.

8 Brusse probably knew the ideas and texts of the Futurists first hand, having worked as a journalist for the *Nieuwe Rotterdamsche Courant* when the Futurists visited Rotterdam in 1913, an event given extensive coverage in the Rotterdam newspapers. On this see Kalmthout, A.B.G.M. van (1998), *Muzentempels. Multidisciplinaire kunstkringen in Nederland tussen 1880 en 1914*, Hilversum: Uitgeverij Verloren, pp. 640-649.

9 Brusse et al. (1938), op. cit. (note 7), pp. XIII-XIV.

10 Brusse et al. (1938), op. cit. (note 7), pp. XIV-XV.

11 Brusse et al. (1938), op. cit. (note 7), pp. XVII, XXV.

12 Brusse et al. (1938), op. cit. (note 7), p. XXII.

13 The information on De Hef in the following section derives from Koot (2001), op. cit. (note 6), pp. 20-44.

14 Reuver, H. de (2000), *Hé, de Hef. Een kranige brug*, Rotterdam: Duo Duo.

15 For examples of De Hef as an urban symbol see Boode, A. de & P. van Oudheusden (1985), *De Hef. Biografie van een spoorbrug*, Rotterdam: Uitgeverij De Hef, pp. 120-125.

16 Wattjes, J.G. (1926), *Nieuw-Nederlandsche Bouwkunst*, Amsterdam: Uitgevers-Maatschappij 'Kosmos', p. VI. As it happens, Wattjes disagrees with this over-simplified categorization.

17 Van de Ven, C.J.M. (1977), 'De Rotterdamse bijdrage aan het Nieuwe Bouwen', *Plan*, 2 (February), pp. 10-24.

18 Interestingly, M. Bienert in his study on the picture constructed of Berlin in the 1920s and '30s distinguishes three almost identical elements with which Berlin sought to present itself as a metropolis: motorized traffic, electric light and tall glass facades. Rotterdam adds the port as a fourth element. 'Never-ending streams of motorized traffic, a sumptuous display of electric lighting, glass facades rising to the skies –

three objective elements combine to give the "visual impression" of a "metropolitan" array of streets.' Bienert, M. (1992), *Die eingebildete Metropole: Berlin im Feuilleton der Weimarer Republik*, Stuttgart: J.B. Metzlersche Verlagsbuchhandlung, p. 105. In truth, these three elements could only be found in a few places in Berlin before the Second World War, according to Bienert.

19 There are several known versions of this film bearing different titles. I later refer specifically to a version in the Filmmuseum in Amsterdam. Information from Floris Paalman gratefully acknowledged.

20 For Berlin specifically see Bienert (1992), op. cit. (note 18), p. 107: 'The "metropolitan traffic" familiar from other metropolises, was less feared than - longed for. Such an accumulation of private vehicles, which few could permit themselves at the time, suggested the modernity and affluence of metropolitan civil society.'

21 Provoost, M. (1995), 'Massa en weerstand 1920–1945', in: M. Aarts (ed.), *Vijftig jaar wederopbouw Rotterdam: Een geschiedenis van toekomstvisies*, Rotterdam: 010 Publishers, pp. 65-96.

22 In 1928 *Groot Rotterdam* had over 100,000 subscribers. See Halbertsma, M. & P. van Ulzen (eds) (2001), *Interbellum Rotterdam: Kunst en cultuur 1918–1940*, Rotterdam: NAi Uitgevers, p. 291.

23 Halbertsma & Van Ulzen (eds) (2001), op. cit. (note 22), p. 291.

24 In 1960 Banham would write of this: 'throughout the Twenties, the U.S.A. continued to offer Europeans, and especially German writers, an image of the Futurist city made real.' Banham, R. (1980 (1960)), *Theory and Design in the First Machine Age*, London: The Architectural Press, p. 298.

25 D'Eramo, M. (1996), *Das Schwein und der Wolkenkratzer. Chicago: Eine Geschichte unserer Zukunft*, p. 13, quoted in: Jazbinsek, D., B. Joerges et al. (2001), *The Berlin 'Grosstadt-Dokumente': A Forgotten Precursor of the Chicago School of Sociology*, Wissenschaftszentrum Berlin für Sozialforschung GmbH (WZB), webpage, http://skylla.wz-berlin.de/pdf/2001/ii01-502.pdf, site visited March 3, 2005, p. 1. Wohl & Strauss 1958 cite two publications in which Chicago is characterized as the most American city: P. de Rousier, *American Life*, New York/Paris 1891 and J. Gunther, *Inside U.S.A.*, New York 1947; Wohl, R.R. & A.L. Strauss (1958), 'Symbolic Representation and the Urban Milieu', *The American Journal of Sociology*, 63 (5) March 1958, pp. 523-532 (p. 530).

26 Quoted in: Jazbinsek, Joerges et al. (2001), op. cit. (note 25), p. 3.

27 Bienert (1992), op. cit. (note 18), pp. 96-102.

28 Jazbinsek, Joerges et al. (2001), op. cit. (note 25).

29 Jazbinsek, Joerges et al. (2001), op. cit. (note 25).

30 'Capital of all modern uglinesses' is how Karl Scheffler described Berlin in 1910. Quoted in: Bienert (1992), op. cit. (note 18), p. 110. Rolf Lindner refers in Lindner, R. (2005), 'Le grand récit des crottes de chien: De la mythographie de Berlin', *Sociologie et Sociétés*, 37 (1), pp. 217-229, to a master's thesis on the ugliness of Berlin: Timm, T. (2003), *Hässliches Berlin: Berlin und sein negatives Image. Eine empirische Untersuchung*, Institut für Europäische Ethnologie, Berlin: Humboldt Universität.

31 R. Blijstra, 'Jong Rotterdam krijgt stad van formaat', *Het Vrije Volk*, November 12, 1952, quoted in: Andela, G. & C. Wagenaar (eds) (1995), *Een stad voor het leven: Wederopbouw Rotterdam 1940–1965*, [Rotterdam:] De Hef, p. 15.

32 Wagener, W.A. (1951), 'Rotterdam', in: C. Oorthuys et al. (eds), *Land en volk: Steden* (*De schoonheid van ons land*; dl. 10). Amsterdam: Contact, pp. 68-73 (p. 73).

33 Cor Wagenaar has shown that this assumption of an unbroken development is unjustified. This does nothing to obviate the fact that this continuity is firmly emphasized in the architectural critical literature. Wagenaar, C. (1992), *Welvaartsstad in wording: De wederopbouw van Rotterdam*, Rotterdam: NAi Uitgevers.

34 Winter, P. de (1988), *Evenementen in Rotterdam: Ahoy' E55 Floriade C70*, Rotterdam: 010 Publishers.

35 These diminutives (paviljoen*tjes*, koepel*tjes*, cafeet-*jes*, kraam*pjes*, winkel*tjes*, eethuis*jes*) all occur in the C70 communiqué: Stichting C70 ([1970]), *C70: Feestelijke ontmoeting van mens en stad*, Rotterdam.

36 Stichting C70 (eds) (1970), *Internationale Gids C70: Rotterdam Communicatie C70 mei-september '70*, Rotterdam: Stichting C70, p. 17.

37 Stichting C70 (eds) (1970), op. cit. (note 36), pp. 8-9.

38 Stichting C70 (eds) (1970), op. cit. (note 36), p. 9.

39 Wentholt, R. (1968), *De binnenstadsbeleving en Rotterdam*, Rotterdam: Ad. Donker, p. 35.

40 Wentholt (1968), op. cit. (note 39), p. 36.

41 Wentholt (1968), op. cit. (note 39), pp. 36, 38.

42 Koerts, A. 'C70 bracht sfeer van vóór 1940', *Het Vrije Volk*, October 1, 1970.

43 De Winter (1988), op. cit. (note 34), p. 113.

44 A term as popular then as it is now, since the rise of the Leefbaar (liveable) political parties, as in Leefbaar Rotterdam and Leefbaar Utrecht (2001). In 1970 the term 'livable' had a quite different charge, as issues of crime and pollution were not yet high on the agenda.

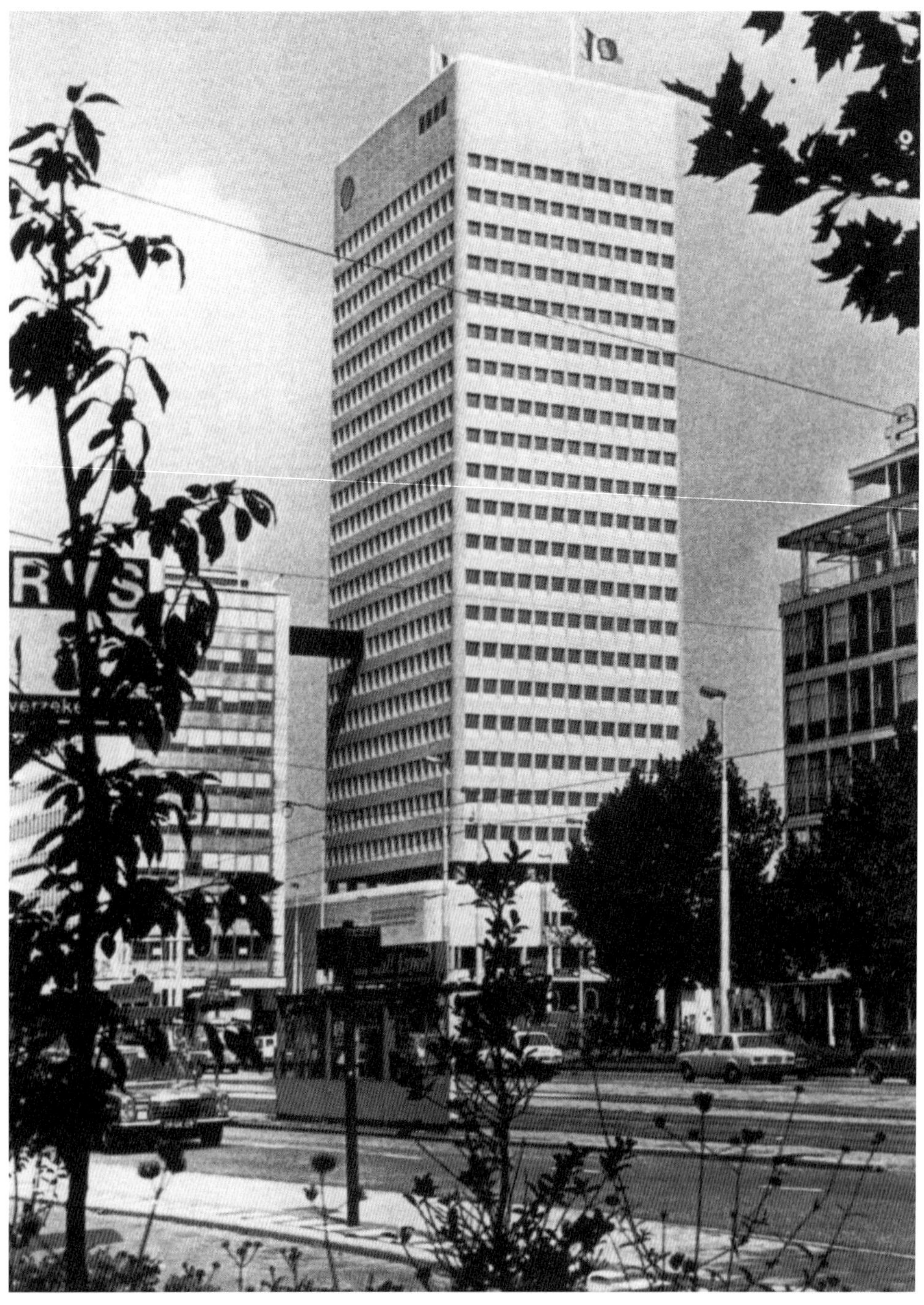

Page from *Het nieuwe Shell-gebouw in Rotterdam*, Rotterdam 1976. Alderman J. Mentink described this 95 metre tall building as a 'capitalist erection'.

Chapter 3

'Modern times are here again.'[1] A new perspective on the city

'I'll risk wagering that Rotterdam will see a metropolitan culture emerge in the '80s, one that will need new ways to measure it.'

(Hans Sleutelaar, circa 1980)[2]

The small scale first experimented with in Rotterdam's inner city during the C70 exhibition would long continue to thread its way through the council's strategy for the city centre. The most fanatical advocate of a small-scale approach was J. Mentink, alderman for physical planning, traffic and public works from 1974 to 1978. Under his governance, aspects of Rotterdam that had been regarded during the inter-war and reconstruction years as pre-eminently modern and metropolitan, and therefore desirable, were toned down one by one. Thoroughfares were made narrower and more winding, a parking policy was to discourage vehicular traffic, the construction of tall buildings was suspended and public space in the centre was filled with small-scale housing: 'The space here serves no purpose after all. You're living and working in a city where the wind blows the clothes from your body!', as Mentink graphically put it.[3] But as the effects of his policy became more visible in the city, another perspective on Rotterdam was unfolding underground so to speak, one that followed on directly from the heroic periods of between the wars and post-war reconstruction; a perspective that looked ahead to the Rotterdam that would begin to take shape in the second half of the 1980s. It is the simultaneous development of these two perspectives that constitutes the subject of this chapter.

The final erection of capitalism

Alderman Mentink's most famous remark concerned the 95 metre tall Shell office tower, which had been handed over in 1976. It was to be the very last 'erection of capitalism' in the centre of Rotterdam if he had anything to do with it. This tough talk appealed so strongly to the public at large that his words took on a life of their own and are repeated to this day.[4] They originated in an interview Mentink gave in February 1977 in *Plan*, a professional journal with a fairly limited circulation.[5] After newspapers reported on the alderman's pithy remarks, his words evidently took flight and reached the general public.[6] Strictly speaking, they have been misquoted as what he actually said in the interview was this: 'The inner city has served as a plaything of the free market economy: anyone wishing to build here can go ahead, and the taller the better! Then you get erections like *that* [pointing outside].'[7] Whatever the case, Mentink called a halt to office construction, designating the as yet unbuilt places in the centre for housing, a 'little park' or a 'little theatre'.[8] He added speed bumps and ramps to Rotterdam's streets and made them narrower and more serpentine wherever possible. His most audacious deed on the traffic front was to reduce Coolsingel from six lanes to four. The exceedingly broad pavements he then graced with plant boxes, additional trees, low walls and pavilions.

Mentink's measures brought him a degree of fame and popularity, as witness the 'Mentink display window' fitted out by the major department store V&D to mark 'Inner City Day' (Binnenstadsdag) in 1977. Yet they were not an isolated gesture but part of the general policy of the College of Mayor and Aldermen. A year after its appointment in 1974, the College had called for everyone to think along with the city council to make the inner city a warmer and more convivial place to be. The response was overwhelming: hundreds of Rotterdammers and non-Rotterdammers submitted their ideas to the city's urban development information service and a selection was published in the so-called *Binnenstadsboek*.[9] The general drift of this 'inner city book' was anything but metropolitan. People's wishes included 'floating gardens', 'lawns on roofs', 'sandboxes', 'more colour in the city', and even a 'hill of flowers and plants decorated with a miniature waterfall' – in short, looking at these '200 ideas for a better inner city' it was abundantly clear that the genie of Flower Power was everywhere except back in the bottle. Not that this was a phenomenon specific to Rotterdam; in the 1970s 'metropolitan' had become a household word with such negative associations as roaring traffic, air pollution, capitalism, and a lack of humanity, and cities all over the world were confronted with a mass exodus to the greener, more tranquil suburbs.[10] Councils, in a bid to stop this outflow of inhabitants, sought to give their cities more of a rural, village-like ambience.[11] Although none of the 200 ideas in *Binnenstadsboek* were carried out literally, the council would continue to act in the spirit of this publication until the early '80s.

In a book published in 1982 reviewing recent urban developments in Rotterdam, the small-scale was regarded not as a fly-by-night trend but as Rotterdam's salvation on the urban design front.[12] The authors of this study, Ids Haagsma and Hilde de Haan, two architecture critics of repute, described Rotterdam as a city that had become 'fuller' and 'greener', a place to 'stray' even, and not 'the modern commercial metropolis' envisaged by the post-war reconstruction planners. According to the jacket blurb, this book had the answers to the following questions: 'How did the dream of a commercial metropolis change into the ideal of the "compact city"? Or, put another way, whatever happened to the plans for a World Trade Centre at Leuvehaven? Why is there still a deer park on Weena, once conceived of as a main boulevard to the commercial centre?' Neither the authors nor the publisher could have foreseen in 1982 that a mere four years later a gleaming, 93 metre tall World Trade Centre would grace Coolsingel and that from 1990 on, one 'erection of capitalism' after another would spring up along Weena.

Yet there was another perspective on Rotterdam in 1982, one developed by people lacking the administrative powers of a Mentink but with powers of imagination instead. Sharon Zukin in her book *The Cultures of Cities* has shown that imagination is a potent resource too. She contends that some groups in the city, though officially not in a position of power, can still be powerful in shaping another viewpoint on that city. Their imaginative powers give them the capacity to guide the city's symbolic economy: 'A look at some of the city's public spaces – shopping streets, restaurants, museums – indicates the importance of artists and immigrants to current processes of defining urban cultures. No one could argue that these are powerful groups. Yet they are so involved in challenging previously conceived ideas about the city's identity that they set a new framework for viewing social life.'[13] To couch this idea in more general terms she turns to Michel Foucault, who has pointed out that power and imagination are inextricably bound together but that it is not always correct to assume that those with power must logically be able to impose an image. According to Foucault it is often the other way round: they who control the images have the power. Zukin applies this train of thought to urban culture of the late 20th century by postulating that whenever a group succeeds in presenting a place in a certain light, this group is often able to claim this place for itself. I shall now illustrate this postulation with concrete examples.

Stadsgezicht

It is hard to say how long artists and other cultural entrepreneurs have nurtured, under wraps, an image of Rotterdam that deviated fundamentally from the small-scale, *gezellig* ideal trumpeted on all sides.[14] However, it is quite clear exactly when this new outlook first reached the public at large. This was on the evening of Sunday, December 25, 1977, when the VPRO broadcasting company televised a short film entitled *Stadsgezicht* as part of an episode of their three-weekly programme *Het Gat van Nederland.*[15] *Stadsgezicht* (Cityscape) is a documentary just under 18 minutes long about Rotterdam as seen through the eyes of the poet and author Jules Deelder and directed by Bob Visser, both of them Rotterdammers. At the same time it is a documentary about Deelder, with Rotterdam as a backdrop. Here, Deelder's identification with Rotterdam, which would quickly reach such proportions as to earn him the unofficial title of 'Night Mayor of Rotterdam', is quite far advanced already. Visser chose Jules Deelder as a guide to Rotterdam because to his mind Deelder manages to express perfectly what is so fascinating about this city's much-maligned unyielding character.[16]

    Stadsgezicht was a remarkable documentary for two reasons. First of all, there was almost nothing on television about Rotterdam or its cultural activities in those days. Deelder later even wrote a poem about Rotterdam's absence 'on the box', which with its mix of put-on and genuine indignation, its language (vernacular with a thick Rotterdam accent) and its hard-hitting humour is typical of Deelder's work in general. The reference to the Second World War, in this case the annual National Remembrance Day (Dodenherdenking) on May 4th and more specifically the two minutes' silence observed at eight o'clock that evening, is an often recurring element in his poetry and prose.

When do you ever see	Wanneer zie je Rotterdam
Rotterdam on the box?	nou op de buis?
Only when they can show	Alleen als ze kunnen laten
that the trams there don't stop	zien hoe hier op 4 mei om
on May 4th at eight o'clock	8 uur de trams gewoon doorrijen
Then all you see is Rotterdam	Dan krijgt Rotterdam nog
being taken down a peg	even gauw de kat
If there's one place where	Nou als er één stad is waar
trams have the right	de trams op 4 mei het rècht
to rattle on, on May 4th	hebben om door te rijen
it's Rotterdam	is het Rotterdam wel
Give us some credit!?![17]	Wat zullen we nou hebben!?!

The fact that Rotterdam did make a television appearance this time, was thanks to the position Bob Visser by now occupied at the VPRO as their Rotterdam reporter. He had begun reporting on Rotterdam for VPRO radio at the beginning of the 1970s. According to Visser, at that time there was no-one else in the media who knew what was going on in Rotterdam; everyone else lived in Amsterdam or close by. In that respect he had cornered a market. The VPRO were only too happy to have a colleague with a feeling for Rotterdam, he says, and this was enough to give him all the space he needed.

Secondly, *Stadsgezicht* the documentary showed a Rotterdam that deviated radically from the prevailing image the public at large had of that city. Rotterdam had been a city with problems, with an identity crisis, a cold, forbidding place with far too much traffic – a city that in fact only vied with the other major Dutch cities through having the 'largest port in the universe', as Mentink mockingly put it.[18] And now there was this agitated figure all in black with shades on day and night, an undiluted Rotterdam accent and – unusual in those hippie days – combed-back gelled hair announcing that Rotterdam was fine the way it was and, what was more, was about to enter 'a fresh and vigorous period of feverish activity'.

How did Bob Visser and Jules Deelder present Rotterdam to the Dutch viewing public? Surprisingly, the beginning of *Stadsgezicht* nails three of the four aspects that acted as standard ingredients in the inter-war years to underline Rotterdam's metropolitanism and modernity: the lighting in the streets, the traffic and the harbour activities. The fourth ingredient, high-rise, would come into its own later in the film. The film opens in almost total darkness; Deelder, barely standing out against the pitch-black background in a long black leather jacket and shades, reads out a text consisting of a résumé of random facts about Rotterdam: 'Rotterdam is a city that has had city rights since 1340; it has 1060 cafés, including 32 with a late-night licence, a flag with three horizontal stripes of green, white and green, 33,000 metres of quayside, 160 million people within a radius of 500 kilometres, 300 shipping lines, 5568 senior citizens in 62 old-age homes, 6 container cranes, 213 infants' schools, the Euromast, a cleanable street surface area of 23 million square metres, 204 restaurants [etc.]'. As Deelder reads on, the evening lights of the city gradually come into view behind him, the street lights, the headlamps, the neon signs.[19] Deelder's voice continues this litany as the setting changes four times. All the locations are clearly in Rotterdam and have to do with traffic. We see Deelder in a train riding through a dockland area, then filmed from the back taking a bike up a long Metro escalator, next reciting his text on a boat moving through the harbour, his face and torso in close-up with a large sea-going vessel behind him, and lastly back on the same escalator but now filmed from the front. In these opening 70 seconds, Rotterdam is shown to be a large, thrilling city continually in motion. Not a beautiful city, and not a *gezellig* city.

Traffic is an often recurring backdrop in the film. When Deelder strolls through the flea market we see the overhead railway and hear the roar of the train above; when Deelder reads a text from his collection *Proza* inside the Park Hotel we see through the window the cars and trams passing by. And at the end of the documentary we see the city after dark filmed from a moving car, giving the effect of an American-style avenue at night. This sequence has its own pulsing rhythm in the accompanying music, the opening bars of the song *Nightclubbing* (1977) by Iggy Pop.[20]

There is more of the city in darkness in *Stadsgezicht*, this time from the perspective of the pedestrian as Deelder wanders with an interviewer through a

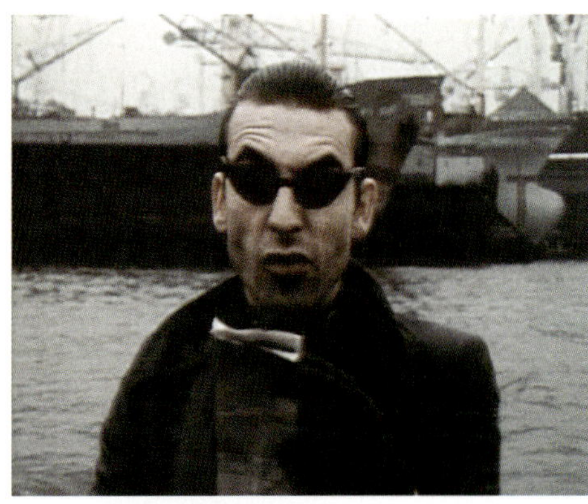
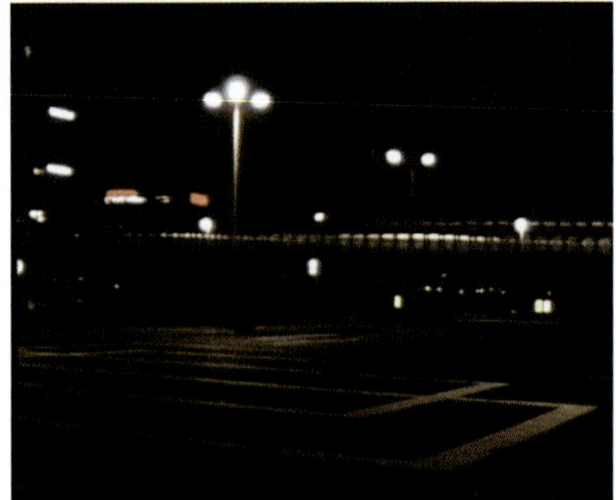
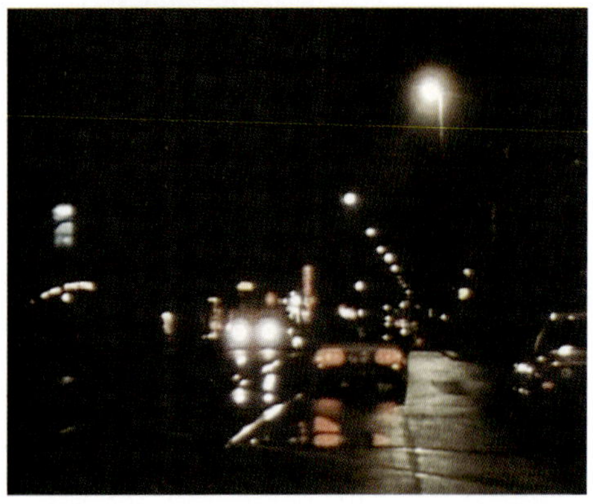
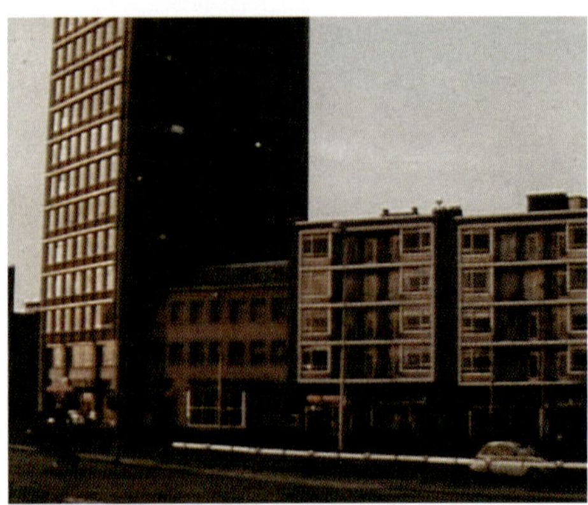
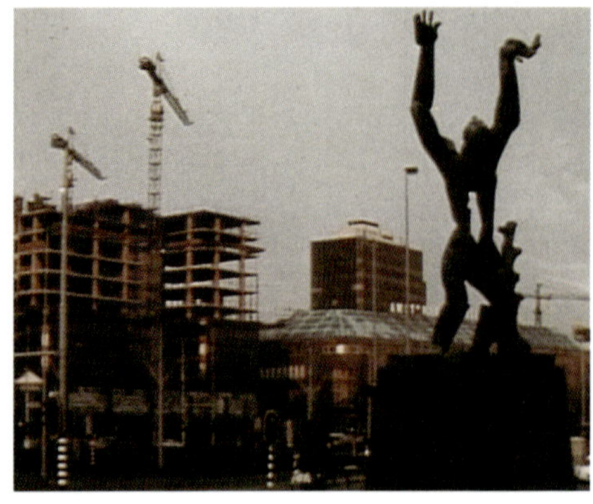

Stills from the Rotterdam documentary *Stadsgezicht*, 1977, dir. Bob Visser.

Top left Jules Deelder, clad entirely in black, reads out a text about Rotterdam as the evening lights of the city come into view behind him; **right** close-up of Deelder with the docks in the background; **middle left** first shot of Schouwburgplein, accompanied by Deelder's remark: 'This for me is the heart of the city. But they want it built up. You can't call it a square then, can you?'; **right** a street after dark with cars and street lamps, musically accompanied by Iggy Pop's *Nightclubbing*; **bottom left** Deelder cycles past a block of flats whose top is beyond the frame, suggesting the towering apartment buildings in his poem; **right** Deelder peddles up Coolsingel with its high rises under construction and Zadkine's *The Destruction of Rotterdam* at right.

nocturnal Rotterdam. The thrill element has returned, particularly as there is almost no-one to be seen. The background music is threatening and makes for a slightly unsettling atmosphere.[21] As the two arrive at an asphalted open space most resembling a car park, Deelder coolly announces: 'This for me is the heart of the city.' They are now in Schouwburgplein, the 'theatre square' whose development had even then been discussed for years to no avail. Deelder likes the square the way it is: 'But they want it built up. You can't call it a square then, can you?' As the music swells ominously and Rotterdam shows its most inhospitable side, Deelder continues excitedly: 'I feel on top of the world here, you know. I really feel at home here. They should stuff all that crap about *gezelligheid* once and for all. (...) It's all so forced. (...) That expression "Hè gezellig" is enough to give me the runs.'

During the conversation in Schouwburgplein the fourth aspect to symbolize modernity and the metropolitan during the inter-war years, high-rise, looms into view. But it only really takes centre stage in the film's final scene, as Deelder cycles through the city centre in the bleak greyness of dawn, alights at Zadkine's large sculpture *De verwoeste stad* (The Destruction of Rotterdam) and recites the poem that gives the documentary its name: *Stadsgezicht*. As the camera follows Deelder as he peddles restlessly on, we see the distinctive, rational modern architecture of Rotterdam passing by. This includes several apartment towers which, as in Andor von Barsy's film of 1928, have been shot so that the tops are out of the picture, suggesting a much taller building. Tall cranes loom alongside buildings under construction. Arriving at Zadkine's large bronze, a human figure reaching upward, Deelder nonchalantly takes up a position behind his bike and recites *Stadsgezicht*:

Presence of mind and realism to the nth degree make merry undisturbed in a road under repair	Tegenwoordigheid van geest en realisme in 't kwadraat vieren onverstoorbaar feest in een opgebroken straat
Tall and diamond-hard the sky with a steely sun or black and low in a wild flurry past skeletons of concrete	Hoog en spijkerhard de hemel met een blikkerende zon of zwart en laag in wilde wemel langs skeletten van beton
Through shut venetian blinds apartment buildings tower stacked tight to the horizon	Doorheen geloken luxaflexen tórenhoog de wooncomplexen stapelen den einder dicht
Post-historic prospect – Rotterdam hewn from marble tilting in the wash of light	Posthistorisch vergezicht – Rotterdam gehakt uit marmer kant'lend in het tegenlicht

This is a poem that deserves closer examination. First of all because in its concise-
ness it touches upon all aspects belonging to the image of Rotterdam and its citizens
as this has been shaped since the beginning of the 20th century and was put into
words by, for example, M.J. Brusse in 1938 – see the passages in question in the previous chapter.[22] The Rotterdam mentality, which Brusse describes as 'unaffected'
and 'forthright'[23], confronts us in the first two lines: 'presence of mind' and 'realism
to the nth degree' can be read as referring to the proverbial Rotterdam directness
and levelheadedness. The use of 'undisturbed' in the third line has much to do with
this. 'Presence' however refers to the emphasis in Rotterdam on the present and
the future, as against the negligible role the past plays in the city. And 'nth degree'
in the original Dutch is *kwadraat*, quadrate, which can similarly be read as a play on
the external appearance of many buildings in the city centre – 'all those building-
block boxes', as Deelder describes them in another poem.[24] 'Road under repair' refers,
via the image of a city where building is being done, to an appetite for enterprise
and an orientation to the future.

The second verse is dominated by words that reflect Rotterdam's toughness:
'diamond-hard', 'steely', 'skeletons of concrete'. By the same token, the city's inhospitable, sinister side, a key element in the TV documentary, is expressed in the words
'black and low in a wild flurry / past skeletons of concrete'. The third verse, about
towering apartment blocks, eulogizes the city's high-rise. In the fourth and last
verse the neologism 'post-historic' once again signifies the typical Rotterdam concern for present and future, for modernity, at the cost of reflecting on the past.
'Prospect' refers to the future but also to the great space in Rotterdam. The poem
ends solemnly and romantically with the lines 'Rotterdam hewn from marble /
Tilting in the wash of light'. Here both the hardness – a city carved from stone –
and the beauty of Rotterdam are the subjects; marble, we should recall, was for
centuries the pre-eminent stone used for decoration.[25] Lastly, the evocative line
'Tilting in the wash of light' evokes the image of an urban silhouette of buildings
so tall that they seem to topple, to tilt. These lines are romantic because of their
exalted manner of exaggerating reality. Marble is certainly a material seldom
found in Rotterdam, but for devotees the materials used by the modernists were
every bit as beautiful as marble. And as for bona fide high-rise, there was nothing
to speak of in the Rotterdam of 1977.

This exaggeration of reality brings us straight to the second reason why
Stadsgezicht deserves to be dwelt on at such length: it is a prophetic poem. It
describes a Rotterdam that didn't exist in 1977 but would take shape during the
1980s and '90s. It also describes aspects of Rotterdam (high-rise, distant prospects,
concrete skeletons) that were condemned and contested in 1977 but would be
reassessed and appreciated by policymakers and the public at large some 10 to 15
years later. The poem was so far ahead of its time that it was quoted in a fairly
recent booklet about present-day Rotterdam in a caption to a panorama photograph
of the city in the year 2003. The author's very words were: 'The view of Rotterdam

from the City Hall corresponds pretty well with what Jules Deelder described in his poem "Stadsgezicht".[26] By that time *Stadsgezicht* was more than a quarter of a century old!

The third, last and possibly the main reason why *Stadsgezicht* deserves a prominent place in a history of the imagined Rotterdam, is that both poem and poet have become an indelible part of what Gerald Suttles has called the texture of local urban culture.[27] Jules Deelder and his *Stadsgezicht* have become collective representations of Rotterdam for the widest audience. *Stadsgezicht* has been printed and reprinted time and again in magazines and collections of poetry.[28] But the poem has gone on to lead a life of its own in circles largely beyond the horizons of literary scholars. Thus, for example, we find in the restaurant of Akropolis, a high-rise apartment complex for seniors in the Schiebroek district of Rotterdam, a large triptych with the Willems Bridge on the left, the Erasmus Bridge on the right, and at the centre Deelder's *Stadsgezicht*. De Hef, the former railway lifting bridge is visible beyond the two new bridges. Remarkably, *Stadsgezicht* appeals in this context as much to the 'Rotterdam feeling' of today through the inclusion of the two new bridges over the Maas, as to the Rotterdam feeling of the generation living in Akropolis, most of whom were born before the Second World War. This can only be explained by the fact that *Stadsgezicht* sits well with clichés that are as old as the inhabitants of this complex.

The history of the poet mirrors that of the poem. Jules Deelder has burgeoned into a national celebrity, a darling of the public at large and, most importantly, 'Mister Rotterdam', for, as Rien Vroegindeweij has written, 'say Deelder and you're saying Rotterdam. His language and accent, his way of thinking and acting, everything about him radiates the idea this country has of Rotterdam: a city of hard workers, the shut-up-and-get-on-with-it mentality, and other such clichés.'[29] Deelder himself professed back in 1986 that 'even in Zutfen' out in the east of the country he could hardly walk ten metres without someone recognizing him. 'Housewives too'.[30] The all-black outfit he is never without is now so familiar that in 2005 he starred in a TV commercial for a washing powder for black clothes! At the same time, Deelder's work is most certainly taken seriously in literary circles.

Stadsgezicht the documentary got its fair share of reactions both informally and in the media, according to its director, Bob Visser.[31] This response can be explained by the fact that Rotterdam got so little television coverage. The documentary moreover showed a side of Rotterdam that was not at all well-known, namely as a city with a cultural life and a cultural identity of its own. For apart from Rotterdam's metropolitan quality *Stadsgezicht* focuses on the culture that flourishes in that metropolitan context. At the flea market the interviewer asks Deelder, once the roar of the train has subsided, 'Is this what you call the breeding ground of neon-romanticism?' 'Yes' comes the reply. Neon-romanticism was the name Deelder gave his own work, as if it were a school. 'It just means I'm not falling back on a earlier tendency (...) Neon-romanticism obviously has to do with neon, the light in which

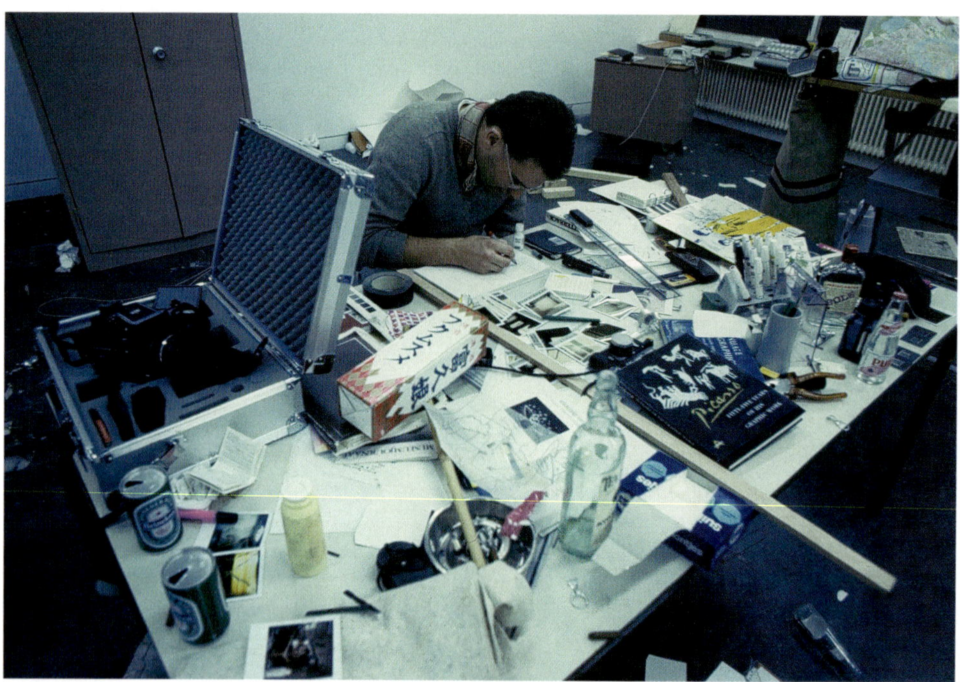

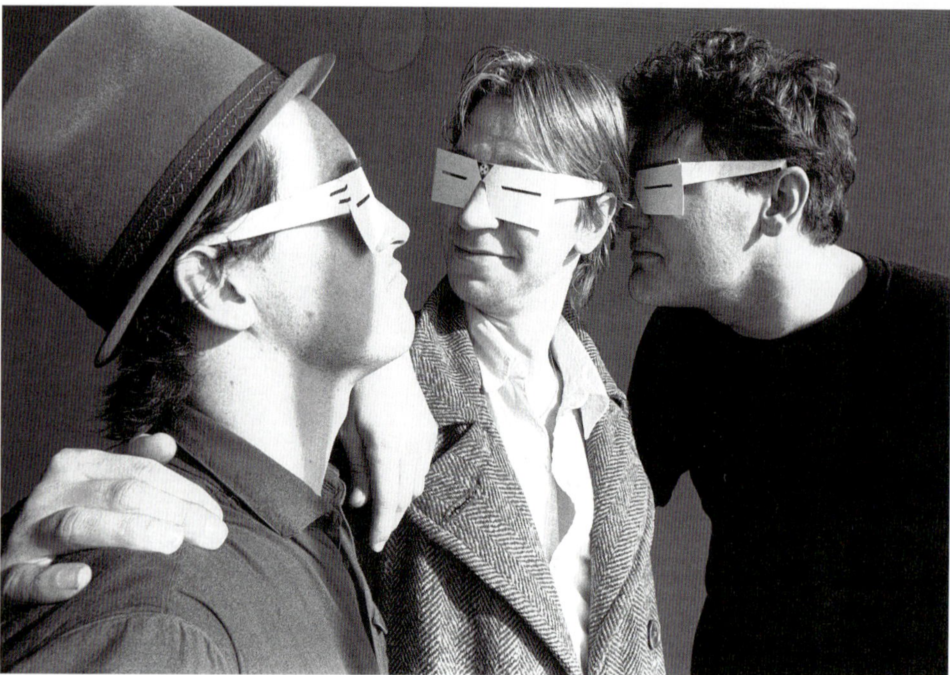

The members of the design studio Hard Werken.
Top Gerard Hadders in the Hard Werken studio on Pelgrimsstraat, 1980; **bottom** from left Tom van den Haspel, Rick Vermeulen and Gerard Hadders as The Presidents, 1979.

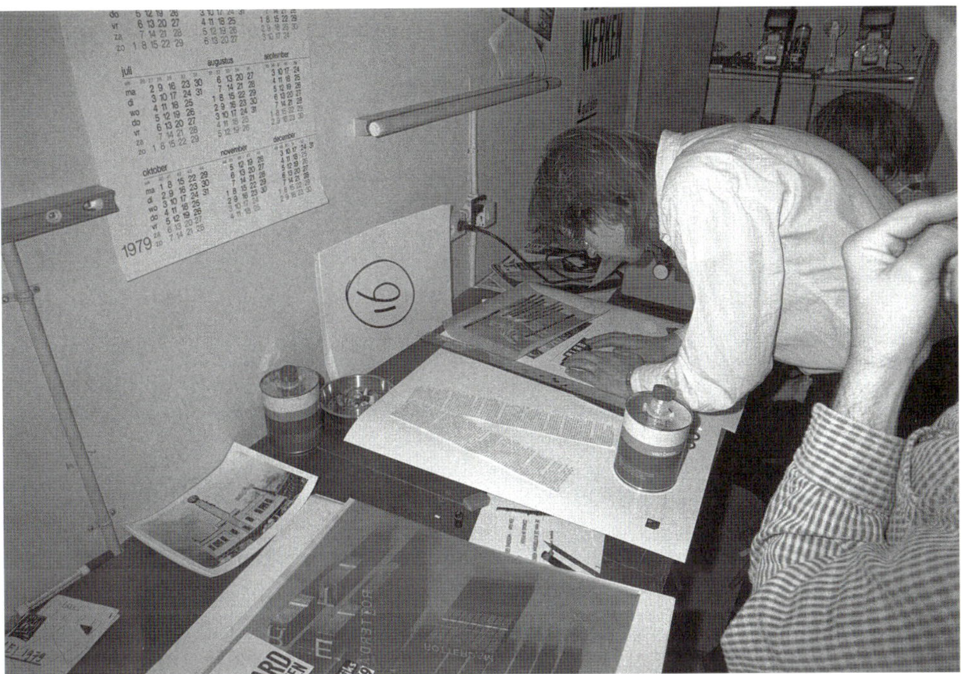

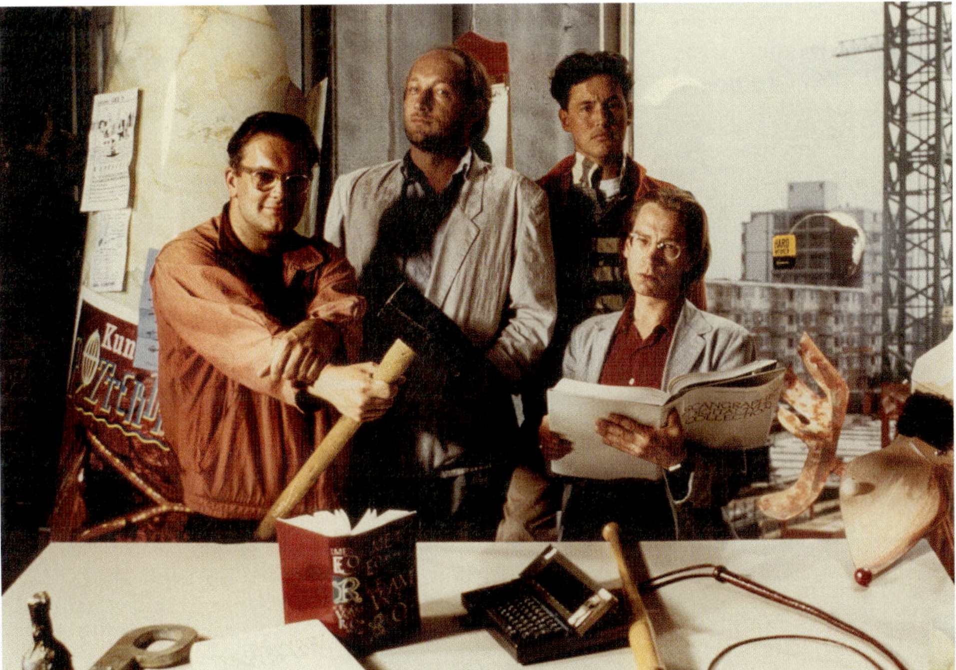

Top Rick Vermeulen typesetting the second issue of the magazine *Hard Werken* in the graphic workshop of the Lantaren, spring 1979; **bottom** group photo in Pelgrimsstraat, mid 1980s, from left: Gerard Hadders, Willem Kars, Tom van den Haspel, Rick Vermeulen.

city life is enacted.'[32] A tendency such as this is only conceivable in a metropolitan
context, and Rotterdam in the documentary is nothing if not metropolitan. The
documentary also attends to Culture with a capital C during a sequence shot in the
Boymans-van Beuningen Museum. There we hear Deelder say that despite 'all that
crazy stuff' about culture having a rough time of it in Rotterdam, he is convinced that
Rotterdam is about to embark on 'a fresh and vigorous period of feverish activity'.
More prophetic words.

Not that Bob Visser and Jules Deelder were lonely voices in the wilderness,
although people outside Rotterdam 'almost shit themselves in amazement' that
this prosaic place turned out to harbour 'another world entirely'.[33] Inside Rotterdam
there were others who sensed that the time was ripe to reassess the city. There
were a few individuals from outside who shared this prophetic feeling, such as the
architect Rem Koolhaas, who in 1978 expressly chose Rotterdam for the Dutch
branch of his Office for Metropolitan Architecture, a revealing name if ever there
was one. The reason, as he explained later, was that he 'had an instinct' that there
was an emerging cultural climate in the city.[34] It is important to stress that people
like Koolhaas were not referring to the official culture of museums, concert halls,
theatres and the like. The budding culture that he and other artists and other cultural entrepreneurs had in mind was a true city culture, a culture that allowed
Rotterdam to be experienced as a world city, as in the programme *Stadsgezicht*. Nor
did they see a contradiction here between Rotterdam the port city on the one hand
and Rotterdam city of culture on the other. On the contrary, its identity as a city of
work sat well with the matter-of-factness they sought, and the docks symbolized
Rotterdam's cosmopolitan character, as they had between the two wars.

As I said earlier, the other perspective on Rotterdam remained an under-
current until the television broadcast of *Stadsgezicht* at the end of 1977. After that
it rapidly came into its own. Nurtured by the creative class, this perspective looked
back to the inter-war years as much as it looked far into the future. Its principal
mouthpiece from 1979 on was *Hard Werken* (literally, hard working). Ten issues of
this deliberately oversized magazine with its Rotterdam cliché of a name were published between April 1979 and January 1982 in a print run of 3000.

Hard Werken

Hard Werken was a real bruiser, not just because of the large A3 format but also
due to its rough-and-tumble design and unabashed sympathy for all things anti-
establishment. The editorial board consisted of a large, fluid group and a hard
core.[35] That second category included Henk Elenga, Gerard Hadders, Tom van den
Haspel, Willem Kars and Rick Vermeulen, who in 1980 set up a design studio which
they also called Hard Werken. They were responsible for the magazine's graphic
design, which basically entailed violating every imaginable typographic precept
obtaining at the time. The fountainhead of those precepts had been the severe

Swiss brand of typography, best known here in a Dutch version wielded by the successful firm of Total Design whose ranks included Wim Crouwel and Friso Kramer. Restraint and dedication to the communicative aspect were the key concepts of this school of graphic design. It meant that every typographic and graphic element had to serve a purpose, and it was this precept that the designers at Hard Werken took most pleasure in throwing overboard. In their magazine, they experimented with all kinds of deliberate imprecisions such as texts and images set at crazy angles and photos framed with ragged or wavy edges; the typography was exuberantly eclectic incorporating letters with a preposterously old-fashioned look; lastly there were all kinds of visual layerings, for example by having forms drawn free-hand as a ground for text or blithely continuing through photos. The magazine's interior was entirely in black, grey and white. This recalcitrant design, applied to graphic work but also to three-dimensional objects and stage sets, would elevate the Hard Werken studio to an international sensation.[36] I should add that most advertisements in the magazine were also designed along radically unorthodox lines by Hard Werken, so that these 'would be in the same (new) vein as the magazine'.[37]

In terms of content, *Hard Werken* combines artistic offerings (poems, literature, photographs, art) with essays about the arts and art policy. But the impression it gives is more one of an artists' magazine than an arts magazine, given its experimental layout and its tendency to deliberately leave out information – even in the ads! The quality of its contents varies between stand-out items of now classic status – such as the prepublication of Jules Deelder's book about the Rotterdam boxer Bep van Klaveren – to forgettable horseplay. Yet the importance the magazine had for Rotterdam is not to be found here but in its aura of cultural vitality. It assumed the role of mouthpiece of a cultural scene expressly associated with Rotterdam though without being provincial. Non-Rotterdam artists and cultural events get as much coverage as the Rotterdam scene. Indeed, the general impression of this magazine with its large pages of large photos (up to A2 format) and its wealth of subjects, is that of an expansive view of the world. With strikingly designed posters bearing the magazine's name pasted all over the city, no-one living in Rotterdam could have been unaware of the arrival of *Hard Werken*.

Hard Werken gave verbal and visual expression to a clear perspective on the city of Rotterdam. Several issues included trenchant critiques of the small-scale architecture being built all over the city centre. This architecture of the *nieuwe truttigheid* (new frumpishness) as Carel Weeber described the tendency towards fiddliness in an interview in the third issue of *Hard Werken* (July 1979), was regarded as an affront to the metropolitanism Rotterdam was valued for.[38] Sander Wissing in the same issue describes the Mentink-driven new-look Coolsingel as a 'chaos of washed concrete slabs'. Before then, he goes on, Coolsingel had been 'the one outstanding metropolitan boulevard in the country'.[39] To prevent Schouwburgplein, the theatre square, from being similarly robbed of its metropolitan ambience, Wissing in his article 'The atmosphere of the city' suggest how this 'void' in the heart of the city should be tackled: 'It will require a sturdy, space-defining architecture to turn this irresolute void into a pleasant place to linger. This calls for monumentality – almost a dirty word these days – also in the handling of materials. For once, the *"gezelligheid"* should depend not on railway sleepers and other junk, nor on cubby-holes, chopped-off corners and little pitched roofs, staggerings in the elevations or other specialities of the new frumpiness, but simply on people. People like visiting places that may not be that *gezellig*, but for the excitement, the atmosphere. The atmosphere of the city.'[40] With these words, Wissing showed himself to be a soul-mate of Jules Deelder, whose poem *Stadsgezicht* had been printed in the second issue of *Hard Werken* (May 1979). Motorized traffic also belongs in Wissing's image of an exhilarating urban atmosphere: 'Karel Doormanstraat should be reopened to traffic, as traffic is part of a city and, odd though it may seem, adds to its vibrancy.'[41] So we see the imagined Rotterdam of the inter-war and reconstruction years resurrected in the pages of *Hard Werken*. The references to the period between the wars are quite literal at times. For example, the cover of the second issue (May 1979) is based on a photograph taken in 1927 by the designer Paul Schuitema,[42] one of the advance guard of Rotterdam artists and designers during the inter-war years. Other photographs, such as Hajo Piebenga's shot of De Hef, are heavily indebted to the New Photography of the 1920s and '30s.

The advertisements exude a similar air of urbanity. According to the editors of the first issue, the intention was to be selective in choosing which ads to publish, and that certainly seems to have been the case. The advertisers were either involved with art or culture, bookshops for example, or with lifestyle, meaning exclusive clothing and shoe shops, hairdressers and the occasional furniture store. For the record, it is by no means always clear what the advertisers are selling! More often than not, the ad is no more than an ambience with an evocative photograph and the firm's name. You have to check the magazine's credits to discover the details. This method of advertising was highly unusual in those days. The fashion ads give a clear picture of what was hip in about 1980: clinging tapering pants, tight-fitting miniskirts or petticoats, pointed shoes or high heels, fifties-style jackets, butterfly glasses and short, semi-spiky hair. This fashion was also known as New Wave after the type of music then popular in Dutch artistic circles, which had been heard and seen early on in Rotterdam. The same outfits can be seen in the ads for record shops.

Founded in 1980, the Hard Werken design studio landed commissions from almost every cultural institution in town. This gave Rotterdam's cultural life a read-ily identifiable signature. Arguably the most famous of these commissions were the posters Hard Werken made for Film International from 1984 to 1994, based on the festival's symbol of a tiger. When in 1984 the Boymans-van Beuningen Museum focused again on art from Rotterdam after a break of many years, it was almost a foregone conclusion that Hard Werken would design the catalogue. Just how famous the Hard Werken style had become can be judged from the many followers it elicited among Dutch graphic designers in the '80s.[43] The design studio no longer

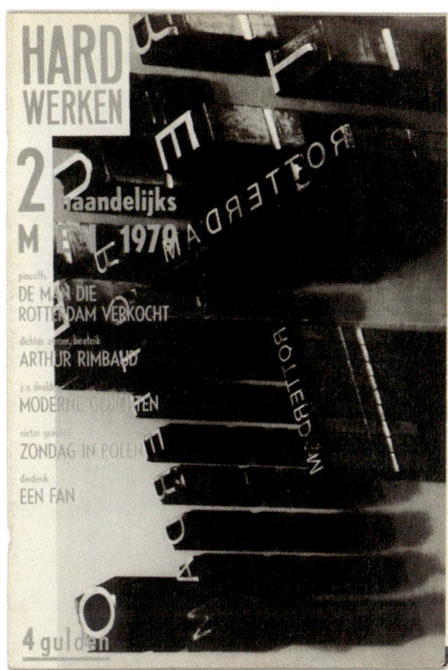

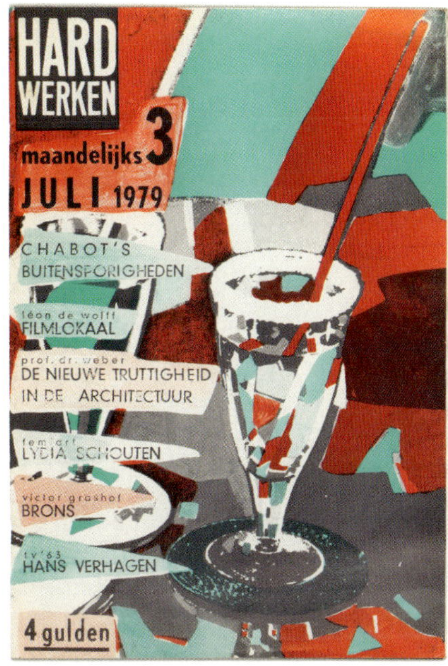

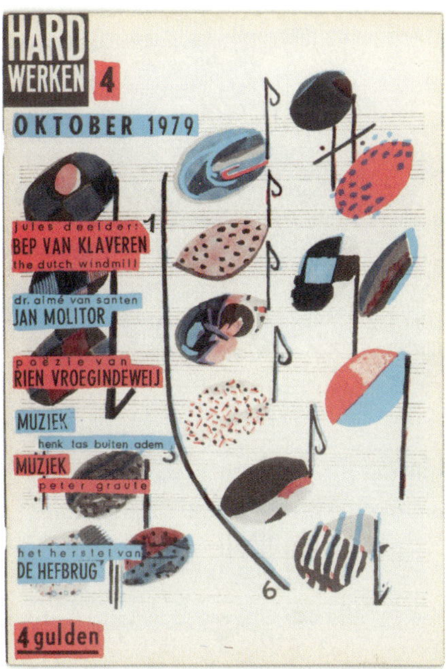

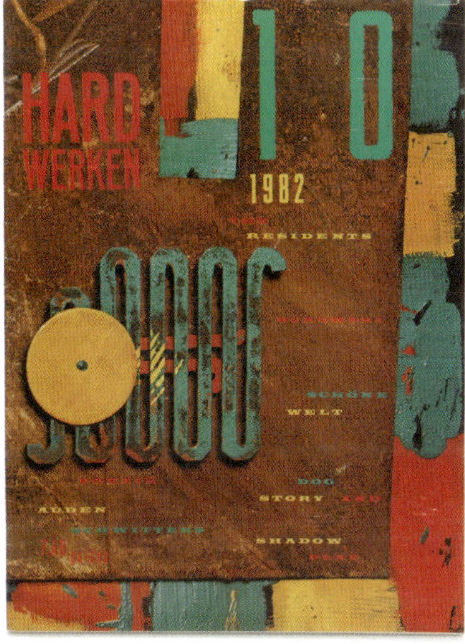

Covers of *Hard Werken* Magazine.

Covers of the magazine *Hard Werken*; **top left** no. 2, May 1979, a cover design based on a photo dating from 1927 by the designer Paul Schuitema; **right** no. 3, July 1979; **bottom left** no. 4, October 1979; **right** no. 10, 1982.

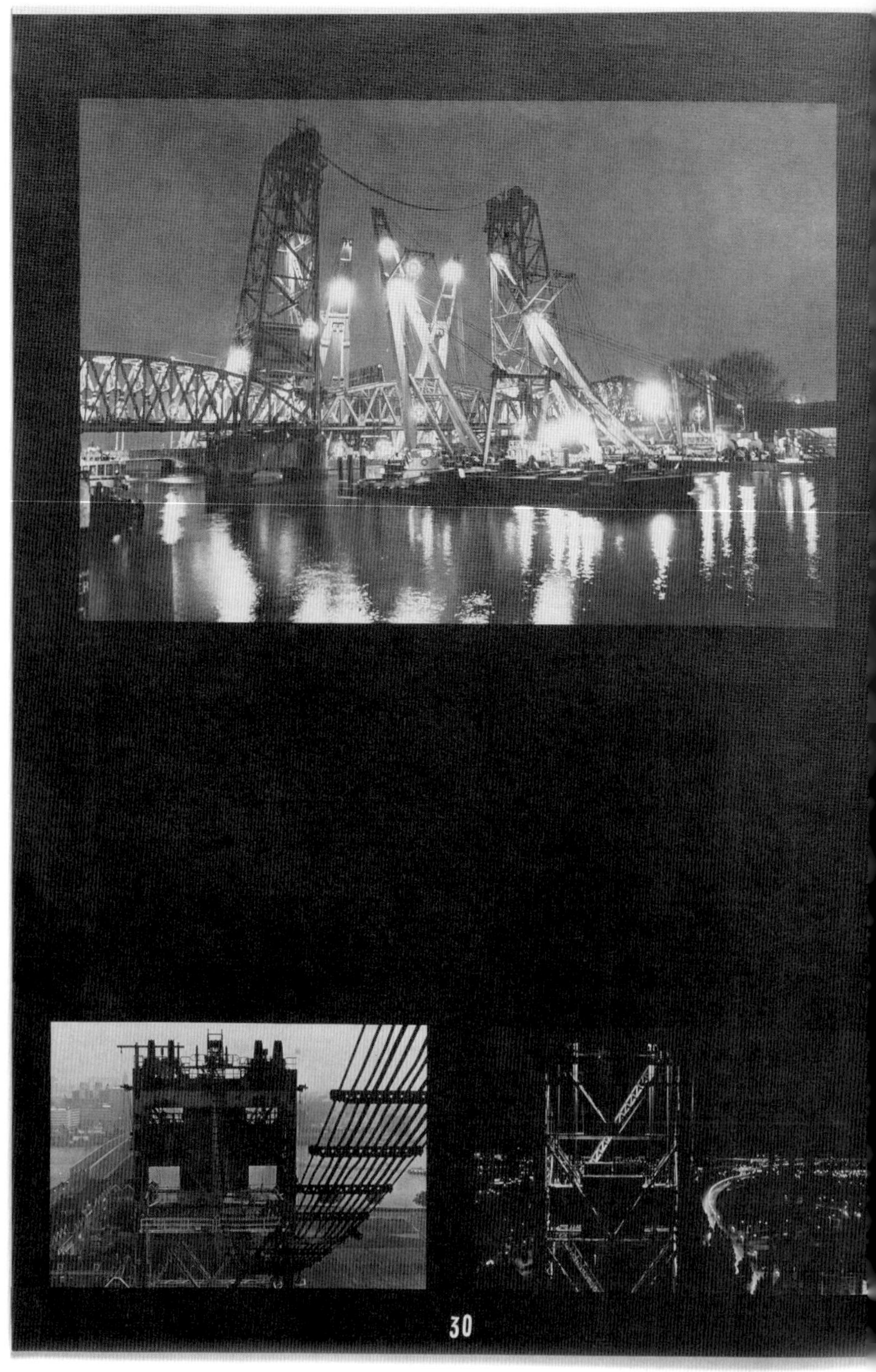

30

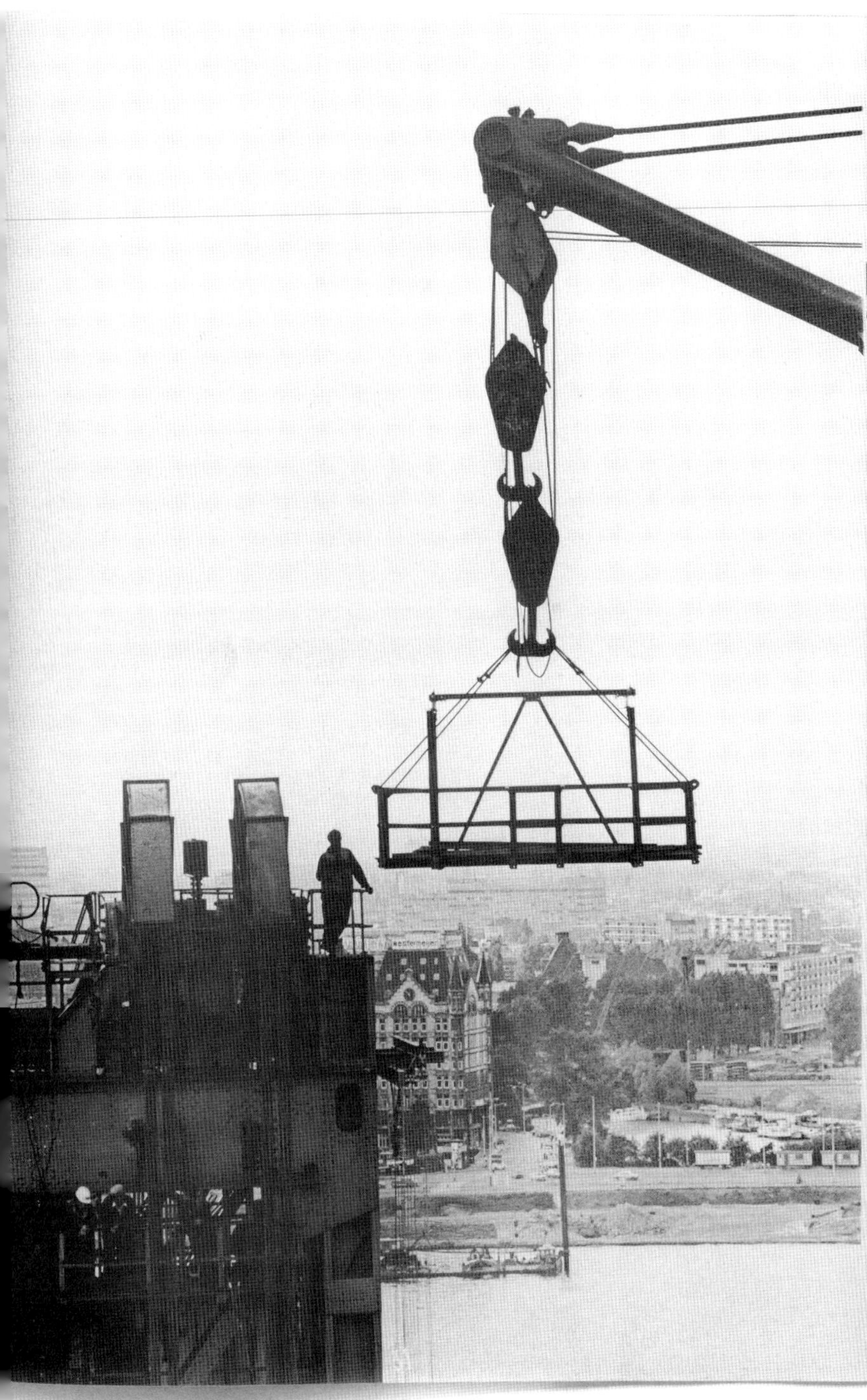

Spread from *Hard Werken*, no. 4, October 1979, with photos by Hajo Piebenga that call to mind the New Photography of the interwar years.

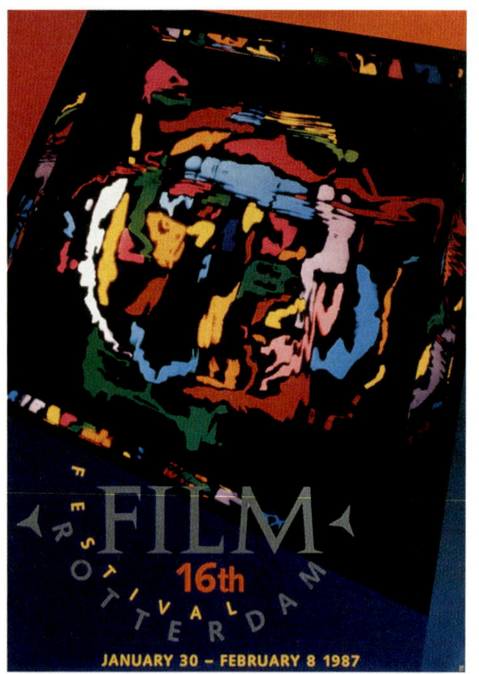

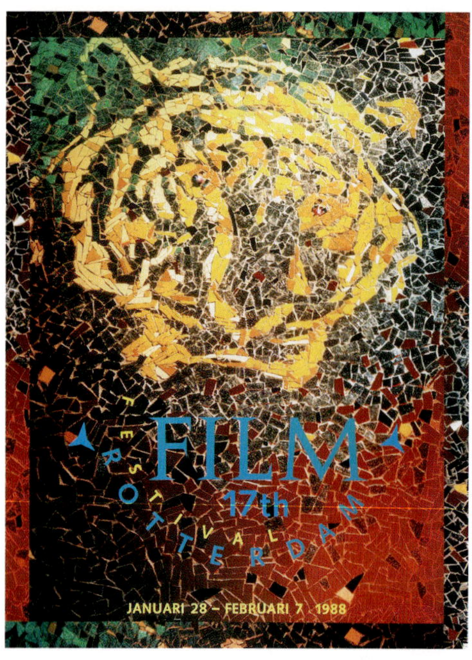

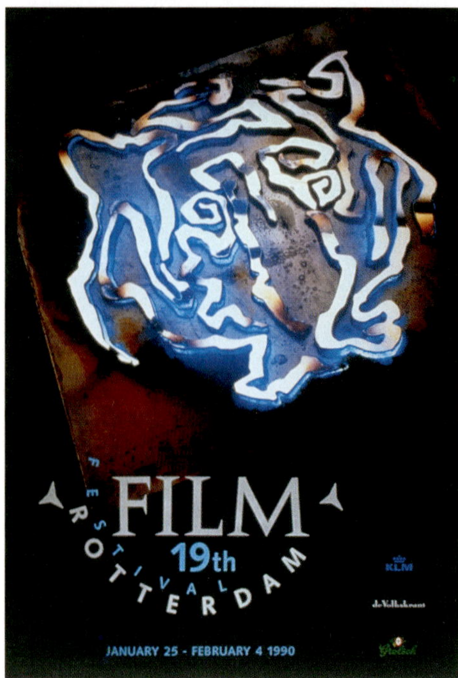

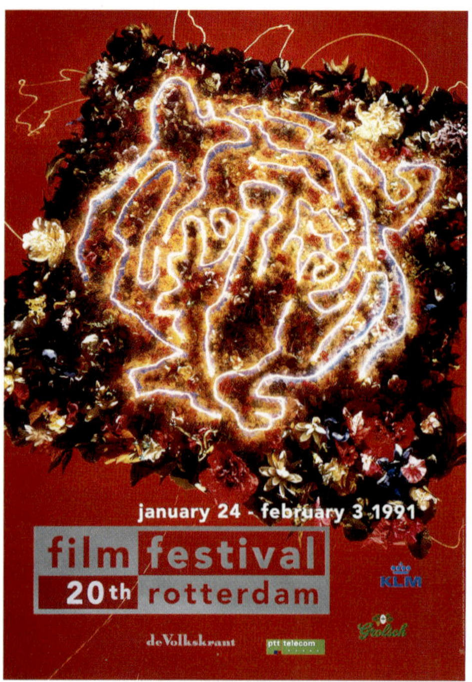

Posters for Film International, designed by Hard Werken.

exists but its members are still active as individuals and some of their designs are internationally famous.

Rotterdam Arts Council

The founders of Hard Werken knew each other from the graphic workshop of De Lantaren art centre, an institution managed by the Rotterdam Arts Council (Rotterdamse Kunststichting or RKS). De Lantaren was established at the start of the 1970s at the instigation of the then director of the Arts Council, Adriaan van der Staay, as an 'arts lab', as he put it, a place where practitioners of the various artistic disciplines could experiment to their heart's content.[44] Willem Kars, whose initiative it was to found the magazine *Hard Werken*, was in charge of the graphic workshop.[45] De Lantaren, later rechristened Lantaren/Venster, also had workshops for film and video, for theatre and for literature, as well as a stage for all kinds of experimental forms of drama, music, dance and literature, two film theatres (Venster 1 and Venster 2) and last but not least a café. Anyone remotely connected with art in Rotterdam in the 1970s visited Lantaren/Venster sooner or later. It was one of the few meeting places for what we now call Rotterdam's creative class. Even the café was mainly frequented by people of artistic talent or ambition, although anyone could visit it. This was where the people who would define Rotterdam's cultural climate in the '80s got to know each other and carried out their first projects. The upshot was an intricate network out of which emerged all kinds of working relationships and joint ventures. Hard Werken was just one of these.

Adriaan van der Staay had already left the Arts Council when the first issue of *Hard Werken* appeared, but in the ten years he was director he had created all the conditions for this and other initiatives to come into full flower.[46] The Rotterdam Arts Council, an independent institution with local government funding, had been founded in 1945 with the aim of stimulating and organizing the Rotterdam art world.[47] This set-up was unique to Rotterdam; no other Dutch city had at its disposal a buffer such as this between the city council and the local art world. The Arts Council had three tasks to fulfil: first to advise the city council and the local art institutions, second to subsidize institutions and projects, and third to advance activities of its own. In his job interview Van der Staay made it clear that the third task, setting up Arts Council activities, was for him the most interesting of the three.[48] He diagnosed a cultural provincialism in Rotterdam that he planned to combat with new enterprises. The city council agreed to his ambitious plans, though was sceptical as to whether they could be achieved: 'Don't forget, Rotterdam isn't London', was the reaction Van der Staay remembers from the city council.[49]

But Adriaan van der Staay saw opportunities for Rotterdam to grow, maybe not into a city like London but certainly into a city with a more worldly presence: 'An unbending principle of my policy was to make Rotterdam a modern international city.'[50] To achieve this he enlisted the services of many new people he considered capable of overhauling and internationalizing the Rotterdam art world. He placed knowledge of a field above organizing skills: 'I only wanted to work with people who were absolutely obsessed with the ins and outs of something.'[51] Under his directorship the Arts Council burgeoned from a tiny company with a handful of staff to a good-sized organization with a 70-strong team.[52] One of his most successful enterprises was to set up two international festivals, for poetry and for film. Poetry International he entrusted to Martin Mooij and Film International to Huub Bals.

In the 60 years of its existence the Rotterdam Arts Council has consistently been caught in the force field between local government administrators and official-dom on one side and artists and other cultural entrepreneurs on the other. Van der Staay was a director who sided more with the artists and organizers. He sought a position from where he and those he employed or supported could enjoy maximum freedom. In this he distanced himself as much as possible from the 'high-handed' running of the Arts Council and left questions of art entirely to the experts whose services he enlisted.[53] Martin Mooij later remembered that freedom as a key condi-tion for major artistic achievements: 'Adriaan was not looking for success in the short term. He wanted a climate where all sorts of activities would develop of their own accord. He was not just looking for strong organizers, there had to be enough room for the things to develop. He knew I wasn't a born organizer, but he felt it was more important that I could create space for others to work in. If you create that space, the most amazing things can happen.'[54]

Also the stuff of legends is the freedom Huub Bals (1937–1988) was given in organizing Film International, which was first held in 1972. Bals in turn was very close to the film-makers (on his tombstone he is described as a *filmkunstenaar*, a film-artist[55]). He was on friendly terms with film directors and actors from all over the world and always put their interests first. Van der Staay trusted implicitly Bals' sense of quality and the future would prove him right. Within five years, Film International had built up a solid reputation nationally and internationally among film buffs and had grown into the best attended festival in the Netherlands.[56] The relationship between Van der Staay and Bals was such that if Bals found an inter-esting new film on one of his many trips abroad and wished to buy it, a phone call to Van der Staay to discuss the price was all that was needed. Mutual trust was the name of the game.[57]

In its first years the film festival was held in Lantaren/Venster, giving this gathering place for artists an international resonance ten days long. One could then sit at the bar with actors and directors from all over the world, not from the com-mercial circuit but from the 'underground or semi-underground scene', 'a highly select group of film freaks, from Dennis Hopper to Jim Jarmusch'.[58] These held the Rotterdam festival in high regard because of the relaxed atmosphere – and because the drinks were free during the first few years. Jacques van Heijningen, who worked at De Lantaren from 1973 on, remembers the first film festivals: 'You could drink there for nothing, spend time there, even live there, soft drugs were allowed, it was heaven on earth. In the early years there was a bar serving free drinks for the special guests at the festival, who sometimes spent 24 hours a day in the bar, ten days long (...). Ali, the Arab in the Fassbinder film [*Angst essen Seele auf*] had to be dragged into the auditorium.'[59]

The fact that Van der Staay's own ideas for Rotterdam, aired during his job interview in 1968, were considered too metropolitan – 'this isn't London' – speaks volumes. His view of Rotterdam in the future was in chime with the prewar vision of a metropolis. In this respect too Van der Staay was closer to artists than to administrators and officials. In an interview in *Hard Werken* in 1979, he relates how on arrival in Rotterdam he was fascinated as many artists have been by its rugged, modern demeanour, in some ways comparable to Eindhoven, the city where he had grown up, but then less provincial: '(...) what I found enthralling about a city like Rotterdam was its twilight-zoney side, its rawness: dilapidated sheds, the cobbled streets of the old dock areas. Although Eindhoven was much more provincial, I do see similarities between the two. A sense of the frontier, border conditions... A city with something new about it because of its late development, something of an American city but also of a German city because of the bombing. It has a cool, artificial centre. I found an incomplete, open situation, much more modern than in many other Dutch cities (...).'[60]

During the Van der Staay era, the Rotterdam Arts Council was an anti-bureaucratic institution fizzing with activity, as many who had dealings with it will verify. A writer like Cor Vaandrager could stroll in at any time, recalls former team member Cees van der Geer,[61] and financial backing was found for every worthwhile idea. Van der Staay set up new specialist departments, 'sections', for those areas of artistic activity that had as yet been unrepresented. The existing sections for literature, the visual arts, music and drama were then joined by sections for dance, architecture, and film and video. The Architecture section, founded in 1974, would be of inestimable value for the image Rotterdam would project. It is to this section that Rotterdam would largely owe the reputation it acquired in the 1980s as a city of architecture. It was manned by architects and experts on architecture who sought to convey their passion for architecture to a wider audience, at a time when architecture could scarcely have been further from the public's mind. Cees van der Geer, a member of the Architecture section in the early years along with Jan Hoogstad, Pi de Bruijn and Reyn van der Lugt among others, recalls inspired meetings that lasted until half-past one in the morning.[62] According to Hans Oldewarris, a publisher of books on architecture who had worked for that section on a freelance basis, it was a 'clique' that 'did its own thing' and it was the architects themselves who set it up: 'It really did come from the architecture world, with Carel [Weeber] and Umberto [Barbieri] as key figures in its conception.'[63]

The downside of Van der Staay's liberal policy was that the Rotterdam Arts Council became increasingly chaotic on the administrative and organizational front. For this reason, but also because the socialist College of Mayor and Aldermen

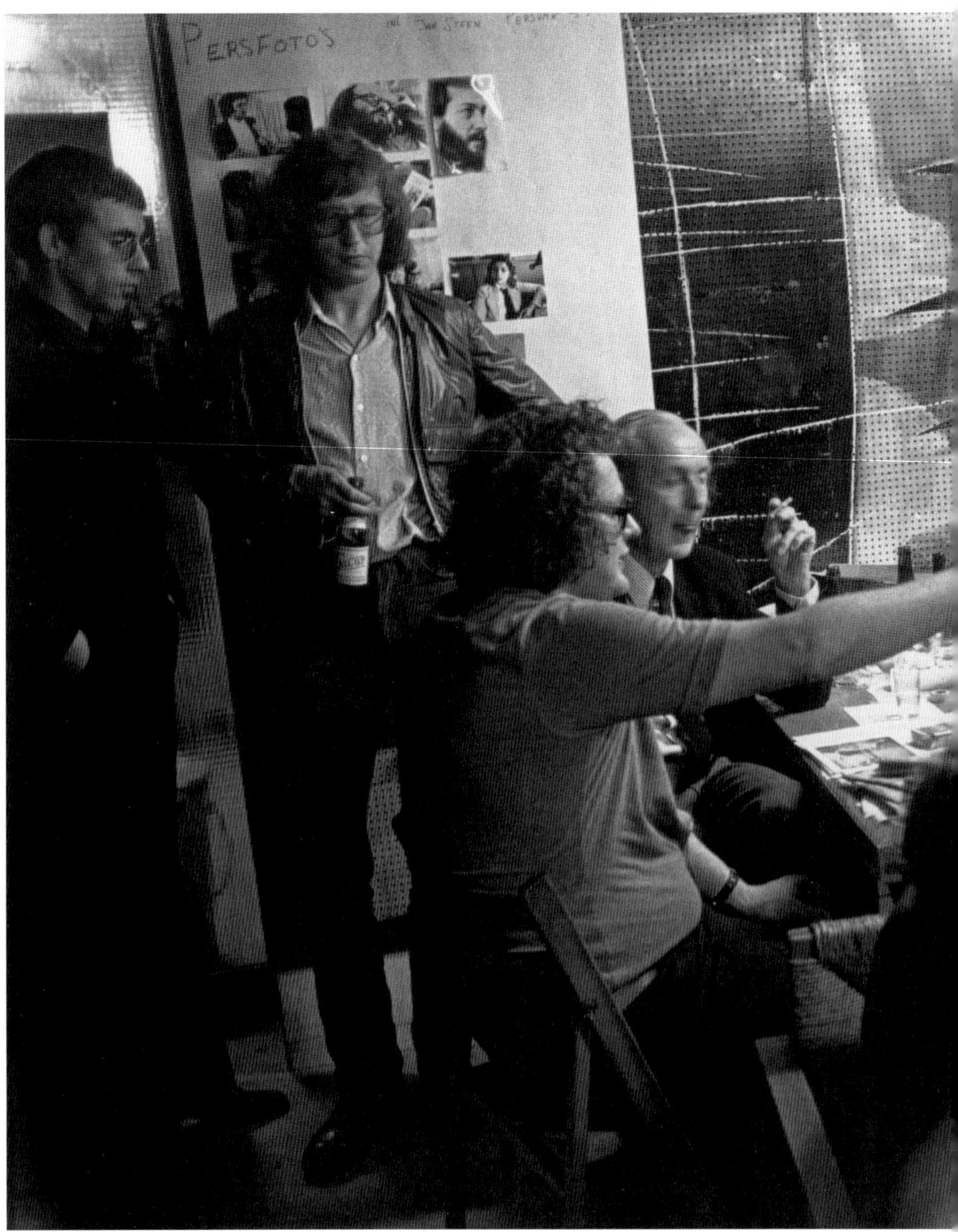
PERSFOTO'S

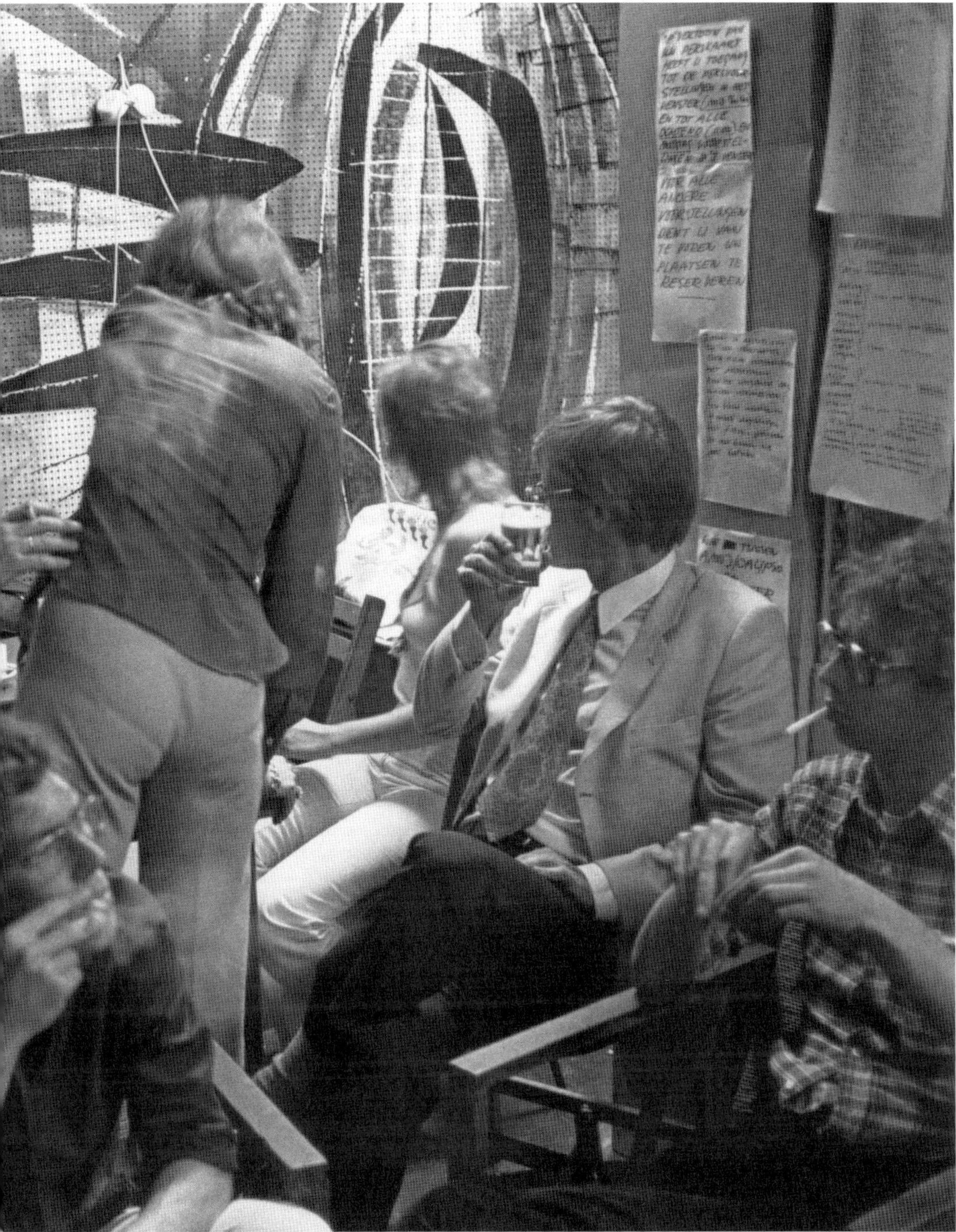

Meeting in the AMVJ Building on Mauritsweg in Rotterdam during Film International, 1972, photo by Hajo Piebenga. Jules Deelder stands at far left, with Huub Bals sitting at left with his arm extended; sitting to his left, the former director of the Rotterdam Arts Council Willy Hofman and on the right (with beer glass) Adriaan van der Staay.

regarded its policy rooted in quality and internationalization as elitist, local government from the mid 1970s on sought to get more control over the Arts Council. This attempt 'to set about limiting the scope of the various cultural institutions and basically seeing the entire cultural sector as a bunch of officials working for local government' (Van der Staay) was one of the factors that prompted Adriaan van der Staay to resign in 1978.[64]

The fact that Van der Staay as director of the Arts Council was always closer to Rotterdam's creative class than to the city council, is made clear by the remarkable fact that the City Hall did not propose a official farewell ceremony and that his departure was marked instead by a going-away party organized by artists. The party was held in Rotterdam's City Theatre (Rotterdamse Schouwburg) with a performance specially put on for Van der Staay's benefit. Shortly before, the dancer Ton Lutgerink had borrowed the light blue jacket that Van der Staay often wore. Lutgerink prepared a dance that was meant to portray Van der Staay, but this failed to register with Van der Staay: 'All at once I saw my jacket on-stage and was naive enough to think: so that's why he needed it. I didn't immediately grasp that it was me he was depicting in his dance.' Lutgerink's dance portrayed Van der Staay 'as someone much given to reflection, an angelic figure who lay down on his back and looked at the heavens'.[65] Since then, Van der Staay has never considered throwing that jacket away.

Van der Staay appreciated this informal farewell enormously. It was attended by just about every artist and cultural entrepreneur who meant something in Rotterdam. Of the city council, only Saskia Stuiveling, the mayor's assistant and a good friend of Van der Staay, was present. During the festivities she awarded him the Wolfert van Borselen Medal, a Rotterdam decoration of great distinction. The fact that members of Rotterdam's creative class took the initiative and not the council is illustrative of the position Van der Staay had come to occupy in the ten years of his directorship. Evidently the creative class had come to regard him as a kindred spirit.

Most of Van der Staay's initiatives as Arts Council director, such as Poetry International and Film International (now International Film Festival Rotterdam, IFFR for short), stayed the course and grew into mega events. The Architecture section, begun when he was in charge, remained active and organized more and more cultural events, such as the first Architecture International Rotterdam (AIR) festival in 1982. When Adriaan van der Staay resigned as director in 1978, the role of the Rotterdam Arts Council changed. Under his successor, Paul Noorman, who was appointed in 1982, the Arts Council was forced to economize and activities such as Poetry International and Film International became autonomous entities.

In the mid 1980s the city council itself became taken with the idea of Rotterdam as a world city. It launched a new policy that was to turn this dream into reality. Although this policy was later interpreted as the starting shot for the new

Rotterdam that emerged during the 1990s, it was just as much a response to all manner of underground enterprises already operating in the city. The following chapter will address council policy from that perspective, as building upon the many activities launched by Rotterdam's creative class, and place that policy in the broader context of a changing view of urbanity.

1 J.A. Deelder in the TV programme *Neon*, directed by Bob Visser, broadcast November 25, 1979, Netherlands Institute for Sound and Vision.

2 Formula for the cultural city paper *Metropool*, printed in Hogerhuis, H. van (1982), 'Metropool: Cultureel stadsblad voor groot-rotterdam', *Hard Werken*, 10, pp. 8-9 (p. 8).

3 Bakker, H. & T. van Hoorn (1977), 'Rotterdamse wethouder Mentink: ik wil over m'n graf heen regeren', *Plan*, 2 (February), pp. 25-32 (p. 28).

4 For instance in the following scholarly publications: Dijk, H. van (1995), 'De gezelligheids-revolutie 1965–1985', in: M. Aarts (ed.), *Vijftig jaar wederopbouw Rotterdam: Een geschiedenis van toekomstvisies*, Rotterdam: 010 Publishers, pp. 161-192 (p. 197); Meyer, H. (1999), *City and Port: Urban Planning as a Cultural Venture in London, Barcelona, New York, and Rotterdam: Changing relations between public urban space and large-scale infrastructure*, Utrecht: International Books, p. 331. Both books fail to acknowledge their source.

5 Bakker & Hoorn (1977), op. cit. (note 3), pp. 25-32.

6 For example in *Economisch Dagblad*, February 28, 1977, and *Rotterdams Nieuwsblad*, February 23, 1977. According to one of the two interviewers, Ton van Hoorn, these words were in many people's mouths shortly after publication, notably at meetings of the Architecture section of the Rotterdam Arts Council. Verbally communicated to the author by Ton van Hoorn, April 16, 2005.

7 Bakker & Hoorn (1977), op. cit. (note 3), pp. 25-32 (p. 28).

8 *Rotterdams Nieuwsblad*, February 23, 1977. On this see also Van Dijk (1995), op. cit. (note 4), pp. 161-192.

9 Haan, H. de & I. Haagsma (1982), *Stadsbeeld Rotterdam 1965–1982*, Utrecht: Oosthoek's Uitgeversmaatschappij B.V., pp. 58.

10 See for example Kloosterman, R. (2001), *Ruimte voor reflectie*, Amsterdam: Vossiuspers UvA, pp. 10-12.

11 Burgers, J. (2002), *De gefragmenteerde stad*, Amsterdam: Boom, p. 9.

12 De Haan & Haagsma (1982), op. cit. (note 9).

13 Zukin, S. (1995), *The Cultures of Cities*, Cambridge MA/Oxford, p. 267.

14 According to the Rotterdam film director Bob Visser (born 1950), none of his generation had problems with Rotterdam's lack of 'gezelligheid'; author's interview with Bob Visser, April 1, 2005.

15 Oudheusden, P. van & H. Verhey (1986), *De Mensch Deelder*, Utrecht/Antwerp: Veen, states that it was telecast during Christmas 1977, more precisely on Christmas Day between 21.10 and 22.45 according to the newspapers. The documentary is also on the DVD celebrating Deelder's 60th birthday, *60 jaar Deelder*, Rotterdam: Neon Film-TV, 2004 (the table of contents dates the programma a year too early, in 1976).

16 Author's interview with Bob Visser, April 1, 2005.

17 Deelder, J.A. & V. Mentzel (1984), *Stadslicht*, Rotterdam: Kreits, p. 34.

18 Bakker & Van Hoorn (1977), op. cit. (note 3), pp. 25-32 (p. 27).

19 Deelder was filmed against the projection screen of the cinema on the top floor of the Wholesale Building (Groothandelsgebouw). That screen could be slid aside from the middle like a curtain for a view across the city. Information from the author's interview with Bob Visser, April 1, 2005.

20 The name Iggy Pop is visible earlier in the film as a sprayed text on a wall.

21 It is an instrumental from David Bowie's album *Heroes* (1977).

22 Brusse, M.J. et al. (1938), *Rotterdam* (*De schoonheid van ons land*; dl. VI), Amsterdam: Uitgeverij Contact.

23 Brusse et al. (1938), op. cit. (note 22), p. XXVI.

24 Deelder & Mentzel (1984), op. cit. (note 17), p. 19. *Blokkendozen* is also a pejorative term for blocks of flats.

25 Rotterdam's beauty was likewise compared to that of marble at the end of the 16th century, see Wagener,

W.A. (1951), 'Rotterdam', in: C. Oorthuys et al. (eds), *Land en volk: Steden* (*De schoonheid van ons land*; dl. 10), Amsterdam: Contact, pp. 68-73 (p. 68).

26 Notenboom, E.W. & B. Maandag (2003), *Metamorfose Rotterdam 2*, Rotterdam: Rotterdams Dagblad/Eppo W. Notenboom, p. 45.

27 Suttles, G.D. (1984), 'The Cumulative Texture of Local Urban Culture', *The American Journal of Sociology*, 90 (2) September, pp. 283-304. On this see chapter 1.

28 For instance in *Hard Werken*, 2, May 1979; Deelder & Mentzel (1984), op. cit. (note 17); Vroegindeweij, R. (ed.) (1990), *Rotterdam gehakt uit marmer, poëzie uit Rotterdam 1940–1990*, Rotterdam: Ad Donker.

29 Vroegindeweij, R. (2004), 'Hij heb een rare kop, maar hij ken wel wat: Jules Deelder zestig', *Algemeen Dagblad*, November 20, 2004, read at http://www.vroegius.nl/artikelen/2004, April 25, 2005.

30 Quoted in: Van Oudheusden & Verhey (1986), op. cit. (note 15), p. 76.

31 Author's interview with Bob Visser, April 1, 2005. I have been unable to locate either previews or reviews of the telecast in the Rotterdam papers.

32 Interview by Piet Piryns with Jules Deelder, May 19, 1984, published at http://www.dbnl.org/tekst/piry001eris01/index.htm, p. 70, site visited April 25, 2005.

33 According to Deelder regarding the reactions to *Stadsgezicht* in an interview with Piet Piryns, May 19, 1984, published at http://www.dbnl.org/tekst/piry001eris01/index.htm, p. 74, site visited April 25, 2005.

34 'I didn't know Rotterdam very well, but I was aware that it was a kind of fairly formless city. And I had an instinct that there was an emerging culture and that, at the same time, it was pretty much a wasteland.' Crimson, P. Gadanho et al. (eds) (2001), *Post.Rotterdam: Architecture and City after the tabula rasa/Arquitectura e Cidade após a tabula rasa*, Rotterdam: 010 Publishers, p. 62.

35 That hard core consisted of Loes Brünott, Henk Elenga, Kees de Gruiter, Gerard Hadders, Tom van den Haspel, Willem Kars, Rick Vermeulen and Rien Vroegindeweij.

36 See Hefting, P. & D. van Ginkel (1995), *Hard Werken Inízio*, Rotterdam: 010 Publishers.

37 *Hard Werken*, 1, April 1979, 'editorial', p. 3.

38 *Hard Werken*, 3, July 1979, p. 16.

39 *Hard Werken*, op. cit. (note 38), p. 32.

40 *Hard Werken*, op. cit. (note 38), p. 33.

41 ibid.

42 According to the credits of no. 2 (May 1979), p. 2.

43 Hefting & Van Ginkel (1995), op. cit (note 36), p. 24.

44 Gaemers, C. (1996), *Achter de schermen van de kunst: Rotterdamse Kunststichting 1945–1995*, Rotterdam: De Hef, p. 125.

45 Hefting & Van Ginkel (1995), op. cit. (note 36), p. 17.

46 His last act as director of the RKS was to grant a subsidy for the magazine *Hard Werken*, according to Van der Staay himself in an interview with the author, July 22, 2005.

47 For a history of the Rotterdam Arts Council see Gaemers (1996), op. cit. (note 44). This book is the source of all information here on the RKS unless otherwise indicated.

48 Author's interview with Adriaan van der Staay, July 22, 2005.

49 Adriaan van der Staay in the documentary *Moois. RKS 1946–2005*, telecast by the VPRO in 2005, production NeON Media. Van der Staay also made mention of this (though wording it differently) during a discussion at the launch of Paul van de Laar's book *Stad van formaat. Geschiedenis van Rotterdam in de negentiende en twintigste eeuw* on March 18, 2000 and during the interview with the author on July 22, 2005.

50 Author's interview with Adriaan van der Staay, July 22, 2005.

51 idem.

52 Gaemers (1996) op. cit. (note 44), p. 79.

53 According to Van der Staay himself in an interview printed in *Hard Werken*, op. cit. (note 37), pp. 16-19 and 22-23 (p. 22). 'The structure as it has developed over the past ten years, was new for Rotterdam too. It was a kind of mix of high-handed bureacratism and expertise. I gave this a deliberate twist when I was there. I separated the managerial side from that of the experts. I don't think Rotterdam's upper crust should say what's good for the arts; that's a matter for the experts in the various sections of the Arts Council.'

54 Hulscher, L. (1994), *De menselijke stem: 25 jaar Poetry International. Sphinx Cultuurprijs voor Martin Mooij*, Zutphen: Walburg Instituut, p. 43.

55 Heijs, J. & F. Westra (1996), *Que le tigre Danse. Huub Bals een biografie*, Amsterdam: Otto Cramwinckel, p. 204.

56 Gaemers (1996), op. cit. (note 44), p. 79.

57 Author's interview with Adriaan van der Staay, July 22, 2005.

58 According to Jacques van Heijningen in an interview with the author, January 19, 2004. Van Heijningen worked at De Lantaren since 1973 and was in charge of the film and video workshop.
59 According to Jacques van Heijningen in an interview with the author, January 19 2004.
60 *Hard Werken*, op. cit. (note 37), p. 22.
61 Author's interview with Cees van der Geer, November 21, 2002.
62 idem.
63 Author's interview with Hans Oldewarris, March 31, 2003.
64 Van der Staay in an interview printed in *Hard Werken*, op. cit. (note 37), pp. 16-19 and 22-23 (p. 23).
65 Author's interview with Adriaan van der Staay, July 22, 2005.

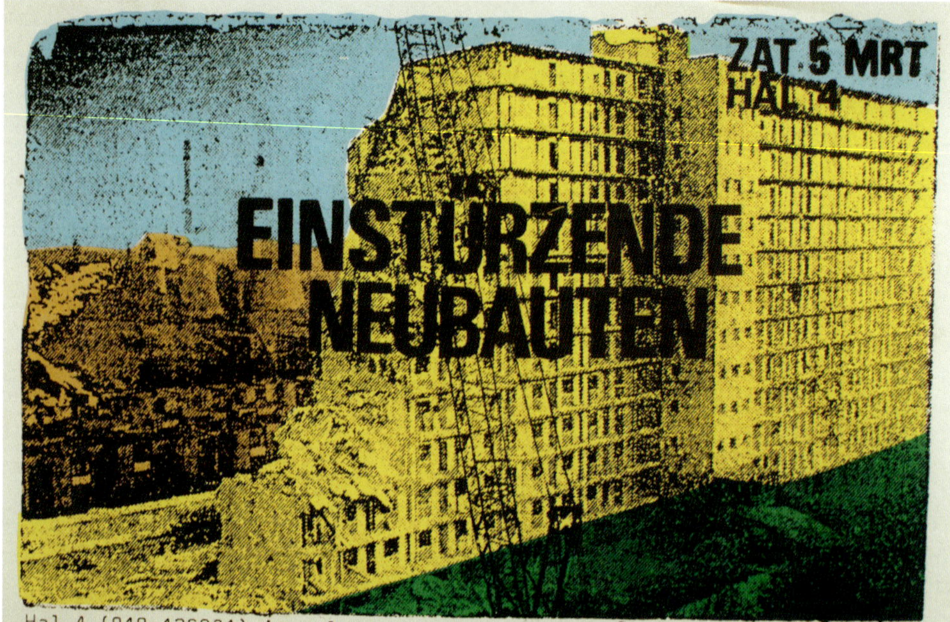

Hal 4 poster advertising a concert there by Einstürzende Neubauten, March 5, 1983, design by Evan van der Most and Hans van den Tol.

Chapter 4

Magical years

Nineteen-eighty seven saw the publication of two reports commissioned by Rotterdam city council that are generally considered a turning point in the policy on tackling the city. *Vernieuwing van Rotterdam* (Renewing Rotterdam), was drawn up under the aegis of the College of Mayor and Aldermen and the other, *Nieuw Rotterdam*, by an independent advisory committee for socioeconomic renewal chaired by W. Albeda. Han Meyer, the author of a study on Rotterdam as a port city, describes 1987 as a 'magical year' for Rotterdam largely because of the publication of these two reports.[1] Irina van Aalst, author of a thesis on the role of culture in the centres of Rotterdam and Frankfurt, likewise regards 1987 as the onset of a new period for Rotterdam.[2] Those directly involved at the time, such as Joop Linthorst, then alderman for the arts, confirm that it is impossible to understand Rotterdam's development in the 1990s without having an idea of the policy set forth in those reports: 'They mark a point. You can't say it all happened in the mid '80s, but if you look back you have to conclude that for Rotterdam a number of fairly crucial milestones were reached or thresholds crossed somewhere around that time, and those reports mark that. (...) For the council too it was a time when we pursued a pretty strong policy, and saw it implemented.'[3] The reports do indeed address various aspects that would be crucial to Rotterdam's continuing development. Thus, for example, the council-sanctioned report mentions for the first time the Kop van Zuid project. The two reports have additionally been important for Rotterdam economically, as both drew attention to the need to pick up on new, global developments as much for the docks as for the city centre: the dock area needed transforming from a large-scale transshipment port into a high-tech logistics hub, and the city's centre had to capitalize on the growth of the business services sector that was supplanting industry throughout Western Europe. Switching from product orientation to the provision of services was regarded as a solution for the high unemployment plaguing Rotterdam – some 50,000 unemployed out of a total population of something over 570,000. Of those 50,000, as many as 30,000 were long-term unemployed.[4]

For Rotterdam to profit from the growth in business services, which basically meant banks, insurance firms and company headquarters, it was necessary to make the city, and its centre in particular, more attractive. Companies set great store by the ambience projected by the city where they are to be domiciled, particularly in the case of a head office. Besides, it is 'common knowledge that a company's place

of business is partly decided by where its director lives'.[5] In other words, if a city has
an attractive residential climate, this indirectly encourages companies to settle there.
A pleasant living climate in a city is also important for attracting qualified staff;
according to Richard Florida, it is even the case in recent decades that employees
first choose a place to live and only then look for a job.[6]

This is not the first time that Rotterdam council wanted to make their city
more attractive, as we saw in the preceding chapters. But attractive now meant
something entirely different from attractive at the time of C70 and the glory days
of alderman Mentink. In *Vernieuwing van Rotterdam* and *Nieuw Rotterdam*, we see
the vision of Rotterdam the metropolis making a comeback. This much is clear from
the covers of the two reports. That of *Vernieuwing van Rotterdam* includes a repro-
duction of a somewhat blurred photograph in grey tints of the illuminated city at
night, an essential part of the iconography of the modern metropolis. The firework
display filling the sky in the photograph shows that the city being portrayed is
bustling with life. The cover of the other report uses high-rise to represent the New
Rotterdam, looming apparition-like in loud though transparent colours printed over
a black-and-white aerial photo of both banks of the river Maas. The siting of these
skyscrapers on Noordereiland, an island lying between the north and south banks,
bears no relation at all to actual plans for this area. Their form is merely outlined, as
if they were elongated coloured perspex blocks. The sole purpose of the high-rise
vision is to illustrate the title 'Nieuw Rotterdam'. The impression is one of a world
city. This is emphasized by the expansive view of the river and the traffic moving in
and over it and by the seemingly endless agglomeration of buildings that make up
this urban landscape.

That this marks a conscious break with the ideal of the small scale that had
dominated local politics since C70, is clear from the explicit rejection in the texts of
the way space was treated in the name of that ideal. The College report mentions
'organizing principles that now look extremely dated, that present open space as a
problem instead of a challenge'.[7] In both 1987 reports, that space regains its positive
status: 'Rotterdam's urban development is rooted in exploiting the city's strong
points and spatial qualities.'[8] Just as space was no longer seen as the cause of
draughty places but as one of Rotterdam's qualities, other aspects of the city, such as
Rotterdam's distinctive modern, rational and international profile, were rediscovered
in these reports.[9] The College report puts it thus: 'Rotterdam is the only Dutch city to
have acquired the image of a city with an internationally tinged, modern appearance.
This character can still be strengthened considerably (...).'[10] Here the swing towards
a positive evaluation of qualities peculiar to Rotterdam is complete.

Underground developments

Important though both reports from the 'magical year' of 1987 undoubtedly have
been for the city, it is incorrect to construe them as the starting shot for the new

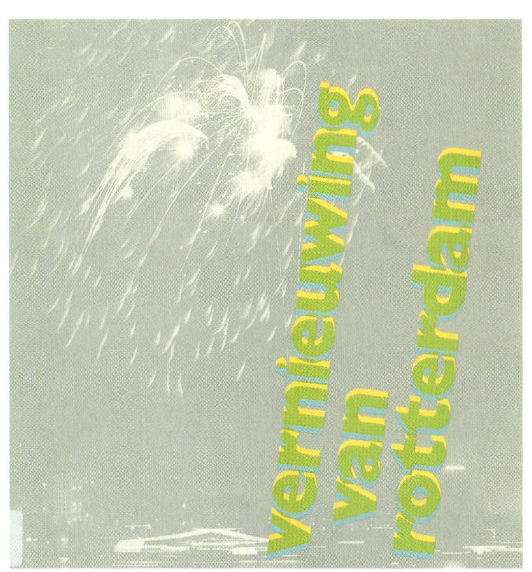

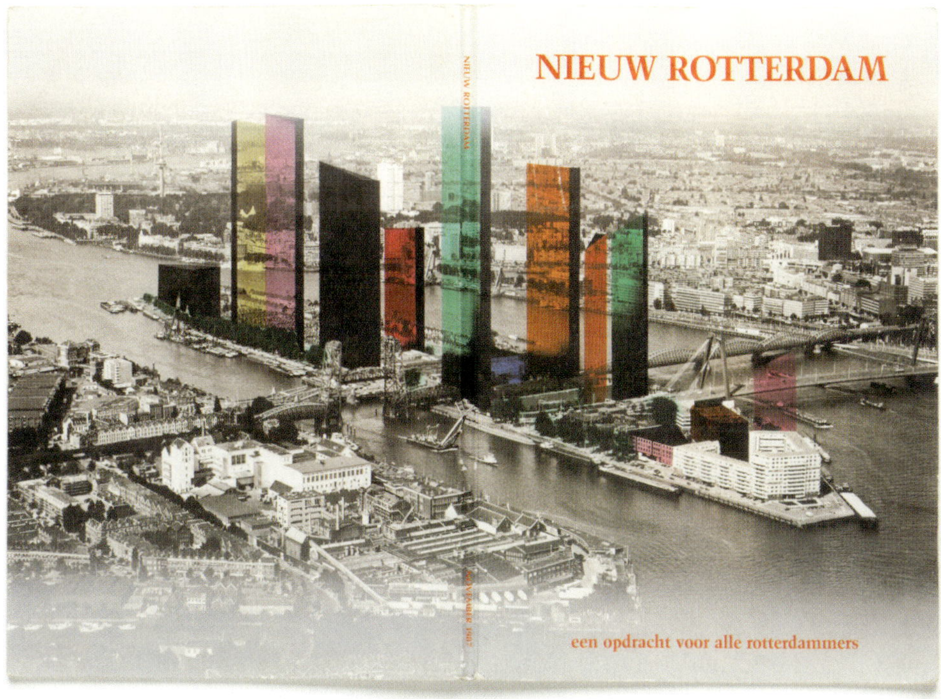

Top cover of *Vernieuwing van Rotterdam*, October 1987, report compiled by the College of Mayor and Aldermen. It shows the illuminated city at night, an essential part of the iconography of the modern metropolis.

Bottom *Nieuw Rotterdam*, 1987, report compiled by a committee chaired by W. Albeda. The cover shows a vision of high-rise that bears no relation at all to actual urban plans.

Rotterdam that would gain shape during the rest of the 1980s and during the '90s. Work had long been proceeding apace preparing the ground for the new council line, preparatory work described in the previous chapter as 'underground'. Such underground developments are certainly no less influential than official policy. In fact this seemingly piecemeal input by individuals and non-official coalitions is of inestimable importance for a city's dynamics. In pre-1987 Rotterdam creative individuals of all kinds had been paving the way forward in no uncertain fashion.

To be fair, the College's own report did not harbour the intention of pointing developments in a wholly new direction. Indeed, accounts from various sources made mention of the fact that the presented policy was a reaction to developments long under way. Yet as a reaction it was none too explicit. These are the opening sentences of *Vernieuwing van Rotterdam*: 'Rotterdam is at the crossroads. Major developments are in progress, developments that require adaptation and renewal on the part of the city.'[11] Which developments they refer to may be distilled in some measure from these words: 'Cities are taking on a new lease of life. New groups of inhabitants and firms are discovering them. Urban functions are reviving and reorganizing. This fresh burst of activity is expected to continue. It all relates to an element of change in culture and in the reception of cities in general.'[12] This refers, if generally, to the renewed interest in urbanity among groups of inhabitants and companies. It goes on to suggest that Rotterdam specifically could benefit from this trend because of all the open space the city had to offer: 'Not all cities will be as successful. Space and spatial qualities are essential requisites.'[13] Joop Linthorst, who as alderman for arts and finance was partly responsible for the College-driven report (*Vernieuwing van Rotterdam*) acknowledges that it not only signalled a new start but was also a summing-up of many ongoing developments: 'In a sense, a report such as this canonizes elements that in fact were already there or that had developed of their own accord. So as the council, you must take care you don't claim it entirely as your own, attribute it all to yourself. A report such as this on the one hand records certain developments and on the other outlines or suggests perspectives for the future. Perspective which, with hindsight, I feel have largely been achieved. And not thanks to the council but often because they were trends, developments in the city that were happening anyway and in the process were simply committed to paper.'[14]

Two trends 'that were happening anyway' and were explicitly and implicitly built upon in the reports of 1987, were introduced in the previous chapter: the reappraisal of Rotterdam's metropolitan aspects and the emergence of all manner of private, 'underground' initiatives on the cultural front. I shall place these turns of events in a broader context in this and the following chapter. The present chapter first of all describes how in 1982 Rotterdam's creative class, organized in the Architecture section of the Rotterdam Arts Council, had called for attention to the image of the city as a whole. A first condition for advancing a comprehensive perspective on Rotterdam is to see the city in its totality rather than as a composition of individual districts. In this chapter, I shall place this reappraisal of urbanity within the context of the new music of those years and the lifestyle that came with it.

The overall image of the city

A fundamental point on which the line suggested by the council in 1987 deviates from the one adhered to since 1970 is a concern for the city image as a whole. The 1970s are typified not only by small-scale architecture but also by a view of the city that zoomed in on constituent aspects. Against that, *Vernieuwing van Rotterdam* and *Nieuw Rotterdam* describe the city as if observed from the air: 'The city's image is defined in particular by its position on the river with a long-drawn-out waterfront, the modern inner city and the distinctive quality of the city's outer ring of residential development. River, inner city and outer urban ring open up exceptional opportunities by Dutch standards.'[15] Yet even this was not new in 1987. It was ushered in by a spate of activities of all kinds organized by Rotterdam's creative class, culminating in the first AIR event of 1982.

AIR is the acronym for Architecture International Rotterdam, an architecture festival instigated by the Architecture section of the Rotterdam Arts Council as a supplement to the existing festivals Poetry International and Film International. As mentioned in the previous chapter, this section was a 'clique that did its own thing'[16] in which the architects Carel Weeber and Umberto Barbieri had a big part to play. Reyn van der Lugt, then head of the Architecture section, was responsible for organizing the AIR festival.

The theme of the first AIR event was 'the image of the city'. This theme was elaborated on for a full year in a welter of activities including exhibitions, competitions, discussions, research and design projects and special publications. That theme, 'the image of the city', was expressly meant as a call to reconsider the grand gesture in architecture and urban design. In the 1970s, architectural practice had been almost exclusively focused on architectural issues at the micro-level. And in the case of social housing, the occupants' requirements had come to carry more weight than the architect's ideas. Even at one of the Netherlands' top architecture schools, that of Delft University of Technology, the 1970s saw the practice of design overshadowed by political issues such as the campaign for affordable homes. According to Hans Oldewarris, himself an architect who studied at Delft, designing was even taboo by then: 'Designing was no longer allowed at Delft (...) that political group called the tune at Delft. It all hinged on housing, low rents. A fine thing in itself of course, but it meant that design was cruelly neglected. (...) AIR 1982 turned it all around, the visual side was back in the spotlight.'[17]

Two components of AIR 1982 in particular expressed the 'image of the city' theme in a way that is well worth considering in the context of this book, as the notion of 'image' was treated symbolically in these two projects. Both presented an image of Rotterdam that reverted to the one formed at the beginning of that century.

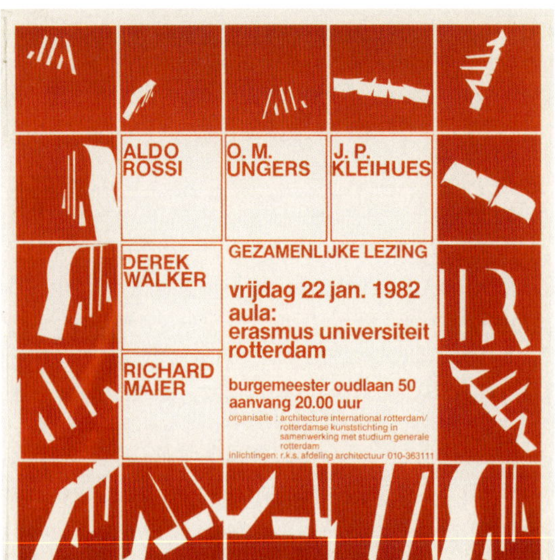

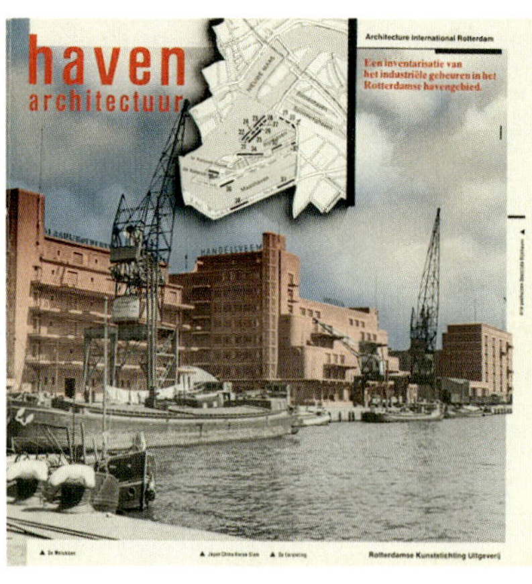

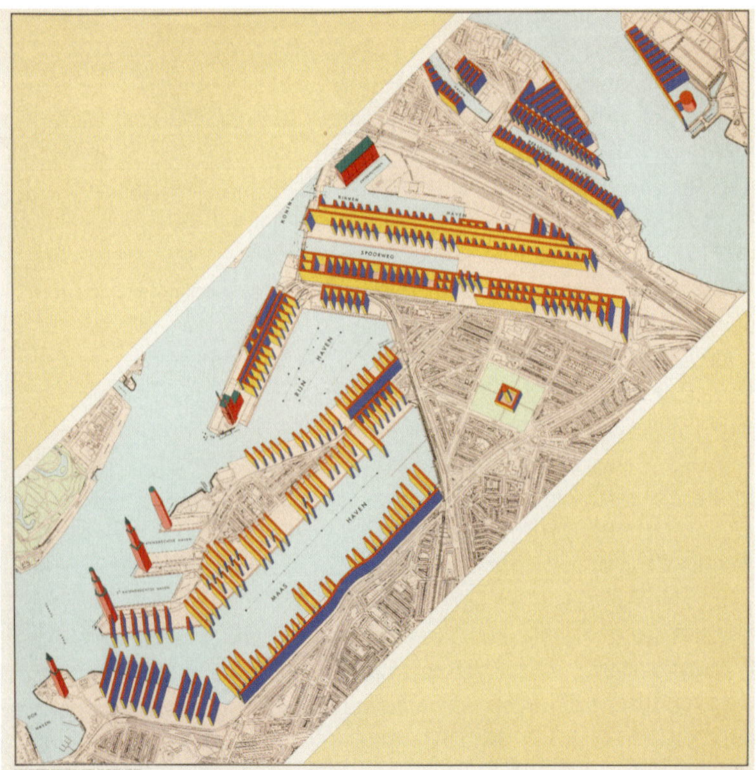

Top left poster for AIR 1982, design by Jan Pesman.

Top right cover of the book *Havenarchitectuur*, Rotterdam 1982.

Bottom Aldo Rossi's design for Kop van Zuid as part of AIR 1982.

The first was an exhibition and accompanying publication on port architecture in Rotterdam. This project put the image of the city of Rotterdam pretty much on a par with that of the port: 'The look of Rotterdam is defined in large measure by the port and port activities. Think of Rotterdam and the port inevitably comes to mind. The Rotterdam Arts Council commissioned an inventory to be made of all the buildings, machinery and structures in the port area so as to capture "the image of the port".'[18] The remarkable thing about this project is obviously not that it regards the port as defining the look of Rotterdam – that would have been a supreme statement of the obvious – but that it treats this fact positively by placing it within the framework of stimulating the city's cultural climate. This means that for the first time in a long while, the port of Rotterdam was held in esteem aesthetically as well as economically, as it had been in the years between the two world wars.[19]

The second AIR project to give 'the image of the city' a symbolic charge was 'De Kop van Zuid'. Kop van Zuid is the customary description for that part of the left bank of the Maas where the river loops quite abruptly to the north, so that on the map the south bank swells polyp-like to form the 'Kop' or head. Developed as a new dock at the end of the 19th century, Kop van Zuid fell into disuse in the 1970s as port activities shifted westward. The council's plans for Kop van Zuid got no further than allocating it as an 'overspill area' for the urban renewal then under way, in other words social housing was to be built there to temporarily house inhabitants whose homes were being renovated or rebuilt.[20] However, the Architecture section of the Arts Council recognized the value of this location for the future look of Rotterdam. To make its qualities more widely known, the section invited five world-class architects from abroad – Aldo Rossi, Oswald Mathias Ungers, Josef Paul Kleihues, Derek Walker and Richard Meier – to give their ideas on how Kop van Zuid should be developed. They were not being asked to make a design or masterplan, but to develop an image, an impression.[21] Though none of these impressions elicited an actual plan, this project has been enormously influential as it brought to light the potentials of this part of Rotterdam. According to Ed Taverne and Cor Wagenaar AIR 1982 made its presence felt far beyond Rotterdam: '(...) AIR's message did meet with a response, particularly in the world of planning and design where the call to address cities as a whole, the Randstad, the entire Netherlands, ushered in not only another practice of design and planning but many new types of publication.'[22] So the concern for the image of the city as a whole, an aspect that became key to council policy from 1987 on, had a lengthy gestation period of ideas and theories of which AIR 1982 was a provisional resumé. So in a sense, 1982 was also a 'magical year'.

Reappraisal of urbanity and metropolitanism

'Cities are taking on a new lease of life,' we can read in the council report *Vernieuwing van Rotterdam* of 1987. 'This fresh burst of activity is expected to continue. It all relates to an element of change in culture and in the reception of cities in general.'[23]

The reappraisal noted here was a conspicuous trend in the 1980s not just in the
Netherlands or Europe, but worldwide. The urban exodus came to a halt and people
one more began opting for a home in the city. Much ink has been spilled over the
social causes of this development and writers are generally agreed as to what these
are.[24] The theory, briefly, is this: there was an increase in one- and two-person households with a greater need than the traditional family for optimum public amenities
for daily subsistence, social intercourse and leisure activities. These would include
larger supermarkets, fast food services, caterers, restaurants, launderettes, cafés
and other leisure-time facilities, theatres, cinemas, attractive shops and museums.
Amenities such as these are by definition concentrated in cities. So settling in the
city is a practical choice for two-income couples and people living alone.

    Demographic developments in Rotterdam bear out this theory. Since 1965
Rotterdam had seen a decrease in its population that would reach alarming proportions particularly in the mid 1970s. Families with children left for the suburbs
where the houses and the residential setting were more to their taste. Between 1965
and 1985 the city's population would drop by almost 22 per cent. From 1985 on, there
were signs of a modest growth occasioned by a decline in population outflow and
a light increase in the number of new arrivals. Families with children however still
preferred the suburbs, whereas the number of one- and two-person households
swelled. In 1989 no less than 75 per cent of the total number of households in
Rotterdam were one- or two-person.[25] These were mostly young people between
the ages of 15 and 30, an age when social activity is a large part of life.[26] This group
would clearly be in need of urban facilities of all kinds.

    Yet in the 1980s there was more involved here than can be put down to
demographic change alone. The fact that more people opted for the urban life at
the beginning of that decade must be placed against the background of other, less
statistically demonstrable social trends. So-called hard factors on site such as all
kinds of amenities played a part too, but these are not enough to explain the
'change in culture and in the reception of cities'.[27] Besides, demographic theory on
the revival of urbanity introduces a chicken and egg dilemma: what came first, the
migration of small households to the city or the resurgence of urban public life?
The small households were allegedly attracted by the amenities on offer in the city,
yet those amenities owed their revived status to those same small households. The
traditional economic paradigm that demand creates supply points to the cityward
migration as the reason for the upsurge in urban amenities. In that case the one- and
two-person households were drawn in by something else. But what?

    In order to answer this question I shall return to the notion of 'aesthetic
conjuncture' introduced by Sharon Zukin.[28] Putting it more simply, urbanity began
coming back into fashion in the 1980s. In his inaugural lecture as professor of urban
studies at Rotterdam's Erasmus University, Jack Burgers follows the same train of
thought, except that he dates the phenomenon slightly later. Without justification,
I feel, as the suburbanization process was definitely past its peak in the '80s. He

writes: 'You could even go so far as to say that the city is fashionable. (...) Where during the heyday of suburbanization in the 1970s and '80s cities wanted to look as rural as possible in a last-ditch attempt to keep their inhabitants from leaving, we now see that smaller towns are trying to assume a metropolitan appearance in the way they design their public space and organize events.'[29] This phenomenon of city life becoming fashionable is intimately connected with the revived vision of Rotterdam the metropolis. Metropolitanism regained its lustre, and this time not only for a handful of artists like Deelder but for the public at large.

Despite all attempts to scale it down, Rotterdam would remain the pre-eminent Dutch city to hold the promise – or threat, in '70s parlance – of a metropolis. More so than Amsterdam, though this last-named was the largest city in the Netherlands. Amsterdam had just come out of a new Golden Age, the age of Provos (a movement dedicated to provoking those in power, hence the name), Kabouters ('serious pranksters' who even briefly sat on the the city council) and hippies. The city had proved an ideal stage set for the social movements that had been making themselves heard since the 1960s, and had built up a reputation well beyond the national borders as a 'magic centre': 'For a time in the 1970's, the era of flower power, Amsterdam was for some people the capital of the world.'[30] Amsterdam was admittedly a large city by Dutch standards but its scaled-down look, predominantly narrow, winding streets, tranquil canals and the charming Vondelpark failed to satisfy the image of a city in the international sense. Of the regular hallmarks of the metropolitan demeanour – traffic flows, high-rise and lights at night – it only had one to its name, the lights at night. With the metropolitan look back in vogue, cities like Rotterdam came to be seen in a better light while the aesthetic conjuncture was less favourable for the likes of Amsterdam. I shall explore these and other oppositions between the images of Rotterdam and Amsterdam more fully in chapter 6.

Music of the city: punk and New Wave

This reappraisal of the metropolitan environment was echoed in the music and lifestyle that steadily gained popularity among young people in the Netherlands from 1977 on, namely punk and the later variant, New Wave.[31] Generally speaking, the hallmarks of punk rock and New Wave music were fast tempos, a high volume, a jagged or distorted sound quality and a minimal melody. The effect is nervous, high-octane and hard-hitting. The manner of delivery is usually highly energetic and full of life – harsh, breathless, shrill. It was with these qualities of dynamism and energy that the music's makers and fans wanted to counter the indolence and listlessness of the hippies. The musical soundtrack to the hippies' leisurely and dreamy attitude to life was on the whole melodious, harmonically complex and with the tempo kept well down. Besides these familiar oppositions between hippie and punk culture there is a more implicit aspect that is worth considering in the present context: the hippie culture's attachment to nature against the metropoli-

tanism of punk culture. In hippie culture love of nature was part of a romantic
escapism centred around a primal, natural existence. Urban life was rejected as
capitalist, wasteful and artificial: 'The hippy dream was one of escape. It was all
about going up country and dropping out and turning on and going to San Francisco
with flowers in your hair, It was idealistic, contemplative, sometimes mystical.
Above all, it was a rejection of urban consumer culture.'[32] This predilection for things
natural was reflected in hippie dress codes. Hair was worn long and loose, make-up
was scarcely used, clothes were loose-fitting and of natural materials, and footwear,
if not absent altogether, was either sandals or prairie boots. Photographs of the
legendary open-air music festival held in 1970 in Rotterdam clearly show these
attributes of hippie dress. The desire to return to some sort of primeval state is
likewise reflected in the poster for this pop festival, which shows Adam and Eve in
Paradise. It was even officially called 'Pop Paradijs', but is much better known as
Kralingen 1970 after Kralingse Bos, the area of woods and clearings in the Kralingen
district of Rotterdam where it was held.

Many lyrics of hippie songs extol the virtues of nature. One obvious example
is *Going Up The Country* from 1968 by the American group Canned Heat. After
Canned Heat had performed this song in the summer of 1969 at the legendary
Woodstock festival, it became something of a hippie anthem. The film later made
about Woodstock begins with the melody of *Going Up The Country*.[33] Canned Heat
performed it again at the Rotterdam festival of 1970. The lyrics are an explicit ode
to the relaxed way of life in rural America: 'I'm going up the country, babe don't you
wanna go / I'm going to some place where I've never been before / I'm going, I'm
going where the water tastes like wine.' The city by contrast is put down as a nerve-
racking, aggressive place: 'I'm gonna leave this city, got to get away / I'm gonna
leave this city, got to get away / All this fussing and fighting, man, you know I sure
can't stay.' Paeans to nature and 'the country' crop up with remarkable regularity in
folk and country music, as Nick Green has shown.[34] But the lyrics of so-called prog-
rock bands like Pink Floyd and Led Zeppelin were also often reflective of an ideal image
of nature or a natural state.[35] Progressive rock music even resorts to imitations of
natural sounds.

Punk rock and New Wave music by contrast use sounds that recall the hubbub of the city. It is less easy, on the whole, to reconcile this music with images of
nature than with that of the 'concrete jungle', the big, tough city. It is for good reason
that New Wave has been described as 'metropolitan funk'.[36] Some bands actually
produced sounds in the street, the most famous of them being the Berlin-based
Einstürzende Neubauten. Their track *Stahlversion* from 1980 was recorded on a
steel bridge, using the bridge itself as a percussion instrument.[37] But there are other
respects in which punk rock and New Wave are urban through and through. The
song lyrics are often about city life, particularly at night. What *Going Up The Country*
was for the hippies, *Collapsing New People* was in a sense for the New Wave generation. The lyrics of this song from 1984 by the British musician Fad Gadget describe

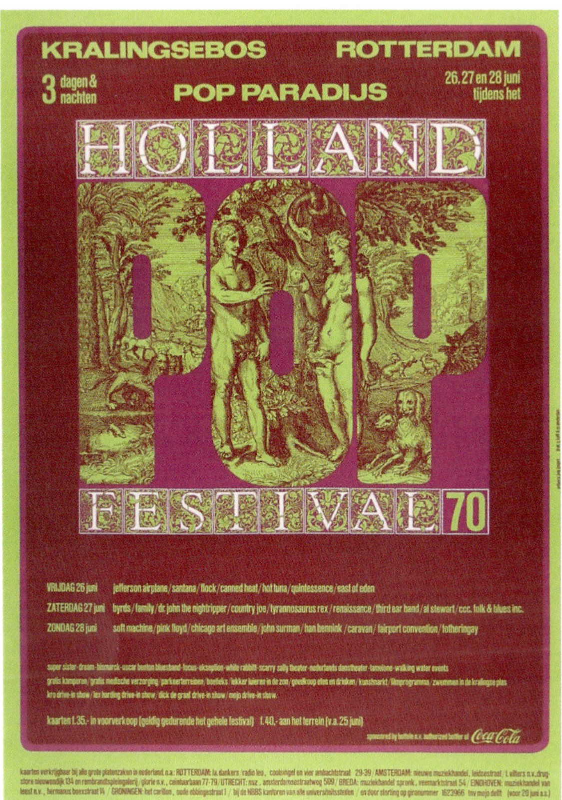

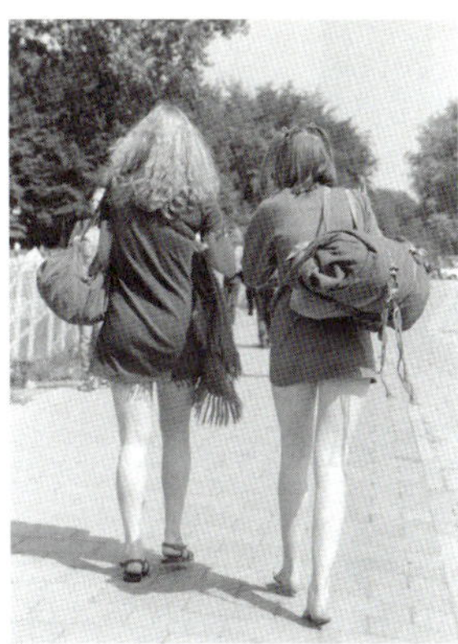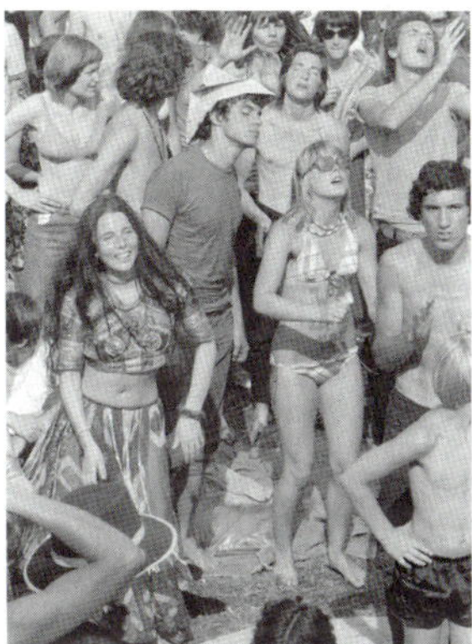

Top poster for Pop Paradijs, June 26-27-28, 1970. Kralingse Bos, Rotterdam, design by Jaap Jongert. The depiction of Adam and Eve in the Garden of Eden reflects the desire cherished by many visitors to return to some sort of primeval state.

Bottom visitors to Pop Paradijs, June 1970, Kralingse Bos, Rotterdam, photo by Herbert Behrens.

the artificiality of life in nightclubs and the flirtation with life in the gutter: 'Stay awake all night / But never see the stars / And sleep all day / On a chainlink bed of nails. Steer clear of the sun / Pancake, sandpaper skin. Takes hours of preparation / To get that wasted look.'[38] A much earlier song of similar bent is *Nightclubbing* from 1977 by Iggy Pop, a singer later drafted into the ranks of punk rock and New Wave. The last verse evokes the same kind of emptiness and futility as *Collapsing New People*: 'Nightclubbing we're nightclubbing / We're walking through town / Nightclubbing we're nightclubbing / We walk like a ghost / We learn dances brand new dances / Like the nuclear bomb'. *Nightclubbing* could also be heard accompanying Rotterdam street scenes at night in the television documentary *Stadsgezicht* (1977, see chapter 3). For the rest, there are many direct and indirect references in song lyrics to life in the street, such as strolling or loitering, as in The Stranglers' *Hanging Around* from 1976, or the individualism traditionally related to city life, as in The Sex Pistols' *No Feelings* from 1977.[39]

The dress codes of punk and New Wave were urban too, from the shoes up. Although punks wore combats boots, stiletto heels were also part of the standard outfit of female punks from early on.[40] The later New Wave look added pointed shoes to the male repertoire. These were not exactly suitable for long hikes through the country, better for short distances across asphalt. Punk and New Wave fashion otherwise takes its cue from clothing originally intended for representative occasions where conventions and appearances weigh more heavily than bodily comfort. The original context of these clothes (jackets, miniskirts, tights, ties) is thrown overboard by combining them with elements suggesting chaos, destruction and indecency such as holes, tears and safety pins. For all these modifications, this dress is still representative in its new context, be it for a different setting of city (especially at night), clubs and street. The hairstyle to go with it was the opposite of hippie hair in every respect: punk and New Wave required short hair that stood up unnaturally and was dyed in vivid colours. Make-up was just as deliberately artificial-looking.

The symbolic function of punk and New Wave

Punk and New Wave would seem to have been a vagary of fashion, judging from the above description alone, yet the stance they took against hippie culture was deep-seated; punk and New Wave stood for the rejection of what was then the established order. Music played an essential part in that stance. Hans Righart, describing the 1960s, has shown how important music can be as a generation's collective means of expression. For the young people who overthrew the existing social standards and values in the '60s, music – in their case rock'n'roll and then beat music – was a value that went far deeper than mere amusement. Music for them had a symbolic function; rock'n'roll and beat music represented a new social order.[41] Righart regards music as the principal element binding young people together in the 'revolution' of the 1960s. He writes: 'Never before had young people identified so strongly with a

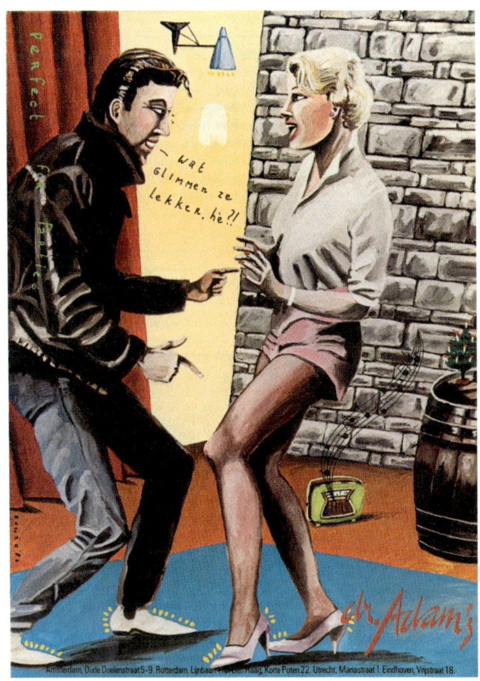

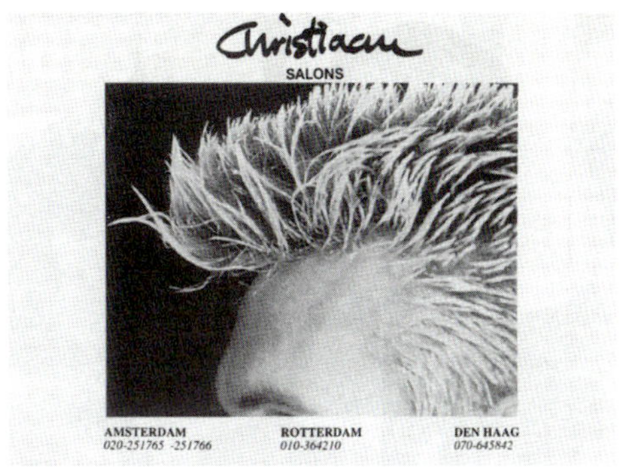

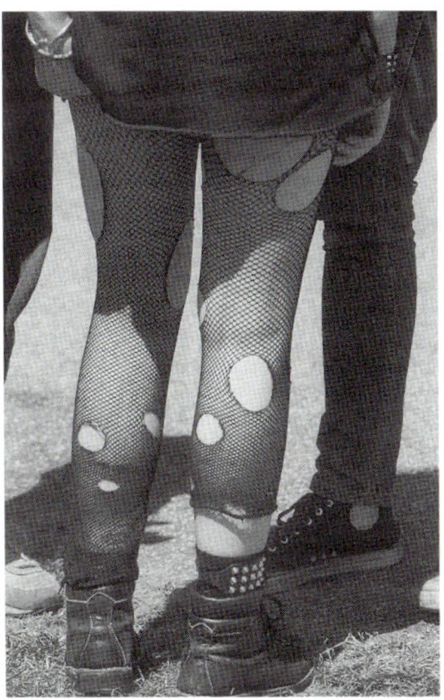

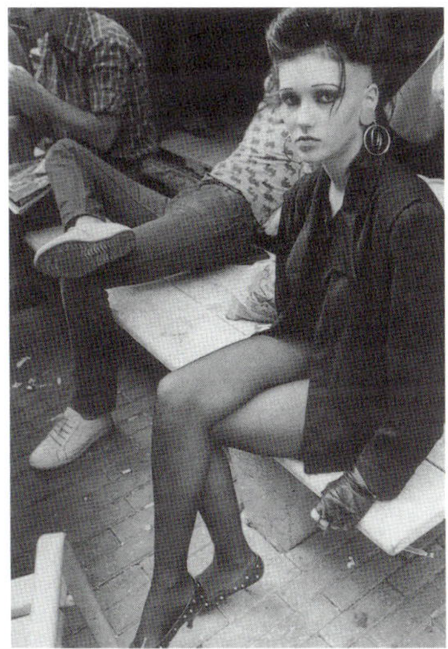

Top left ad for Dr. Adam's shoe shop, January 1983, back cover of the music magazine *Vinyl*. Stiletto heels for women and pointed shoes for men were part of New Wave dress code.

Top right ad for Christiaan the hairdresser's, October 1981, from *Vinyl*.

Bottom left legs of a female punk at Park Pop Festival, The Hague, 1980; **right** female New Waver, 1980s, photo by Ed van der Elsken. The hair standing up unnaturally, excessively heavy make-up, the jacket, miniskirt and stiletto heels are typical attributes.

music genre; never before had the symbolic function of music been so great.'[42]

Although the general opinion is that the insurgency that found expression in punk and New Wave can in no way be compared with the sea change that took place in the 1960s, I would still like to make that comparison, at all events as regards the symbolic function of the music. Punk and New Wave, in the Netherlands too, were the expression of the young generation's discontent with the ideals of the generation before theirs, those same hippies described above. A hatred of hippies was one of the few constants in punk ideology. They were the enemy and the phrase 'dirty hippies' became commonplace. Now, the literature on punk repeatedly points out that for all this self-created opposition, there are many similarities to be found between hippiedom and punk.[43] This observation is true of the early days of hippiedom, but not at all in the second half of the 1970s, when hippie culture had become institutionalized. It was these settled hippies and their now modified and politicized body of ideas that punks and their affiliates were so vehemently opposed to. It was, at root, a conflict between generations and Hans Righart in his study into the 1960s in the Netherlands shows that a clash of generations was the core of the matter at that time too; indeed, the subtitle of his book translates as 'History of a generation conflict'. But the clash around 1980 was much less severe than then and the social repercussions less far-reaching.

That the music of around 1980 had a symbolic function for youngsters militating against the prevailing social order, comes across loud and clear in the young people's programme *Neon*, broadcast by VPRO Television in 1979 and 1980. It was a collage of scraps of documentary, scraps of fiction, interviews and home videos. It was hard to discern an overarching theme besides the fact that anyone who was against the established order could be on it, from a Dutchman who had himself filmed defecating over a balcony in protest against the demolition of the block of flats where he lived, to supporters of the Baader-Meinhof Group. This exceedingly diverse material was glued together with videos of punk and New Wave concerts by Dutch as well as foreign bands. *Neon* was directed by Bob Visser, who had made the Rotterdam documentary *Stadsgezicht* with Jules Deelder two years before. Deelder also contributed to this new programme as a commentator, eliciting several crowning moments in his career as a television performer. *Neon*, then, was a Rotterdam product, made by a Rotterdam director with a Rotterdam presenter and with relatively many Rotterdam subjects and images shot in Rotterdam. This was not entirely coincidental, as punk and New Wave had a special meaning for Rotterdam and Rotterdam was an important platform for punk and New Wave.

The soundtrack of Rotterdam

Punk and New Wave's great significance for Rotterdam is all down to the harsh urban quality of the music. If in a general sense it was symbolic of an energetic, down-to-earth outlook on life, put in the Rotterdam context the music more specifically symbolized Rotterdam's rationality and dynamism. Peter Graute, owner of the legendary alternative record shop Backstreet Records launched in 1979 on Boomgaardstraat in Rotterdam, in that same year drew attention in an interview in *Hard Werken* to the instinctive affinity between punk and Rotterdam. When asked by the interviewer, Willem Kars, why the punk movement was more firmly rooted in Rotterdam than in, say, Amsterdam, Graute answered: 'Actually it caught on in Amsterdam first, but more because of the international scene there, which saw punk as a great gimmick. But it's more firmly rooted here due to the social climate: here you simply have to work hard and keep your mouth shut.'[44] Punk rock and New Wave music, as it were, formed the right soundtrack for celebrating Rotterdam as a metropolitan, raw but also dynamic environment. This is evident from the fact that all artists and cultural practitioners who worked together during the period in question on making the vision of a metropolitan Rotterdam a reality, identified with this music to an extreme degree.

The identification obtained not just for the music but also for the outfit that went with it; according to a remark made by Henk Elenga, in May 1979 it was no longer the done thing to have long hair in the *Hard Werken* scene.[45] The dress codes in general can be made out from advertisements for hairdressers and clothes shops found throughout *Hard Werken*, but also in, say, the New Wave music magazine *Vinyl*. Looking at these ads, it is striking that some leading clothes shops such as Brutus and Lady Day only had Dutch outlets in Amsterdam and Rotterdam. Rotterdam obviously counted in this context, and there was even a colloquial term (*modernico*) used locally to describe a Rotterdammer who dressed and wore his or her hair New Wave style.[46]

It was in fact mainly artists who first appreciated punk rock and New Wave in the Netherlands: 'The trendy art academy types latched onto it first, the same as with House later on. Punk in this country was not brought on by social developments; we were too well off here, certainly compared to other countries. It was more a wave of recognition shared by a bunch of people.'[47] Their identification with this music caused many artists to set up bands themselves. As the harmony was pretty basic and the vocals preferably none too melodious or in tune, it didn't matter if you lacked musical training. The ones who didn't play listened to records or attended concerts, preferably by the latest, most obscure groups. Peter Graute had a pivotal role in all this, not just through his record shop, where many people often came just to listen, but because he organized concerts. Very early on, he was bringing to Rotterdam and other towns in the Netherlands and beyond, bands who would later become world-famous on the alternative circuit. He names some of them in the interview in *Hard Werken*: The Red Crayola, Scritti Politti, Teenage Jesus and the Jerks (featuring Lydia Lunch), Adèle Bertei of the former Contortions and This Heat. He arranged gigs for them in Heavy, a café on downtown 's-Gravendijkwal. For devotees these were unforgettable occasions, not least because it all happened in such a small space.

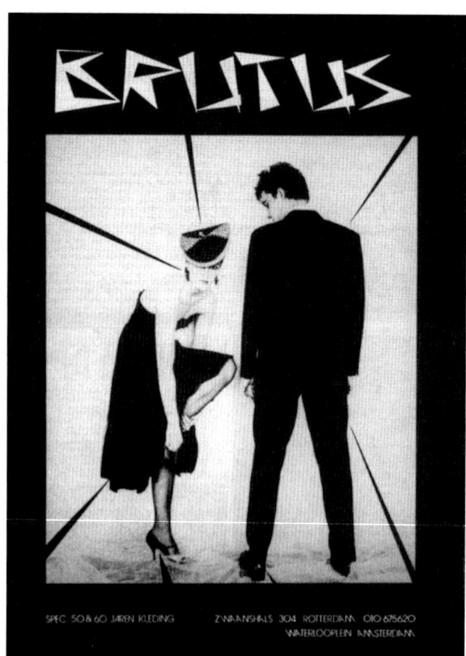

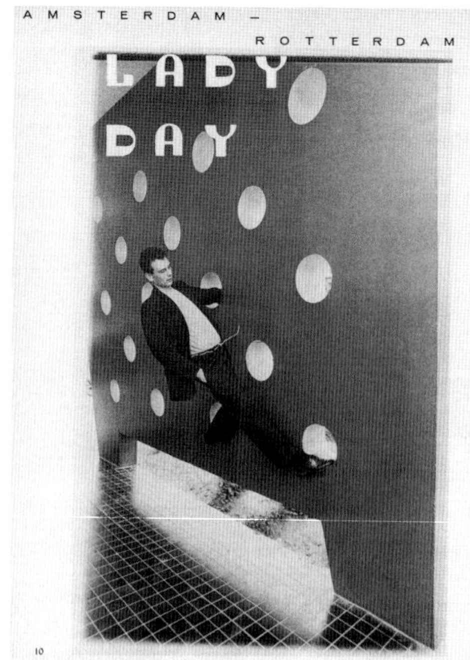

Top left advertisement for Brutus clothes shop, June 1981, back cover of the music magazine *Vinyl*. This trendsetting shop had just two outlets, in Amsterdam and Rotterdam; **right** advertisement for Lady Day clothes shop in *Hard Werken* no. 9, 1981. The ads in *Hard Werken* were designed by the editors.

Right full-page ad for Haddock Records, a Rotterdam record shop, in the national music mag *Vinyl*, no. 15, April 1982. In those years Haddock Records regularly placed large ads such as this in *Vinyl* with a regular change of photos which show Rotterdam as a dark, thrilling metropolis.

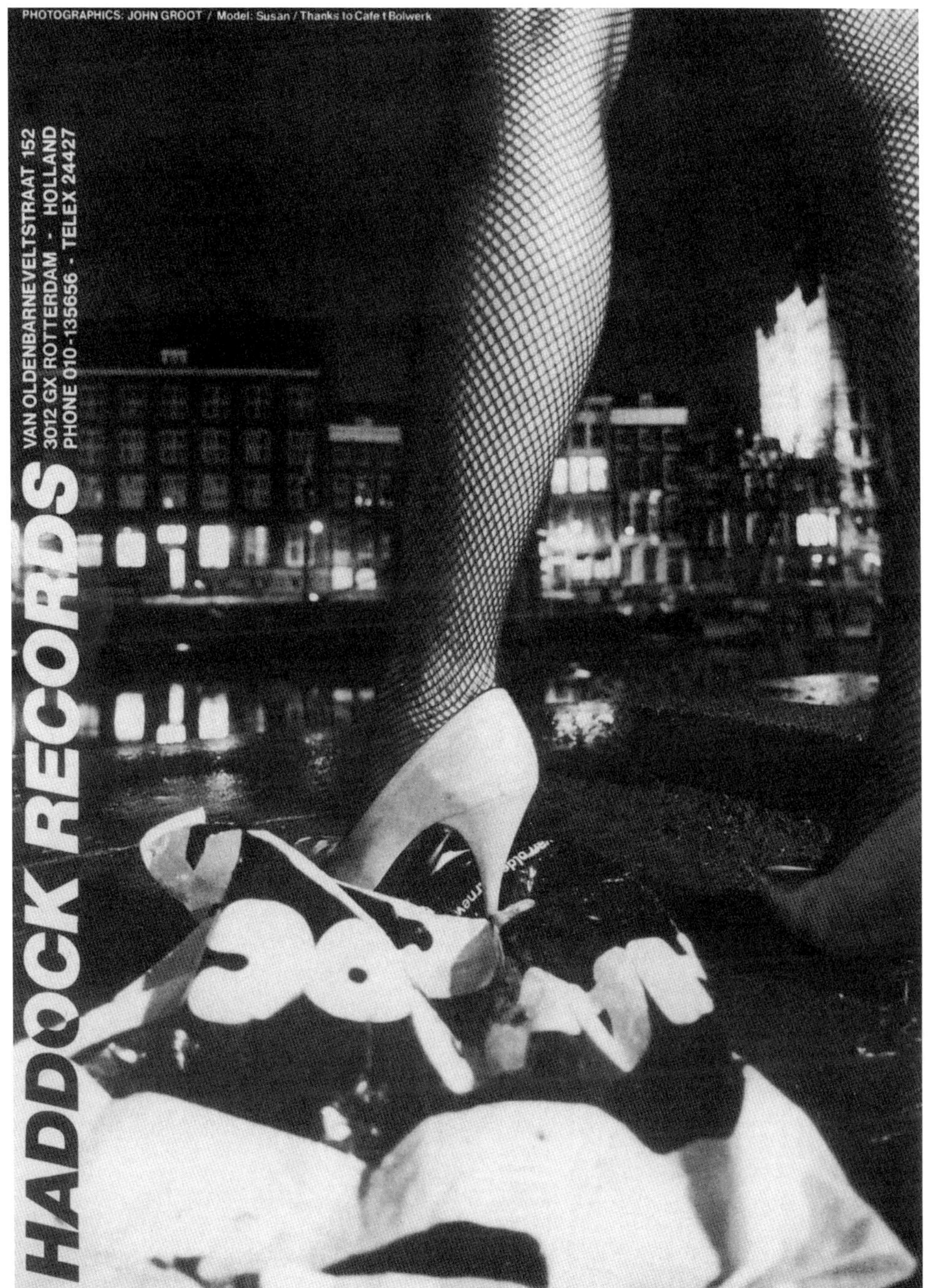

PHOTOGRAPHICS: JOHN GROOT / Model: Susan / Thanks to Cafe t Bolwerk
HADDOCK RECORDS
VAN OLDENBARNEVELTSTRAAT 152
3012 GX ROTTERDAM - HOLLAND
PHONE 010-135656 - TELEX 24427

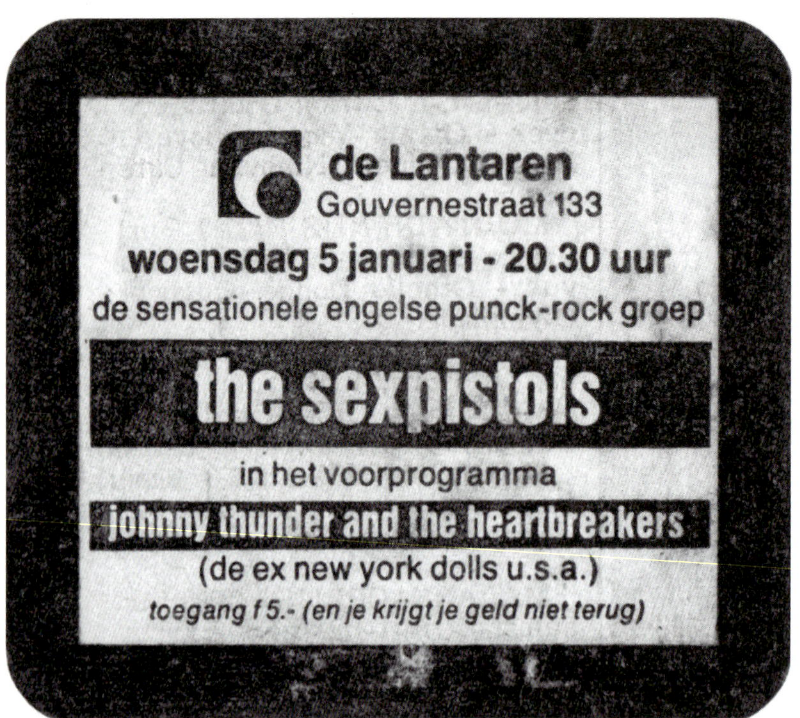

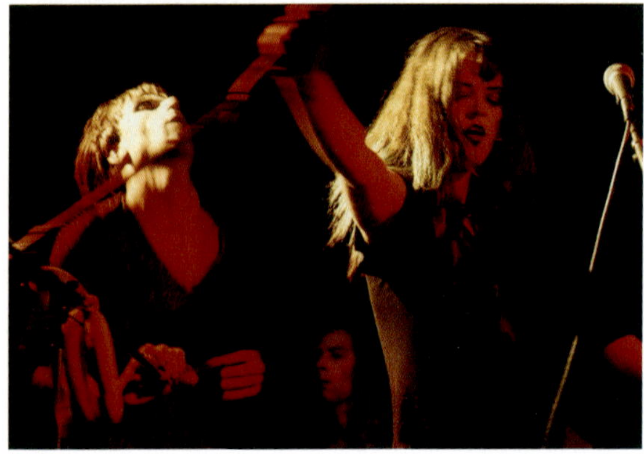

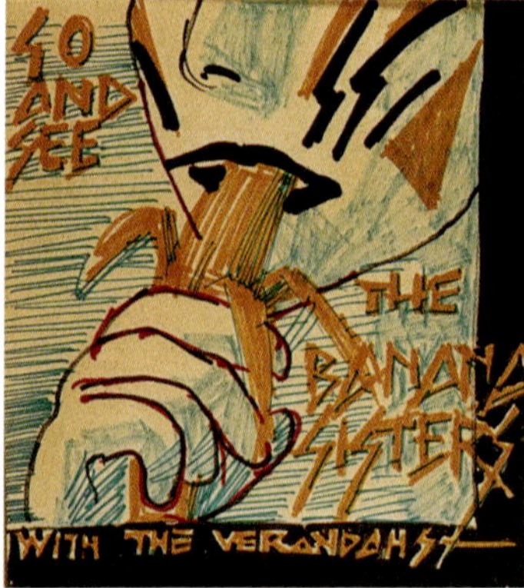

Top announcement of a performance by The Sex Pistols in Lantaren, Rotterdam, January 5, 1977.

Bottom left performance by The Banana Sisters, a punk band set up by members of Utopia; **right** sketch for a poster for The Banana Sisters, design by Chiel van der Stelt.

There were others in Rotterdam who had their ears firmly to the ground when it came to the latest developments on the alternative music front. A mood of excitement and curiosity gripped artists' circles about the many new bands sprouting up and there was always a mad scramble to be the first to mention them. For example, in 1979 the artist Henk Tas, the photographer Pieter Vandermeer and the designer Henk Elenga reported in *Hard Werken* on the music they had heard in hip New York clubs like Hurrah's, CBGB's, Max's Kansas City and the Mud Club. *Hard Werken* regularly alerted its readers to interesting new bands and even had its own record label, Hard Werken Records. The poet and writer C.B. Vaandrager, who explored the diamond-hard Rotterdam scene in both his work and his life, identified with what he calls the 'dislocating, raw city mentality of punk and New Wave', although he was slightly older than the generation foregrounded in this book. He was a good friend of the New York singer Lydia Lunch, who performed in Rotterdam on many occasions and lodged with Vaandrager and his girlfriend Marian.[48]

The young Rotterdam impresario Beerend Lenstra knew exactly which bands were promising and brought them across to the Netherlands. The in-house music programmer for the Eksit youth centre in Rotterdam from 1971 to 1974, he had gone on to organize concert tours. Looking at the names of the bands Lenstra brought to Rotterdam in the late 1970s and early '80s, he must have had an exceptional sense of quality - and exceptional contacts. The Ramones, Talking Heads, Jonathan Richman & The Modern Lovers, Joy Division, U2, Simple Minds, Depeche Mode - they could all be seen and heard on small Rotterdam stages, often shortly before they turned to playing large venues like Ahoy.[49]

Lenstra set up a Dutch tour for archetypal UK punk band The Sex Pistols on two occasions. The first time was in January 1977, the second in December of that year, when the Pistols' fame was 'on a par with that of The Beatles'.[50] The second tour was a resounding success, despite the short time left to prepare for it. The Mojo concert agency rang Lenstra asking him if could organize a string of performances by The Sex Pistols a mere two days before the tour was to open. He had no trouble booking concerts, 'there was nothing to fall back on but that didn't matter, you were sure to sell the lot in one go'.[51] So The Sex Pistols performed nine times in a row from December 5th to the 14th in small venues right across the Netherlands from Maastricht to Winschoten.[52] The rush on tickets was so overwhelming that in Lenstra's words it was 'simply a madhouse': 'At every venue there would be 3000 to 4000 people at the door and you had, like, the Eksit Club for instance, which could only hold 300. That was actually a no-go situation. And when the show was over, there was a car crushed completely flat outside the entrance, absolutely nothing left of it.'[53]

With hindsight Lenstra signals a measure of kinship between the outlook on life of punk and New Wave and the urban setting typical of Rotterdam. He searches for his words when pressed on the significance New Wave has had for Rotterdam: 'If you're talking about New Wave, particularly the more underground

bit, there was the sense of a connection with New York, both being port cities and
having an unsettling side to them. You had a whole bunch of these American clubs
where you could hear the underground aspect to New Wave and those groups, they
definitely felt more comfortable here than in Amsterdam, you could see that. (...)
James White, The Heartbreakers, The New York Dolls, a whole string of groups like
these had all kinds of connections here in town. Tuxedo Moon even made a film with
Bob Visser, a Rotterdam film-maker, and James White lived here for a while and then
you had (...) Lydia Lunch who spent a much longer time living here. But I must say
this really was the seamier side of life. I did some concerts with James White, and
that wasn't exactly a barrel of laughs!'[54] This dark and doomy side of Rotterdam
comes across well in the ads placed by Haddock, a Rotterdam record shop, in the
New Wave magazine *Vinyl*. Launched in 1981, this was a national monthly music
publication with an average run of about 10,000, and the impact of these full-page
photographs of staged situations with a Rotterdam location as backdrop should
not be underestimated.

Many of the bands who could be seen performing in the television programme *Neon* were also booked by Lenstra. The footage was in fact shot at the New
Pop festival which Lenstra organized in Rotterdam every year from 1977 to 1981, once
again with a selection of groups whose names are familiar today, such as The Cure,
The Specials and The Ramones. *Vinyl*, which only targeted the latest alternative
music, described New Pop in 1981 as 'one of the most interesting festivals in the
country for the groups they have'.[55]

In 1979 Rotterdam gained one more hot spot for the latest music, Hal 4
(hall four). Lenstra had organized the first two concerts there, by Garland Jeffreys
and Fischer Z, after which the programming was taken over by Mike Pickering, who
hailed from Manchester where he had close ties with the music scene centring on
the Factory Records label, whose most illustrious groups were Joy Division (later
New Order), A Certain Ratio, Cabaret Voltaire and Orchestral Manoeuvres In The Dark.
Promising groups from other British cities and from Germany, Belgium and America
were enticed to Rotterdam through Pickering's international network, once again
mainly bands that have since attained legendary status: The Cure (1980), The Human
League, Bauhaus, Theatre of Hate, This Heat, Palais Schaumburg, The Birthday Party
(1982), Einstürzende Neubauten, Tuxedo Moon.[56] In Hal 4 as well public interest often
exceeded the venue's capacity, which was about 800.

Taken as a whole, it would be safe to say that regular visitors to pop concerts
in Rotterdam between, say, 1977, the year of the first New Pop Festival and The Sex
Pistols' concert in Lantaren/Venster, until 1983 would have been treated visually
and orally to the absolute cream of international punk, New Wave and rock. Not just
that, but Rotterdam had several punk bands of its own, notably the internationally
known Rondos.[57] Evan van der Most, director of Hal 4 since its inception, feels, as do
Peter Graute and Beerend Lenstra, that it wasn't just the luck of the draw that this
music was received in Rotterdam so early on and with such enthusiasm: 'Yeah...

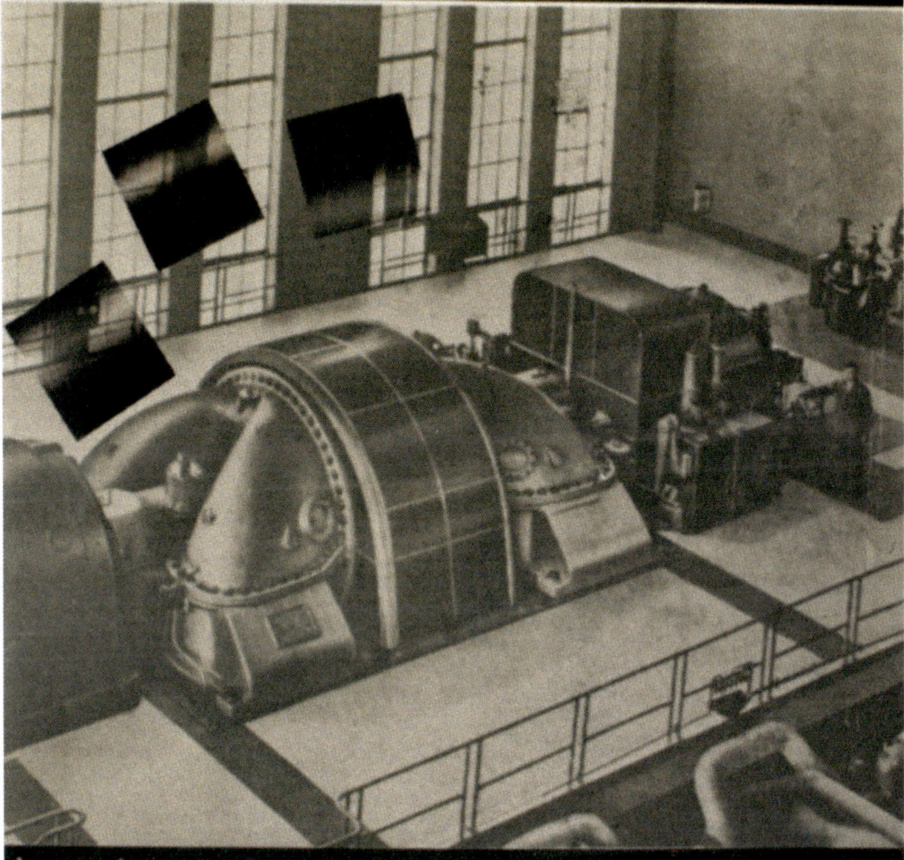

Poster announcing performances in Hal 4 by groups from Factory Records, October 30, 1980, design by Alan Turnbull. Mike Pickering, who did the programming for Hal 4, had close ties with the New Wave scene in Manchester.

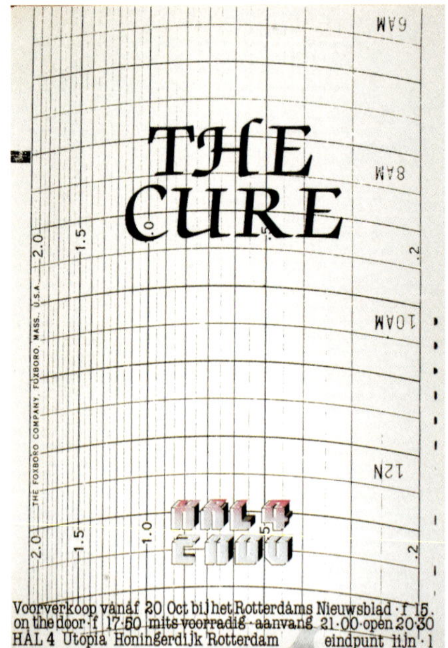

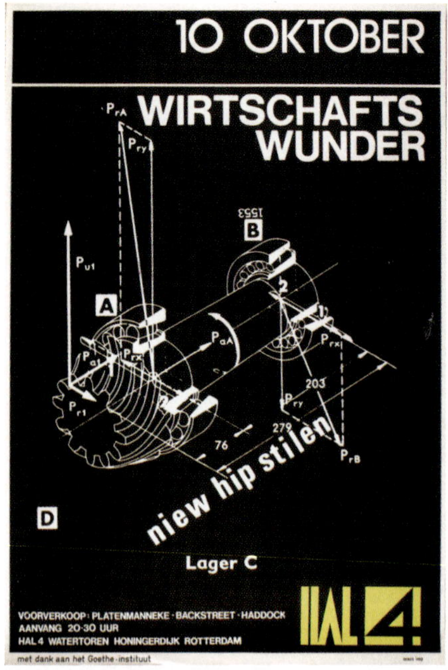

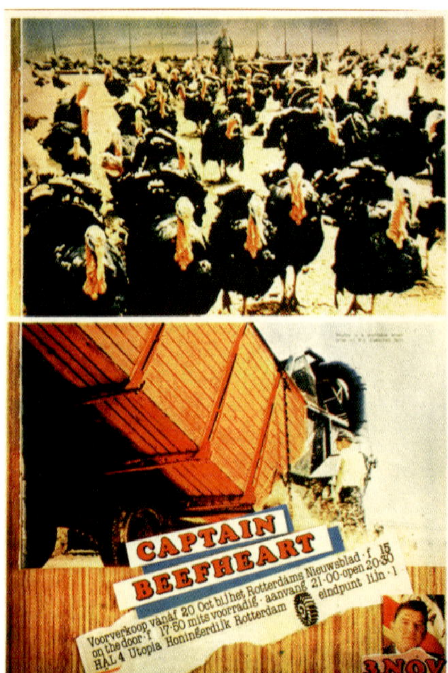

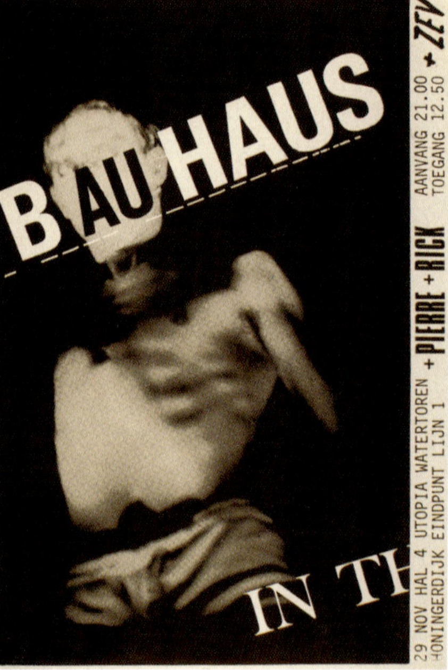

Posters for performances in Hal 4.
The Cure, November 2, 1980, design by Alan Turnbull; Wirtschaftswunder and Nieuw Hip Stilen (a New Wave band from Rotterdam), October 10, 1982, design by Hans van den Tol and Hans Werlemann; Captain Beefheart, November 3, 1980, design by Alan Turnbull and Hans Werlemann; Bauhaus, November 29, 1980, design by Hans van den Tol and Hans Werlemann.

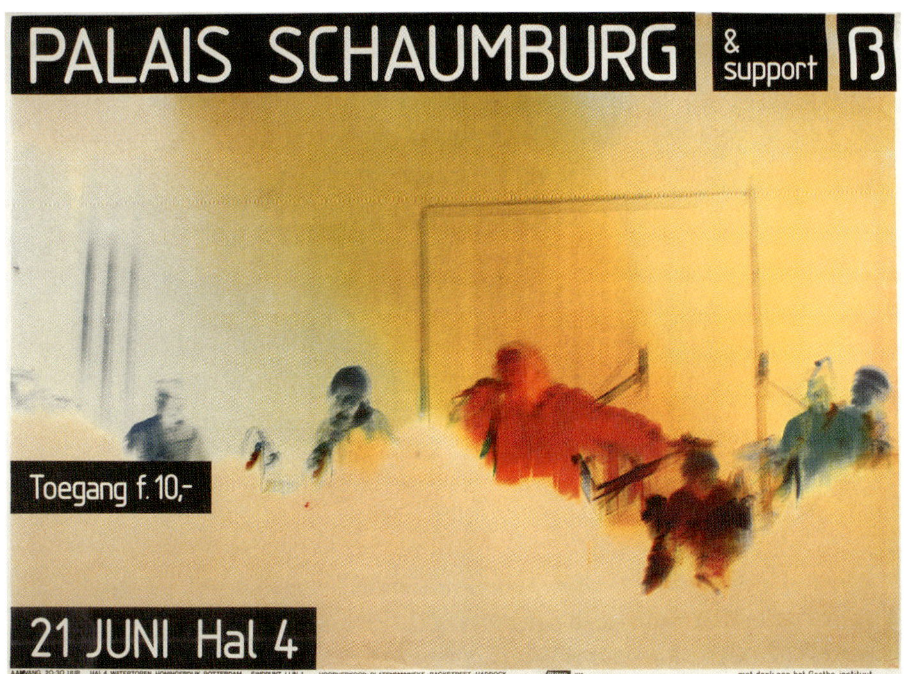

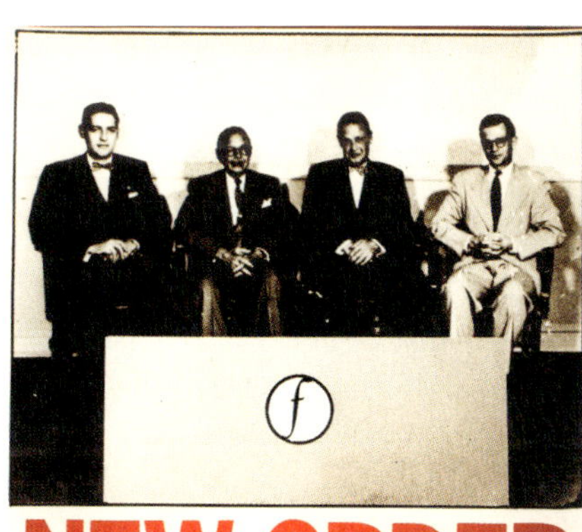

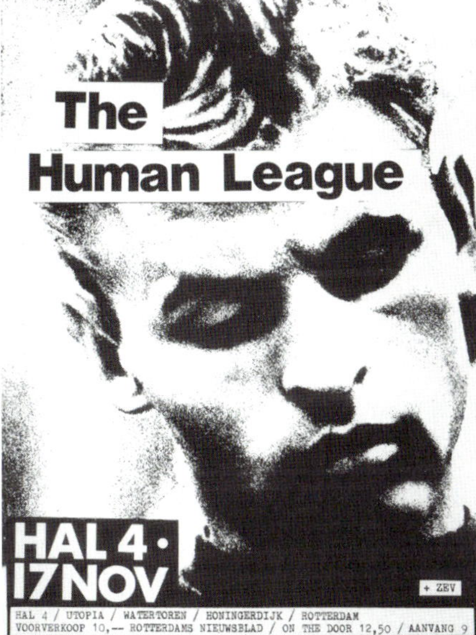

Palais Schaumburg, June 21, 1982, design by Hans van den Tol; New Order, December 13, 1980, design by Alan Turnbull; The Human League, November 17, 1980, design by Alan Turnbull and Hans Werlemann.

right… I don't know why exactly… what I mean to say… thing is, we thought of Amsterdam as… well they were all nice and snug there and we associated that with hippies and warmth and homeyness and being snug together and, well, Rotterdam wasn't warm and homey and snug, there was a different atmosphere.'[58] According to Van der Most, the Amsterdam venues for new music, amongst them the internationally renowned Paradiso, began lagging behind their Rotterdam counterparts from 1980 on. In Amsterdam they were still fully focused on punk rock at a time when this was considered old hat in Rotterdam. In Rotterdam by contrast the latest practitioners of New Wave and No Wave (a short-lived New York variation) could be seen sometimes even earlier than in their own country. Thus, for example, the English group New Order, formed from the ashes of the legendary Joy Division, played their very first concert in Rotterdam's Hal 4. According to Van der Most the years 1980-1983 marked the heyday of New Wave in Rotterdam: 'It didn't last that long, but between say 1980 and 1983 Rotterdam was the place where it all happened.'[59]

Subculture

This identification with punk and New Wave in the late 1970s, early '80s by Rotterdam's creative class had all the resonance of a subculture. It was only insiders who had access to information about the latest music and the lifestyle that came with it. You won't find anything in the music mags about the concerts in, say, Heavy. And many ads left out all the particulars, giving just a name and projecting a mood. Knowing the name of the latest upcoming group, where they could be seen playing, which record shops had their single, where to be seen oneself and what clothes to wear were all a question of knowing the right people. Almost all information was by word of mouth. Sarah Thornton describes having such inside information at one's disposal as 'subcultural capital', a variation on Pierre Bourdieu's cultural capital.[60]

This Rotterdam subculture, then, took an interest in the production, distribution and consumption of the new music. Of these three activities the first, production, was not uppermost in Rotterdam. There are no Rotterdam bands from this period with a long-term international reputation, although the Rondos are legendary in some circles. What counted in Rotterdam was distribution – selling records and organizing performances – and consumption – buying records and attending performances. This might seem a sign of weakness, the word 'consumption' having a particularly passive ring. But it should be looked at another way. In those years and given this underground music, the consumer had an important and extremely active role to fulfil. Fact is, almost all this music was brought out by small production companies, small independent record labels or even by the groups themselves. This was one of the achievements of punk rock and later New Wave; it broke the hegemony of the major companies. With technology much more generally available, in principle anyone could bring out a record. There was a thriving trade in cassette

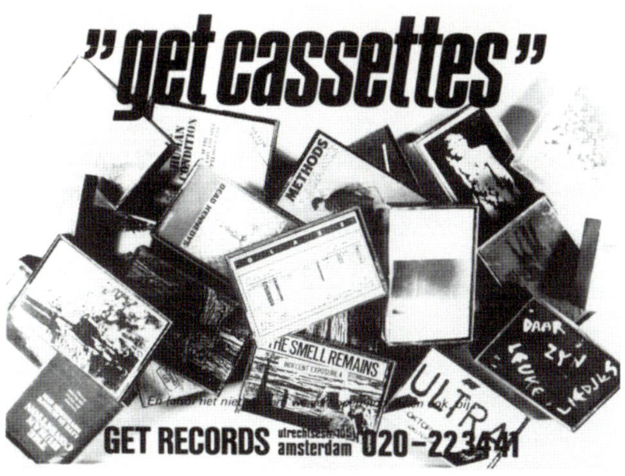

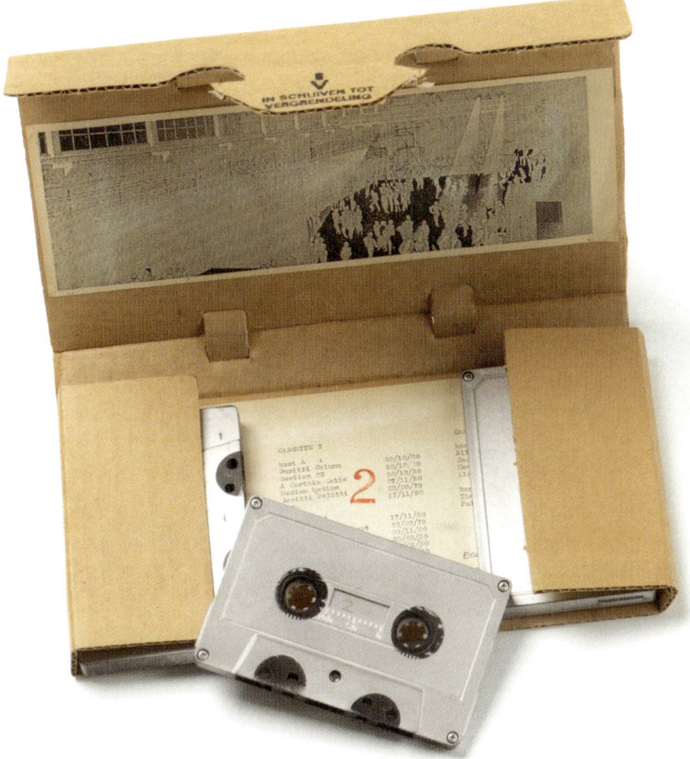

Top advertisement for cassette tapes from the music magazine *Vinyl*, no. 9, December 1981. The thriving trade in cassette tapes made it easy to produce music independently.

Bottom special issue (including audio cassettes) of *Revista*, Utopia's own magazine, compiled by Hans Mesman, with recordings of concerts in Hal 4, 1980-1982.

tapes, the generally available medium par excellence. This did mean, however, that
the groups had no promotion department dealing with advertising and radio spots.
So it was all done by word of mouth, with the record-buying public in a starring
role. Rotterdam was an important place for many bands, not least because it had a
smattering of specialized records shops such as the aforementioned Backstreet
Records run by Peter Graute as well as Haddock, Platenmanneke and Pathefoon.
Backstreet Records was much more than a record shop, it was an information centre.
What Rotterdam meant at that time for new music is in some measure comparable
with what Hamburg meant in the early 1960s. Hamburg was then legendary as a
centre of pop music, not for the home-grown music but because of the groups you
could hear there, The Beatles being the obvious example.[61]

The reappraisal of Rotterdam as a metropolitan city as expressed in the two official
reports of 1987, was prepared by Rotterdam's creative class. The Architecture section
of the Rotterdam Arts Council had drawn attention theoretically to the city's overall image, while punk and New Wave expressed the metropolitan feeling intuitively.
Just as Futurism had provided the parameters in which the metropolitan aspects of
Rotterdam could be assessed in a positive light in the inter-war years, so the music
and attitude of punk and New Wave performed a similar duty in the late '70s and
early '80s.

There is another aspect of punk that may explain why this music in particular and the lifestyle attendant on it made such an impact on Rotterdam artists and
other members of the creative class. Punk happened to arise out of a do-it-yourself
mentality, out of a conviction that everyone who wanted to could start up and
manage an enterprise even if they had had no prior training. One such enterprise
was to start a punk or New Wave group – a swipe at the progressive and symphonic
rock groups who had become so dependent on sound engineers – but the DIY attitude
extended to many more activities.[62] Although the golden age of punk was well past
by the early '80s and had ceded musically to New Wave (the term 'art rock'[63] has
also been bandied about here as elsewhere), this DIY ideology lived on. The Rotterdam
magic of the late 1970s and early 1980s can largely be attributed to such DIY initiatives. In the next chapter I shall describe with the aid of examples how individuals
fuelled by the DIY mentality engaged in joint ventures of varying combinations and
established a creative network in Rotterdam in the process.

1 Meyer, H. (1999), *City and Port: Urban Planning as a Cultural Venture in London, Barcelona, New York, and Rotterdam: Changing relations between public urban space and large-scale infrastructure*, Utrecht: International Books, p. 352.

2 Aalst, I. van (1997), *Cultuur in de stad: Over de rol van culturele voorzieningen in de ontwikkeling van stadscentra*, Utrecht: Jan van Arkel, p. 143. There are other authors who consider the year 1987 as a watershed, including: Neill, W.J.V., D.S. Fitzsimons et al. (eds) (1995), *Reimaging the Pariah City: Urban development in Belfast & Detroit*, Aldershot/Brookfield (USA)/Hongkong/Singapore/Sydney: Avebury, p. 20 and Hitters, E. (1996), *Patronen van patronage: Mecenaat, protectoraat en markt in de kunstwereld*, Utrecht: Jan van Arkel, pp. 154-155.

3 Author's interview with Joop Linthorst, January 12, 2004.

4 Albeda, W., W.S.P. Fortuyn et al. (1987), *Nieuw Rotterdam: een opdracht voor alle Rotterdammers*, Rotterdam: Adviescommissie Sociaal-Economische Vernieuwing Rotterdam, pp. VI and 69; Wiardi Beckman Stichting (1988), *De grote steden, hun stadsgewesten en het compacte-stadbeleid*, Amsterdam: Wiardi Beckman Stichting, p. 43.

5 Albeda, W., W.S.P. Fortuyn et al. (1987), op. cit. (note 4), p. 29.

6 Florida, R. (2002), *The Rise of the Creative Class: And How It's Transforming Work, Leisure, Community and Everyday Life*, New York: Basic Books.

7 Straasheijm, W. & S. Buijs (1987), *Vernieuwing van Rotterdam*, Rotterdam: Gemeente Rotterdam, college van burgemeester en wethouders, p. 24.

8 Straasheijm, W. & S. Buijs (1987), op. cit. (note 7), p. 99.

9 Straasheijm, W. & S. Buijs (1987), op. cit. (note 7), pp. 74, 76.

10 Straasheijm, W. & S. Buijs (1987), op. cit. (note 7), p. 23.

11 Straasheijm, W. & S. Buijs (1987), op. cit. (note 7), p. 4.

12 Straasheijm, W. & S. Buijs (1987), op. cit. (note 7), p. 23.

13 ibid.

14 Author's interview with Joop Linthorst, January 12, 2004.

15 Straasheijm, W. & S. Buijs (1987), op. cit. (note 7), p. 23.

16 Author's interview with Hans Oldewarris, March 31, 2003.

17 idem.

18 Text on the printed invitation to the exhibition 'Rotterdamse havenarchitectuur', Hans Oldewarris archive.

19 Winter, P. de, J. de Jong et al. (eds) (1982), *Havenarchitectuur: Een inventarisatie van industriële gebouwen in het Rotterdamse havengebied*, Rotterdam: Rotterdamse Kunststichting Uitgeverij.

20 This view of the area would persist until well into 1985, see DROS GB GW (1985), *Struktuurschets Kop van Zuid*, Rotterdam, DROS GB GW.

21 Barbieri, U. et al. (1982), *De Kop van Zuid: Ontwerp en Onderzoek*, Rotterdam.

22 Taverne, E. & C. Wagenaar (2003). 'Tussen elite en massa: 010 en de opkomst van de architectuurindustrie in Nederland / Between elite and mass: 010 and the rise of the architecture industry in the Netherlands', in: H. Oldewarris & P. de Winter (eds), *20 jaar/years 010 1983–2003*, Rotterdam: 010 Publishers, pp. 29-68: p. 54.

23 Straasheijm, W. & S. Buijs (1987), op. cit. (note 7), p. 23.

24 Jobse, R.B., H.M. Kruythoff et al. (1990), *Stadsgewesten in beweging: Migratie naar en uit de vier grote steden*, Utrecht: Rijksuniversiteit Utrecht/Delft: Technische Universiteit Delft/Amsterdam: Universiteit van Amsterdam; Mik, G. (ed.) (1989), *Herstructurering in Rotterdam: Modernisering en internationalisering en de Kop van Zuid*, Amsterdam: Koninklijk Nederlands Aardrijkskundig Genootschap/Rotterdam: Economisch-Geografisch Instituut Erasmus Universiteit Rotterdam; Knaap, G.A. van der & W.F. Sleegers (1990), 'Stedelijke vernieuwing en structuurverandering van de bevolking in Rotterdam', *Geografisch Tijdschrift*, XXIV (3), pp. 212-223; Ostendorf, W., J. Buursink et al. (1988), *Atlas van Nederland: Deel 3: Steden*, 's-Gravenhage, Staatsuitgeverij.

25 Mik, G. (ed.) (1989), op. cit. (note 24), pp. 45, 56, 136.

26 Mik describes a heavy overrepresentation of 15- to 29-year-olds among the newcomers (60% in 1987) and a light overrepresentation of 20- to 30-year-olds in the number of residents. Mik, G. (ed.) (1989), op. cit. (note 24), pp. 56, 61.

27 Straasheijm, W. & S. Buijs (1987), op. cit. (note 7), p. 23.

28 Zukin, S. (1982), *Loft Living: Culture and Capital in Urban Change*, Baltimore/London, The Johns Hopkins University Press, p. 15.

29 Burgers, J. (2002), *De gefragmenteerde stad*, Amsterdam: Boom, p. 9.

30 Kloos, M. (ed.) (1988), *Amsterdam: An Architectural Lesson*, Amsterdam: THOTH, p. 11.

31 On punk in the Netherlands see: Goossens, J. & J. Vedder (1996), *Het gejuich was massaal: Punk in*

Nederland 1976–1982, Amsterdam: Jan Mets.

32 Palmer, M. (1981), *New Wave Explosion: How Punk Became New Wave Became the 80s*, London/New York: Proteus Books, p. 51.

33 The film is from 1970, directed by Michael Wadleigh.

34 Green, N. (2005), 'Songs from the Wood and Sounds of the Suburbs: A Folk, Rock and Punk Portrait of England, 1965–1977', *Built Environment*, 31 (3), pp. 255-270. Examples he gives include the album *Songs from the Wood* from 1977 by Jethro Tull and the song 'Goodbye Yellow Brick Road' from 1973 by Elton John.

35 For example Pink Floyd, 'A Pillow Of Winds', from the album *Meddle*, 1971; Led Zeppelin, 'Going to California', from the album *Led Zeppelin IV*, 1971.

36 Keunen, B. (2001), 'Artistic subcultures in the metropolis and the chaotic city experience: The case of the New York music scene of the 1980s', in: H. Krabbendam, M. Roholl & T. de Vries (eds), *The American Metropolis: Image and Inspiration*, Amsterdam: VU University Press, pp. 225-235 (p. 225).

37 Einstürzende Neubauten, *Stahlversion*, 12" single, June 1980: 'Releases on first single recorded in a hollow overpass using the sound of the bridge itself and drumming on its steel sides'. Later included on the LP *Strategien gegen Architekturen/Strategies against Architecture*, 1980–1983 (Mute Records); information from the private collection of Louis Verschoor.

38 With thanks to Louis Verschoor.

39 For an interesting overview of early examples of metropolitan themes such as individualism, isolation and alienation see Williams, R. (1985), 'The metropolis and the emergence of Modernism', in: E. Timms & D. Kelley (eds), *Unreal City: Urban experience in modern European literature and art*, Manchester: Manchester University Press, pp. 13-24.

40 For a good picture of the early fashion see Anscombe, I. (1978), *Not another PUNK! book*, London: Aurum Press Ltd.

41 Rock'n'roll was city music too: 'Rock and roll was perhaps the first form of popular culture to celebrate without reservation characteristics of city life that had been amongst the most criticized. In rock and roll, the strident, repetitive sounds of city life were, in effect, reproduced as melody and rhythm.' Gillett, C. (1983 (first edition 1970)), *The Sound of the City: The Rise of Rock and Roll*, London: Souvenir Press, p. viii.

42 Righart, H. (1995), *De eindeloze jaren zestig: Geschiedenis van een generatieconflict*, Amsterdam [etc.]: Arbeiderspers, p. 28.

43 See for example Coon, C. (1977), *1988: The New Wave Punk Rock Explosion*, London: Orbach and Chambers Limited/New York: Hawthorn Books, Inc., p. 4.

44 Kars, W., 'Correcties voor New York', *Hard Werken*, 4, October 1979, pp. 26-27 (p. 27). That punk was treated as a gimmick is clearly legible in the 1977 issues of the fortnightly Amsterdam pop magazine *Muziekkrant Oor*, whose front page was invariably emblazoned with sensation-seeking reports about punk bands though with little or nothing serious to say about the music and the ideas that shaped it.

45 *Hard Werken*, 2, May 1979, Rotterdam: Stichting Hard Werken, p. 26.

46 There is no recorded mention of this term other than by word of mouth.

47 Fer Abrahams, quoted in: Goossens, J. & J. Vedder (1996), op. cit. (note 31), pp. 10-12.

48 Schenke, M. (2005), *Vaan. Het bewogen bestaan van C.B. Vaandrager*, Amsterdam: De Bezige Bij, p. 392.

49 Talking Heads and The Ramones, May 10, 1977 in Lantaren/Venster, source *Muziekkrant Oor*; Jonathan Richman and The Modern Lovers, September 26, 1977 in Lantaren/Venster, source *Muziekkrant Oor*; Joy Division, January 16, 1980 in Lantaren/Venster, source http://www.waterrat.com/jd_gig.htm, site visited August 22, 2005; U2, February 13, 1981 in Eksit, source http://www.ecst.csuchico.edu/~edge/u2/speechs/concerts.html, site visited October 7, 2002; The Simple Minds, February 28, 1982 in Lantaren/Venster, source programme paper Lantaren/Venster, GAR; Depeche Mode, March 28, 1982 in Lantaren/Venster, source programme paper Lantaren/Venster, GAR.

50 http://www.geocities.com/SunsetStrip/Palms/3829/engtour.html site visited August 22, 2005; http://www.portaldorock.com.br/especialsexpistols3.htm site visited August 22, 2005; author's interview with Beerend Lenstra, May 19, 2003.

51 Author's interview with Beerend Lenstra, May 19, 2003.

52 To be more precise: December 5, Eksit Club, Rotterdam; December 6, Maastricht; December 7, Pozjet Club, Tilburg; December 8, Stokvishal, Arnhem; December 9, De Effenaar, Eindhoven; December 10, Huize Maas, Groningen; December 11, Maf Centrum, Maasbree/Venlo; December 13, De Klinker, Winschoten; December 14, Eksit Club, Rotterdam. Sources: http://www.geocities.com/SunsetStrip/Palms/3829/engtour.html site visited August 22, 2005;

http://www.portaldorock.com.br/especialsexpistols3.
htm site visited August 22, 2005.
53 Author's interview with Beerend Lenstra, May 19, 2003.
54 idem.
55 *Vinyl*, August [1981], Amsterdam: Stichting Vinyl, p. 44.
56 Author's interview with Evan van der Most,
January 5, 2004; overview of Hal 4 activities in Hans
Oldewarris archive.
57 See Ritsema, M. (2000), 'Muziek', in: P. van Ulzen
(ed.) (2000), *90 over 80: Tien jaar beeldende kunst in
Rotterdam: De dingen, de mensen, de plekken*,
Rotterdam: NAi Uitgevers/Stichting Kunstpublicaties
Rotterdam.
58 Author's interview with Evan van der Most, January 5,
2004.

59 Email from Evan van der Most, July 4, 2006.
60 Thornton, S. (1995), *Club Cultures: Music, Media and
Subcultural Capital*, Cambridge: Polity Press.
61 See Krüger, U. & O. Pelc (eds) (2006), exh. cat. *The
Hamburg Sound: Beatles, Beat und Große Freiheit*,
Hamburg: Hamburgmuseum/Ellert & Richter Verlag.
62 '(...) the pre-eminent punk ideal [was] doing it
yourself. This DIY attitude entails subordinating tech-
nical skills to the immediacy and spontaneity of the
moment: you don't need suitable training to make
music, create art, bring out a film or a magazine – just
do it.' Goossens, J. & J. Vedder (1996), op. cit. (note 31),
pp. 32-33.
63 See the programme papers of Lantaren/Venster, GAR.

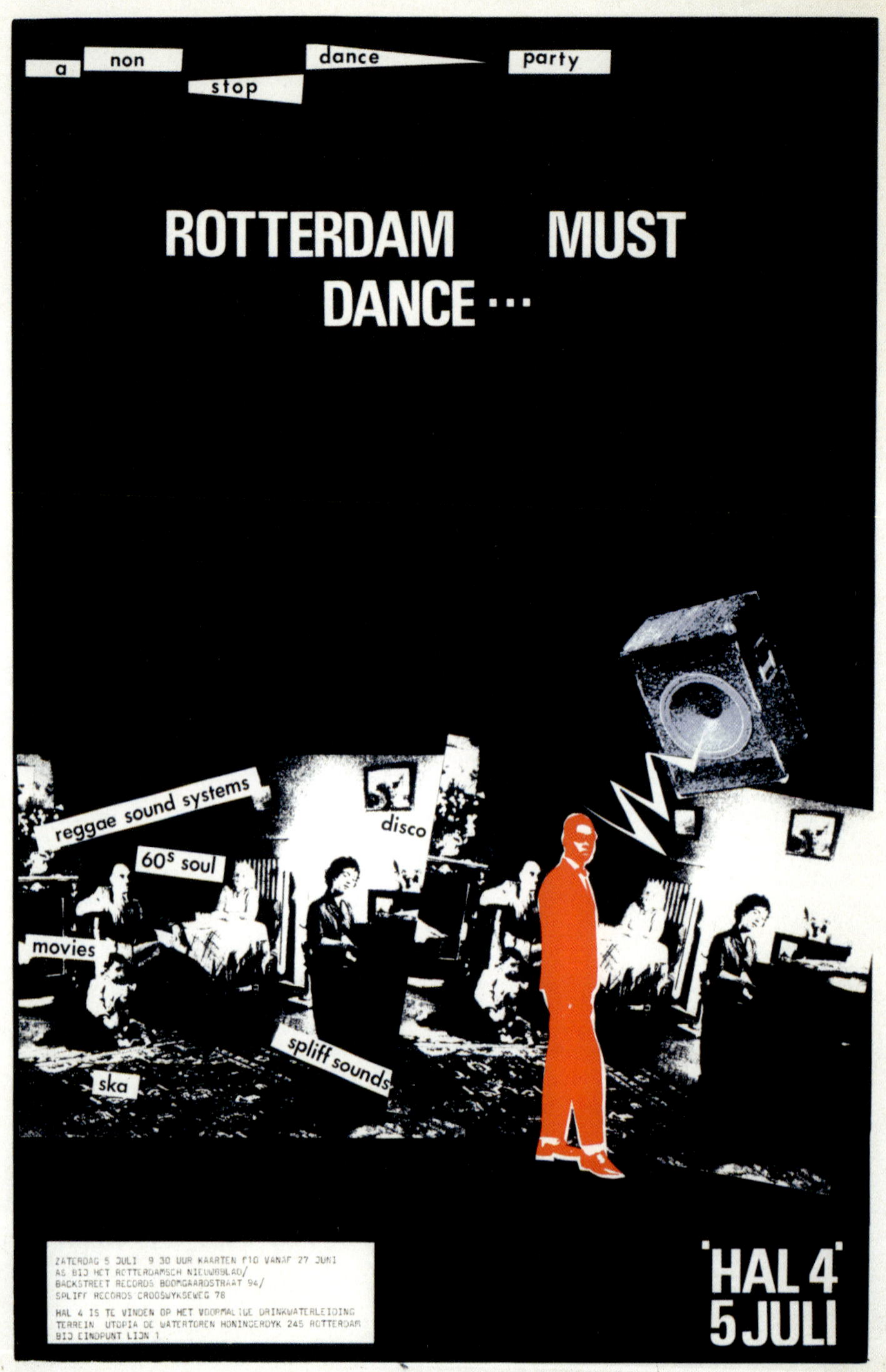

Poster announcing a party in Hal 4, July 5, 1980, design by Alan Turnbull.

CHAPTER 5

Do it yourself. The emergence of Rotterdam's creative network

Until well into the 1980s, for the members of the creative class highlighted in this book Rotterdam must have been something of a playground where the new challenges could be picked out at will. This saw them entering into an ever-changing array of working relationships. Out of these coalitions grew a complex, far-flung network of artists and cultural entrepreneurs. In part these were people already living in Rotterdam, in part newcomers to the city. They shared an almost impetuous desire for enterprise as well as a view of Rotterdam as a large, tough, modern, down-to-earth and exhilarating city.

In this chapter I shall unpack three examples of such impetuous ventures. The first is the founding of the live-work community Utopia at the site of the former Rotterdam waterworks in Rotterdam's Kralingen district. The second is Ponton 010, an initiative of Utopia in association with artists and entrepreneurs active in Rotterdam for a longer time. The third is the several cafés Daan van der Have founded at places throughout the city, setting the trend for a new type of Rotterdam café.

New blood: Utopia

In 1988 a research report was published entitled *Wie verhuist er naar Rotterdam?* (Who moves house to Rotterdam?) It was the outcome of a survey held among the 16,987 people who in 1986 had moved to Rotterdam from elsewhere in the Netherlands. One of its questions concerned the reason for moving to Rotterdam, the respondents choosing their answer from a set list. One of the answers to this multiple-choice question, along with the obvious practical reasons for moving, was the desire to live the metropolitan life in 'the big city of Rotterdam', as the survey described it. Remarkably, as many as 29.9 per cent of the interviewees chose this answer.[1] Two other striking facts emerged from the survey besides this trend towards big city living: among those who moved to Rotterdam from elsewhere in the Netherlands in 1986 was a comparatively large group with an advanced education (higher vocational or university), 25 per cent of all males and 17 per cent of females. These percentages were much smaller among the existing Rotterdam population, 11.2 and 11 per cent respectively. In line with this, the percentage of high-income groups among the domestic newcomers was also higher than that among the longer-term Rotterdammers.[2] Furthermore, a striking number of those who had just moved in were young people; no less than 68 per cent was under 30, and this excluded children still living at home.[3] When the city council noted in 1987 that new groups of residents were discovering Rotterdam, they probably had this swelling group of young, well-educated people in mind.[4] Of course, these are welcomed by every municipality because of the favourable effect they can have both economically and culturally on the urban climate.

The founders of Utopia also satisfied the above criteria, even though they had moved to Rotterdam much earlier, in 1978. They too were young and well-educated and were attracted to big city life. Indeed, they could be regarded as the heralds of a broad trend that would only make itself known much later. Artists and other cultural practitioners are often in the front line of such developments, as pointed out in chapter 1.

Most members of Utopia were still studying at the Architecture faculty at Delft University of Technology, or had just graduated from it. Many of their former fellow students had gone to work for Rotterdam city council at the Town Development department, but pen-pushing for officialdom held no interest for the future Utopians. During their time at Delft they had actively made space for the creative and theoretical sides of the architectural profession, amongst other things by publishing the periodical *Utopia*, and on graduating wanted nothing other than to continue reflecting on architectural and urban design. And for this, Rotterdam literally had all the space they needed.[5]

The seventh issue of *Utopia* was devoted to water towers and solar energy. It was through this that Hans Oldewarris, architecture student and editor of the periodical, came to learn of an attractive plot of vacant urban land, the former premises of the Rotterdam waterworks (the so-called DWL site) in the Kralingen district. 'Someone told me there was an amazing water tower standing empty along the Maas in Rotterdam.' He decided to take a look, this was autumn 1976: 'I went there by bike. It was marvellous weather. That water tower was out of this world. Sixteen hectares of grounds and a porter's lodge, all nicely fenced in. Could I have a look, I asked. It was completely empty. All those magnificent buildings, just standing empty like that. What were they going to do with it? "Well sir, nothing actually."

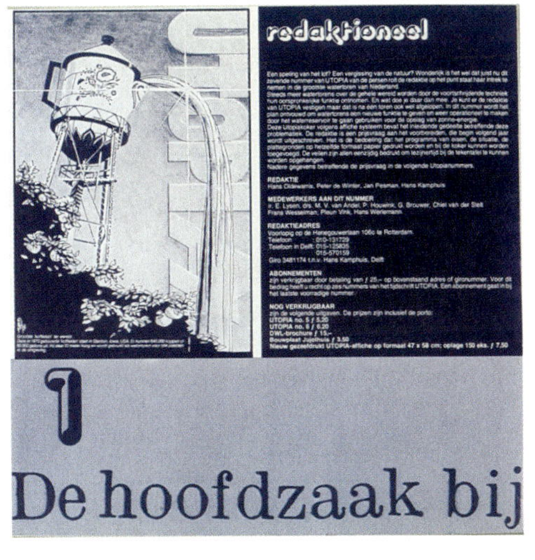

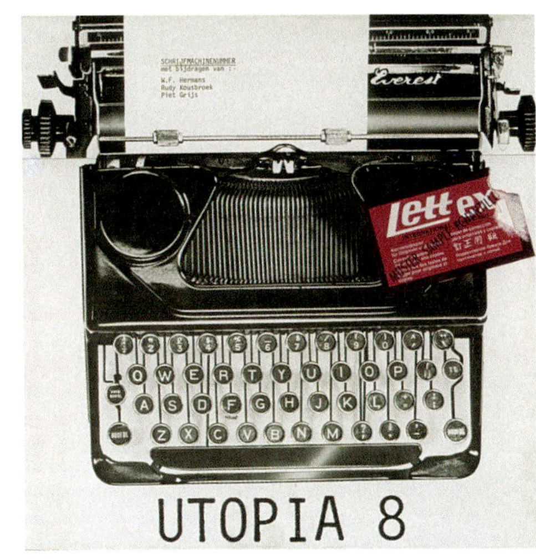

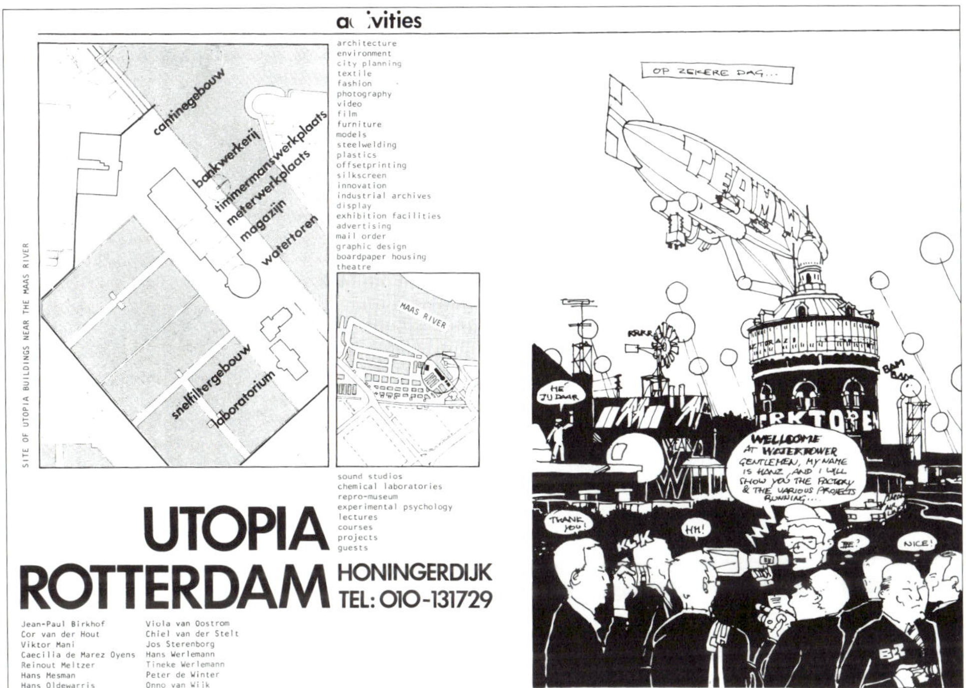

Top covers of the magazine *Utopia*; **left** no. 7 on water towers and solar energy, August 1977; **right** no. 8 on typewriters, December 1977.

Bottom pages from the *DWL-brochure* with the proposal to set up a work community in the water tower complex on the site of the former Rotterdam waterworks, February 1977.

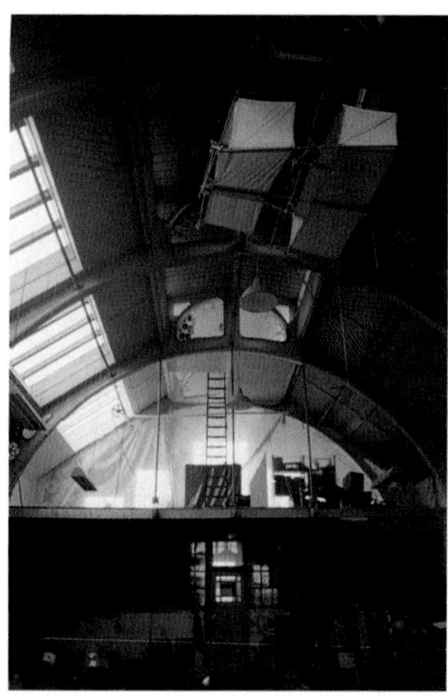

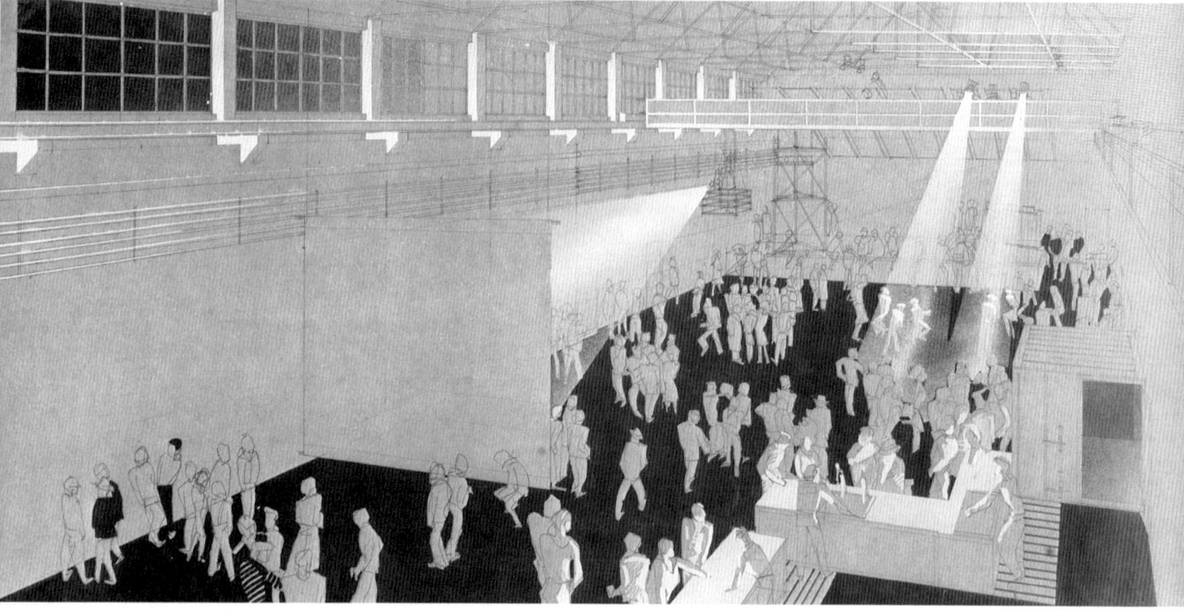

Top Living quarters in Hal 3 of Utopia, 1978.

Bottom Drawing of Utopia's Hal 4 as a black box for concerts, performances, events, congresses etc, c. 1980.

PP. 138-139 group photo of the members of Utopia with partners and family in Hal 4, 1983, photo by Hans Werlemann. From left, on the overhead crane: Peter de Winter, Offa de Winter, Haiko Dragstra; standing on the stage: Henk Jan Kamerbeek, Trubus Sanwirtjatmo, Claudi Cornaz, Walter Vincent, Hans Oldewarris, Joke van der Spek, Cor van der Hout, Albert van Tour, Betty van den Boogert; sitting on the stage: Hans van den Tol, Anna Furtak, James Rubery, Hans Mesman, Karin de Bock, Frans Werlemann (suspended in mid-air), Reinout Meltzer; standing and sitting in the front row: Herman Helle, Judith Bovenberg, Herma van der Knaap (with Dieter de Winter), Hans Werlemann, Agnes Roozenburg (with Tim van der Hout), Tineke Werlemann, Marja Minderman, Viola van Oostrom, José Loos, Viktor Mani, Caroline Meltzer, Chiel van der Stelt.

They were obviously not going to tear down something as fine as this. But the council had no idea what they should do with it. It was a complete impasse.' Impasse or not, these buildings were on the point of being demolished when at the beginning of 1977 the College of Mayor and Aldermen gave its wholehearted support to a plan to build an amusement park there, glorifying in the name Lagorama.[6] The city council gave this the thumbs-down, however, and the DWL site reverted to the limbo-like state it had been in since the mid 1960s when it had become clear that there had to be a new waterworks at another location.

By now the group associated with the magazine *Utopia* knew very well what they wanted with that plot of land. Oldewarris had reported on his visit to Rotterdam and everyone was 'over the moon about the location'. It was decided to set up a work community. This would be the basis for all kinds of small business ventures operating at the interface between art and technology, such as architecture, urban design, scale-model building, woodwork, photography, film, video, graphic design, screen printing, industrial design, textile design and computer technology. Their inspiration was the Bauhaus school of before the war. With this rudimentary plan in the back of their minds the Utopians asked to discuss the matter with the alderman responsible for the DWL site, W.J. van der Have of Economic Affairs. He rejected their proposal but because the group was clearly not intending to take no for an answer, he turned the matter over to his fellow alderman Jan Riezenkamp, who was responsible for Culture. The subsequent discussion with Riezenkamp was much more of a success. Oldewarris recalls the proceedings as follows: 'He seemed to like us, I think, and thought the plan was an interesting one. (...) And then Jan Riezenkamp came up with something along the lines of a College resolution, to be able to give us the key. So we were just given the key, without going through all the democratic channels, no contract, nothing – it was never put before the council, not to my knowledge anyway. There was absolutely nothing on paper. "You can stay there for a while". They really had no idea what they were going to do with it. Maybe they just thought at least now it would be occupied.' Jan Riezenkamp's own version more or less confirms this state of affairs: 'According to my colleague Pim Vermeulen [then alderman for Urban Renewal and Public Housing] I let those people from Utopia in through the bathroom window; I quite knowingly let them occupy those grounds – I don't know if the concept of squatting existed then. (...) My slogan has always been who cares if it's a fiasco as long as it's an interesting fiasco. So I felt it was worth risking, administratively of course it was a liability.'[7] Some months later, the council did agree on a loan to Utopia to get the site into workable shape, which meant that Utopia was now formally the tenant.[8]

These days, much thought is given to the importance of so-called free states (*vrijstaten*), places where the city's creative spirit has free rein. A number of Dutch cities now even have an official 'cultural incubator policy' (*broedplaatsenbeleid*), whereby vacant properties or former brownfield sites are allocated for artists and cultural entrepreneurs who can set up projects for low accommodation costs.[9]

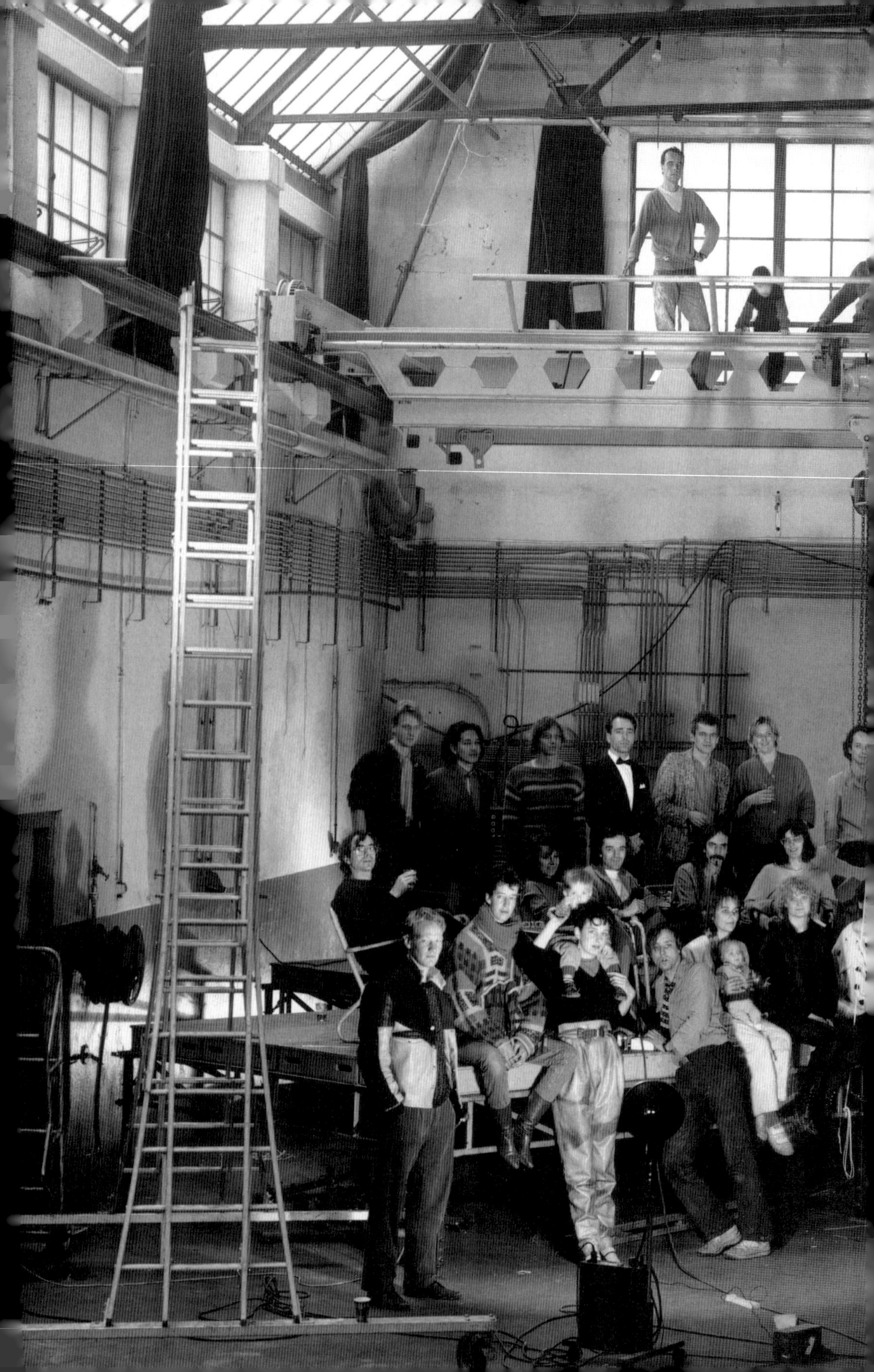

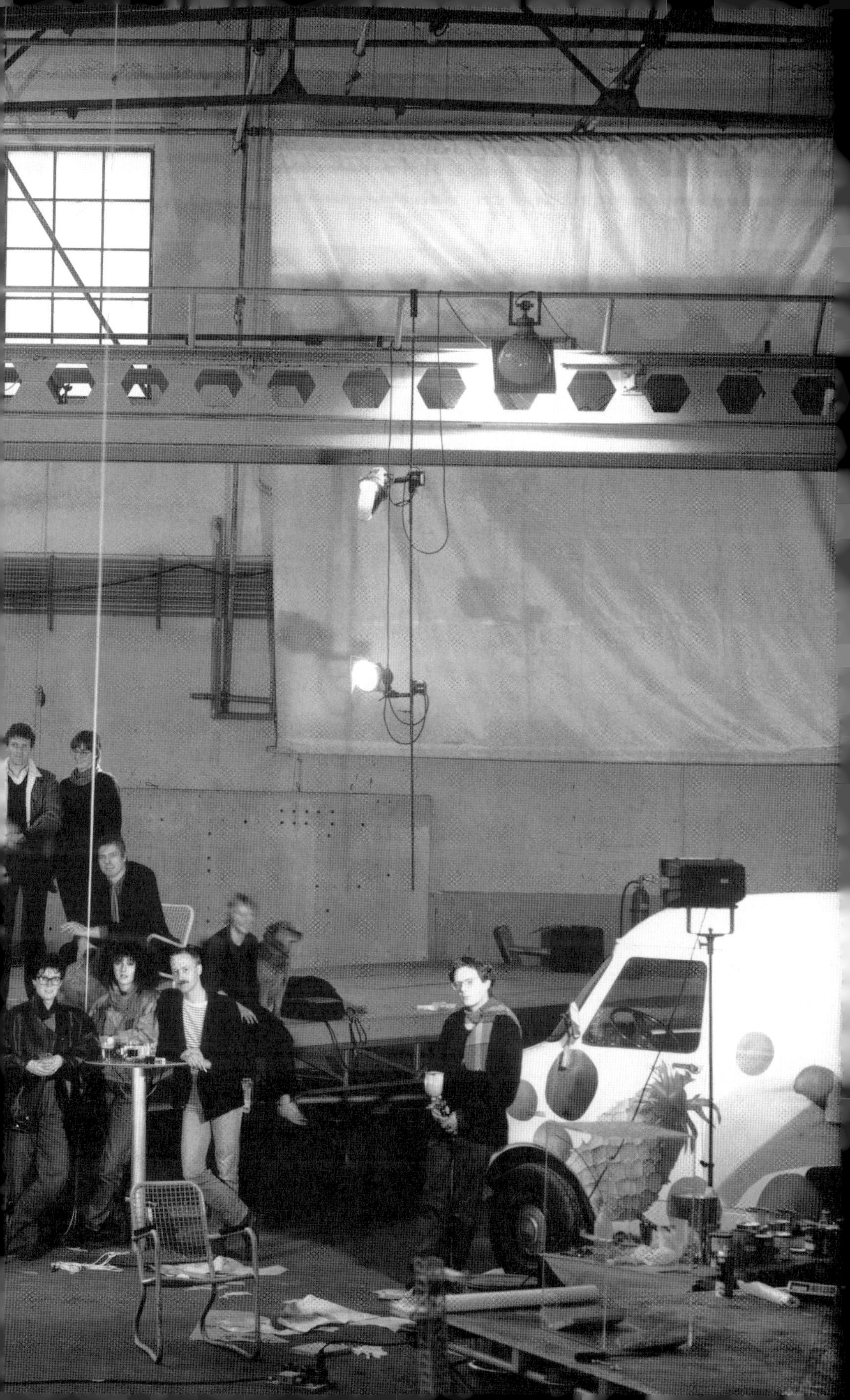

There was no question of this in 1977. Riezenkamp was way ahead of his time when he estimated that this group of enterprising people would be a 'shot in the arm for the city'.[10] Remarkably, the alderman's official policy on culture as articulated in two reports in 1978, attests to another viewpoint altogether.[11] Instead of the *laissez faire* principle he recalls as his administrative guiding principle, the reports smack more of a move towards greater council control over art and culture. For the record, the reports have had few consequences to speak of. The opposite is true of the ad hoc decision to give the key of the DWL site to the folks from Utopia.

In February 1978, the Utopians began moving into the 19th-century dwellings still intact in the water tower and started refurbishing the other buildings on site and laying out the piping and conduitry for gas, electricity and water.[12] It is close to a miracle that a mere two years later everyone and all the enterprises were housed more or less to their satisfaction and even a concert hall had been opened there, the aforementioned Hal 4. Miraculous not least because the members of Utopia had to do all the laying out and building themselves, from providing running water which meant digging channels to and from the street, to internal constructional interventions of all kinds, also in the depths of winter without heating.

In the autumn of 1979 Utopia organized a big housewarming party in Hal 4 with the express intention of 'inviting Rotterdam'. This immediately put them in touch with other artists and cultural entrepreneurs in Rotterdam. The Utopia group had little affinity with the visual artists who had commanded such attention in the 1960s and '70s, such as Woody van Amen, Mathieu Ficheroux, Hans Verwey and Louis Looijschelder.[13] This was largely due to the difference in age but also to their utterly different approaches to art and the role of the artist. The members of that older generation each went about their own discipline in complete independence whereas the Utopians were interested in a confluence of disciplines and in applied forms of art. And where the freewheeling Rotterdam artists accepted the existing infrastructure for presenting art, the members of Utopia sought to make their own conditions in which to produce and present their work. This forged an immediate bond with other pioneers in the city, such as the architect Rem Koolhaas, the cultural entrepreneur Beerend Lenstra, the members of Hard Werken, the artists of Kunst en Vaarwerk, the visual artist and organizer Wink van Kempen, the future director of Now & Wow Ted Langenbach, and the pioneers in catering and hospitality Joop Hakvoort and later Daan van der Have. Working relationships sprang up, some of which would continue into the 21st century. For example, Hans Werlemann, one of the founders of Utopia, has been the regular photographer for Rem Koolhaas's Office for Metropolitan Architecture since 1980. Rick Vermeulen and Gerard Hadders of Hard Werken's graphic design team did the design work for the publishing house begun by Hans Oldewarris and Peter de Winter in the grounds of Utopia in 1983.[14] Joop Hakvoort and Daan van der Have approached Viktor Mani and Chiel van der Stelt, two Utopians who together constituted the architecture firm BOA, to refurbish their cafés and redesign the interiors. Ted Langenbach, who in the 1990s would

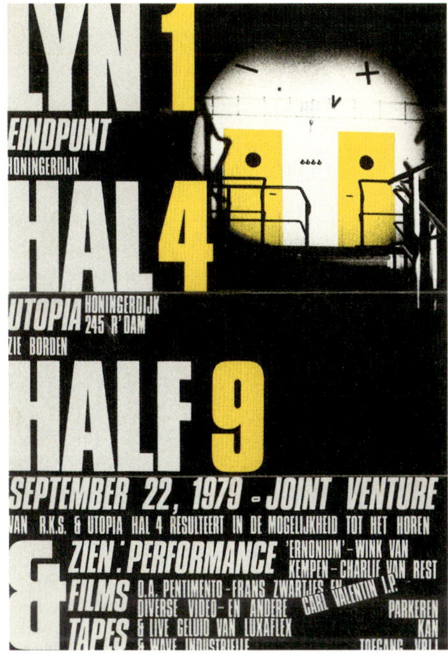

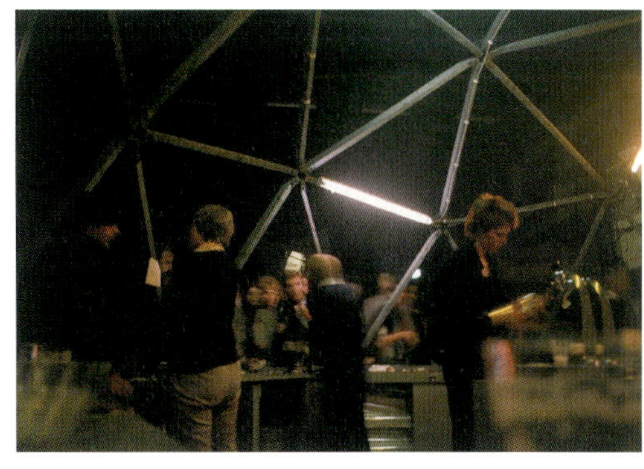

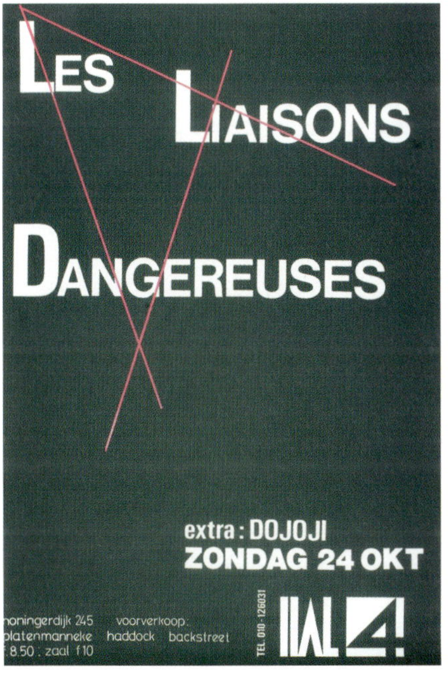

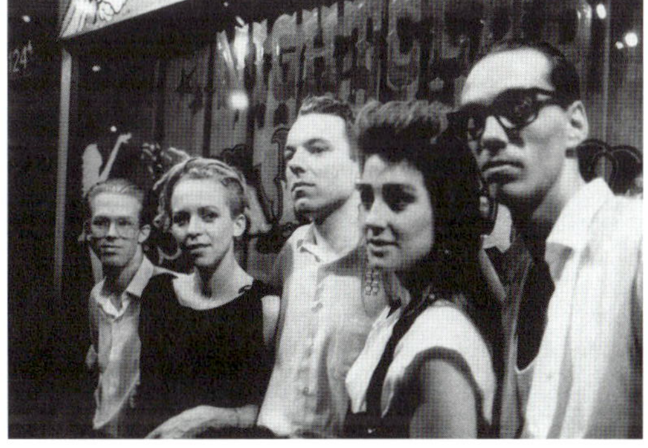

Top left poster for Utopia's inaugural party in Hal 4, September 22, 1979, design by Chiel van der Stelt and Hans Werlemann; **right** photo taken during the party.

Bottom left Hal 4 poster announcing the band Dojoji who were opening for Les Liaisons Dangereuses, October 24, 1982, design by Hans van den Tol; **right** the band Dojoji with Ted Langenbach.

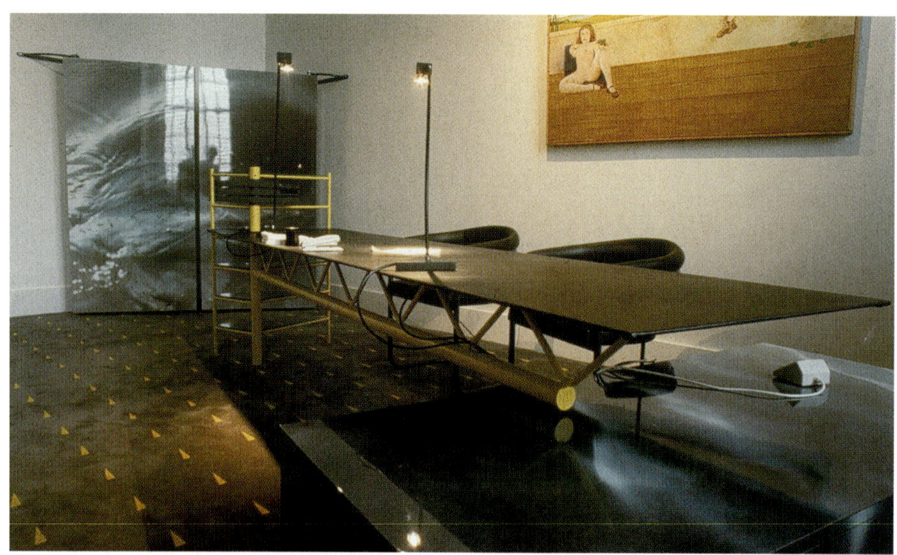

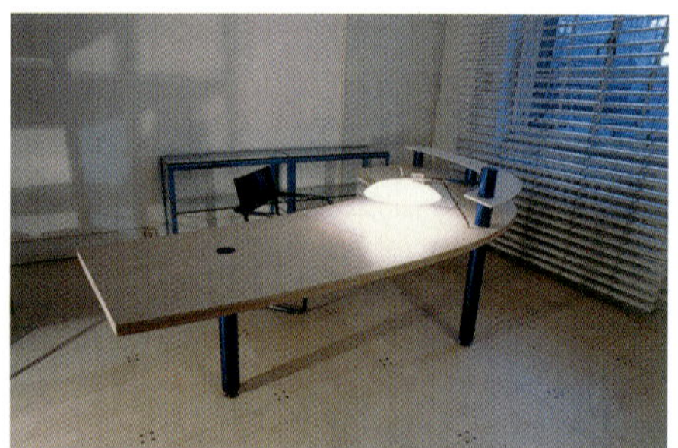

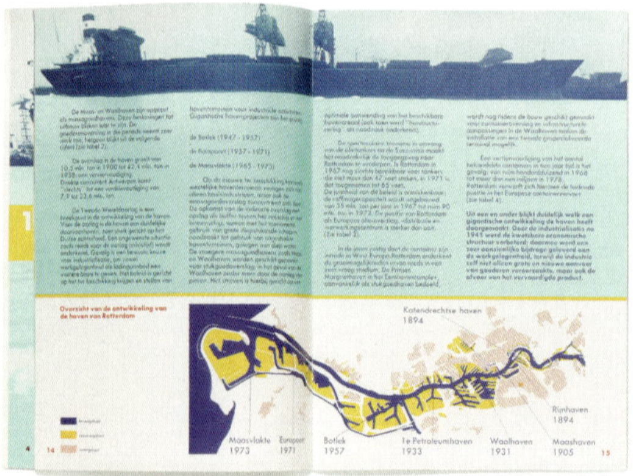

Top room of alderman for port affairs Jan Riezenkamp, design by BOA Contractors (Viktor Mani and Chiel van der Stelt) and Ed den Hollander, 1981.

Middle room of alderman for finance Pim Vermeulen, with ten-cent coins glued in the floor, design by BOA Contractors (Viktor Mani and Chiel van der Stelt), Hans Oldewarris and Hans Werlemann, 1980.

Bottom opening from Jan Riezenkamp, *Havennota*, 1979, design by Reinout Meltzer.

grow into the Netherlands' most celebrated organizer of dance parties, performed in Hal 4 with his band Dojoji and held his first parties there.

Just how tight and complex this network of enterprising people was can be illustrated by an in-depth description of Ponton 010. This exceptional project was the outcome of varying coalitions of artists, architects and organizers who had been requested by the Rotterdam Port Authority to examine ways of strengthening and visualizing the relationship between city and port. Among these coalitions were the members of Utopia and others such as the three artists who had joined forces in 1978 as Kunst en Vaarwerk, namely Hans Citroen, Willem van Drunen and Cor Kraat.[15] It is unusual on the face of it to find the Port Authority turning to architects and visual artists to illustrate the relationship between port and city, but it can be explained by the fact that the former alderman for culture Jan Riezenkamp had been appointed alderman for Port Affairs in 1978. In this new function he would keep up contact with the folks from Utopia and get them such commissions as the interior design of two aldermen's chambers (in 1978)[16] and the design of a port policy document.[17] Not only that, the director of the Port Authority, Henk Molenaar, was well-disposed towards the arts out of a personal interest and commitment. Molenaar was moreover profoundly aware that even something seemingly driven entirely by economic forces as the port would benefit from a favourable image, firstly because a port needs to be sustained by a society to be able to function and secondly because the image it has can influence a company in its decision to settle there.[18] So we see that the more or less coincidental personal preferences of two administrators gave a considerable boost to cultural life in the city. And we can conclude as well that the reports Riezenkamp drew up as alderman for Cultural Affairs have had less real influence than his informal interest in art, this time as port alderman. It was not the first time, as it happens, that Riezenkamp's and Molenaar's 'hobby' led to something of an unofficial arts and culture policy: when more and more harbour buildings and dock areas became empty in the 1980s as port activities shifted steadily westward, these were consistently passed on to artists for a low or non-existent rent. According to Riezenkamp, the Port Authority was at one time doing more business in studio hire than anyone else in the city, including the DGK and (since 1987) the SKAR, two municipal bodies officially entrusted with providing accommodation for art and artists.[19] Many studio complexes that have included noted Rotterdam artists, such as those on Vierhavenstraat and Quarantaineterrein, were called into being by this practice.

Ponton 010

Of all the projects born of the rapprochement between Port Authority and artists, much the most complicated and spectacular was Ponton 010. Its complexity required experts in a wide array of fields to make it a success. At its core was a *ponton* or flat-bottomed boat which was converted into a tier of seating for 1100 people plus

a stage and a bar. The idea came from Utopia, more specifically from Hans Oldewarris
and Peter de Winter. Fellow Utopians Viktor Mani and Chiel van der Stelt of BOA
Contractors provided the architectural design. Others involved in the organizational
side were Ole Bijster, Beerend Lenstra and Hans Werlemann.[20] Joop Hakvoort and
Daan van der Have, joint owners of the successful jazz café Dizzy, took care of the
catering for Ponton 010 both at its moorings on Parkkade and during voyages.[21]
Ponton 010 made a total of ten such voyages in the summer of 1980. The 'floating
stand' was then pulled by tugs to numerous places in the docks. The port was the
principal spectacle in all this though there were always on-board performances
during the trips. As co-organizer, Beerend Lenstra had broad experience in organizing concerts for new foreign bands and thanks to his contacts the very latest and
greatest in New Wave music could be heard on several occasions aboard Ponton
010, including The Gang of Four and The Slits from the UK as well as local punk and
New Wave bands like Kotx and Willy Nilly. But you could also hear high-quality
experimental music and jazz performed live.

Ponton 010's voyages through the docks got plenty of coverage in the local
papers and also from the national station Radio 3. On August 5 1980, for example,
the VARA company broadcast a pop concert, and on the evening of Friday August 22
the VPRO company broadcast a four-hour programme live from Ponton 010, presented
by author and interviewer Ischa Meijer with performances by nationally renowned
entertainers amongst whom Johnny van Doorn, Freek de Jonge and Jules Deelder.
As said earlier, there was little media interest in Rotterdam generally speaking
because all the media and television people lived in Amsterdam. So the impact of
such a transmission on the nation's image of Rotterdam can only be imagined. Not
to forget dyed-in-the-wool Amsterdammer Ischa Meijer's inevitable swipe at 'that
godawful place' Rotterdam, which only served to strengthen Rotterdam's profile as
essentially different from that of Amsterdam. Ponton 010 also received publicity on
a truly generous scale in the seventh issue of the magazine *Hard Werken*, getting a
full four pages of text, plans and photographs devoted to it.[22]

What was so important about Ponton 010, apart from the fact that it brought
Rotterdam into the public eye as a city where they experimented with out-of-the-
ordinary cultural projects?[23] First of all, Ponton 010 gathered together people who
would later work together and inspired others to indulge in similarly ambitious
activities. Ted Langenbach for one sees Beerend Lenstra as someone who has taught
him plenty: '(...) Beerend Lenstra was of course an example of how Rotterdam had
to be. And Beerend always had that attitude of that's cool, let's do that, let's get it
in place. Beerend is one of my big heroes.'[24] Of course Ponton 010 wasn't the only
example of Lenstra's influence, as there were many other projects he had set up.[25]
Secondly, Ponton 010 forged a bridge not only between city and port, the premise
underlying that project from the beginning, but also between art and port and so
between Rotterdam the city of culture and Rotterdam the port city. For the generation of artists and entrepreneurs who collaborated on this project, it was easy enough

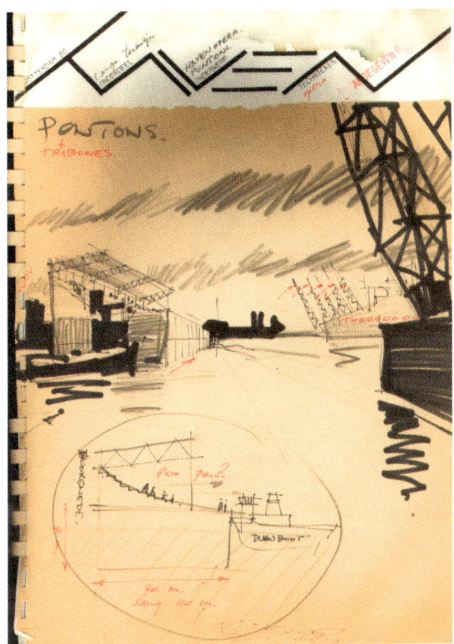

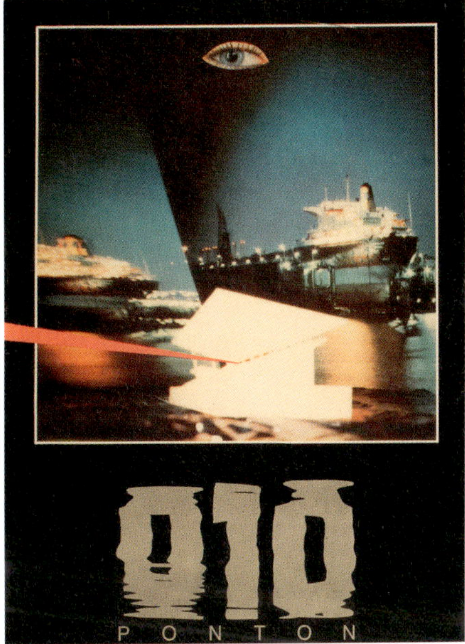

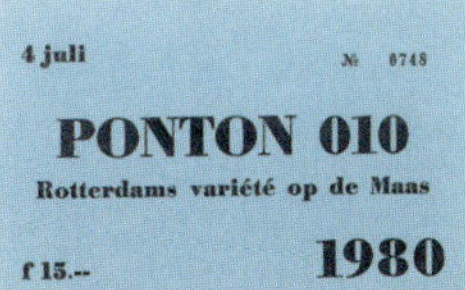

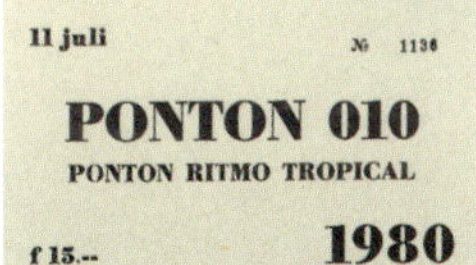

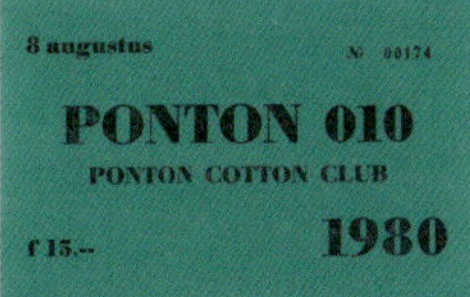

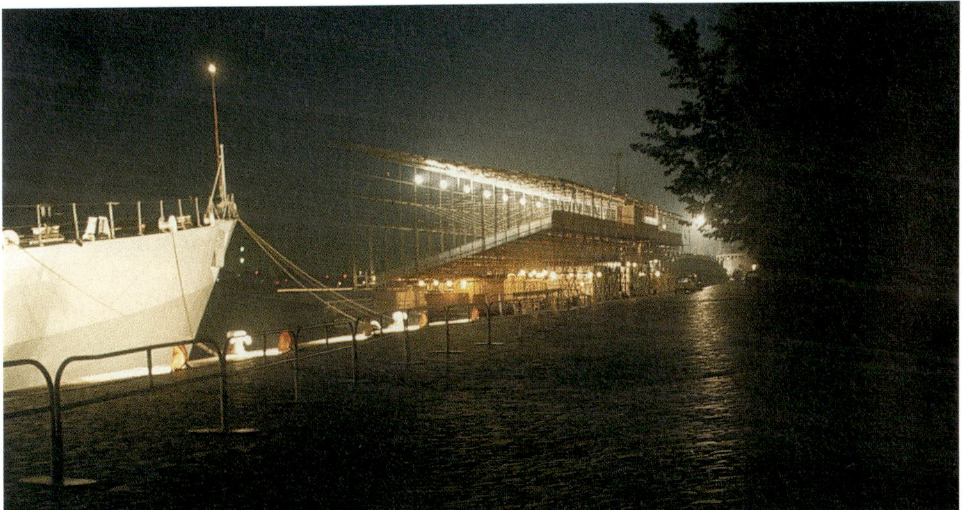

Ponton 010, 1980. **Top left** draft study, drawing by Chiel van der Stelt; **right** poster, design by Alan Turnbull and Hans Werlemann; **middle** tickets; **bottom** the moorings at Parkkade, with a voyage scheduled every Friday.

PP. 146-147 drawing/photomontage of Ponton 010, 1980, design by Chiel van der Stelt, Alan Turnbull and Hans Werlemann. **Inset at bottom left** final design by BOA Contractors (Viktor Mani and Chiel van der Stelt).

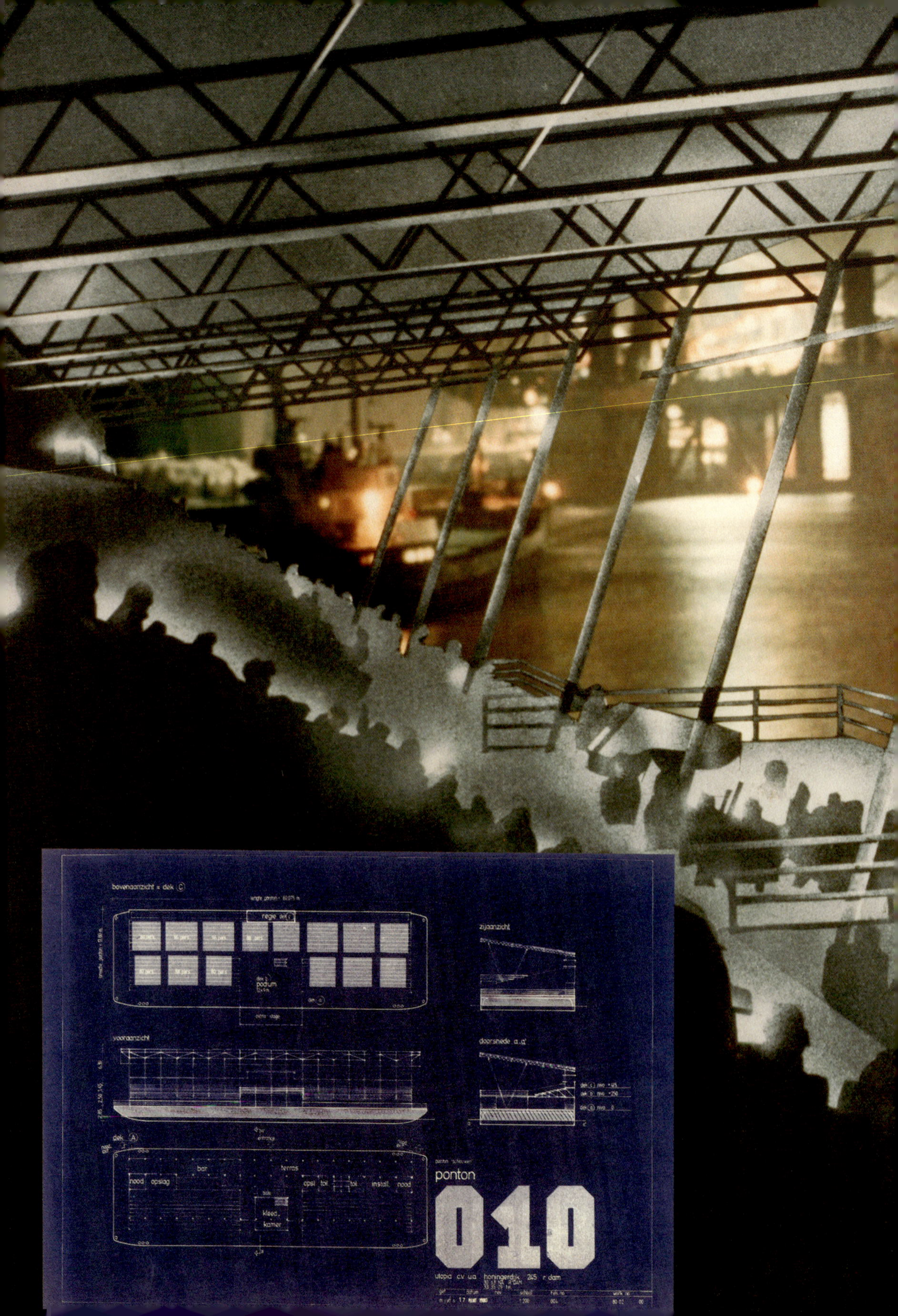
bovenaanzicht x dek
regie dek
zijaanzicht
podium
extra etage
vooraanzicht
doorsnede
dek A
bar
terras
nood opslag
opsl toi toi inslaf nood
kleed kamer
ponton
010
utopia c.v. u.a. honingerdijk 245 r.dam
17 mei 1980

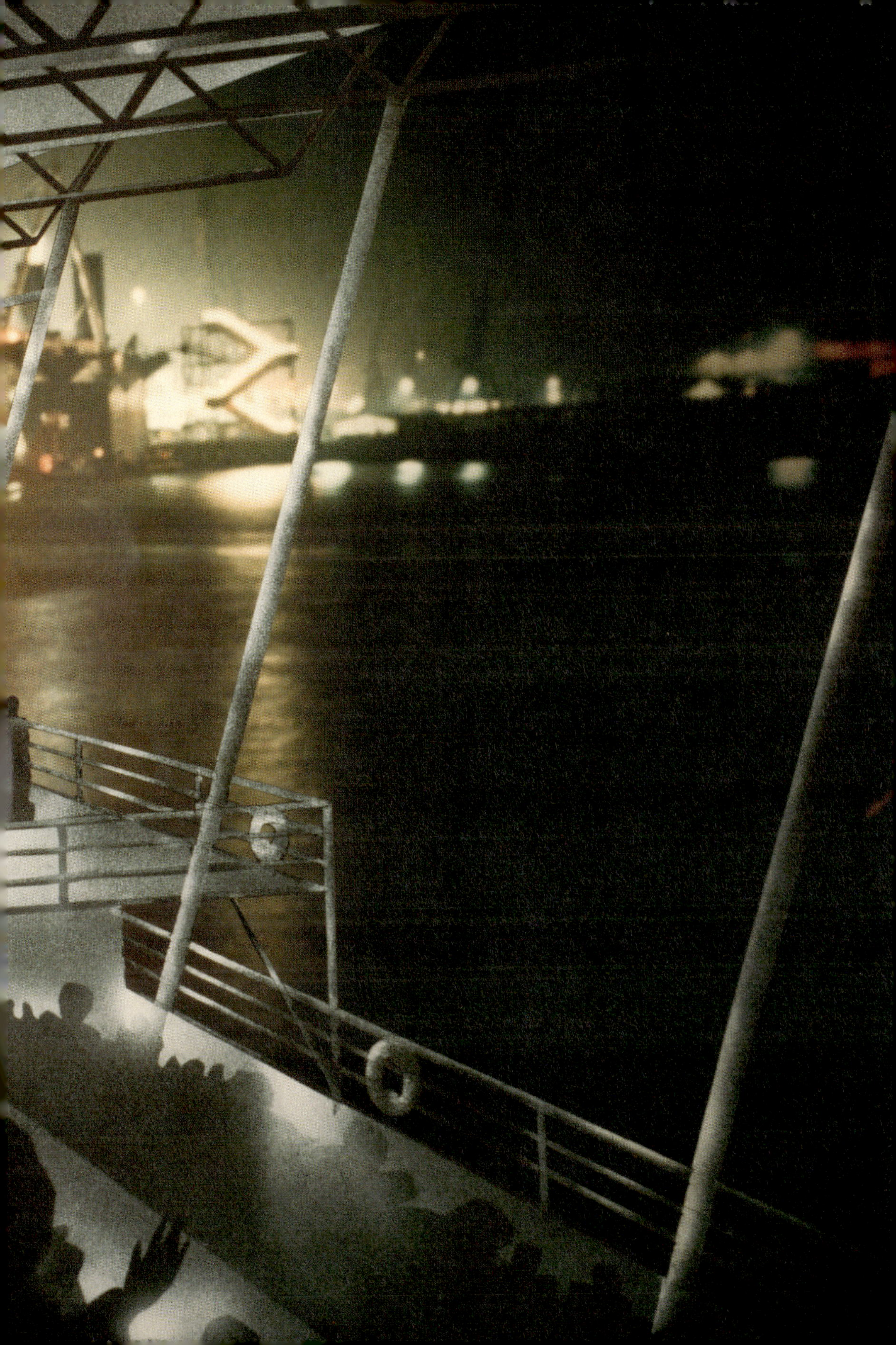

to see the city of culture and the port city along one front, as this approach to the port as spectacle – Ponton 010 as the seating, the port as the performance – was in perfect keeping with interests that were theirs anyway. Aspects like the rough aesthetic of utilitarian edifices, the awe-inspiring impact of structures whose workings are beyond most of us, and the sheer expanse and unfathomable nature of water also played strongly in the Utopians' enthusiasm for the DWL site. Ponton 010 offered, as it were, a modernized successor to the romantic image of the docks, an image that could no longer be found in the city, much to the regret of many.[26] There was nothing nostalgic about this project, just a clear expression of their love of the hypermodern, big, noisy, smelly machine that the port of Rotterdam had become. One of Ponton 010's voyages even had 'Night of the Stench' as its theme.[27] The text announcing Ponton 010 in *Hard Werken* of May-June 1980 illustrates perfectly this contrast between the old and new port: '... 0.00 o'clock ... Ponton 010 arrives at the Gusto wharf and moors alongside the frigates of the Dutch East India Company, the smell of spices. Romance... The bombardment. Jet fighters roar above the sheds. Helicopters illuminate the abandoned grounds.... Explosions and the sounds of Concert For Factory Sirens (Russia 1920)... Nine grain elevators like elephants in the dark of night. Beacons, buoys, cranes, fanned out across the sulphur-scented expanse. Container trucks in a row, high-kicking as in Moulin Rouge... 4500 gas masks are handed out... The opera commences...'.[28] This new perspective on the port making it an object of aesthetic appreciation as it had been in the inter-war years, laid the basis for the growing popularity of the docks among artists and other cultural practitioners.

A positive aesthetic appreciation of the port is essential if one is to have a good understanding of Rotterdam's cultural advances in the 20th century. We already examined this aspect of the inter-war years in chapter 2. But since the end of the 1970s until the present the docks have been a source of inspiration – in many cases even a reason to stay in the city – for artists, designers, architects and in fact everyone who contributes to Rotterdam's cultural climate. The most illustrious among Rotterdam's artists, designers and architects positively drool at the mention of the docks.

The designer Richard Hutten, whose studio is in a dockland area, was quoted in the home design magazine *Eigen Huis & Interieur* in 1999 as having said that the docks make him feel good.[29] Landscape architect Adriaan Geuze when asked in 2001 why his practice, West 8, is domiciled in Rotterdam replied: 'For us Rotterdam is a very obvious place to work because we really like the rhythm of the river and the harbour.'[30] Asked for 'tips for a day out' in *NRC Handelsblad* of July 20/21, 2002, visual artist Joep van Lieshout recommended the harbour route set out by the ANWB, the Dutch automobile association, especially in the evening: 'Make sure you don't return through the harbour before dusk. The refineries have futuristic lighting at night.' And his favourite picnic spot turns out to a hillock on a spit of land overlooking the Maasvlakte, Hoek van Holland and the sea ships sailing by.[31] In stark contrast to the above, council policy is dogged by a polarizing discourse that distinguishes between

Rotterdam the city of culture and Rotterdam the city of docks and work. The authorities would love to drop the port and work city image, or would have throughout the period covered by this book.[32] This opposition also crops up time and again in studies by historians or sociologists on Rotterdam's cultural climate. When Paul van de Laar speculates on the possibility of Rotterdam ever becoming a city of culture, he unquestioningly assumes that this can only be done if the city loses its image of toil and sweat: 'The image of a city of work has not been erased, though it is high time it was replaced by that of a city of culture.'[33] Willem Frijhoff suggests that Rotterdam can only become such a city once it has developed 'an authentic urban culture', and to explain what he means by that he refers to Amsterdam, where, as he puts it, 'all cultural activity has been magnificently integrated into the world of the city as we see it'.[34] The possibility that Rotterdam's urban culture might well have a character utterly unlike that of Amsterdam, and that Rotterdam the city of culture is closely bound up with Rotterdam the port city, is simply not a part of Frijhoff's mindset. Rotterdam's urban culture to his way of thinking is not rooted in '(...) the megalomaniac, anaemic discourse on metropolis and port we keep hearing, and that the farther the port is from the city, the farther it slips from the real world of Rotterdammers.'[35] It should be clear from this book that the discourse on metropolis and port is anything but anaemic. Irina van Aalst is another to assume a work/port city-culture city contradiction when in her dissertation *Cultuur in de stad* (Culture in the city) she writes about the cultural policy of Rotterdam city council in the 1980s: 'Investments in the cultural infrastructure are part of a strategy to replace this image [of a work and port city] with a "new" one.'[36] Such polarizations are adopted more out of habit than as well-considered definitions, but it does show how persistent this opposition is.

Ponton 010 went so far as to present the docks themselves as art. Its organizers were fully aware that in doing so they were building upon ideas advanced by Futurists, Constructivists and other modernist artists between the two wars.[37] So the reference to the *Concert For Factory Sirens* by the Russian Futurist Vladimir Mayakovsky in the above excerpt from *Hard Werken* is more than a happy coincidence.[38] In 1980, Utopians Chiel van der Stelt and Bert van Veldhuizen organized in association with Martin Aarts and architect Kees Christiaanse an exhibition inspired by Futurism entitled 'Helix, film, rrumoerr, transparant'.[39] There is as well a clear connection between Futurism and punk and in particular with New Wave music as heard on Ponton 010. Much New Wave music made use of sounds that evoke associations with the hubbub ('rrumoerr') of heavy industry and traffic. Some New Wave music is even termed 'industrial music' for this reason, such as the two UK bands named below. Remarkably many groups of artists and musicians of those days chose names suggesting a connection with the art of the inter-war years: the Marinetti's (a Rotterdam-based artists' initiative, named after the Futurist Filippo Tommaso Marinetti; Cabaret Voltaire, a British 'industrial' band, named after the legendary nightclub where Dada was born); and Bauhaus, a post-punk proto-gothic band, also

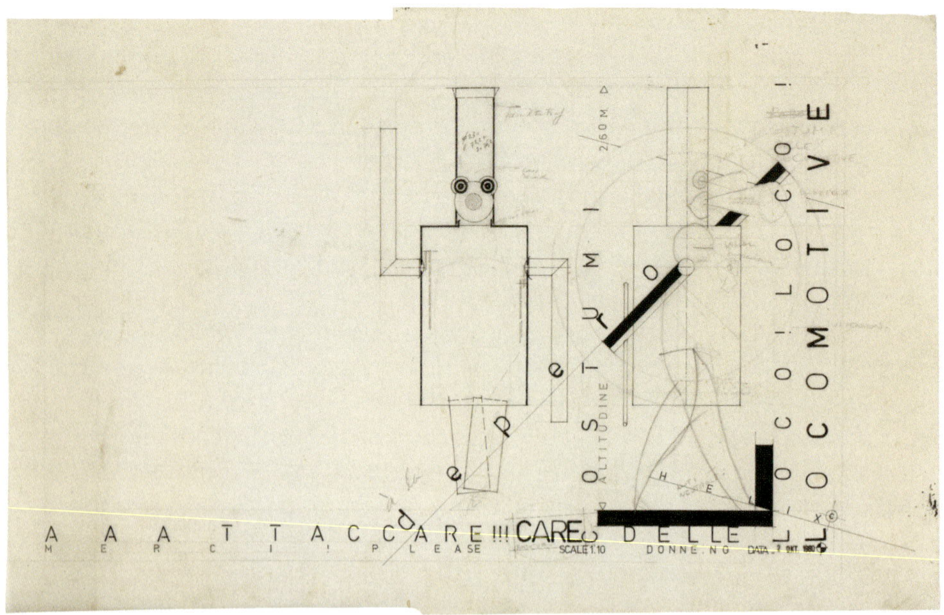

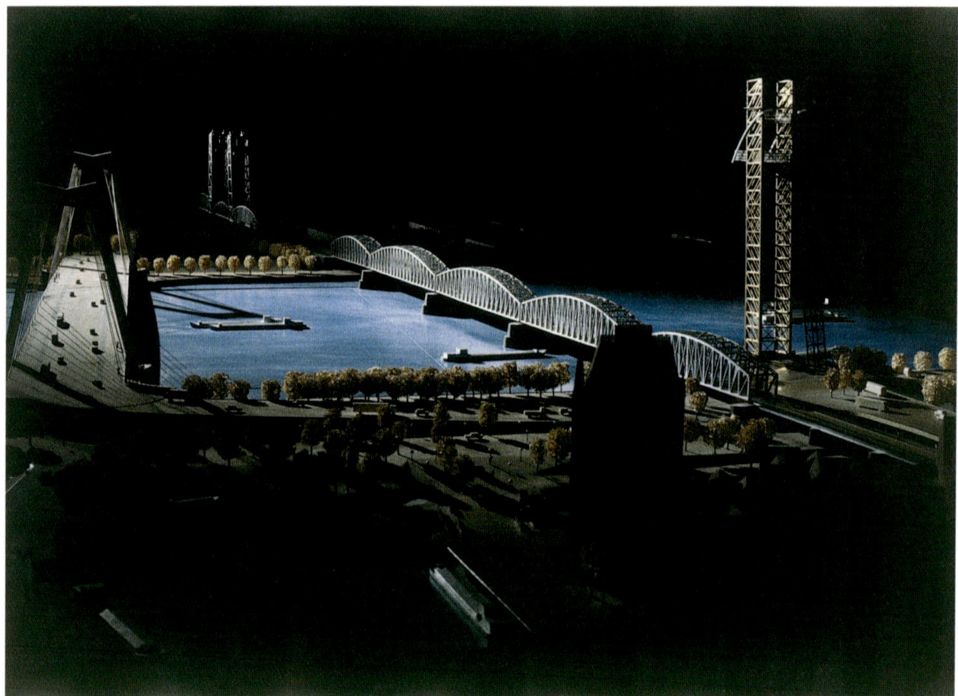

Top Chiel van der Stelt, design for locomotive costumes for futurists, for the exhibition 'Helix, film, rrumoerr, transparant', Lijnbaancentrum, 1980.

Bottom Rem Koolhaas / Office for Metropolitan Architecture, design for a building on the Maas, 1981.

from the UK, named after the pioneering art and architecture school in Germany.

There was a similar resurge of interest around 1980 in a wide range of inter-war isms among architects outside the Utopia group. Rem Koolhaas was one who in 1981 designed a building on the Maas river in Rotterdam that makes direct reference to the famous *Lenin Tribune* of 1920–1924 designed by the Russian Constructivist El Lissitzky. Koolhaas made his design at the behest of the city council though it was never built. It did provoke much discussion, though, and was published extensively, also in *Hard Werken*.[40] This renewed interest on the practical front was mirrored by a similar concern from the theory side; in the 1980s the academic staff of Dutch museums and architecture scholars in general turned their attention to modernist architecture and urbanism for the first time in years. In 1982 and '83 five museums hosted exhibitions on the Modern Movement in architecture, each with its own accompanying book. Nor did these shows focus alone on the 'heroic age' between the wars but covered the run-up to modernism in the 19th century as well as the post-war period up to 1960. Their concern for the reconstruction era is note-worthy, as the modernist architecture of those years had long been reviled and ignored. Separate exhibitions and publications were devoted to the contributions by Amsterdam and Rotterdam.

The new type of café that became popular at the onset of the 1980s can likewise be seen as an ode to the inter-war years. The new Rotterdam cafés were generally large like the *grand cafés* of the '20s and '30s, and their interiors brought back the Modern Movement with tubular steel furniture, glass and other hard materials.

The new Rotterdam café

Two establishments were responsible for setting the trend for a new type of Rotterdam café. These were Dizzy and Lux, neighbours on 's-Gravendijkwal. Both were owned and managed by Joop Hakvoort and Daan van der Have, the latter con-tinuing with them after Hakvoort's death in 1983. Dizzy had been a successful jazz café since 1977. It was enlarged out of necessity at the end of 1982 when the premis-es of what used to be Heavy (see chapter 4) were added to it and the interior was redone entirely by the BOA architectural practice. This new-style Dizzy, whose interior has changed little as of this writing, was for those days extremely spacious, bright and modern with a long bar, tubular steel furniture, a roomy stage for live perform-ances and a large garden terrace. Although not touted as such, Dizzy can be regarded as Rotterdam's first grand café since the reconstruction era. With its mondaine atmosphere, it was nothing like the traditional Dutch 'brown café'. Indeed, it was tailored to an urban lifestyle, serving breakfast as well as lunch and dinner.

Lux, which opened its doors in November 1983, was much smaller than Dizzy but far more radical in its modernity. If Dizzy's interior clung on to warmer materials such as a wood floor, Lux was as cool as ice in its combination of steel,

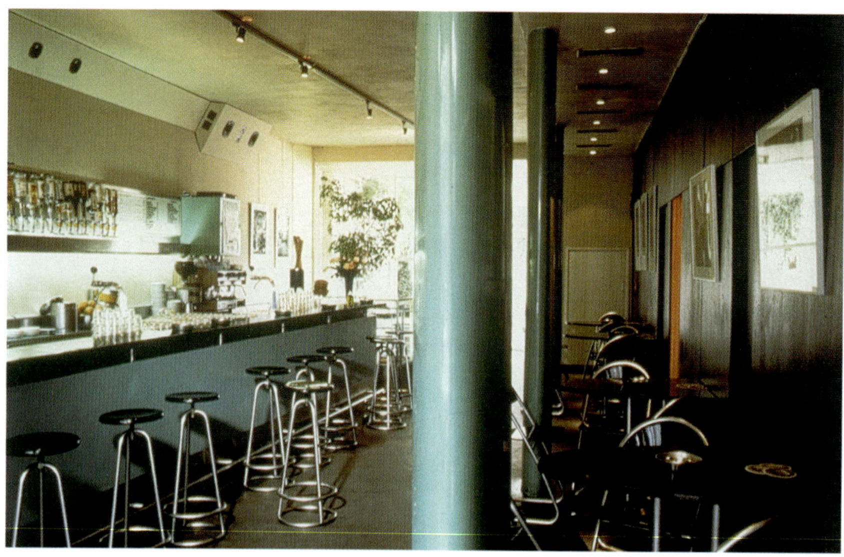

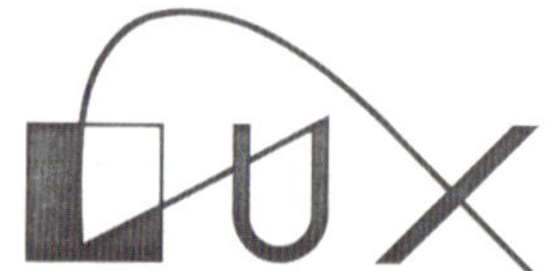

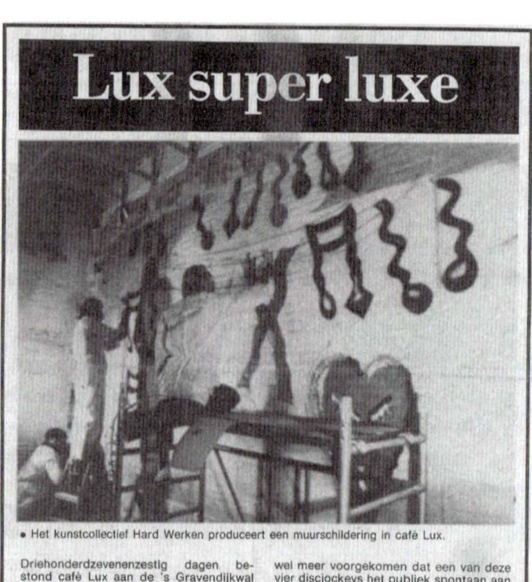

• Het kunstcollectief Hard Werken produceert een muurschildering in café Lux.

Driehonderdzevenenzestig dagen bestond café Lux aan de 's Gravendijkwal zaterdag en dat moest gevierd. Het café, dat veel high-tech (wat staat voor héél en zéér modern en niet smal der geest) publiek naar zich toetrekt, vierde in die sfeer feest.

Italiaanse hapjes, exotische cocktails, het personeel aan de andere kant (de verkeerde kant dus) van de bar en echte disco-muziek, verzorgd door de vier meest bekende discjockeys uit Rotterdam waaronder ex-Heavy draaier Peter van Gameren.

Disco in een high-tech café? ,,Nou ja, disco'', bromt Wob Rombouts, werkzaam in Lux en organisator van het feest. ,,Noem het maar dansmuziek. Het is trouwens wel meer voorgekomen dat een van deze vier discjockeys het publiek spontaan aan het dansen kreeg. En dat voor een café!'' Super-de-lux dus dat Lux zaterdag. Mannen en vrouwen in smoking, nippend aan de cocktails en het kunstkollektief maar werken. Jawel, de enige kale muur die nog over was kreeg zaterdag een heus kunstwerk. De stichting Hard Werken, een Rotterdams kunstenaarskollektief, maakte met behulp van air-brush een prachtige muurschildering.

Het werk werd vastgelegd op video en polaroids. ,,Ik heb wel voor de zekerheid twee potten witkalk gekocht'', vertelde Wob Rombouts. ,,Wanneer we het niet mooi vinden, is het zo weer weg.''

Top café Lux shortly after opening in 1983. Design by BOA Contractors (Viktor Mani and Chiel van der Stelt); **right** logo of Café Lux, design by Chiel van der Stelt.

Bottom members of Hard Werken working on an airbrush painting in Café Lux, *Rotterdams Nieuwsblad*, November 12, 1984.

glass, cool colours and black, the whole brightly lit with countless halogen spotlights. More so than in Dizzy, one could feel a man or woman of the world in Lux with its reasonably priced cocktails and constant supply of appetizers on display. Lux was soon claimed by youngish creative professionals in their twenties and early thirties. For them Lux's ambience added to their experience of Rotterdam as a rational, dynamic, worldly, modern city. The members of Hard Werken were regular visitors from the beginning. Their affinity with Lux can be gauged from their contribution to the party celebrating the café's first full year: one wall bore a mural painted by airbrushing, a technique deriving from graffiti art, a typically metropolitan phenomenon itself. A local paper typified the clientele of Lux as 'high-tech', 'which means as modern as can be and not narrow-minded at all'.[41] A national newspaper described its customers as 'post-punks, New Wavers and yuppies'.[42]

The example of Lux and Dizzy was soon followed up on all sides, to such a degree in fact that as early as 1986 a Rotterdam newspaper devoted an article to the unstoppable rise of 'the modern Rotterdam café': 'Hardened café-goers who swear by their local brown café, its meatballs, its boiled eggs and the familiar mug of hot strong coffee, will probably feel little for the latest catering adventure in Rotterdam. But there's no stopping the trend now, the future has arrived. The modern café is everywhere.'[43] The anonymous author of these words went on to describe the attributes typical of the new, 'ultra-modern' café: '(...) there's an espresso machine, an ever-changing selection of contemporary art on the walls, you can have lunch, a hot meal and sometimes even breakfast, and there are live performances on a regular basis. But the most striking thing about it is the interior: the new café has a bright and modern design. Its ambience comes from the use of contemporary materials. Not dark timber but stainless steel, no dimmed lighting to convey cosiness but neon.'[44] If at that time Dizzy and especially Lux appealed largely to a select band of pioneers, by 1986 'the modern Rotterdam café' had become much more widely popular: 'People still find it amazing that the new trend has caught on with an extremely wide audience, but it has meant that modern cafés are now springing up everywhere and that more and more proprietors of the "normal" variety are getting their cafés redone. It's not like it was in the '60s when a new establishment opened for a particular segment of the public and an old establishment somewhere else lost its clientele.'[45]

It is hard to explain this renaissance in Rotterdam's catering and hospitality sector in economic terms. Unemployment rocketed in the first half of the 1980s, more and more jobs moved out of the city and the council was forced to cut down on costs. Curiously, this failed to impact negatively on Rotterdam's after-hours activities and nightlife – in fact the catering industry flourished and cultural events enjoyed an increase in popularity. A comparison with the crisis years of the 1930s springs to mind, when Rotterdam experienced the same paradoxical situation: a slump in the economy coupled with a burst of cultural activity.[46] One explanation of the paradox in the 1980s is the accommodating attitude of the social security department in those days towards those with a creative profession who were considered eligible for supplementary benefit. In Rotterdam in the 1980s the social services had a special ruling for artists and others in the cultural sector who were unable to live from what they earned. They were not obliged to apply for every available job, and professional costs could be deducted from their income before this was declared.[47] This worked as a stimulant on the professional segment engaged in creative work. Artists and entrepreneurs dependent on a social security benefit now had the money and the time to work or even, as was repeatedly the case in Rotterdam in the 1980s, set up a studio complex, maybe with an exhibition area.[48]

The emergence of new cafés in Rotterdam was a subject of national interest, which did indicate that it was a phenomenon peculiar to Rotterdam. An article on Daan van der Have in the national daily *NRC Handelsblad*, gave to understand that even Amsterdam cafés were taking a keen interest in the successful Rotterdam formula: 'The big boys in Amsterdam's catering sector had asked him if he could furnish them with a few ideas and even wanted to set up shop in Rotterdam. For catering entrepreneur Daan van der Have (35) there is no more eloquent example of the emergent café culture in Rotterdam.'[49] Traditionally Amsterdam had been the trendsetter in entertainment and nightlife, not Rotterdam. By then Van der Have had launched many more eating and drinking establishments in Rotterdam besides Dizzy and Lux, including two with a cultural thrust: Zochers, a café-salon-restaurant whose activities included live musical performances and discussions on cultural subjects, and De Unie, a café that was to host activities organized by the Rotterdam Arts Council.

Daan van der Have is a typical exponent of the aforementioned DIY mentality and someone with an eye for the specific qualities of Rotterdam. After secondary school and two years mainly spent travelling, he actively chose Rotterdam, as 'Rotterdam is an unbelievably cool place in terms of atmosphere'.[50] After learning the trade from Dizzy's founder Joop Hakvoort, from 1982 on he launched one Rotterdam café after the other at a white-hot pace.[51] Although these establishments differed in terms of set-up and ambience and whether they were combined with a restaurant or not, they were united in responding to one or other phenomenon peculiar to Rotterdam, either in their spaciousness, rationality, modern interior layout or in their setting which drew attention to a characteristic place in the city, as in the case of Zochers in Het Park and Loos in the old shipping quarter (Scheepvaartkwartier). In stressing these qualities of Rotterdam Van der Have made a contribution of inestimable value to a new perspective on the city. Although he collaborated rewardingly with some council officials and aldermen, he steadily became sceptical about council policy where it relates to developing a perspective on Rotterdam. He feels that official promotion campaigns all too often label Rotterdam inappropriately and fail to see the real potential to be found in the city.

By the end of the 1980s, then, Rotterdam could boast a relatively small but highly active and burgeoning creative network of people who had become hugely proficient in organizing events and setting up small enterprises of all kinds, often working closely together. There had been a succession of well-attended festivals and events in Rotterdam long before the 'festival city' tag appeared in city brochures and long before a foundation (Stichting Rotterdam Festivals, 1993) was established to organize and coordinate such festivals. In the January 1988 issue of the entertainment monthly *Magazijn* the festival tag is already in evidence: 'Rotterdam is the city of festivals, no two ways about it. Ten years ago they only talked about Film and Poetry International. Today, in 1988, festivals are the order of the day.' They certainly were: by then Rotterdam had a Summer Carnival (since 1984); Celluloid Rock, a film music festival (since 1987); an Afro-Caribbean festival; Teatro Fantastico, a theatre festival (since 1987); a 'romantic music day' (since 1987); the Poetry Park Festival (since 1977); the Heineken Jazz Festival (since 1984); the Theater Festival; and many smaller festivals besides.[52] The members of the creative class responsible for all this shared the ideal that the received qualities of Rotterdam could be brought out better. Although they took the DIY mentality as their frame of reference, they did collaborate with the council and municipal bodies yet this was almost always informally or semi-officially. I have already referred to the 'underground' role filled by alderman Riezenkamp. Carel Alons, director of the Rotterdam Theatre or Stadschouwburg, was another to enjoy informal contact with some members of the network of cultural entrepreneurs, which resulted in concrete plans. Teatro Fantastico and Floor theatre café were both the result of brainstorming sessions with Beerend Lenstra and Daan van der Have.[53] All those involved describe it as an open network; anyone with good ideas could plug into it, as long as Rotterdam's interests were uppermost.

The magic fades: Rotterdam 1990

It is all the more remarkable, then, that the 1980s closed with a festival that was a failure in almost every respect. This was 'Rotterdam 1990', organized to mark the city's first 650 years. It should have ended that decade with a bang but it became a fiasco of stupendous proportions. The level of underachievement among its organizers was so serious that the council commissioned an independent investigation into the state of affairs. Published in the beginning of 1991, the resulting research report focused most firmly on the blunders committed by the council when organizing this festival. It failed to mention by name one of the most fundamental causes of the debacle, namely that when organizing Rotterdam 1990 little if any use was made of the expertise evident in the city. Instead the council took control of all aspects – ideas, planning, organization and promotion.

According to the author of the report, Anton Zijderveld, it was all wrong from the start; '(a) the plans failed to mesh, (b) they revealed a level of ambition that was unrealistic in financial terms let alone any other, (c) they took little account of the time factor, that is, with the fact that 1990 was not far off.'[54] A foundation,

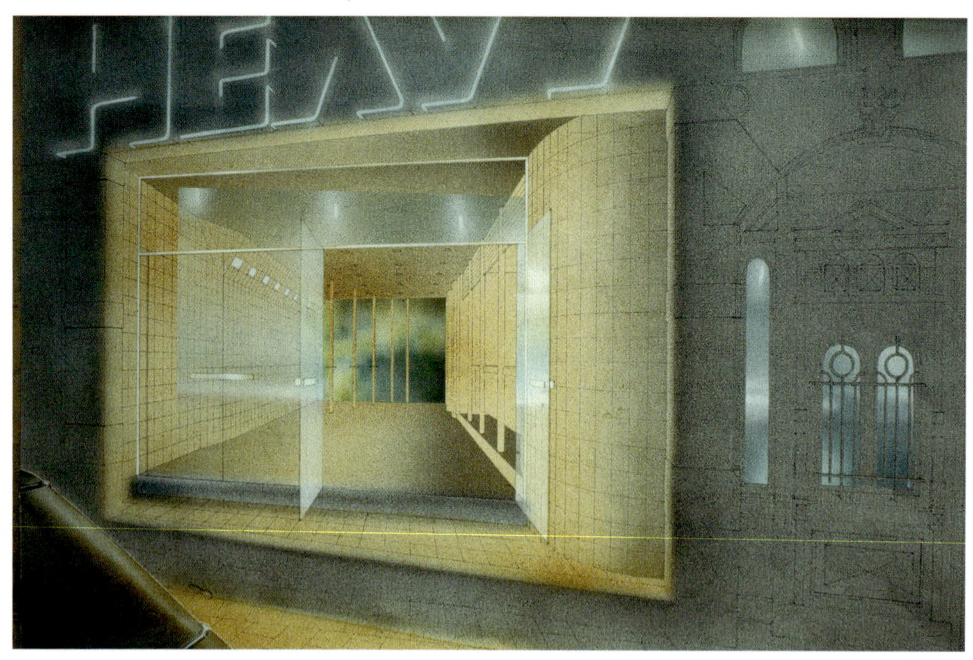

Design proposal for the night-time café Heavy, design by BOA Contractors (Viktor Mani and Chiel van der Stelt), 1981, unexecuted. During the day Heavy was an alley linking 's-Gravendijkwal with the garden of Dizzy, the café next door. Closed off with metal roller shutters during the day, the bar in the side wall opened at night so that the alley became a café.

Stichting Rotterdam 1990, was set up to organize the festival, but Zijderveld points out that this foundation could scarcely act independently of the local council as the foundation's board of directors was chaired by the mayor and included the council secretary and an alderman among its number. Not just that, the head of the council's External Relations department, Kees Bode, who on paper had only one medium-sized project under his belt, made the entire festival so much his concern that many had the impression that he was far more responsible than was actually the case. Or, as Zijderveld puts it: '(...) informally and as the mayor's right-hand man the head [of ER] was everywhere at all times!'[55] Unfortunately Bode could talk of nothing else than the 'un-Dutch air' the festival should have, yet according to Zijderveld his plans were invariably variations on the same theme and highly unrealistic to boot.[56] All the same, Zijderveld places the ultimate responsibility with the mayor, Bram Peper, who in his double role of mayor and chairman of the foundation's board of directors, should have trimmed the controls of his head of External Relations. That he failed in this was held against him in the report, as was the failure to communicate adequately how Rotterdam 1990 was organized and how it was progressing. According to Zijderveld he was so wrapped up in the hassles dogging Rotterdam 1990 that the council came to regard the festival as the 'mayor's party'.[57] In mid 1990, the council made one last effort to make the best of a bad job with an additional financial injection of almost a million guilders, but even this failed to prevent what was to have been the festival's major crowd-puller, the Rivoli mega-fair on Müllerpier, from closing prematurely. Zijderveld's report contains humiliating stories about parts of the festival programme on that pier that were opened by the mayor to 'an almost empty room'.[58]

Meanwhile Rotterdam's creative class looked on despairingly at the succession of blunders perpetrated with a budget many times greater than the ones they themselves were used to. Beerend Lenstra recalls how he and the director of the Mojo concert agency were there when the mayor announced the planned performance by The Rolling Stones too early, which effectively put paid to it: 'Bram Peper announced that the Stones were coming while I was sitting there with the director of Mojo. We looked at each other and knew: they won't be coming now. You have to keep that kind of thing secret until it's absolutely certain. The Stones were planned as part of the programme for 1990, but when the mayor announces it in public when the negotiations are still in full swing, with a group of that calibre it's just not done, I should say not, it stops there and then as basically there's nothing left to negotiate. And that's it, end of story. And the whole year was like that. An embarrassing business all round.'[59] For Beerend Lenstra, Rotterdam 1990 was a reason to stop organizing Teatro Fantastico, the successful theatre festival in tents that he had helped launch and whose director he had by now become. More than ten years and many successful events later, he is still seething: 'I do see 1990 as a turning point (...). Because I was so angry with the council for the way it had all gone, I grabbed the opportunity to get out of the city for a time; that was the year I said I was leaving Fantastico and the best of luck. It lasted one more year and that was the last of it. It's still a shame, but every time there was all that work getting the money organized, and of course it's really frustrating when on the other hand you just see the council frittering away at least 60 million in a single year.'[60] Lenstra explains the fact that the organizers of Rotterdam 1990 passed over the city's pool of talent as follows: 'That's civil servants all over, they think "this looks fun, I can earn something out of this" and then trot out their own plans along the lines of "we can do that too".'[61] Daan van der Have had the same experience, that there are times when officials enter into competition, so to speak, with private entrepreneurs.[62] For the record, Lenstra himself organized various large-scale events for the council later in the 1990s, such as the opening of the Erasmus Bridge in 1996 and the reception for President Clinton in 1997.

Even in the face of an economic recession, Rotterdam enjoyed many enchanted years long before the so-called magical year of 1987. That magic was largely owed to an enterprising and resourceful group of artists, architects and entrepreneurs who worked together and were inspired by one another. Yet when preparations began on Rotterdam 1990, a major celebration of their city, their talents were largely overlooked. The findings of the independent commission into the failure of Rotterdam 1990 meant that it was the mayor and his cronies whose reputations suffered most. The image of the city as a whole, however, was able to take a few knocks at the time. These were also Kees Bode's sentiments in an interview of some years later, looking back on what went wrong in that disastrous year of 1990: 'Let's say that 1990 was an incident, a ripple, a huge ripple perhaps, for myself and a number of others, but it had no effect on Rotterdam's development as a whole. It gave the municipal council some negative publicity, those "stupid" officials, but not the city. No-one says that nothing ever happens in Rotterdam and that 1990 is evidence of this.' When going on to name the issues of real importance for the public's image of Rotterdam, he implicitly pays a compliment to Rotterdam's creative class: 'But Rotterdam at that time had already made its mark with those festivals, with the new buildings, with the fact that we were getting the architecture institute and the Kunsthal. Thank goodness you couldn't take those achievements away. Otherwise 1990 would really have been a hard pill to swallow.'[63] It was not only the festivals, then, but also the 'new buildings' – no doubt a reference to Rotterdam's burgeoning reputation as a city of architecture – and the forthcoming architecture institute that can in large measure be traced back to the actions of members of that same creative network.

It is no accident that the likes of Beerend Lenstra, Daan van der Have, Adriaan van der Staay and the members of Hard Werken and Utopia furthered their own cause in Rotterdam and not in another Dutch city. Almost every member of the city's creative class chose to set up practice in Rotterdam, the country's second largest city. Given their predilection for metropolitanism, it is remarkable that they failed to choose the largest city in the Netherlands, Amsterdam. The following chapter will chart the deliberations and sensitivities underlying this decision.

1 Zundert, A. van (1988), *Wie verhuist er naar Rotterdam? Analyse van de binnenlandse vestiging*, Rotterdam: Gemeentelijk Bureau voor Onderzoek en Statistiek, unpaged. The survey was conducted using the stratified sampling method. The total net response was 900.
2 Jobse, R.B., H.M. Kruythoff et al. (1990), *Stadsgewesten in beweging: Migratie naar en uit de vier grote steden*, Utrecht: Rijksuniversiteit Utrecht/ Delft: Technische Universiteit Delft/Amsterdam: Universiteit van Amsterdam, p. 119.
3 Van Zundert (1988), op. cit. (note 1).
4 Straasheijm, W. & S. Buijs (1987), *Vernieuwing van Rotterdam*, Rotterdam: Gemeente Rotterdam, college van burgemeester en wethouders, p. 23.
5 Unless stated otherwise, all the following information and quotes come from an interview by the author with Hans Oldewarris, March 31, 2003.
6 Provoost, M. (1991), 'Het DWL-terrein op de driesprong', in: H. Berens & D. Camp (eds), *DWL-terrein Rotterdam*, Rotterdam: 010 Publishers, pp. 32-39.
7 Author's interview with Jan Riezenkamp, March 2, 2004.
8 For this see various items in the private archive of Hans Oldewarris.
9 Verhelst, M. et al. (eds) (2001), *Agora: Tijdschrift voor sociaal-ruimtelijke vraagstukken*, theme issue on 'free states', 17 (4). Utrecht: Stichting Tijdschrift Agora.
10 Author's interview with Jan Riezenkamp, March 2, 2004.
11 Riezenkamp, J. (1978), *Kunstbeleid in Rotterdam: Deel 1: persoonlijke beschouwingen*, Rotterdam; Riezenkamp, J. (1978), *Kunstbeleid in Rotterdam deelnota: beeldende kunst*, Rotterdam: Gemeentedrukkerij Rotterdam.
12 The founders of Utopia were, in alphabetical order, Jean-Paul Birkhof, Willem Broer, Carla Carlier, Constance van Duinen, Viktor Mani, Hans Mesman, Hans Oldewarris, Viola van Oostrom, Jos Sterenborg, Hans Werlemann, Tineke Werlemann and Peter de Winter. Three of them – Willem Broer, Carla Carlier and Jos Sterenborg – withdrew before Utopia made its home in the tower; Tineke Werlemann did move into the tower (together with her husband Hans) but never became a member of Utopia. The initial group in fact consisted of the following eight people (in alphabetical order): Jean-Paul Birkhof, psychologist from Amsterdam; Constance van Duinen, fashion designer from Delft; Viktor Mani, architect from Rotterdam; Hans Mesman, architect and sound engineer from Delft; Hans Oldewarris, architect from Rotterdam; Viola van Oostrom, textile designer from Rotterdam; Hans Werlemann, photographer from The Hague; and Peter de Winter, urban designer from Delft. This initial group was soon expanded with new members: Haiko Dragstra, mechanical engineer from Delft; Cor van der Hout, carpenter from The Hague; Reinout Meltzer, industrial designer from Delft; Chiel van der Stelt, architect from Delft; Onno van Wijk, computer technician from Delft; and a few months later James Rubery, audiovisual technician from Rotterdam.
13 Told to the author by Hans Oldewarris.
14 For the history of 010 see: Oldewarris, H. & P. de Winter (eds) (2003), *20 jaar/years 010 1983–2003*, Rotterdam: 010 Publishers.
15 See Jagt, E. van der (2000), 'Kunst en Vaarwerk (1978–heden)', in: P. van Ulzen (ed.), *90 over 80: Tien jaar beeldende kunst in Rotterdam: De dingen, de mensen, de plekken*, Rotterdam: NAi Uitgevers/Stichting Kunstpublicaties Rotterdam, pp. 96-97.
16 Utopia Contractors, minutes of a meeting held on Jan 28, 1978, Hans Oldewarris archive, and author's interview with Hans Oldewarris, March 31, 2003.
17 An invoice sent by J.A. Oldewarris to Grafisch Ontwerpbureau Meltzer, 01-11-1979, for working drawings for a port policy document, Hans Oldewarris archive; Riezenkamp, J. [1979], *Havennota* [unplaced].
18 Author's interview with Henk Molenaar, February 27, 2004.
19 Dienst Gemeentelijke Kunstgebouwen and Stichting Kunst Accommodatie Rotterdam respectively. Author's interview with Jan Riezenkamp, March 2, 2004. See also Balvert, F. (2000), 'Ateliersituatie', in: P. van Ulzen (ed.), *90 over 80: Tien jaar beeldende kunst in Rotterdam: De dingen, de mensen, de plekken*, Rotterdam: NAi Uitgevers/Stichting Kunstpublicaties Rotterdam, pp. 24-25.

20 Brochure Ponton 010, black and white copies, typed, unpaged, Hans Oldewarris archive; author's interview with Hans Oldewarris, March 31, 2003.

21 Copy of a newspaper cutting, '"Ponton 010": drijvende tribune aan de parkkade', *Rotterdams Nieuwsblad*, May 20, 1980, Hans Oldewarris archive.

22 *Hard Werken*, 7 (May-June), Rotterdam: Hard Werken.

23 Although Ponton 010 made no further voyages after 1980, the project has a heroic reputation. For example, during the 'diners pensants' organized by urban designer Riek Bakker on the occasion of the Rotterdam-Maaskant Prize awarded to her in 1994, Ponton 10 was described as a 'successful project' in the category 'miscellaneous', alongside projects granted a much longer life such as Hotel New York and the ship *De Maze*. Bakker, R. (1994), *Ruimte voor verbeelding*, Rotterdam: 010 Publishers/Stichting Rotterdam-Maaskant, p. 148.

24 Author's interview with Ted Langenbach, November 7, 2003.

25 Festivals Lenstra was involved in setting up and/or organizing include Rotterdam New Pop Festival, Sunday afternoons in Het Park, Poetry Park Festival, Film International, Teatro Fantastico, the Heineken Jazz Festival, the Antillean Summer Carnival, and Boulevard of Broken Dreams; Beerend Lenstra's CV, Beerend Lenstra archive.

26 For an analysis of the port's nostalgic or romantic image see: Klamer, A. & D. Kombrink (2004), *Het verhaal van de Rotterdamse haven: Een narratieve analyse*, Rotterdam: Stichting Economie & Cultuur.

27 Kok, J., 'Ponton 010 wil haven bij bevolking brengen: Eerste afvaart vrijdag 13 juni a.s.', *Het Zuiden*, June 11, 1980.

28 *Hard Werken*, op. cit. (note 22), p. 36.

29 *Eigen Huis & Interieur*, September 1999, Hoofddorp: VNU, p. 58.

30 Crimson, P. Gadanho et al. (eds) (2001), *Post.Rotterdam: Architecture and City after the tabula rasa/Arquitectura e Cidade após a tabula rasa*, Rotterdam: 010 Publishers, p. 68.

31 Nieuwstadt, M. van, '24 uur in Rotterdam', *NRC Handelsblad*, July 20/21, 2002.

32 This discourse has remained uppermost to this day. Take the debate on Rotterdam as a creative city held on February 24, 2005 at the instigation of Café De Unie in Rotterdam, whose participants included the councillors for culture in Rotterdam (Stefan Hulman) and Amsterdam (Frits Huffnagel). Port city and creative city were treated in this discussion as mutually exclusive phenomena, even though practice has shown that 'creative types' appreciate Rotterdam precisely because it is a port city. The same sentiment reared its head again during the closing discussion of the international conference 'CityLive2005conference, Hart voor Rotterdam', November 11, 2005, Rotterdam. One of the panellists, Jean Baptiste Benraad, director of a Rotterdam housing corporation, suggested that Rotterdam's reputation as a non-creative city rests on its image as a city of work and port activity. As he put it, 'It was always the harbour, that's something we have to shake off'.

33 Laar, P. van de (2000), *Stad van formaat. Geschiedenis van Rotterdam in de negentiende en twintigste eeuw*, Zwolle: Waanders, p. 589. See also Laar, P.T. van de (1998), *Veranderingen in het geschiedbeeld van de koopstad Rotterdam*, Rotterdam [: the author], p. 3.

34 Frijhoff, W. (1993), 'Beelden, verhalen, daden: stadscultuur', in: A.D. de Jonge & M.D. de Wolff (eds), *De Rotterdamse cultuur in elf spiegels*, Rotterdam: 010 Publishers, pp. 9-18 (pp. 16, 12).

35 Frijhoff (1993), op. cit. (note 34), pp. 9-18 (p. 17).

36 Aalst, I. van (1997), *Cultuur in de stad: Over de rol van culturele voorzieningen in de ontwikkeling van stadscentra*, Utrecht: Jan van Arkel, p. 188.

37 Author's interview with Hans Oldewarris, March 31, 2003.

38 *Hard Werken*, op. cit. (note 22), p. 36.

39 Opening of Lijnbaancentrum Rotterdam on Friday, December 12, 1980 at 20.30, copy of the invitation in Hans Oldewarris archive.

40 Wissing, S. (1982), 'OMA', *Hard Werken*, (1982) 10, pp. 42-47.

41 'Lux super luxe', *Rotterdams Nieuwsblad*, November 12, 1984.

42 Roer, R. van de, 'Ontbijten met opera', *NRC Handelsblad*, November 7, 1986.

43 'Neon en roestvrij staal verdringen de bruine kroeg', *Het Vrije Volk*, June 14, 1986.

44 ibid.

45 ibid.

46 Halbertsma, M. & P. van Ulzen (eds) (2001), *Interbellum Rotterdam: Kunst en cultuur 1918–1940*, Rotterdam: NAi Uitgevers.

47 According to a letter sent to the author by M.J. Toet, director of operations relating to the Social Assistance Act (Abw) of the Department of Social

Affairs and Employment Agency of Rotterdam City
Council, dated April 8, 2003, this ruling was a form of
'*gedoogbeleid*' (a policy of condoning violations) and
had 'no basis in law and legislation'. Toet called the ruling 'the so-called Haarlem model' whose core was that
artists were to be treated as an exception. I know from
my own experience however that non-artistic, one-
person professions were also admitted to the ruling.
The Rotterdam artist and former artists' gallery coordi-
nator Enno de Kroon claims in a personal, unpublished
document of February 17-21, 1999 that the ruling had
been devised not in Haarlem but in Rotterdam: 'For the
first time the BKR [the 'one per cent of building costs for
art' scheme] had been dispensed with, and something
had to be done with the vast stock of artists; in
Rotterdam you could be counselled by the "self-employ-
ment agency" of SoZaWe [Social Affairs and Employment]
which in the first instance had no experience at all in
dealing with artists but had mainly applied themselves
to these matters at the instigation of Hanneke van der
Grienten. A policy was developed in Rotterdam that
would later become famous as "the Rotterdam model".
It entailed that young artists would be given the opportunity to work 20 hours a week on their art and for the
remaining time make themselves available for "wage
employment". On top of that, being self-employed they
had to invest the profits from sales in their career,
enabling them to buy materials and develop their skills
further. This "Rotterdam model" was developed by
Hanneke van der Griendt but it had no real legal basis.'
48 Jagt, E. van der (2000), 'Kunstenaarsinitiatieven',
in: P. van Ulzen (ed.), *90 over 80: Tien jaar beeldende
kunst in Rotterdam: De dingen, de mensen, de plekken*,
pp. 100-101.

49 Van de Roer, op. cit. (note 42).
50 Author's interview with Daan van der Have,
January 14, 2003.
51 To be precise: the refurbished Dizzy (1982); Lux
(1983); Zochers (1986); De Unie (1986); Loos (1988);
Floor (1988); Hotel New York (1993); Westerpaviljoen
(1993). With thanks to Lenie de Jager.
52 Information derived for the most part from
Beerend Lenstra's CV, Beerend Lenstra archive, and
partly from: *Magazijn: Cultureel Maandblad voor
Rotterdam*, no. 171 (January-December 1988),
Rotterdam: Rotterdamse Kunststichting/Stichting
Kunstzinnige Vorming Rotterdam, p. 4; Hagendijk, W.
(1994), *10 jaar zomercarnaval Rotterdam*, Rotterdam:
Museum van Volkenkunde/Van de Rhee.
53 Author's interviews with Beerend Lenstra, May 19,
2003, and Carel Alons, January 15, 2004.
54 Zijderveld, A.C. (1991), *Rotterdam 1990: Analyse en
evaluatie van de bestuurlijke gang van zaken*,
Rotterdam, p. 11.
55 Zijderveld (1991), op. cit. (note 54), p. 26.
56 Zijderveld (1991), op. cit. (note 54), pp. 26-27.
57 Zijderveld (1991), op. cit. (note 54), p. 23.
58 Zijderveld (1991), op. cit. (note 54), p. 25.
59 Author's interview with Beerend Lenstra, May 19,
2003.
60 idem.
61 idem.
62 Author's interview with Daan van der Have,
January 14, 2003.
63 Bakkes, J., et al. (eds) (1996), *De stad aan de man
gebracht: Vijftig jaar gemeentevoorlichting in
Rotterdam*, Rotterdam: Voorlichting Bestuursdienst
Rotterdam, p. 120.

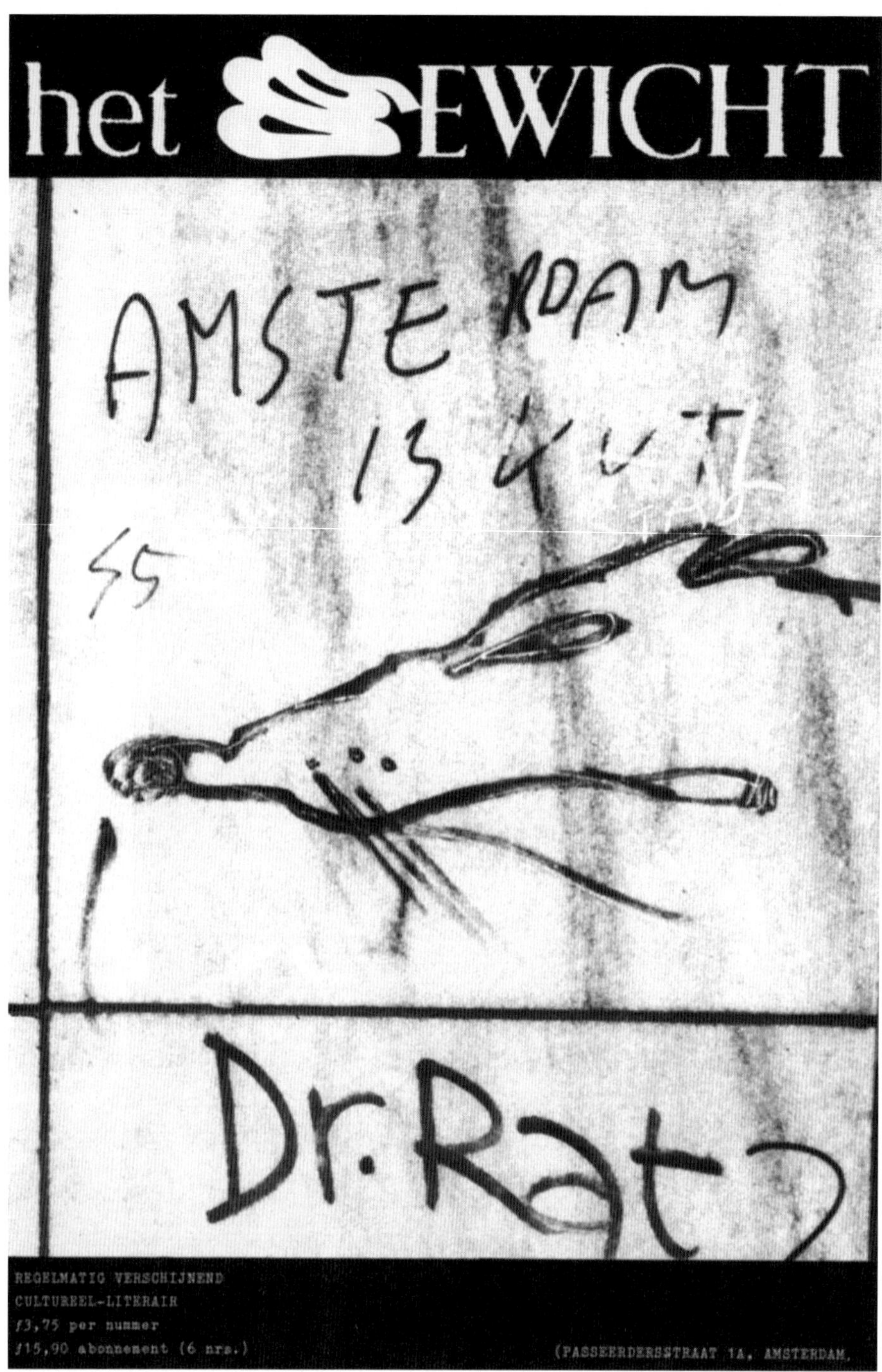

Advertisement for the magazine *het Gewicht* including the graffiti text 'Amsterdam is kut' (Amsterdam is shit), from *Hard Werken* no, 2, May 1979.

CHAPTER 6

The wasteland versus the womb. Why some artists and cultural entrepreneurs choose Rotterdam above Amsterdam

Many artists, architects, designers and others active in Rotterdam's cultural domain, have deliberately opted to live and work in this city. They like the metropolitan air, the space, the openness, the dynamism, the rationality, the modernity – in short, the hallmarks that have typified Rotterdam since the period between the two wars. To press home their argument in favour of Rotterdam, the name of the Netherlands' capital and largest city, Amsterdam, crops up with remarkable regularity. Amsterdam is then described as the absolute opposite of Rotterdam – provincial, oppressive, introverted, drowsy, dreamy and old-fashioned. By describing Amsterdam in these terms, the listed qualities of Rotterdam take on an even more positive air. This polarization between the two cities is no mere rhetoric: for many members of Rotterdam's creative class it is founded on fact. They go on to brand the inhabitants of the two cities as opposites: Amsterdammers are arrogant, Rotterdammers modest, Rotterdammers work hard, Amsterdammers just talk, Rotterdammers like to work together, Amsterdammers are competitive, and so on.

Just how much of all this is true is less important than the fact that creative people evidently are influenced by stereotypes when choosing a city. And it is by no means only smaller fry who see the two cities this way. The international starchitect Rem Koolhaas has repeatedly spoken out on Amsterdam in the most negative terms, clichés and all. He rails against the city's inward gaze and the conservatism he sees as uppermost there.[1] He later described his reasons for choosing Rotterdam when opening a Dutch office for his architecture firm in 1978 (there was already an office in London) in the following terms: '(...) when I first came [back] to Holland I was confronted with the choice of where to open an office. In Amsterdam or in Rotterdam. I had spent most of my time in Holland in Amsterdam and I really didn't like Amsterdam. I think Amsterdam is too claustrophobic, you are always turning in circles. I didn't know Rotterdam very well, but I was aware that it was a kind of fairly formless city. And I had an instinct that there was an emerging culture and that, at the same time, it was pretty much a wasteland.'[2] Koolhaas says this in a book from 2001 about Rotterdam's architecture firms. Other architects besides Koolhaas explain in the book why they are domiciled in Rotterdam. Remarkably, four of the nine explanations include an argument based on a comparison with Amsterdam. Keep in mind that the interviewer doesn't even mention the word Amsterdam in his brief question 'Why Rotterdam?'. Willem Jan Neutelings of Neutelings Riedijk Architects praises the slogger's mentality of Rotterdam, pitting Amsterdam against it as a leisure city: '(...) Amsterdam is really a city for culture, leisure and tourism. Rotterdam is really known as a city of workers, related to the harbour. So, this particular atmosphere, which is rougher on the level of architecture, but also on the level of the people, makes it a very pleasant, inspiring city to work in.'[3] Erick van Egeraat mentions other stereotypical oppositions, namely the international, liberal mentality that is said to prevail in Rotterdam as against the more crystallized and therefore more hardened culture of Amsterdam: '(...) when I moved to Rotterdam [from Delft in 1995]... to have a sign on a billboard announcing my work and it says my name and the word Rotterdam after, suddenly makes things, let's say international, let's say airy, spacy. Completely opposite to what Amsterdam does. To me Amsterdam is very much a city which is cultural, but it is also a city with a lot of opinions... Rotterdam has this very open minded kind of approach...'.[4]

Amsterdam proved to be an inevitable topic during the interviews I conducted for this book as well. Almost everyone I interviewed launched spontaneously into the subject of Amsterdam.[5] After rolling out the familiar clichés, they added when pressed that all clichés about both cities are true. The following potted selection is representative. Ted Langenbach, director of the Rotterdam club Now & Wow since 2001 and an organizer of dance parties since the 1980s, finds Amsterdam 'oppressive'. Hans Oldewarris describes Amsterdam as 'self-satisfied', 'provincial' and 'given to navel-gazing'. Jacques van Heijningen, director of the Rotterdam Film Fund, refers contemptuously to the creative Amsterdammers who can't survive without the 'placenta that is Amsterdam' and the 'womb feeling' the city gives. He has more respect for artists and cultural entrepreneurs who visit the 'wasteland' of Rotterdam. In Amsterdam they spout too much 'hot air'. Bob Visser is another with no time for the Amsterdam artist scene, which he encountered from the inside when making a television programme with the Amsterdam writer and television presenter Boudewijn Büch. What irked him most was how little contact there was with people outside your circle and that you measured your achievements against the judgement of the others in that circle. Beerend Lenstra regards working in Amsterdam as 'a disaster'. He explains: 'Amsterdam is pretty slow on the uptake when it comes to events and development, (...) it's half-baked and lethargic.' Curiously, interviewees one would have expected to have a more balanced view of the two cities, having lived or worked in both, endorse the stereotypes with as much conviction. Former Rotterdam alderman Jan Riezenkamp, who owns a house in both cities, considers Amsterdam to be 'more provincial' than Rotterdam: 'Because you only have to leave your front door and the whole village is out there in the square to greet you. In Rotterdam you melt into the crowd. The concentration of people in the artistic sector, or who think they're in it, is much greater in Amsterdam, so it all clings together more and to my mind is less open. Here in Rotterdam it's so spread throughout the city that (...) it's much more diluted. And so you have more space for individuality as an artist, you can do far more without everyone watching your every move.' A statement made in 1986 by Gerard Hadders, one of the Hard Werken designers, bears out Riezenkamp's perspective: 'But then this needs to be said too: I think it's extremely important for us that we're based in Rotterdam. We can do our own thing here in a way. I mean there isn't some designer behind every lamp post who's either your friend or your enemy, which is how it is in Amsterdam.'[6] When Adriaan van der Staay began working in Rotterdam in 1968 he was in a good position to compare the two cities, as he knew many people from Amsterdam's cultural field and had been involved in launching the Sigma Centre, which later spawned the Paradiso and Melkweg music venues. The conclusion drawn from these experiences was: 'I could never have worked in Amsterdam. (...) They did a lot of talking there but nothing got done, one council report after the other, (...) officialdom in Amsterdam tended towards writing exceedingly many reports and doing exceedingly little.' Against that, the mentality in Rotterdam is, in the words of Hans Oldewarris, 'shut up and get on with it, a typical Rotterdam cliché that really is true'.

Jules Deelder, the self-styled 'Night Mayor of Rotterdam', has even made the opposition between Rotterdam and Amsterdam part of his identity. His success as the personification of Rotterdam is in large measure due to the exaggerated aversion to Amsterdam which he flaunts at the drop of a hat. Deelder takes every available opportunity to make Amsterdam look ridiculous. When presenting an instalment of the television programme *Neon* from Dam Square in Amsterdam, he began as follows: 'We're now in the tragic centre, also known as Amsterdam', sending

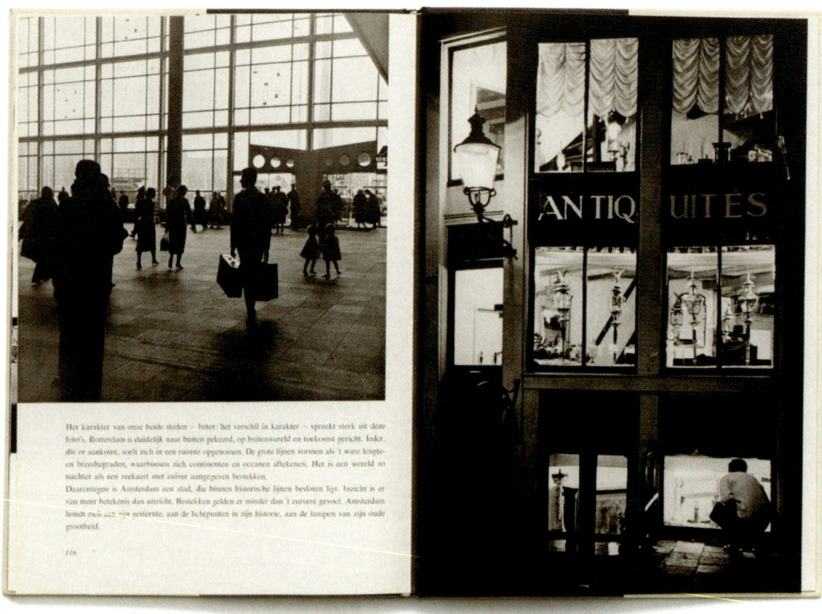

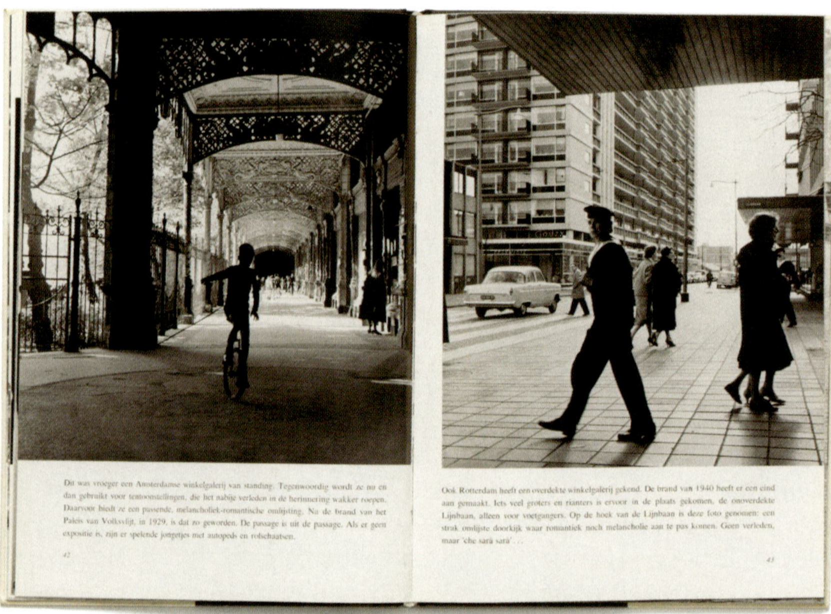

Pages of photos of Rotterdam and Amsterdam from Aart Klein (photos) and Herman Besselaar (text), *Amsterdam-Rotterdam, Twee steden rapsodie*, Baarn [1959].

Top left Rotterdam Central Station; **right** an antique shop on the Singel in Amsterdam.

Bottom left gallery behind the former Palace of Industry in Amsterdam; **right** the Lijnbaan in Rotterdam.

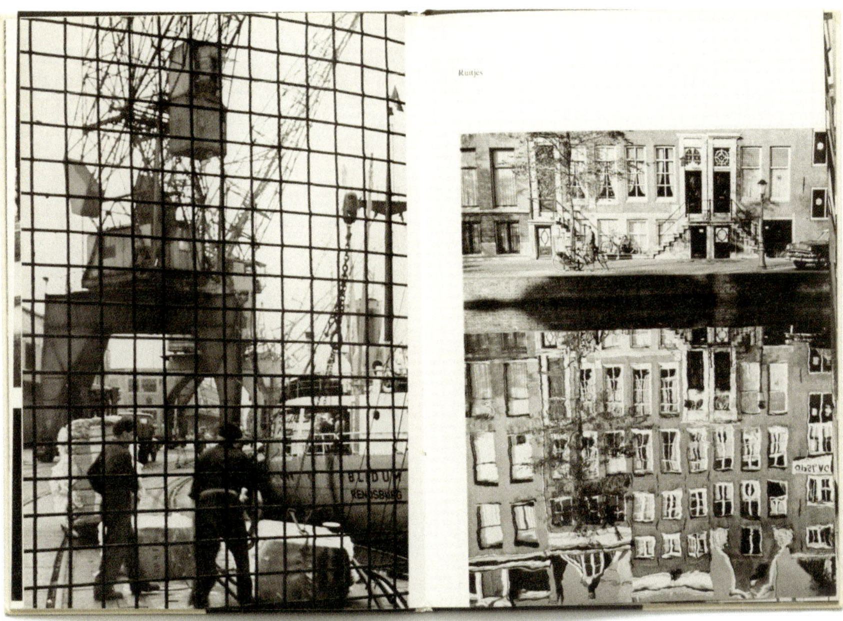

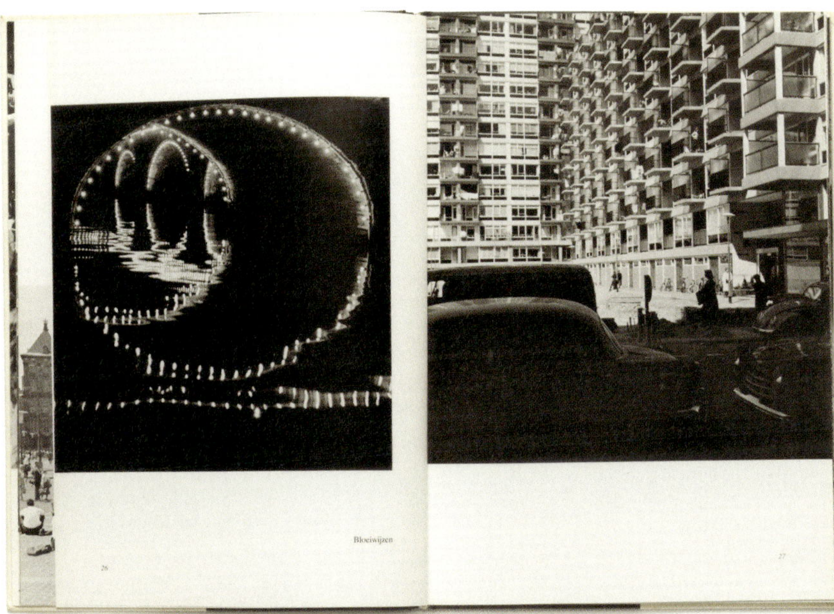

Top left a quayside in Katendrecht, Rotterdam; **right** Prinsengracht in Amsterdam.

Bottom left festive lighting on Reguliersgracht in Amsterdam; **right** a block of flats along the Lijnbaan in Rotterdam.

up the honorary title of 'magic centre' which Amsterdam had borne with pride since
the turbulent Sixties.[7] In the same programme he declared that the undeniably
phallic National Monument in Dam Square, 'or the prick of Amsterdam', should be
stashed away in 'the prick of Rotterdam', the Euromast, 'which of course is much
longer'. The rivalry between Rotterdam and Amsterdam also keeps cropping up in
his poetry and prose, explicitly and very much to the point at times, as in the
following poem:

Not that I've anything	Niet dat ik wat tegen
against Amsterdammers	Amsterdammers heb
Quite the contrary	Integendeel
they're decent folk	't Zijn beste mensen
They have a good heart	Ze hebben een goed hart
Only it should be cooked	't Moest alleen gekóókt
and hung on their back	op hun rug hangen
(nice and low so that	(en dan zo laag dat
the dogs can get at it)[8]	de honden erbij kennen)

and implicitly at other times, as in the first verse of *Rotown Magic*:

You can't pin Rotterdam down	Rotterdam is niet te filmen
The images change too fast	De beelden wisselen te snel
Rotterdam has no past,	Rotterdam heeft geen verleden
no stepped gables in town.[9]	en geen enkele trapgevèl.

On the face of it, it is astonishing that creative intellectuals feel the need to indulge
in clichés about Amsterdam and Rotterdam that scarcely rise above the level of
bar-room gossip. It makes more sense if we examine these clichés in another, less
tawdry light. The clichés refer to images of both cities and in the foregoing chapters
it transpired that artists and other cultural practitioners are those best equipped
to recognize these images and help give form to them. Seen in these terms, then, it
is not that surprising that precisely this creative elite steps off from clichés when
choosing between cities. They are pre-eminently sensitive to what Rolf Lindner has
called 'the urban imaginary'.[10] Already in chapter 1 we saw that the imaginary city
cannot simply be disposed of as not real or not true. It is an essential link in organizing the wealth of impressions got from the real city. But there is more to it than that.
The constantly reiterated verdicts on the assumed mentality of Amsterdammers

and Rotterdammers have the effect of a self-fulfilling prophecy. Those clichés attract a certain type of person to one of the two cities. These people warm to one another because of certain characteristics typical of Amsterdam or Rotterdam they themselves possess, whereas others at variance with these qualities have difficulty fitting in. This way we see reality accommodating itself to the stereotyped image! In the experience of Joop Linthorst, former alderman for the arts, such a self-regulating selection mechanism does exist in Rotterdam. Whenever there was a vacancy in local government, he could name beforehand those who would apply and those who would not: 'I sincerely believe there is a strongly selective element involved in shaping the cultural elite or upper crust, that the city chooses its own people who stay on or work here; I also noticed it in the selection procedures for jobs: you knew beforehand who would be in the market and who wouldn't.'[11]

In short, the supposed opposition between Amsterdam and Rotterdam is so persistent as to have real consequences for both cities. This has everything to do with the long history of polarization. The two cities have been compared ever since becoming first and second cities of the Netherlands in the 17th century. And the idea that Rotterdam might well knock Amsterdam off its throne has been around for just as long. In 1713, for example, Claas Bruin, an accountant by trade and a dramatist and poet by inclination who himself lived in Amsterdam, described in verse the strong competitive position occupied by the Rotterdam docks: 'O flourishing Rotterdam! O splendid monarch on the Maas! / Looking upon all fleets tacking to your harbours, / Out and in, with their trove from East, North, West: / here the Merchant can found his seat of trade, / Straightway in Gijsbrecht's Town [= Amsterdam], that Pearl upon the IJ, / Whom you with all your sea power all but surpass.'[12] That Amsterdam and Rotterdam were locked in this relationship of first and second cities for so long, explains in part the qualities attributed to them. Amsterdam can boast of an illustrious past and has done well in preserving the status quo. This explains the accusations of arrogance and circumspection levelled at it. Rotterdam by contrast, as second city has continually had to prove itself and as a result positively thrives on change. This explains the city's energetic, dynamic image. Rotterdam, in the words of an Italian visitor in the 1870s, 'undertakes like a young and adventurous city' whereas Amsterdam 'begins to doze over her treasures.'[13] In other words, Rotterdam shows great promise for the future, Amsterdam is the result of occurrences in the past. These are characteristics common to other first and second cities.[14] In the case of Amsterdam and Rotterdam this opposition is all the greater because of the contrast between the old heart of Amsterdam and Rotterdam's modern centre.

Forever locked in rivalry

The rivalry between Amsterdam and Rotterdam was economic to begin with. This aspect slipped into the background as the 20th century progressed. After the Second World War Rotterdam took on so much industry and its port grew so furiously that

Amsterdam was forced to acknowledge Rotterdam as its superior on the economic front. The struggle then spilled over into other channels including art and culture. Amsterdam was and is the cultural capital of the Netherlands but Rotterdam had ambitions of its own in that field, and still has. In the 1980s Rotterdam succeeded in collaring a number of key national cultural institutions. These days both cities are keen to attract and keep as many members as possible of the creative class. Since the American economist Richard Florida showed in his book of 2002, *The Rise of the Creative Class*, that the presence of the creative class – the term is his invention – is essential for the urban economy, Dutch municipal councils have become aware of the importance of inhabitants with a creative profession.[15] The TNO, the Netherlands Organization for Applied Scientific Research, drew attention to the presence in the first two Dutch cities – Amsterdam in 2004 and Rotterdam in 2005 – of a 'creative industry', explained in the resulting report as three sectors, firstly the arts, secondly media and entertainment and thirdly business services.[16] Predictably, Amsterdam came out of this flags flying as the most creative city in the Netherlands. Less predictably, and more than a little alarming for Amsterdam, the creative industry was seen to be growing faster in Rotterdam than in Amsterdam.[17] This fact is the latest breeze to fan the flames of the eternal rivalry between the two cities.

This rivalry has constantly shifted its focus in terms of city aspects over the years, but in effect it all boils down to jealousy on the part of the second city, which would love to be the first, and pride on the part of the first city, which intends to keep that position. Although Rotterdam overtook Amsterdam in the port city stakes more than a century ago, it rankles Amsterdam to this day. Very recently, in 2001, the Amsterdam docks were enlarged with the Ceres Paragon container terminal, suitable for handling the very largest sea containers. The City of Amsterdam invested 282 million guilders in the project.[18] But even when the first plans for this terminal became known back in 1999, the Netherlands Bureau for Economic Policy Analysis (CPB) and members of parliament expressed doubts as to the viability of an Amsterdam container terminal so close to the major container ports of Rotterdam and Antwerp.[19] These doubts proved well-founded, for the terminal lay idle for years, until mid 2005.[20] According to Henk Molenaar, former director of the Rotterdam Port Authority, the construction of the Amsterdam container terminal can only be understood in terms of the deep-seated rivalry with Rotterdam.[21] That powerful emotions were behind this seemingly rational, economic manoeuvre are made clear by the speech Mark van der Horst, then deputy mayor of Amsterdam, made on September 30, 2005 on the occasion of the signing of the first contract for the terminal. In it he called Amsterdam 'the port of all ports' and predicted that in ten years' time all negative publicity about the container terminal lying idle would be forgotten: '(…) I am full of admiration for the vision and the courage of my political predecessors and the councillors who had the nerve to make a decision that went way beyond "the next election". They must have thought: "Surely it cannot be true that Amsterdam, in historical terms the port of all ports, the port that can take the credit for the Golden Age, that this port is not going to take full advantage of the greatest logistic development in centuries?" (...) in ten years' time, it is not be the headlines of the past few years that will spring to people's minds; it will be the many ships that sail into port.'[22]

Rotterdam for its part refuses to accept that Amsterdam is the cultural and creative hub of the Netherlands. Since the 1980s Rotterdam has been whittling away at this seemingly unassailable position occupied by Amsterdam. The immediate cause was the plans of the Minister of Health, Welfare and Culture (WVC) to establish two new national cultural institutions, an architecture institute and a museum of photography. While Amsterdam as usual assumed that both would fall inside its own municipal boundaries to supplement the other state institutions in the city, Rotterdam ignored the status quo in cultural matters and claimed both the architecture institute and the museum of photography for itself. With success too. The following paragraphs relate how Rotterdam managed to pull this off.

The battle for the Netherlands Architecture Institute

In September 1983 minister Eelco Brinkman of WVC announced his intention to finance a national architecture museum.[23] It was to result from the fusion of three existing bodies concerned with researching and documenting architecture: Stichting Architectuur Museum (SAM), the Netherlands Documentation Centre for Architecture (NDB) and Stichting Wonen. As all three were then domiciled in Amsterdam, most parties involved assumed that this new museum would be sited in that city too. Not Rotterdam city council, however. It commissioned the Rotterdam Arts Council to examine the possibility of accommodating a national architecture museum in Rotterdam. In January 1984 the Arts Council presented a report which more or less claimed the architecture museum for Rotterdam.[24] It had three arguments for this claim: first, Rotterdam is under-endowed when it comes to state institutions – it doesn't even have one state museum; second, the architectural climate has been right for it since the beginning of the 20th century and particularly in recent years; and third, Rotterdam already has the premises for the new museum in the former building of the city's central public library. The council later commissioned Rem Koolhaas to design the modifications and enlargement for the library in readiness.[25] In the protracted and intensive public discussion that followed this report, it was the least concrete of the three arguments, namely the favourable architectural climate of Rotterdam, that figured most prominently. In justifying his decision in Rotterdam's favour when it came, minister Brinkman himself spoke highly of the city's vibrant climate in architectural terms. Clearly, Rotterdam had managed to exploit its reputation as 'city of architecture' to the full. The struggle between Amsterdam and Rotterdam for the architecture museum, then, was above all a tussle between those cities' images. Rotterdam, besides pursuing the shrewdest of tactics, could now reap the benefits of all those years of activity on the architectural front.

First off in its report, the Rotterdam Arts Council contended that an architecture *institute* rather than a museum was more suited to Rotterdam. There was a clear stance behind this choice of name: Rotterdam was not to approach architecture from a museological angle, the past was not merely to be preserved but would be placed in relation to the present and the future. This aspect was brought into sharper relief in the letter written by Arts Council director Paul Noorman to accompany the report sent to alderman Joop Linthorst. In it, Amsterdam was, or so it seemed, casually brushed off as a city whose architecture could only be approached historically: 'In Amsterdam with its illustrious history of architectural culture, this culture is mainly approached from an art-historical standpoint. In Rotterdam by contrast it is the coupling of history, the current state of play and the future that counts most. We feel it would be a good thing to stress this distinction in the College's continuing discussions with the Ministry of WVC.'[26] And indeed, the authorities lapped up this distinction, probably because it was in perfect keeping with the received picture of Amsterdam as city of the past and Rotterdam as city of the future. So inexorable was this opposition between the two cities in the discussion that at one point there were calls to divide the forthcoming institute into an Amsterdam department for the past and a Rotterdam department for the future![27] Many too adopted the idea of an institute rather than a museum, which implicitly gave to understand that the dispute had already been decided in Rotterdam's favour.

Rotterdam, city of architecture

Indeed, there was more going on architecturally in Rotterdam than in Amsterdam, simply because Rotterdam had plenty of space left over to build. But that was not the only reason why Rotterdam's architectural climate had such a good name. As we saw in chapter 2, since the inter-war years Rotterdam had been regarded as the pre-eminent modernist city, a reputation strengthened after the Second World War by the reconstruction of its centre in modernist style. So strong was Rotterdam's association with modernism that the term 'Rotterdam School' was raised as the opposite of the Amsterdam School, an architectural strand whose formal idiom was in many ways the antithesis of modernism.[28] The Rotterdam Arts Council's Architecture department, which had been active since 1974, had seen to it that Rotterdam's modernist past was back in the public eye. Exhibitions, talks and debates on Rotterdam's architecture were held and books on buildings from the inter-war years published, some including a card model.[29] But modernism had also regained a foothold in contemporary Rotterdam architecture. The first tangible evidence of this was the housing erected in 1980 on Kruisplein to a design by the fledgling architecture firm Mecanoo.[30] Before then, modernism had been taboo in the Netherlands after post-war districts such as Bijlmermeer had been branded as woeful errors. Mecanoo were the first to dare to apply modernism, in particular the principles of Le Corbusier, in housing and in a city centre. The architects succeeded in putting in place an appealing, trendy building that worked well. The design attracted much local attention, having originally been a competition entry, and was noticed by the professional press. Architecture critic Hans van Dijk regards 1980 as a turning-point for Rotterdam architecture thanks to this building: '(...) since 1980 [Rotterdam has been seeking] to reconnect (...) with its prewar reputation as a city of "modern" architecture'.[31] In the years that followed more and more modernist-style buildings sprang up in Rotterdam and other Dutch cities, this time with modernism as one possible architectural style among many and no longer the only true architecture as it had been in the 1920s. Architectural historians Ed Taverne and Cor Wagenaar see a general revival of interest in architecture at the start of the 1980s, and place Rotterdam at the cutting edge of this turn of events, particularly in terms of revivifying modernism: '(...) Dutch architecture embarked on a new lease of life with the city of Rotterdam in a vanguard position. With this renaissance came the persistent idea that Rotterdam was the cradle of architectural modernism, both before the war and during the post-war reconstruction. Hadn't Rotterdam always been a bastion of modernity?'[32]

As we have seen, a key tool in promoting Rotterdam as a bastion of modernism was the spate of publications issued by the Rotterdam Arts Council. It was Hans Oldewarris, architect and a co-founder of Utopia, who was responsible within the ranks of the Arts Council for producing and distributing these books. When the director of the RKS, Paul Noorman, made known at the end of 1982 his decision to abandon these publishing activities, Oldewarris decided to found an independent publishing house together with the urban designer and fellow Utopia founder Peter de Winter.[33] Taking the name 010, after the dialling code for Rotterdam, the firm made its home in the Utopia grounds. Since its inception 010 Publishers has specialized in books on urbanism, architecture and design. Since then too, 010 has worked as a promotion machine for Rotterdam. This can be gleaned from the subjects of its books, remarkably many of which have to do with Rotterdam – the Arts Council publications were also made part of its catalogue – but it is patently obvious from one of the first interviews with the two fledgling publishers that for them the driving force was to beef up the cultural climate of Rotterdam. Here again the rivalry with Amsterdam was immediately brought into play: 'Amsterdam has 180 publishers and Rotterdam about 18. That says a lot about how far behind we are here, and that something needs to be done about it.'[34]

This promotion of Rotterdam is also referred to by Taverne and Wagenaar in their essay on the history of 010 Publishers as an aspect most prominent in the firm's early years, most notably its promotion of Rotterdam as a city of modern architecture: '010 Publishers is one of the channels along which this definition (or redefinition) of Rotterdam as locus of modernity was elevated to a universal project.'[35] They name as an example a book from 1983 edited by S. Umberto Barbieri on architecture and planning in the Netherlands between 1940 and 1980[36]: 'Number one on the 010 catalogue shows most clearly the link between the promotion of Rotterdam as a

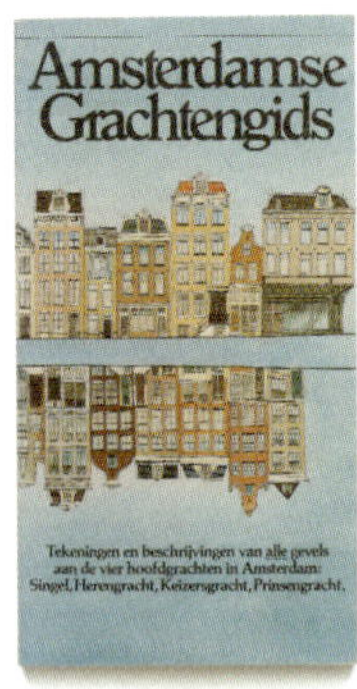

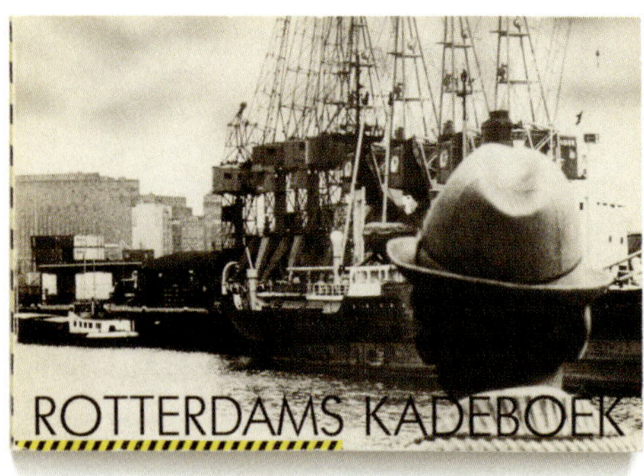

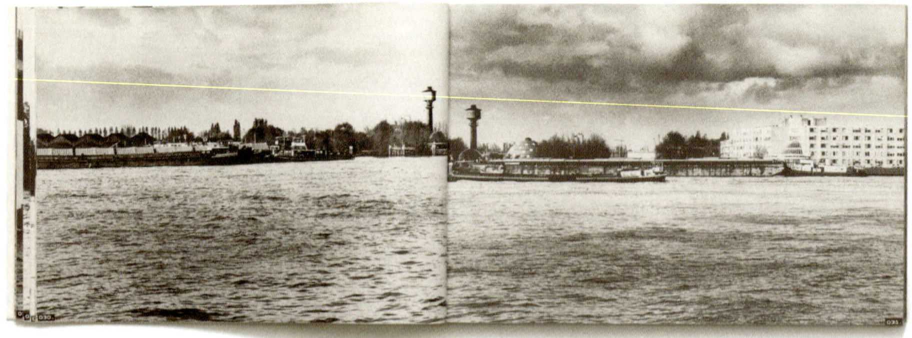

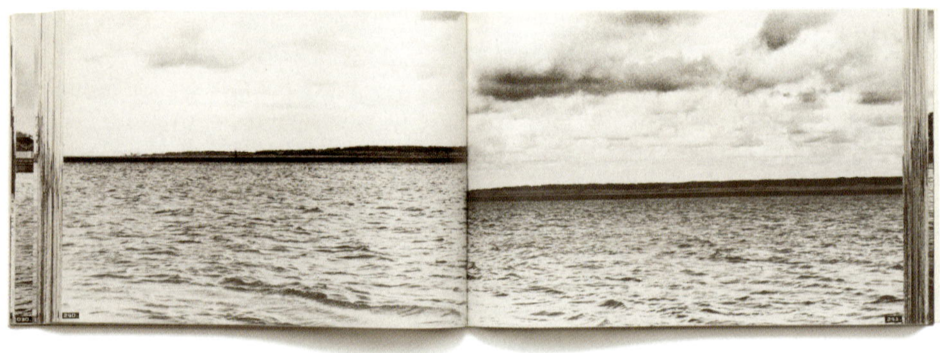

Top left *Amsterdamse Grachtengids*, Utrecht/Antwerp 1978.

Cover (top right) and pages from *Rotterdams kadeboek*, Rotterdam 1983, photos by Hans Werlemann and Alan David-Tu.

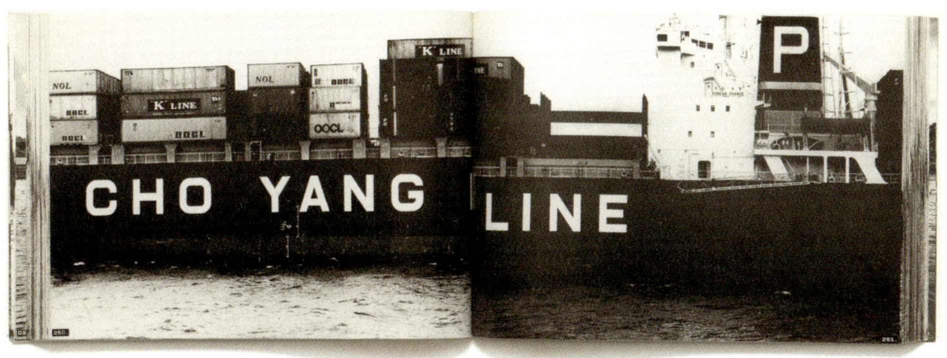

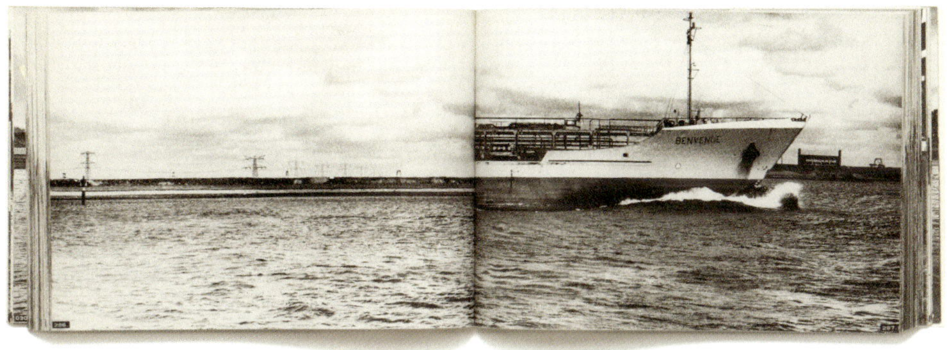

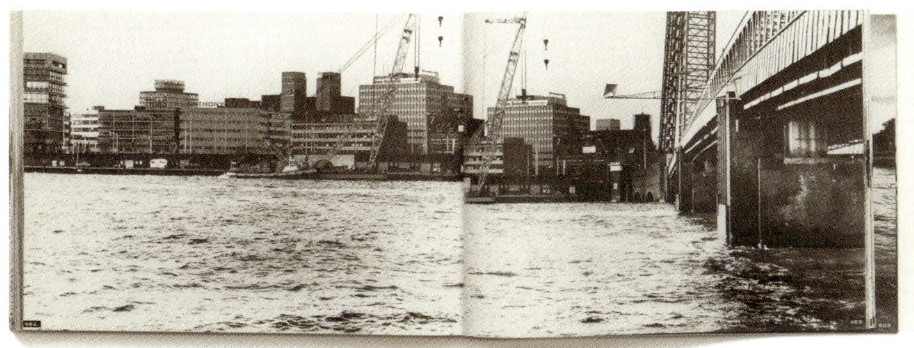

city of modern architecture and the emergence and coming into full flower of
010 Publishers.'[37] In this connection I would like also to draw attention to another
book from the publishing house's first year, a book that features Rotterdam less as a
city of architecture than as a modern, rational city, and as the antithesis of historical,
poetic Amsterdam. *Rotterdams kadeboek*[38] was designed to be that city's answer to
the original 18th-century 'Grachtenboek' featuring Amsterdam's canals.[39] If the
Grachtenboek contains copperplate etchings of 'all the houses and wonderful
buildings on the Keizersgracht and Herengracht in the city of Amsteldam [sic]',
Rotterdams kadeboek is a matter-of-fact report in 500 black-and-white photographs
on the two banks of the Maas, from the city of Rotterdam to where the river enters
the North Sea at Hoek van Holland. *Rotterdams kadeboek* can be regarded as a
statement about Rotterdam. It is an ode to spacious, open, rational, dynamic, modern,
'Great Rotterdam' – a total of 70 kilometres of quayside, Amsterdam eat your heart
out! – in short a paean to the image of Rotterdam fostered by many artists and cultural entrepreneurs.

A specialized and soon highly respected architectural publisher, new high-
profile architecture, the presence in the city of the renowned architect Rem Koolhaas[40]
not to forget a renewed awareness of Rotterdam's modernist architectural heritage:
all told, architecture was 'in the air' in Rotterdam. From the discussions round the
founding of the architecture institute it transpires that because of all these qualities,
Rotterdam's image as the number one city of modern architecture had become
generally accepted, all the way up to ministerial level. A noteworthy detail in this
respect is that the minister who ultimately decided that the architecture institute
should be based in Rotterdam, had written a foreword in the very first book from
010 Publishers.[41] There were unpleasant inferences that the minister was biased
and was not overly fond of Amsterdam.[42] Similarly, the director-general of Cultural
Affairs at the ministry, former Rotterdam alderman Jan Riezenkamp, was branded a
member of the Rotterdam camp because of his earlier dealings with Rotterdam.[43]

Pro-Amsterdam opinion leaders and those directly involved were shocked
by Rotterdam's claim on the architecture institute. Rational arguments against its
siting in Rotterdam alternated with hysterical threats. 'The choice of Rotterdam
would do irreparable damage to relations with the universities and relations in
Amsterdam'.[44] The Academy of Architecture in Amsterdam announced that it would
not be handing over documentation to Rotterdam, as such material would then be
inaccessible for academic research.[45] The Amsterdam daily *Het Parool* of December
11, 1984 reported that 'four famous Dutch architects or their descendants are considering withdrawing their archives if the Netherlands Institute for Architecture
and Urbanism is domiciled in Rotterdam'.[46]

After a year or so of speculations and heated discussion minister Brinkman
broke the news that the architecture institute was to be housed in Rotterdam. This
signalled a political victory for Rotterdam council but, more importantly, Rotterdam
had scored a major point against Amsterdam in the image stakes. Rotterdam

emerged from this symbolic struggle as the most modern, forward-looking and promising of the two cities, not least in the cultural field. Brinkman made known his decision on December 19, 1984 at the groundbreaking ceremony for the new city theatre (Rotterdamse Schouwburg). A photograph of the ceremony shows a laughing minister hobnobbing with the equally jovial alderman Joop Linthorst, both sporting hard hats, and the mayor Bram Peper. Visible in the photo is a billboard to be found at various places in Rotterdam at this time, bearing the words: 'Rotterdam makes it'. This slogan smacked of the rivalry with Amsterdam, being a riposte to the campaign to promote Amsterdam whose own slogan was 'Amsterdam has it'. The Netherlands Architecture Institute, as it would be called, in the end was not housed in the old library the council had made available for it free of charge but in a prestigious new building within a stone's throw of the Boijmans Van Beuningen Museum. The Amsterdam-based foundation Stichting Wonen had remained reluctant to hand over its collections if the new institute were to be housed in the converted Rotterdam library and made newly built premises a condition.[47] In a competition held for this purpose the design by architect Jo Coenen was chosen – and not that of Rem Koolhaas, to the disappointment of many.[48] The building was delivered in 1993, on the corner of busy Rochussenstraat and Verlengde Mathenesserlaan, now rechristened Museumpark.

An institute and a museum of photography

Two years later, history would repeat itself with the inter-city tug-of-war to land the Dutch national institute of photography (Nederlands Foto Instituut or NFI). In Rotterdam photography had long been making serious waves as an art form thanks to Perspektief, a gallery founded by a handful of photographers in 1980.[49] It was partly through their efforts that the national photographic archives (Nederlands Fotoarchief or NFA) had already settled in Rotterdam in 1990. The council therefore named the favourable climate for photography in Rotterdam as a reason for siting the NFI there. Once again, public debate raged and feelings ran high, with Amsterdam cultural bodies and photographers threatening sabotage if the institute were to be housed in Rotterdam, and once again Amsterdam ultimately lost out.[50] But the opening of the Nederlands Foto Instituut on March 30, 1994 in the 'house of photography' in Witte de Withstraat in Rotterdam did not signify the end of the tussle. Nineteen ninety-seven saw a new juicy bone tossed between the scrapping dogs, to wit a legacy of ten million euros to found a museum of pohotography.[51] Several Dutch cities vied for this legacy from the amateur photographer Hein Wertheimer, but Amsterdam and Rotterdam once again were the most likely candidates. Their fourth joust for a cultural institution began.[52]

This time the time-honoured rivalry seemed initially to have been suppressed in favour of resolving the issue together. Four Rotterdam-based bodies and one in Amsterdam tabled a joint plan for investing the Wertheimer legacy. Instead of a

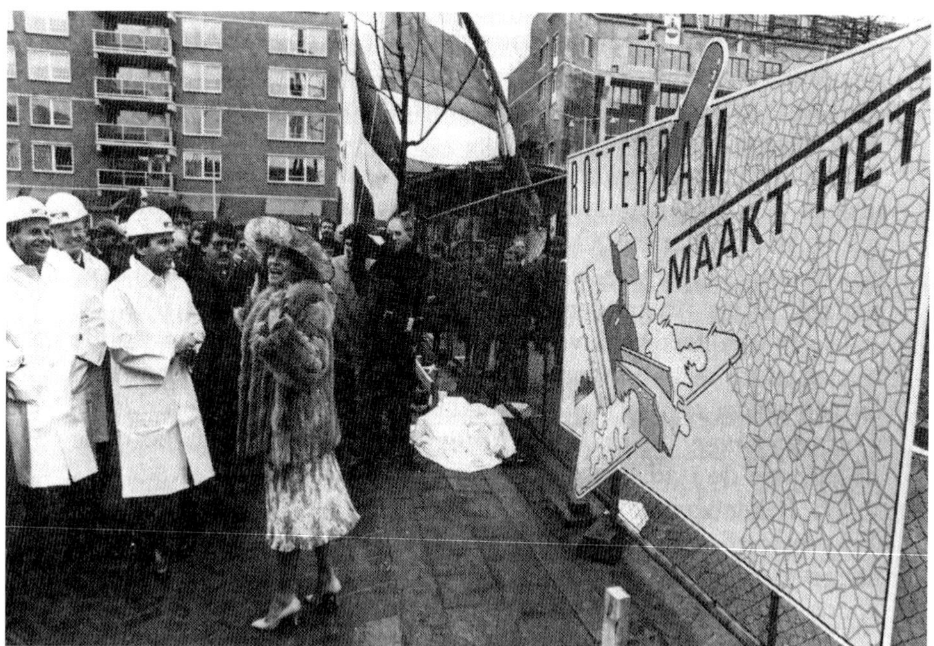

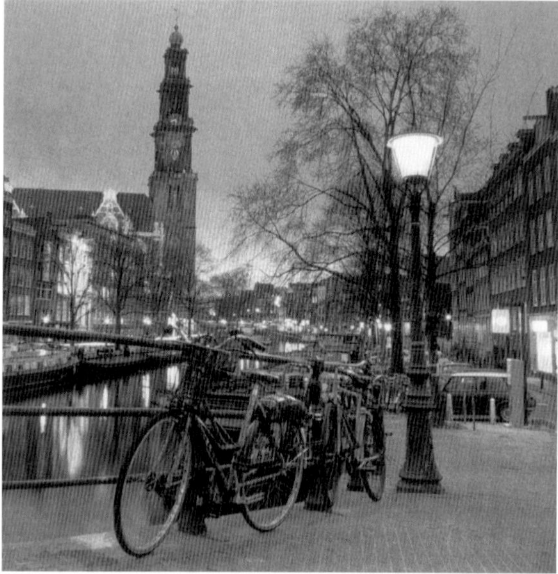

Top festivities to mark the groundbreaking ceremony for the new city theatre, December 19, 1984. Note the board bearing the words: 'Rotterdam makes it'. Actress Pauline van Rhenen performed for an audience that included the mayor Bram Peper, minister Eelco Brinkman and alderman Joop Linthorst. It was then that minister Brinkman of Welfare, Health and Culture broke the news that the architecture institute was to be housed in Rotterdam.

Bottom picture postcard of Prinsengracht in Amsterdam, photo by P. van der Meer, design by Max Leser ('A Paper Mill Product'), bought on Damrak, December 2003. This is a stereotypical representation of 'old Amsterdam'.

traditional museum of photography they proposed embedding photography in the broader context of an 'Institute of Visual Culture'.[53] The umbrella term visual culture (*beeldcultuur*) was included in the name of the institute to stress that it contained not only what was considered 'art' but the entire spectrum of images produced by the media of film, photography and electronics. The instigators were a photographic conservation studio (Nationaal Fotorestauratie Atelier), the NFA, the NFI, and V2_ Organisation (an 'institute for the unstable media'), all four from Rotterdam; and from Amsterdam the Nederlands Filmmuseum, the largest of the five with a 140-strong staff. The top brass of these five organizations were entirely in agreement on what the objectives of the new institute were to be, and where it was to be sited: in Las Palmas, a former warehouse at Kop van Zuid in Rotterdam. Las Palmas would also be the name of the new institute. The public facilities of the Filmmuseum in Vondelpark in Amsterdam would be kept up.[54] State Secretary for Culture Rick van der Ploeg supported the plan wholeheartedly and held out the prospect of a sizeable subsidy.

But then it all got unstuck. The board of the Filmmuseum began voicing objections to the move to Rotterdam and mobilized a lobby of worthies in Amsterdam's cultural sector to protest against this collaboration with Rotterdam.[55] These presented the Las Palmas plan as if it meant the demise of the Amsterdam Filmmuseum and as an uncertain adventure that had still to be fully financed. They launched signature campaigns to keep the Filmmuseum in Amsterdam.[56] National and local dailies kept close track of each clash. If the Amsterdam camp consisted of Filmmuseum executives and a swelling band of supporters, the museum's director Hoos Blotkamp and deputy Ruud Visschedijk were consigned to the Rotterdam camp. Their attempts to present rational arguments for collaborating with Rotterdam were drowned out by a rising tide of emotions whose source went back a long way, as we have seen. On January 20, 2000 the 'high drama'[57] reached a provisional peak that in fact meant curtains for the Amsterdam-Rotterdam joint venture. The board called together the Filmmuseum's staff and its chairman Dig Istha informed them that the Filmmuseum would no longer be party to the Rotterdam scheme of things. Not just that – according to Blotkamp Istha had sworn that the word 'Rotterdam' would never be mentioned in the Filmmuseum again![58]

Hoos Blotkamp and his deputy director Ruud Visschedijk had already been nudged out of the proceedings by being prohibited from either acting or speaking on behalf of the museum, but now the two reported sick. Despite strong support in the press for their services – 'Keep Hoos here' was a headline in *NRC Handelsblad* of March 3, 2000 – they never returned to their posts. The Wertheimer money was, after all, eventually assigned to Rotterdam to found the Nederlands Fotomuseum.[59]

Amsterdam in opposition

Amsterdam's position as the Netherlands' cultural capital is no longer the natural thing it used to be, for itself as well as for others, since Rotterdam's quadruple vic-

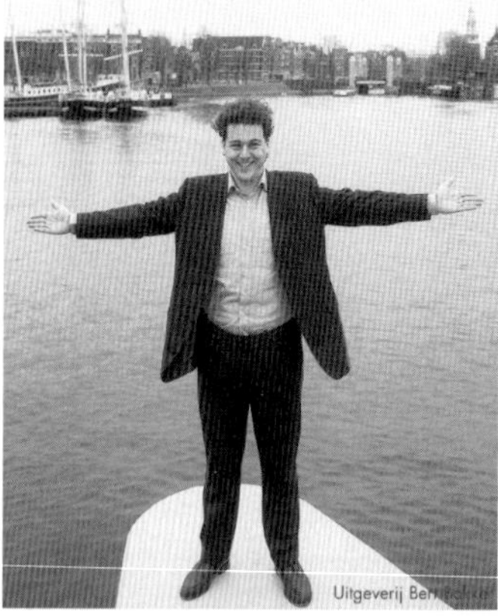

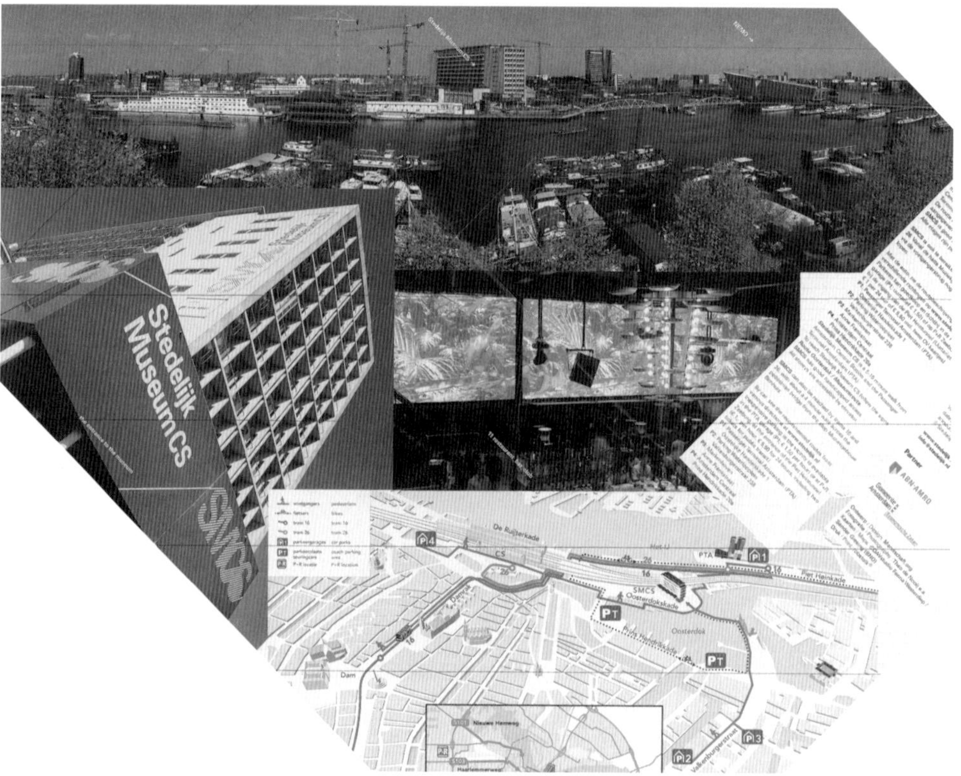

Top cover of Lodewijk Asscher, *Nieuw Amsterdam: De ideale stad in 2020*, Amsterdam 2005.

Bottom information folder for Stedelijk Museum CS, 2005. The panoramic view out over the IJ represents the new Amsterdam.

tory in the cultural institutions stakes (NAi, Nederlands Fotoarchief, Nederlands Foto Instituut, Nederlands Fotomuseum). Since then, even the smallest sign that Rotterdam has scored in the cultural field is met with jitteriness from Amsterdam and whoops of triumph from Rotterdam. Outsiders lap up the ongoing rivalry and are even wont to take malicious pleasure at Amsterdam's misfortunes. As the underdog Rotterdam usually has the public's sympathy.

A recurring matter of concern for Amsterdam since the 1990s is the exodus of artists and other cultural practitioners from the city. The main reason they give for leaving is the lack of inexpensive live/work accommodation there. Many cheap premises in Amsterdam where artists lived and worked were demolished in the 1990s. According to reports in the media their preferred destination is Rotterdam.[60] In a bid to turn the tide Amsterdam city council in 2000 launched a so-called cultural incubator policy (*broedplaatsenbeleid*) of providing funds to convert old buildings into studios to replace premises that had been demolished. But whereas the old studio complexes had come about spontaneously, often in squats, these new studios were being officially meted out. Doubt soon arose as to whether these new premises would indeed act as 'cauldrons of creativity' where fledgling artistic talent could develop undisturbed. The subject of whether there is any point to this policy is still far from closed.[61]

After Richard Florida's ideas about the importance of the creative class for cities hit the Netherlands in late 2003, the issue of Amsterdam's dwindling attraction for artists and the like became more pressing still.[62] In June 2004 a network of business people and creative professionals, the Club van Amsterdam, was founded to address the matter.[63] That matter, meanwhile, was regarded more and more as a crisis, for instance in the weekly *Volkskrant Magazine*, which reported on the Club's first meeting: 'Amsterdam is not the attractive place for creative people it used to be. Land is too expensive and commerce is commandeering all the good spots. "The city will bleed dry if we're not careful".'[64] That the city was at the same time going through an identity crisis can be discerned from a promotional campaign for the city entitled 'I Amsterdam', which was launched in October 2004. One of the image problems this campaign was to tackle was that Amsterdam is largely known to foreigners as a city where you can buy drugs and sex of all kinds, described euphemistically by the Berenschot campaign agency as 'sex, drugs and rock'n'roll'.[65] This image arose in the 1960s and '70s when Amsterdam was a focus of hippie culture. The campaign was geared to strengthening and popularizing other aspects of the city such as its creative side, its residential milieu, its commercial activity and its concentration of knowledge.[66]

Remarkably, this reflection on the image of Amsterdam runs parallel to a new mode of presenting the city. The first meeting of the Club van Amsterdam took place on the eleventh floor of the former post distribution centre next to Amsterdam Central Station, the so-called Post CS Building whose contents include a club restaurant. The photos of this meeting, published at the Club van Amsterdam web-

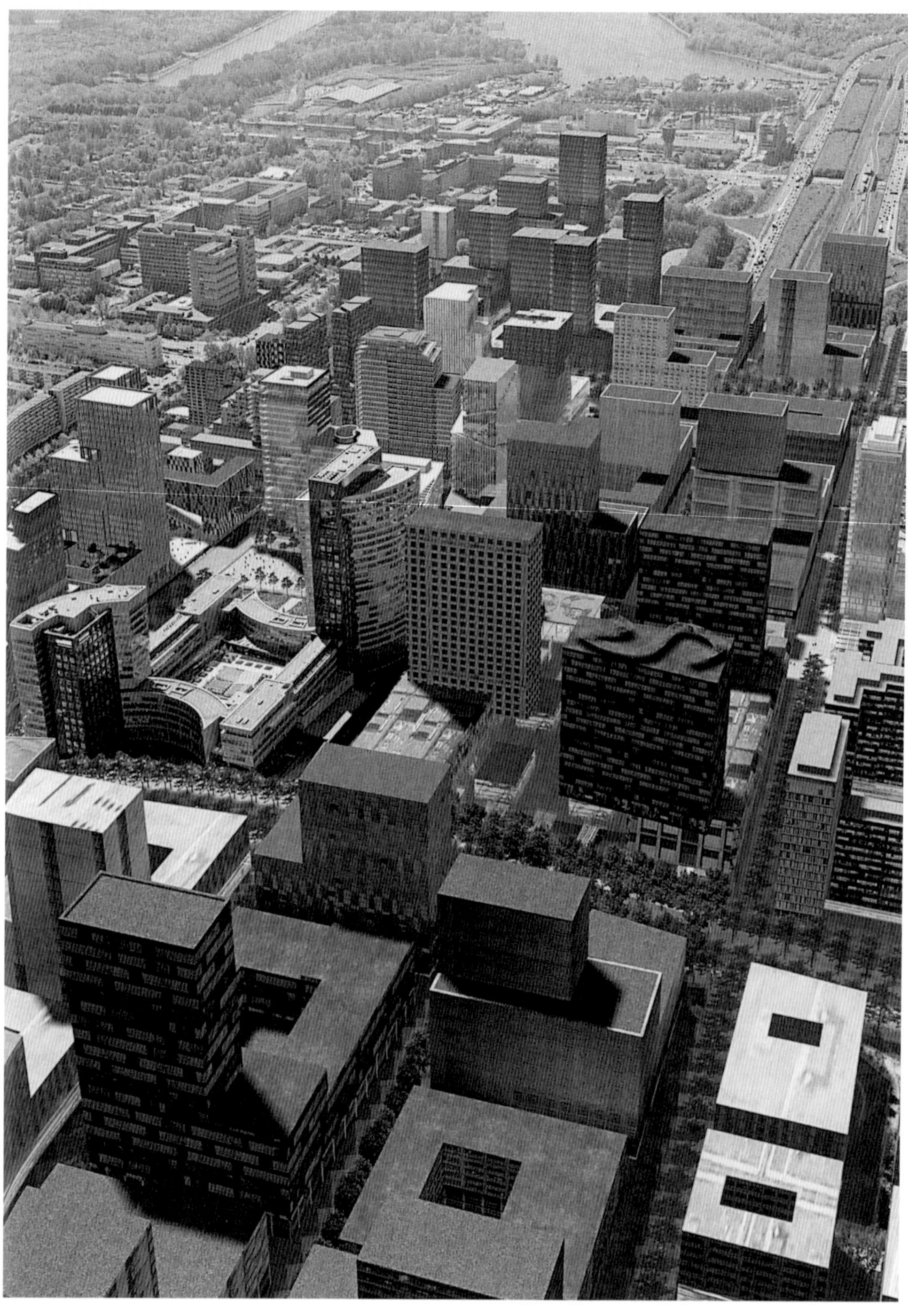

Proposal for high-rise on Amsterdam's Southern Axis (Zuidas), in W. Salet and S. Majoor (eds), *Amsterdam Zuidas European Space*, Rotterdam 2005.

site, show not just the invitees but also the view from the building.[67] That view is vast and spacious, looking over the railway tracks, the waters of the IJ Inlet and industrial buildings. It differs fundamentally from the image of Amsterdam shown by the tourist postcards, that is, a small-scale, snug and fine-grained city where time seems to stand still. The purpose of including at the Club website shots of the view enjoyed by those exchanging ideas on the future of Amsterdam is of course metaphorical: a new perspective on the city. It is evident from other sources too that for the creative inhabitants of Amsterdam the city's historic image has had its day. In an article ominously entitled 'Chased out of town' in *de Volkskrant* of October 4, 2001 visual artist Fendry Ekel pours scorn on the olde-worlde charm of his city: 'Amsterdam is becoming a kind of Disneyland, a Madurodam at actual size.' Amsterdam's Stedelijk Museum, which has been criticized for some years now for being behind the times and no longer at the cutting edge, was another institution to use another, ahistorical image of the city in its publicity material. In a museum information folder from early 2005 the diagonal of the paper is used for a panoramic photograph of the southern shore of the IJ, where the museum is temporarily housed in the same Post CS-building where the Club van Amsterdam met. Besides showing the museum's temporary accommodation the photo includes the water, ships, post-war high-rise, cranes and a train. At the far left can be seen just a glimpse of the old centre of Amsterdam. The Post CS-Building itself gets a second low-angle shot that emphasizes the height of this post-war quasi-modernist structure.

Another example of Amsterdam presented in more spacious terms is the front cover of the book *Nieuw Amsterdam*, written by councillor (now deputy mayor) Lodewijk Asscher on the eve of local elections in early 2006. Asscher himself, arms flung wide open, is in the photo which bleeds off the front cover to continue briefly on the back. Extending beyond him are the waters of the river Amstel, which seem vast. Right in the background we can recognize the distinctive gables of old Amsterdam. The 'New Amsterdam' Asscher describes in this book, his personal dream of how the city should be in 2020, is visualized with water and space. It does seems as though the intended transformation of Amsterdam will be preceded by a new way of presenting the city, just as we have seen in the case of Rotterdam. The two most recent flagship projects on the urbanistic front – the IJ embankment project and the Southern Axis development corridor (Zuidas), both still under construction, add to this new, spacious, modern image of Amsterdam.

The Rotterdamming of Amsterdam

Ironically, the new-style presentation of Amsterdam tends to bring Rotterdam to mind. The great expanse of the waters of the IJ surrounded by high-rise, cranes, new-build and recycled harbour sheds, is something we know from Rotterdam. The high-rise projected on Zuidas recalls Rotterdam's Weena boulevard. The press was quick to seize on this resemblance to Rotterdam. After the opening of the Muziekgebouw, a new music centre on the IJ, a journalist writing in *Trouw*, a national daily newspaper, was lyrical about this 'muscular building' with a 'tough, almost Rotterdam-like air about it'.[68] Machteld van Hulten, writing in another national daily, *de Volkskrant*, on February 23, 2006, went a step further. 'The Rotterdamming of Amsterdam' was the phrase she used in connection with the ongoing development of the banks of the IJ. Van Hulten drew attention to the fact that since the Stedelijk Museum's move to the aforementioned Post CS-Building and the opening of 'the spectacular Muziekgebouw' the IJ embankment has become a trendy, culturally tinged place with – if you please – a Rotterdam-like character: 'Ten years ago this was a no-go area, a streetwalkers' district you dared visit only rarely for some down-at-heel dance party in a warehouse. All at once it was the place to be, where the cultural and intellectual elite hung out of an evening. Followed by the rest of Amsterdam. Here was a new side to Amsterdam. No longer the blown-up miniature village with its quaint streets, winding canals and arched bridges. This was Rotterdam! Big ships, windy quays, great space.'[69]

On the face of it, it is a victory for Rotterdam that its big brother – or maybe sister, the opening words in the photobook accompanying the 'I Amsterdam' image campaign being 'Amsterdam is a woman' – was now taking after its smaller sibling for a change. But in the end Rotterdam would have little to gain if Amsterdam were to become too spacious, modern and rational. As we clearly saw at the beginning of this chapter, the opposition with Amsterdam was a key facet of the image built up around Rotterdam. Rotterdam needs Amsterdam, not in a practical sense but so as to define itself for the world. This would seem to be the destiny of all 'second cities', that their identity is shaped in part by the first.[70]

Rotterdammers who dream of Rotterdam becoming a cultural or creative hot spot like Amsterdam, should realize that if that dream came true it would mean the end of the cultural climate peculiar to Rotterdam. Many members of Rotterdam's creative class would probably move to a new empty city. Beerend Lenstra is one who even now looks back with a twinge of sadness to the time when Rotterdam was much emptier than it is today: 'Of course the disadvantage is that that space and the way you experience it, it'll all pass. Coolsingel, for example, at one time you could take a stroll there on Sunday. But try doing that now, it's no fun at all. On the one hand it's a pity, that sense of great space is getting less all the time of course, and on the other it's the consequence of what happens and how things develop. But that feeling of space you used to have, there's less of it now.'[71]

The clichés about Amsterdam and Rotterdam are partly true and partly untrue. Like all clichés they are over-simplified caricatures. But from the above we can see that they have tremendous staying power and can have dramatic consequences for both cities. Creative people let themselves be guided by it in choosing one city above another,[72] cultural policy is influenced by it at the highest level, even economic decisions are informed by emotions that can only be explained in terms of the polarization between the two cities. Artists and other cultural practitioners are pre-eminently sensitive to stereotypical qualities of cities, but they are also the ones who are able to give these a new thrust, as Jules Deelder and many others after him have done for Rotterdam.

In the next chapter I shall show that the development of Kop van Zuid, a former dock area on Rotterdam's south bank, can be regarded as the crowning achievement of the new perspective on the city as this has been evolved by Rotterdam's creative class. At the same time chapter 7 attends to the pioneering activities cultivated here by artists and cultural entrepreneurs before the area was redeveloped.

1 Koolhaas, R. (1988), 'Epilogue', in: M. Kloos (ed.), *Amsterdam: An Architectural Lesson*, Amsterdam: THOTH, pp. 108-118. Koolhaas is also extremely negative about Amsterdam in: Kwinter, S. (ed.) (1996), *Rem Koolhaas: Conversations with Students*, Houston, Texas: Rice University School of Architecture/New York: Princeton Architectural Press, p. 57: 'It is a vast tourist trap that in the high season is intolerable for one reason and in the low season is intolerable for other reasons. (…) In Holland, a city like Rotterdam is ten times more interesting or promising.'

2 Crimson, P. Gadanho et al. (eds) (2001), *Post.Rotterdam: Architecture and City after the tabula rasa/Arquitectura e Cidade após a tabula rasa*, Rotterdam: 010 Publishers, p. 62.

3 Crimson, Gadanho et al. (eds) (2001), op. cit. (note 2), p. 74.

4 Crimson, Gadanho et al. (eds) (2001), op. cit. (note 2), p. 98.

5 The exceptions were Riek Bakker, Daan van der Have, Joop Linthorst and Bas Vroege. They did mention Amsterdam, but for reasons other than putting it in opposition to Rotterdam. See the list of interviewees at the back of this book.

6 Ruarus, P. (1986), 'De permanente strijd van Hard Werken tegen eenvormigheid', *Graficus*, 68, February 6, pp. 4-13 (p. 13).

7 *Neon*, 8, broadcast on April 13, 1980, tape in the Neon Media archive, Rotterdam.

8 Deelder, J.A. & V. Mentzel (1984), *Stadslicht*, Rotterdam: Kreits, p. 4.

9 From the collection *Interbellum*, 1987, quoted from: Deelder, J. (1994), *Renaissance: Gedichten '44–'94*, Amsterdam: De Bezige Bij, p. 466.

10 Lindner, R. (2006), 'The Gestalt of the Urban Imaginary', *European Studies*, 23 (2006), pp. 35-42.

11 Author's interview with Joop Linthorst, January 12, 2004.

12 'O bloejend Rotterdam! O schoone Maasvorstin! / Wat ziet ge al vlooten naar uw havens, uit en in / Laveeren, met den schat van Oosten, Noorden, Westen: / hier kan de Koopman ook zijn handelzetel vesten, / Gelijck in Gijsbrechts Stad, die Paerel aan het IJ, / Die gij bijnaar, door al uw zeemacht, streeft voorbij.' Quoted in: Klein, A. & H. Besselaar ([1959]), *Amsterdam Rotterdam: Twee steden rapsodie*, Baarn: In den Toren, p. 62. For the dating of this poem see Hazewinkel, H.C. & J.E. van der Pot (eds) (1942), *Vier eeuwen Rotterdam: Citaten uit reisbeschrijvingen, rapporten, redevoeringen, gedichten en romans*, Rotterdam: W.L. & J. Brusse's Uitgeversmaatschappij N.V., pp. 43-44.

13 Edmondo de Amicis, who travelled through the Low Countries in 1873, wrote this in his book *Olanda*, quoted in: Klein & Besselaar ([1959]), op. cit. (note 12), p. 63.

14 See, for instance, the papers on numerous international examples at the 'Second Cities' conference, University of Glasgow, April 30-May 1, 2004. The characteristic relationship between first and second cities also obtains at a regional level.

15 Although Florida asserts that in principle people from all professional groups can belong to this creative class so long as they use their creativity in their work, in public discourse in the Netherlands only those people with a creative profession are counted among the creative class. Florida, R. (2002), *The Rise of the Creative Class: And How It's Transforming Work, Leisure, Community and Everyday Life*, New York: Basic Books.

16 Rutten, P., W. Manshanden et al. (2004), *De creatieve industrie in Amsterdam en de regio*, Delft: TNO, p. 2. Manshanden, W., P. Rutten et al. (2005), *Creatieve industrie in Rotterdam*, Delft: TNO, p. 9.

17 Metz, T., 'Creativiteit is geld waard: Terwijl de economie cultureel wordt, wordt de cultuur commercieel', *NRC Handelsblad*, February 18, 2005.

18 See *Christos Kritikos in Amsterdam, een portret*, telecast February 24, 2002 in the series of VPRO documentaries '7 dagen'; also on http://www.vpro.nl/programma/7dagen/afleveringen/, site visited November 10, 2005.

19 Centraal Planbureau (1999), *Randvoorwaarden voor een economische onderbouwing van een verbeterde zeetoegang voor het Noordzeekanaalgebied*, [The Hague:] Centraal Planbureau; 'Vragen PvdA over subsidie containerterminal Amsterdam', July 2, 1999, from Nieuwsbank: Interactief Nederlands persbureau (http://www.persbericht.nl, site visited November 10, 2005).

20 See 'Ceres finally scores', published June 2, 2005, on http://www.worldcargonews.com/htm/w20050602.324540.htm, site visited November 10, 2005.

21 Author's interview with Henk Molenaar, February 27, 2004.

22 http://www.amsterdam.nl/gemeente/college/mark_van_der_horst/opening, site visited November 10, 2005.

23 *NRC Handelsblad*, September 22, 1983, cutting in the press documentation department of the Netherlands Institute for Art History (RKD), The Hague, NAi folder. Brinkman made his announcement through former Rotterdam alderman Jan Riezenkamp, Director-General of Cultural Affairs at the then Ministry of Welfare, Health and Culture (WVC).

24 Architecture section of the Rotterdam Arts Council (1984), *Rapportage betreffende de vestiging van een architectuurmuseum in Rotterdam*, Rotterdam: Rotterdamse Kunststichting, sectie Architectuur. The architectural historian Maarten Kloos, who lives in Amsterdam, wrote on March 9, 1984 in *de Volkskrant*: 'Rotterdam (...) has more or less demanded that the architecture institute should be site on its territory.' Cutting in the press documentation department of the Netherlands Institute for Art History (RKD), The Hague, NAi folder.

25 Brouwers, R. (1998), 'The NAI – the history of a design task', in: R. Brouwers et al. (eds), *The Netherlands Architecture Institute*, Rotterdam: NAi Publishers, pp. 64-83 (p. 66). According to Joop Linthorst, 'bringing in his name was a way of getting one up on minister Brinkman'; author's interview with Joop Linthorst, January 12, 2004.

26 Letter from Paul Noorman (RKS) to Joop Linthorst (alderman for Art Affairs), January 26, 1984, press documentation department of the Netherlands Institute for Art History (RKD), The Hague, NAi folder, added to *Rapportage*, op. cit. (note 24).

27 According to *Het Parool*, December 11, 1984, cutting in the press documentation department of the Netherlands Institute for Art History (RKD), The Hague, NAi folder.

28 See Ven, C.J.M. van der (1977), 'De Rotterdamse bijdrage aan het Nieuwe Bouwen', *Plan: Maandblad voor ontwerp en omgeving*, (2), pp. 9-24.

29 The books accompanied by card models featured J.J.P. Oud's Café De Unie and the Superintendent's Office, S. van Ravesteyn's Feyenoord Freight Office, El Lissitzky's Lenin Tribune, J.H. van den Broek's Villa Gestel, R. van 't Hoff's Villa Henny and Adolf Loos's House for Josephine Baker; see the 'Complete Catalogue' in Oldewarris, H. & P. de Winter (eds) (2003), *20 jaar/years 010 1983–2003*, Rotterdam: 010 Publishers, pp. 175-178.

30 For this see Dijk, H. van (1995), 'De gezelligheidsrevolutie 1965–1985', in: M. Aarts (ed.), *Vijftig jaar wederopbouw Rotterdam: Een geschiedenis van toekomstvisies*, Rotterdam: 010 Publishers, pp. 161-192 (pp. 169-171).

31 Van Dijk (1995), op. cit. (note 30), p. 169.

32 Taverne, E. & C. Wagenaar (2003), 'Tussen elite en massa: 010 en de opkomst van de architectuurindustrie in Nederland/Between elite and mass: 010 and the rise of the architecture industry in the Netherlands', in: H. Oldewarris & P. de Winter (eds), *20 jaar/years 010 1983–2003*, Rotterdam: 010 Publishers, pp. 29-68 (p. 30).

33 Oldewarris & De Winter (eds) (2003), op. cit. (note 29), p. 12; author's interview with Hans Oldewarris, March 31, 2003.

34 Hans Oldewarris in *Het Vrije Volk*, July 6, 1983, printed in facsimile in Oldewarris & De Winter (eds) (2003), op. cit. (note 30), pp. 0-1.

35 Taverne & Wagenaar (2003), op. cit. (note 32), p. 30.

36 Barbieri, S. Umberto (ed.) (1983), *Architectuur en planning: Nederland 1940–1980*, Rotterdam: 010 Publishers.

37 Taverne & Wagenaar (2003), op. cit. (note 32), p. 33.

38 Werlemann, H. & A. David-Tu (1983), *Rotterdams kadeboek*, Rotterdam: 010 Publishers.

39 Author's interview with Hans Oldewarris, March 31, 2003. Originally published in Amsterdam by Mourik, 1768-1771.

40 Koolhaas had yet to rise to the international fame he enjoys now, but his book *Delirious New York* from 1978 had attained mythical status among insiders both in and out of the Netherlands. Kloosterman and Stegmeijer contend that Koolhaas has been the pre-eminent factor in Rotterdam's growth as a 'city of architecture' and in its concentration of successful architecture firms, but it is more probable that he was just one factor in the 'architecture city' stakes alongside the others named in this chapter. Kloosterman, R. & E. Stegmeijer (2004), 'Cultural Industries in the Netherlands – Path-Dependent Patterns and Institutional Contexts: The Case of Architecture in Rotterdam', *Petermanns Geographische Mitteilungen*, 148 (4), pp. 68-75.

41 In Barbieri (ed.) (1983), op. cit. (note 36), p. 6.

42 Halbertsma, M. (2000), 'Amsterdam, de eeuwige strijd met', in: P. van Ulzen (ed.), *90 over 80: Tien jaar beeldende kunst in Rotterdam: de dingen, de mensen, de plekken*, Rotterdam: NAi Publishers/Stichting Kunstpublicaties Rotterdam, pp. 22-23.

43 *Het Parool*, December 11, 1984, cutting in the press documentation department of the Netherlands Institute for Art History (RKD), The Hague, NAi folder.

44 Van Rooy, Max (1984), 'De voordelen van de Beurs', *NRC Handelsblad*, CS, September 14, 1984.

45 Koopmans, Jaap (1984), 'Rotterdam heeft recht op architectuurmuseum', *Haagsche Courant*, October 30, 1984, cutting in the press documentation department of the Netherlands Institute for Art History (RKD), The Hague, NAi folder.

46 Cutting in the press documentation department of the Netherlands Institute for Art History (RKD), The Hague, NAi folder.

47 Brouwers (1998), op. cit. (note 25), p. 66.

48 Brouwers (1998), op. cit. (note 25), pp. 64-83.

49 Cornelissen, M. (2000), 'Perspektief (1980–1993/1995)', in: P. van Ulzen (ed.) (2000), *90 over 80: Tien jaar beeldende kunst in Rotterdam: De dingen, de mensen, de plekken*, Rotterdam: NAi Publishers/Stichting Kunstpublicaties Rotterdam, pp. 136-137.

50 For this see Marsman, E. (1995), 'Voltooid. De moeizame geschiedenis van het Nederlands Foto Instituut', in: H. van Dulken et al. (eds) *Stilstaande beelden: ondergang en opkomst van de fotografie* (*Jaarboek Kunst en beleid in Nederland*; dl. 7) Amsterdam: Boekmanstichting/Van Gennep, pp. 33-53; Cornelissen, M. (1995), *Perspektief in Rotterdam 1980–1993*, Master's Thesis Vakgroep Kunstgeschiedenis, Utrecht: Universiteit Utrecht; Marsman, E. (2005), 'Ieder voor zich en niks voor hen allen: Ontbrekend fotografiebeleid in Nederland', *Boekman*, 5 (63), pp. 11-31.

51 Nederlands Foto Instituut, Nederlands Fotoarchief, et al. (2001), *Blauwdruk voor het Nederlands foto-museum*, Rotterdam: Nederlands Foto Instituut, Nederlands Fotoarchief, Nationaal Fotorestauratie Atelier.

52 To wit, the Netherlands Architecture Institute (1), Nederlands Fotoarchief (2), Nederlands Foto Instituut (3) and now the museum of photography (4). For the battle over the Wertheimer legacy see also Nuchelmans, A. (2005), 'Een felomstreden erfenis: Het Wertheimer-legaat als splijtzwam', *Boekman*, 5 (63), pp. 68-77.

53 Filmmuseum, Nationaal Fotorestauratie Atelier et al. (1999), *Las Palmas Het Plan: Internationaal Centrum voor Foto, Film & Mediatechnologie*, Rotterdam: Projectbureau Las Palmas/Communicatie-team Kop van Zuid. All the following information derives from this plan except where otherwise specified.

54 Filmmuseum, Nationaal Fotorestauratie Atelier et al. (1999), op. cit. (note 53). Open letter from Hoos Blotkamp (director, Filmmuseum) and Ruud Visschedijk (adjunct director, Filmmuseum), December 13, 1999, in reaction to the 'Filmmuseum letter' from 30 prominent members of Amsterdam's cultural sector to the 'permanent committee on cultural affairs' of the House of Representatives (lower house), December 9, 1999, Hoos Blotkamp archive.

55 Open letter from Blotkamp & Visschedijk, op. cit. (note 54).

56 See Hoos Blotkamp's own report on events occasioned by the Las Palmas plan of January 1999-January 2000, January 30, 2000, Hoos Blotkamp archive.

57 As characterized by Beerekamp, H., 'Houdt Hoos hier', *NRC Handelsblad*, March 3, 2000.

58 idem note 56. Istha had indeed set great store in retaining the Filmmuseum for Amsterdam, as is evident from an email sent to the author on March 29, 2006 in which he says he is still proud of the fact that he prevented the Filmmuseum from leaving that city.

59 The final decision fell on February 20, 2003. It was front-page news for many Dutch papers, one headline screaming 'Rotterdam wins race on photographer's legacy: Wertheimer's millions for Fotomuseum', *NRC Handelsblad*, February 20, 2003.

60 Verhelst, M. et al. (eds) (2001), *Agora: Tijdschrift voor sociaal-ruimtelijke vraagstukken*, 17 (4), p. 14, theme issue on free states and law-free zones; Loorbach, L., 'Brandveiligheid remt bloei cultuur: Broedplaatsen kunnen niet voldoen aan eisen', *Het Parool*, January 28, 2005; Jungmann, B., 'Uit de stad gejaagd', *de Volkskrant*, October 4, 2001; Loorbach, L., 'Project Broedplaatsen', *Het Parool*, November 17, 2005.

61 See the public discussion in *Het Parool*, November 17, 21, 22 and 23, 2005; *de Volkskrant*, November 24, 2005.

62 This was after Florida's first presentation in the Netherlands on September 26, 2003 in Amsterdam.

63 Luyten, M. (2004), 'Verzin een list: Creatief Amsterdam gaat ten onder', *Volkskrant Magazine*, June 19, 2004, pp. 28-32; http://www.clubvanamsterdam. nl/cva/cva_nl_home.html

64 Luyten (2004), op. cit. (note 63), p. 29.

65 Gehrels, C., O. van Munster et al. ([2003]), *Choosing Amsterdam: Brand, concept and organisation of the city marketing*, Amsterdam: Gemeente Amsterdam.

66 Gerlings, M. (2004), 'Amsterdam is een vrouw: Fotoboek in het schap buitenland als mini-billboard', *Recreatie & Toerisme*, October 30, 2004; Heeg, R. (2004), 'Sobere stad van "viezigheid"', *Adformatie*, October 7, 2004.

67 www.clubvanamsterdam.nl, site visited July 4, 2006.

68 Lange, H. de & P. van der Lint, 'Jazz en klassieke muziek aan 't IJ: Muziek gebouw', *Trouw*, May 24, 2005.

69 Hulten, M. van, 'De grote sprong: Amsterdam breidt uit tot over het IJ', *de Volkskrant*, February 23, 2006.

70 The idea of Rotterdam as 'second city' has aroused indignation among many Rotterdammers. This was once again made clear at an international conference held on November 11, 2005 in Rotterdam and organized by CityCorp, a joint venture between local housing corporations. At the mention of the term 'Second City' in the closing discussion, the Rotterdam businessman Michael Lints retorted testily, to spontaneous applause from the audience: 'If Rotterdam decides to be "second best", I'm moving.'

71 Author's interview with Beerend Lenstra, May 19, 2003.

72 This also emerges from a study with a more quantitative approach than mine: Kamp, M. van de (2003), *'One eye sees, the other feels': Het locatiekeuzeproces van kleine culturele ondernemingen in Amsterdam en Rotterdam*, Faculty of History and Arts, Department of Culture and the Arts, Rotterdam: Erasmus Universiteit.

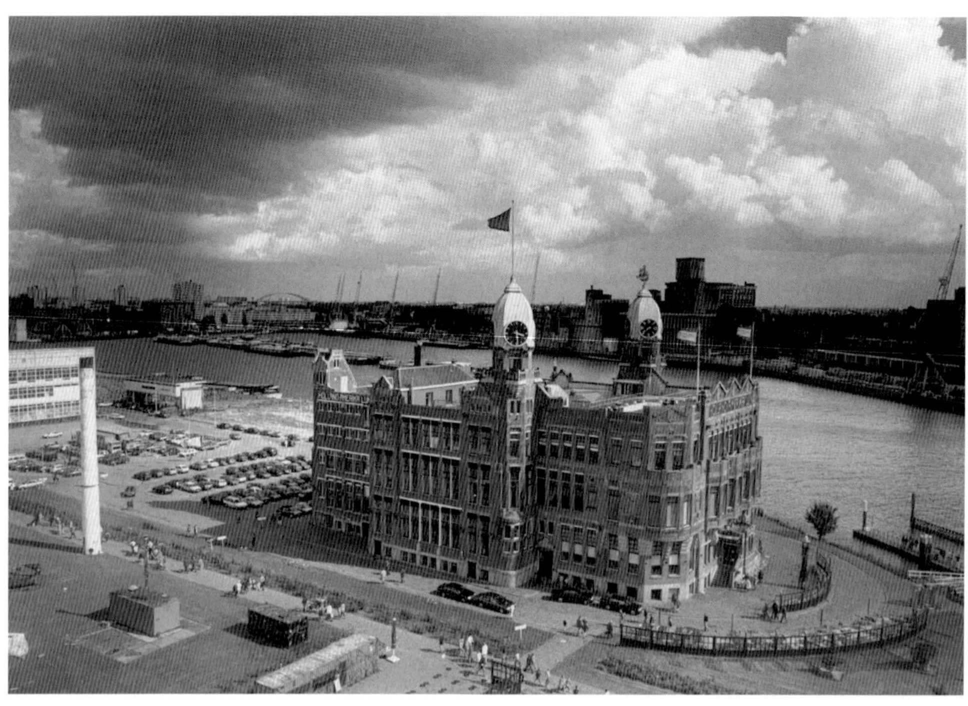

Hotel New York, Wilhelminapier Rotterdam, photo by Hajo Piebenga, 1994.

Chapter 7

A dream come true: Kop van Zuid

*'The dream of all urban designers is
to see the city achieve a heroic splendour
that exceeds their expectations.'*[1]

Riek Bakker

It is impossible to imagine Rotterdam at the turn of the millennium without Kop van Zuid. This name, which literally translates as 'head (*kop*) of South (Rotterdam)', is given to a former dock area on the south bank of the Maas. Rotterdam-Zuid, the entire urban segment south of the river, traditionally has been regarded more as a hanger-on than a regular part of town. The project to renovate and develop Kop van Zuid, and in particular to erect a bridge between it and the north bank, was an attempt to combine at least the northernmost part of Rotterdam-Zuid with the existing city centre across the river. Whether this has succeeded in all respects is difficult to judge so soon after the event. What is indisputable, though, is that Kop van Zuid has immediately and seamlessly become an integral part of the image of Rotterdam as it has evolved. This is particularly true of Wilhelminapier and the Erasmus Bridge (Erasmusbrug) which connects two major boulevards, Coolsingel on the north bank, via Schiedamsedijk, and Laan op Zuid in the south. Opened in 1996, the Erasmus Bridge has become a trademark for the city, gracing street maps and tourist guides, and is used in media of all kinds to visually get the message across that 'this is about Rotterdam'. The Euromast, which used to symbolize the city, has been almost entirely upstaged by the Erasmus Bridge.[2]

That Kop van Zuid has become such an iconic factor for Rotterdam might be construed as a happy if serendipitous side-effect of this urban initiative. This is

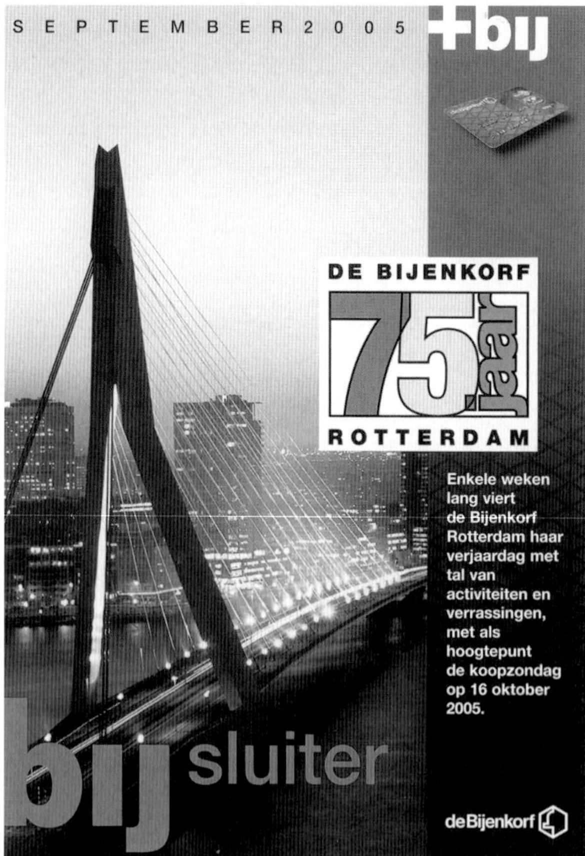

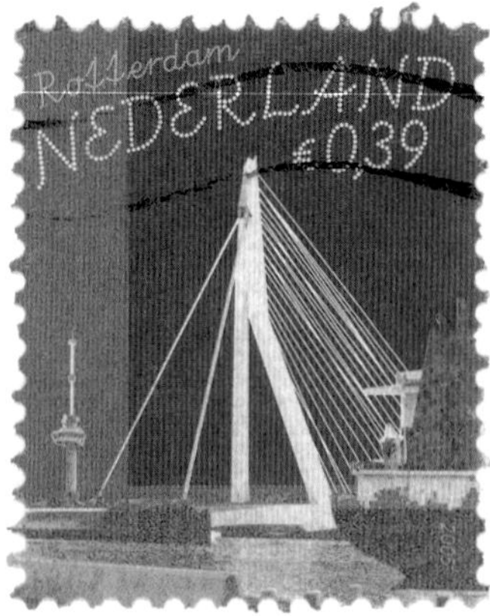

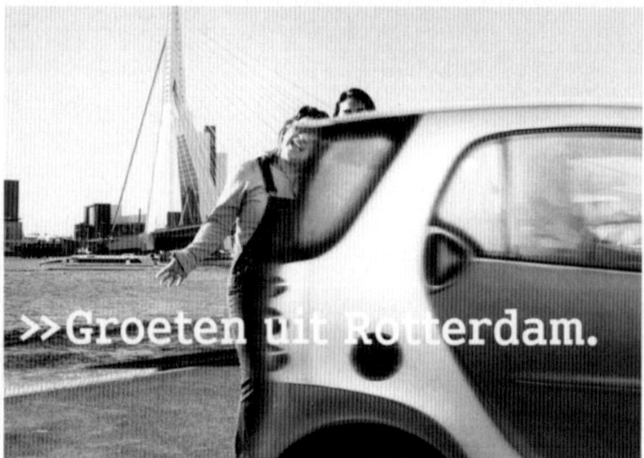

The Erasmus Bridge in various roles as an urban icon for Rotterdam: **top left** front page of a Bijenkorf brochure marking the first 75 years of the Rotterdam branch of this department store, September 2005; **right** postage stamp, 2005; **bottom** picture postcard for an advertising campaign for the Smart Car, c. 2002.

not the case however. If we look at the history of Kop van Zuid and the motives driving the people who have given the area a new future, it was clearly concern for Rotterdam's image that laid the basis for the urban plans. The Kop van Zuid project is, so to speak, the crowing achievement of years of evolving a new perspective on the city. It is the embodiment of a dream fostered by Rotterdam's creative class since the end of the 1970s. In Kop van Zuid, Rotterdam presents itself as a spacious, rational, modern, worldly city, with high-rise on both river banks creating an imposing sky-line. This is the Rotterdam evoked in Deelder's poem *Stadsgezicht*. This is as well the Rotterdam artists envisage when eulogizing Rotterdam as an open city, the antithe-sis of introverted Amsterdam. And this image has since found favour with the public at large, as we saw in the introduction to this book.

Once again, artists and cultural entrepreneurs were the first to realize what Kop van Zuid could mean for the image projected by Rotterdam. The AIR project of 1982 discussed in chapter 4 had got the ball rolling. These ideas had yet to catch on with the local authorities. As late as 1984, a municipal 'structural concept' drawn up for Kop van Zuid sniffily dismisses the significance of AIR 1982 as 'merely relative'.[2] The 'principal objectives' formulated for the area by three municipal departments – Physical Planning and Urban Renewal (DROS), Public Works (GW) and City Develop-ment (GB) – focused most finely on the need for affordable housing. According to the structural concept, AIR 1982 had made it clear 'that it is impossible to construct an urban masterplan for Kop van Zuid that can encompass and manage the entire area'.[4] It was only when a new director was appointed in 1986 to what was by then Rotterdam's Urban Development Unit (Dienst Stadsontwikkeling) that a visionary approach to the former dock area made its appearance at council level. That director was Riek Bakker. Her name will in all probability be forever linked with Kop van Zuid, and rightly so. Her creative talent and bracing arguments brought alive the vision of Kop van Zuid for her own department, for the city council, for the people of Rotterdam and for the national government, who would part-finance the project.

In this seventh chapter, however, I would like to draw attention to individ-uals and groups who are often left unmentioned in the literature on Kop van Zuid yet had much to do with its success. At a time when plans for Kop van Zuid were no more than a shadow pantomime of scale models, drawings and descriptions, there were artists and cultural entrepreneurs engaged in setting up concrete projects there. So Kop van Zuid had linked arms with the city centre psychologically before there was any visible activity on the urban planning horizon. This chapter seeks to give these pioneers the well-deserved place in history they have lacked until now.

The city as a whole

When Riek Bakker was approached by a headhunter in 1985 to take over directorship of Urban Development, no-one could have foreseen the crucial role she would fill in developing what would become known as 'the New Rotterdam'. Indeed, Bakker herself says that the powers that be thought they were enlisting the services of a warm and affable lady who would leave things largely as they were.[5] They would be in for a surprise.

Since 1976 Bakker had run a successful agency for garden and landscape design together with Ank Bleeker in Amsterdam. Her work at Bakker & Bleeker had taught her to present plans in such a way that the client would get the right picture and wax enthusiastic. This knowledge would serve her well in her new position.[6] It was this concern for presentation and communication that would help to make such a success of her career in Rotterdam. This success began immediately with her campaign to give her department greater prestige.[7] She soon discovered that the department she was now in charge of carried little weight within the council and was even threatened with closure. According to Bakker, this was because no-one in the department considered the city as a whole. Everyone had a project to be getting on with, a building or an area, but no-one had an overall picture of the city. As a result, the department had no clear standpoint on that issue. So in June 1986 Bakker organized a month of brainstorming sessions with her staff. The questions around which these sessions revolved were simply these: What's good about the city and why? What isn't good about the city and why? And what should be done to change things for the better?[8] The upshot of this 'June project' was that projects could be placed in a broader context: 'We started talking about how projects could be clustered and made to relate, so that big problems could generate big solutions. This meant that area development took over from project development.'[9] But the most important thing was that the department could now communicate an overall perspective on the city: 'We now had a standpoint on the city in its entirety, one that picked up on the needs that were felt at the time. We had a story we could tell to the outside world.'[10]

The 'story' was favourably received by the mayor and the five aldermen who together constituted the council's Urban Restructuring group. This 'sub-College' and two others like it were founded to develop plans to infuse new life into the city, plans which would ultimately lead to the two reports (*Vernieuwing van Rotterdam* and *Nieuw Rotterdam*) of 1987.[11] Many of Bakker's ideas, particularly her focus on the city as a whole, would end up in *Vernieuwing van Rotterdam*.

A view from the window of a hotel on the Maas

Kop van Zuid was designated in the 1987 'June project' as one of the areas it would be interesting to develop. But Bakker's Kop van Zuid dream dates from two years earlier. On accepting the position of head of the Urban Development Unit in 1985, she decided to spend a week of the Christmas recess in a Rotterdam hotel for her first taste of the city. The window of her hotel room offered a view of the Maas and Kop van Zuid. She could scarcely believe her eyes when she looked out. For her the idea of making this area part of the city centre was so obvious that she failed to understand why this hadn't been done long ago. First of all, the area had more than enough vacant land a stone's throw from the existing centre to take up the city's inevitable growth, and second, a centre straddling both banks of the river would square well with Rotterdam's image as a world port city. She recalls that moment in her characteristically direct way: 'I looked and thought you're all nuts. Why on earth aren't you doing anything there? And why didn't you set about it long ago? You must be bonkers if you don't want to add that bit.'[12] Having made enquiries, she learnt that the division between North and South Rotterdam, or Noord and Zuid, was something of a sensitive issue. Rotterdammers north of the river felt they were a cut above their fellows in the South and some southerners made it a question of honour to never once set foot in North Rotterdam. It was not knowing about this invisible barrier that had allowed her to let her imagination run free.

The story about the glimpse from the hotel window is not just an amusing anecdote, it illustrates how one of Rotterdam's key urban initiatives began with a a view of the city sooner associated with a photographer or painter than with an urban designer. The iconic strength of Kop van Zuid is not something accidental but is owed to that glimpse. Major urbanistic changes can have their origins in the right person being in the right place and gazing at the city in the right way. It was that gaze that put Rotterdam in a whole new perspective, a perspective which then needed to be given shape in drawings, photographs and scale models to open the eyes of others to the new imagined Rotterdam.

Bakker realized that the comprehensive plan she had envisaged would only get support if it were pumped up to the max. 'I'll never pull it off if I don't make something that grabs people visually and emotionally', as she later voiced her thoughts at the time.[13] This was one reason why, when given permission to bring in an external agency, she chose an Almere-based architecture firm headed by Teun Koolhaas. She was convinced that Koolhaas could visualize a plan in such a way that the political world would warm to the idea. As she put it later somewhat one-sidedly: 'It wasn't even that important whether it was a good plan or not, what *was* important was whether it could be got across.'[14] In October 1986 the city council commissioned Teun Koolhaas Associates to make an urban masterplan for Kop van Zuid.[15] At the beginning of 1987, the firm presented a design, one with a clear story to tell about the city, just as Bakker had expected. That story was part verbal, part visual; the plan consisted of a written description, a scale model, masses of drawings and – unusual at the time – a slide show.[16]

Koolhaas's language in the description is particularly evocative and unashamedly exploits Rotterdam's image as as metropolis and a port city with all the attendant qualities, amongst them rationality and spaciousness. Koolhaas conjures up for the reader a 'fully-fledged metropolitan centre' on both banks of the Maas, typifying the former dock area in the South as 'tough' and 'peculiar to Rotterdam'.[17] A noteworthy aspect is his concern for the best possible view of the city and the river, for instance from the quays in Kop van Zuid. Similarly, the bridge

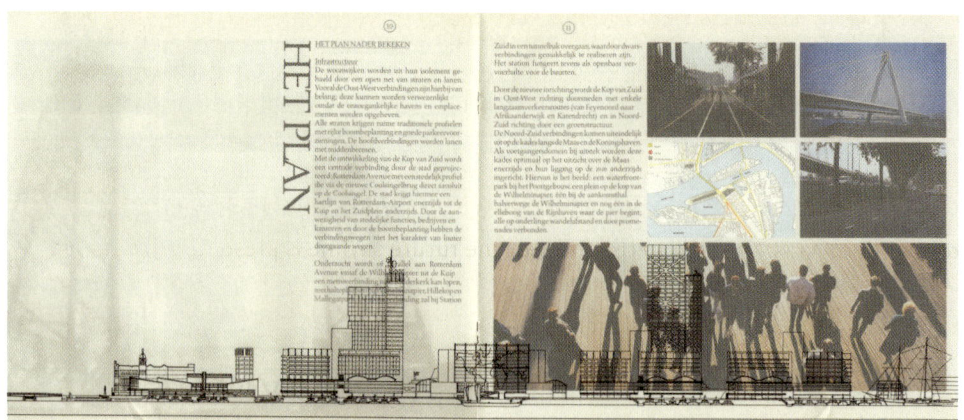

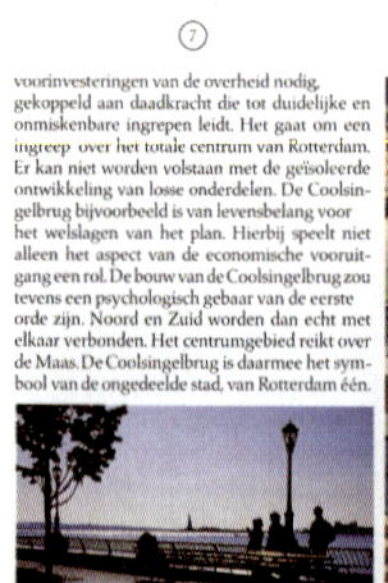

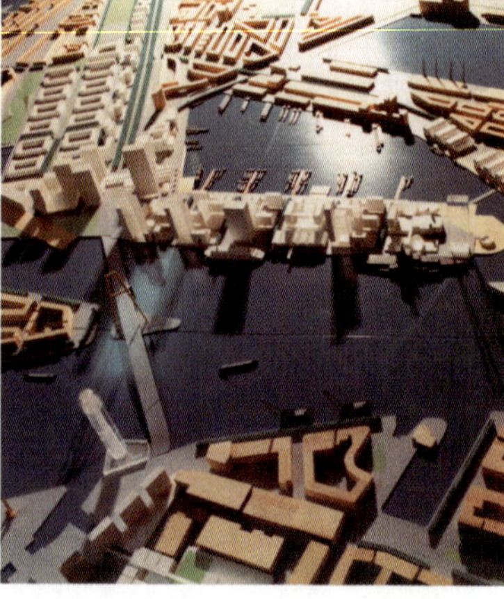

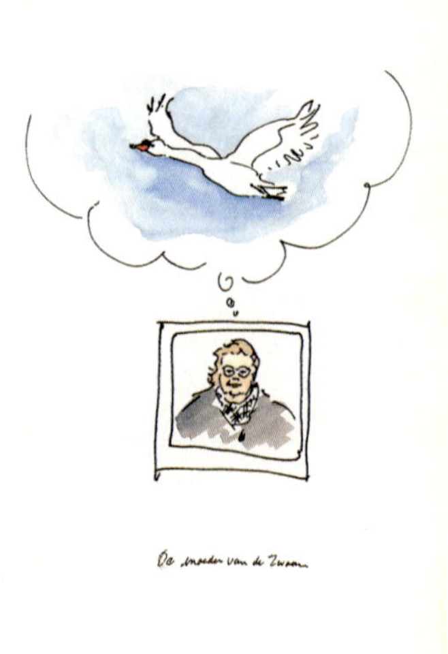

Top an impression of the skyline on tracing paper in *De Kop van Zuid: Een stedebouwkundig plan*, Rotterdam [1987], with photos suggesting a metropolis on the underlying pages.

Bottom left impression of the future Kop van Zuid, reproduced in *De Kop van Zuid: Een stedebouwkundig plan*, Rotterdam [1987]. New York is a source of inspiration, judging from the photo on the left.

Bottom right 'De moeder van De Zwaan' (Mother of The Swan), Riek Bakker and the Erasmus Bridge drawn by Dicky Brand, reproduced in G. Bekaert et al., *De brug. Poëzie en kunst*, Rotterdam 1996.

is more than a traffic corridor between North and South: 'Joining Noord and Zuid is a segment of centre that reaches across the Maas. But it is more than that just a means of conveying traffic. Stand on Zuidbrug [the future Erasmus Bridge] in the middle of the city centre, in the open, liberating landscape of the river and look west and you'll feel part of the world.'[18] This high-flown description is reflected in the visuals. The scale model presents a shadow play of high-rise against the flush backdrop of the Maas. The silhouette effect of the future skyline is presented in detailed drawings done with a fine-tip black pen on semi-transparent paper through which colour photos shine to suggest an urban dynamic.[19]

The design's message got through to the press. To underline its metropolitanism, a journalist from *Rotterdams Nieuwsblad* described the plan as 'Manhattan on the Maas'.[20] That alliteration went on to lead a life of its own: 'Manhattan on the Maas' has since become a standard term for describing Rotterdam's metropolitan demeanour. To give the plan social and political clout, Riek Bakker launched an intensive promotional campaign by organizing different evenings for different interest groups. These were then deluged with visual material that stressed the importance of the Kop van Zuid plan for the city's image as a whole. At the centre of the proceedings was the bridge that was to join Zuid to Noord.

The bridge

It was crystal-clear to Bakker and Koolhaas that they needed a bridge if their plan was going to succeed. But the enormous costs were an initial stumbling block to general acceptance. The council's traffic department for one failed to see the need for a bridge: 'The traffic department saw it as wildly extravagant. Granted, we didn't need it in terms of traffic, but we certainly did in terms of image.'[21] To overcome the deadlock Riek Bakker and her supporters within the College of Mayor and Aldermen thought up a ruse: they had two engineers design a bridge apiece, the aim being to fuel a discussion about which of the two was to be built rather than whether there should be a bridge at all.[22] And it worked. The lively public discussion that ensued was ended on November 14, 1991 when the council decided to implement Ben van Berkel's design.[23] Remarkably, their argument behind this choice was that Van Berkel's bridge was the most attractive of the two. Functional and budgetary considerations came second. The council was likewise taken by what Bakker called the 'magic of images'.[24] In that respect Bakker had everything going for her. An almost euphoric mood permeated the College and the council regarding the transformation Rotterdam was to undergo. For Bakker, then, the administrative climate in Rotterdam was most invigorating: 'It was energizing, it was a Mecca in a way it hasn't been since.'[25] Bakker sees the mayor, Bram Peper, as the motor behind this administrative vitality, but also describes the aldermen of those years as 'strong', particularly Roel den Dunnen, Pim Vermeulen, René Smit, Joop Linthorst and Hans Simons, 'the chosen few, you might say'.[26]

Council documents on Kop van Zuid show that the College of Mayor and Aldermen and many on the council were aware that the new city bridge would henceforth be of seminal importance in representing Rotterdam. In the College's proposal for the area's infrastructure it spoke out strongly in favour of Van Berkel's design: 'This bent single-pylon bridge has enormous additional impact compared to the developers' "four-poster".'[27] That the 'bent single-pylon bridge' cost the council an extra 15 million guilders was not a prohibitive objection, the College felt, as: 'This powerfully modelled bridge renders in concrete form the salient fact that here, at this central position in the city, the distance between right and left banks of the river is at its greatest, and is a symbolic as well as a physical link between the two halves of the city.'[28] Riek Bakker moreover had the foresight to inform the municipal council that the single-pylon bridge could become the city's new trademark, according to the minutes of a meeting of the municipal committee for Spatial Planning, Traffic and Transport.[29]

The visual aspect of the plans for Rotterdam appealed to a wide audience. According to a councillor 'the picture of little Manhattan' was familiar throughout the country as early as 1989.[30] Even before it was built, the Erasmus Bridge was known colloquially as 'The Swan'.[31] Its shape does indeed recall a stylized silhouette of a swan, an association strengthened by the bridge's white finish. It is an asymmetrical design with many diagonals, suggesting movement. The swan looks as though it could take to the air or water at any moment, and in a way reflects the motion of the river and the ships. Much more than a neutral link in Rotterdam's infrastructure, this bridge was regarded by many as the triumphant symbol of a dynamic Rotterdam. The official opening was celebrated with a cavalcade of festive events which expressly sought to involve the local population. One of the stand-out activities was a brunch held on the Erasmus Bridge for 5000 Rotterdammers from all segments of the population. These opening festivities were organized by B-produkties BV, an agency run by Beerend Lenstra from the first wave of Rotterdam cultural entrepreneurs.[32]

Shortly after the opening, Rotterdam Public Works published a slim volume which placed all emphasis on the bridge's poetic and visual qualities. In it visual artists, photographers and poets variously report on 'how the Rotterdam cityscape was changing as a result of the building of the Erasmus Bridge'.[33] The bridge's symbolic meaning looms equally large in the introductory essay by Geert Bekaert. This well-respected Belgian architecture critic describes the bridge in exalted terms: 'It represents the ultimate fulfilment of a deficiency, the unexpected realization of a dream. The city that was never "finished", is hereby complete. It becomes a city at a time when cities are disappearing. There is more to the Erasmus Bridge than the simple matter of a bridge or, put another way, it is Rotterdam's first real bridge. Such a bridge is not conceived in the first instance in functional and structural terms. It is not a question of utility or necessity. It does not simply span the watery deep; does not just connect shores and bring them together. It is genesis. It begets. It conjures both the old and the new, the known and the unknown.'[34] Bekaert points out that interpreting the bridge along such poetic lines is in the spirit of the bridge's designer, the architect Ben van Berkel. Van Berkel has repeatedly made clear that he considers aesthetics more interesting in the long run than technology. He has, Bekaert explains, placed the Erasmus Bridge fairly and squarely in the world of imagination by quoting in his design notes the French writer Maurice Blanchot: "'One could say", writes Blanchot, "that someone who is fascinated no longer perceives any real object, any real form, because he no longer belongs to the world of reality but to the indeterminate realm of fascination itself.(...)".'[35] Over and above that, Bekaert identifies cosmopolitan ambitions in the design for the Erasmus Bridge: 'For the Erasmus Bridge aspires to join the ranks of those world-famous bridges: the Charles Bridge in Prague, the Pont-Royal in Paris, the Tower Bridge in London, the Ponte Vecchio in Florence, the Rialto in Venice but also the Brooklyn Bridge in New York and even the Golden Gate Bridge in San Francisco.'[36] In short, the bridge was the finishing touch to Rotterdam's image as a world city.

When the Erasmus Bridge was taken into use in September 1996, construction work at Kop van Zuid had only just begun. More than just a necessary link, the bridge was a promise of what was to come. Not that the bridge led then to a no-man's-land – far from it, thanks to the trailblazing activities a handful of creative individuals had been engaged in here since the end of the 1980s. As a result, many Rotterdammers as well as many from outside were familiar with Kop van Zuid before the bridge arrived. One of the ventures from those pioneering years, Hotel New York, has remained a tourist attraction to this day.

Squatters, exhibitions and parties

Out of the entire Kop van Zuid, Wilhelminapier has always been the feature that has appealed most to plan-makers – from the organizers of AIR 1982 up to and including Riek Bakker. This is most likely because of its prominent visual presence from the north bank, but is also due to the wealth of narratives connected with this pier. For Wilhelminapier is the site of the former office and departure hall of the Holland-America Line (HAL), the shipping company that until 1972 carried passengers to the United States. The office dates from 1901–1920; the terminal building is a modernist design by the famous Rotterdam architects J.H. van den Broek and J.B. Bakema and was built in 1949.[37] From here thousands of hopefuls left for the New World to start a new life there. Here, too, thousands took their leave of their loved ones. Literally giving onto the open sea, symbolically the HAL complex stands for the contacts Rotterdam enjoys with the rest of the world. These instinctive associations aside, the HAL buildings are of great architectural value and marvellously situated. The former office building stands on the outermost tip of the pier with its front towards the sea. It is this front facade with its Jugendstil decorations in which the building's architectural worth largely resides. The most immediately striking features of the office building are the two towers with green domes of oxidized copper. One contains a circular clock, the other a circular weathervane. These tall and conspicuous towers render the building visible from many places across the city. The post-war terminal building has a much more rational air about it. A radical, modernist structure, it is oversailed by six shell roofs each with a span of 18 metres giving the building a strong effect of waves when seen in silhouette. The 135 metre long quayside facade consists almost entirely of square panes of glass.

There were HAL staff still working in the former office building with the copper domes until 1984.[38] From then on, it lay vacant until September 1988 when a group of artists squatted the building and used it for living and working. They organized themselves into a foundation with the ambitious name of Groot-Manhattan (Great Manhattan). Their ideal was to turn the building into a cultural gathering place where exhibitions could be mounted and dance and drama performances put on. They immediately opened the building to the public by throwing parties and organizing exhibitions and allowing visitors in between two and five every afternoon. The building's owner, a property developer (Cityproject), left them alone as it had failed to find a buyer or renter for the seriously dilapidated premises.[39] According to one of the squatters, Cityproject offered to sell the premises to the council for 28 million, but the council was willing to pay no more than half that.[40] The council did buy it eventually in 1989 and the squatters left. The building continued to to be used for cultural ends, hosting exhibitions that included the second Rotterdam Photography Biennale in 1990.[41] In 1992 work began on converting the former office into a combined hotel and restaurant.

Meanwhile, artists had discovered the HAL departure hall. In 1988 the photo gallery Perspektief held the first Photography Biennale there.[42] The large unobstructed spaces in this building with its breath-taking prospect of the Maas and the city on the north bank proved admirable for exhibitions. It was also home for a number of years for the popular, ever larger dance parties Ted Langenbach had been organizing in Rotterdam since 1986 or thereabouts. In 1993 Langenbach organized here the first 'MTC party'. The letters MTC – short for 'Music Takes Control' – were something of an institution in the world of Dutch nightlife and the parties' organizer, Ted Langenbach, was already 'a living legend in party-land'.[43]

Ted MTC

Ted Langenbach was part of the Rotterdam creative network of the 1980s described in previous chapters. He was particularly close to the visual artist Gerald van der Kaap, who together with some members of Hard Werken produced an unorthodox photographic magazine entitled *Zien* (see). Though only nine issues were published between 1980 and 1986, it was held in high esteem by the photography and visual arts world as it drew attention to new developments at a very early stage.[44]

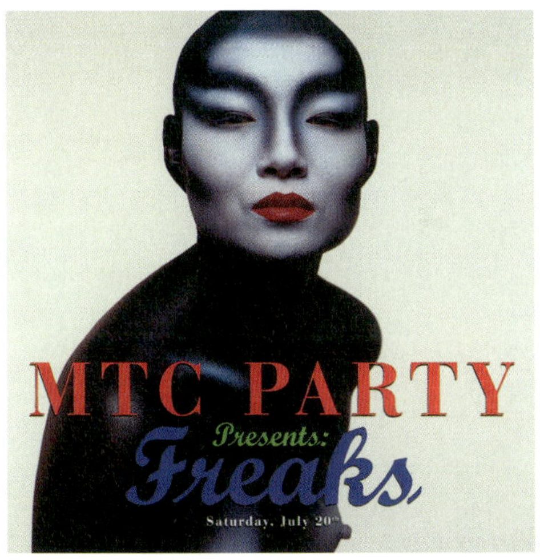

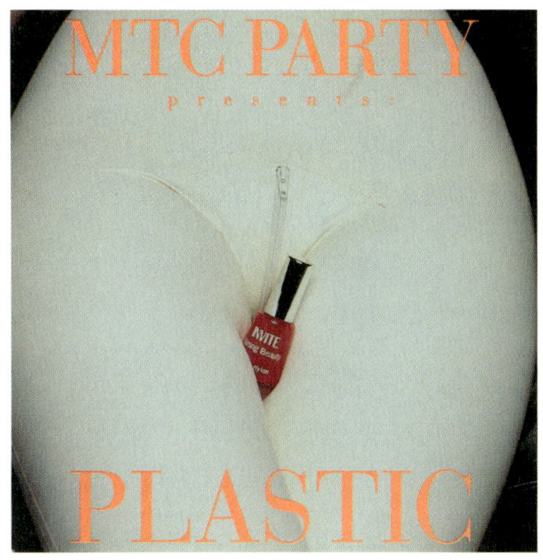

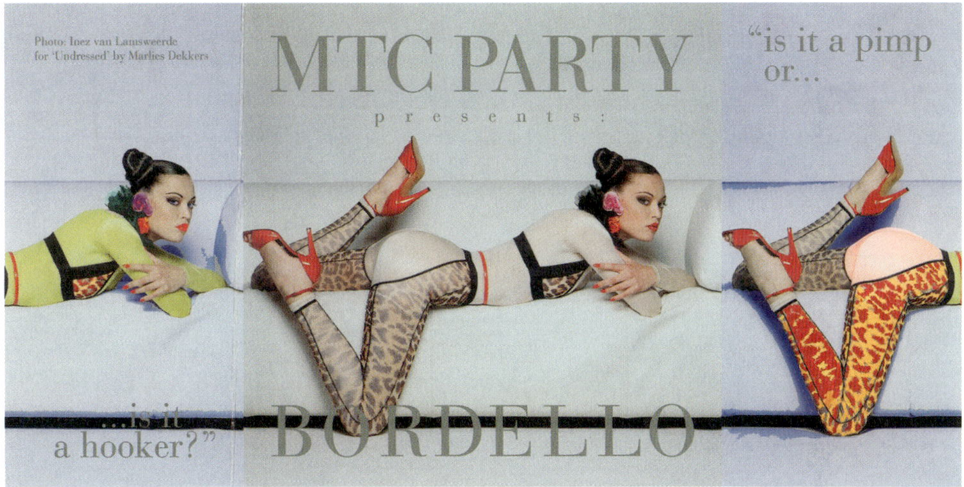

Flyers for MTC parties in the HAL departure hall, photos by Inez van Lamsweerde, graphic design by Verhey & Associates; **bottom** flyer announcing the 'Bordello' party, July 1994, where Marlies Dekkers presented her 'Undressed' range of lingerie.

Together with Van der Kaap Langenbach organized parties and exhibition previews in galleries in the 1980s. An opening put people in the mood for a party and 'then Ted was called in with his bag of records'.[45]

From 1987 on, Langenbach visited House parties in London, Barcelona and Germany, the real thing in those days.[46] He was also often to be found at the Roxy in Amsterdam, a club where the Dutch DJ Eddy de Clercq familiarized the Dutch party-going public with House music. There was scarcely anywhere in Rotterdam where you could go to dance: 'If you wanted to let your hair down in Rotterdam, you usually ended up in seedy dives or places that were much too small. And a lot of people don't feel comfortable in discos.'[47] So in 1988 Langenbach organized together with his girlfriend Monica van Leeuwen the first genuine Rotterdam house party in the style of what he had seen abroad. It was a modest affair, held in the canteen of an out-of-the-way garage big enough to accommodate 200 party-goers.[48] Langenbach came from a visual artists' scene that was still heavily into New Wave. The fact that he played House 'horrified' some visitors.[49] Outside his collaboration with Van Der Kaap, he worked on occasion with Beerend Lenstra. In 1990 they organized a major party in the former HAL office to round off the exhibition 'Stadstimmeren' in festive style. Lenstra remembers with amusement how a serious cultural public found themselves mingling with the faithful following of pleasure-loving 'beautiful people' that Langenbach had attracted by then.[50]

Langenbach achieved major recognition as Ted MTC or 'Tante Ted' (Aunt Ted!) when he began organizing parties in Nighttown, a medium-sized pop venue in the centre of Rotterdam. The director, Fons Burger, had already brought London DJs to Nighttown and wanted to hold more of such dance parties: 'Ted was one of the few people in Rotterdam engaged in organizing cutting-edge parties. So he was the man for us.'[51] Music was only one aspect of the MTC parties at Nighttown, which were whacked-out all-in affairs that included fashion shows, special dress codes and performances. Held every month or so in 1990 and 1991, these parties were exceedingly popular with a young alternative public. Each usually had a theme and there were often two rooms with different ambiences and styles of music. Ted himself described one of the Nighttown parties as follows: 'My apologies to all those hundreds of people who had to queue up in the rain. Try to arrive a little earlier next time. ("Start of the programma [sic] 9 p.m., you have to know that"). The "Love and Seduction" party kicked off in two rooms (House Room and Jazz & Soul Room) with a choice selection of acts such as the fashionperfo [sic] of ELL=BELL, Blue Man (bodypaint), E.D.C., House of Venus, House of Diva, Tin Tin, dr. Soul, erotic yoghurt act, Dolpho (jazz-dancer) etc. etc. The show went on until the early hours after which many visitors once again ended up in unfamiliar beds.'[52]

In 1993 Langenbach was invited to hold MTC parties in the HAL departure hall on Wilhelminapier.[53] There he had so much space at his disposal that he could fit out several rooms. By now, House was only one of numerous types of music being played. At a party in July 1994 with the theme 'Bordello' Jules Deelder played jazz records in a room fitted out like the famous cartoon bar The Coconut Club from the Panama of the 1950s.[54] These parties had the fashion shows, performances and theatre-type stage sets the MTC public had come to expect. Noted Rotterdam fashion designer Marlies Dekkers showed her first lingerie designs at an MTC party in 1994.[55] The invitations and flyers were crafted with similar care, and included memorable photographs by the now internationally famous duo of Inez van Lamsweerde and Vinoodh Matadin.[56] Tickets for the parties were not cheap at 40 guilders apiece, yet were often sold out a week before.[57] Somewhere between 2000 and 3000 people would attend.

Meanwhile, another new attraction was packing them in further along the pier in the former HAL offices. This was Hotel New York. It has always been more than a hotel, boasting a vast restaurant area with a café and bar. If Ted Langenbach's clientele were a young and fashion-conscious crowd who wanted to be seen, people of all ages and social standing ate and drank at Hotel New York, from Ruud Lubbers (the Dutch prime minister until August 1994) to 'Uncle Gerrit from Zuid'.[58] Even Amsterdammers made the trip to Rotterdam just to visit it.[59]

Hotel New York

The story of Hotel New York began, once again, with a canny look into the future. Daan van der Have, director of the Dizzy concern with its numerous Rotterdam cafés and restaurants, and a group of fellow entrepreneurs were looking for an indoor space that would be suitable as a venue for progressive pop and rock, with a hall able to seat about 1000. It was 1988, and at that time Rotterdam had no medium-sized auditorium for pop and rock concerts. Their eye fell on the former HAL office building and one of them said: 'Good grief, it's like a hotel.' This remark made in passing evidently took root and grew into a crazy scheme to begin a hotel with a restaurant and café here in this thoroughly dilapidated building in its thoroughly dilapidated surroundings.[60] The pop/rock venue they had originally been looking for became Nighttown, which opened its doors in September 1988 on West-Kruiskade in the city centre.

Van der Have together with business partner Hans Loos and artist/designer Dorine de Vos, approached the council, who already had a plan of their own for developing Wilhelminapier. There they were confronted with Riek Bakker, director of the Urban Development Unit, Jan Doets, director of OBR, the city's development corporation which advises on business accommodation, and Jan Laan, alderman for Spatial Planning, Traffic and Transport. According to Van der Have, Riek Bakker immediately recognized the plan's potential: 'That's what we should do.'[61] Van der Have and Loos had already shown their worth as catering entrepreneurs with a number of successful cafés and restaurants in Rotterdam. They had brought in Dorine de Vos to design the interiors and furnishings for the café-restaurants Zochers, Loos and Floor. Now they wanted to sell all these properties to get the hotel-restaurant off the ground.

Riek Bakker remembers how the plans for Hotel New York were originally greeted with disbelief, a disbelief that gradually gave way to faith: 'Those guys had good ideas, enormous drive, everyone trusted them.'[62] According to Bakker, it was their plan that saved the HAL headquarters from being demolished: 'That building was saved in the nick of time. It was letting in rain everywhere, squatters were living there and it was touch and go whether or not it would be torn down.'[63]

The council granted the three entrepreneurs a loan (3.5 million guilders) and a subsidy (1.5 million) to repair and convert the premises.[64] Alderman Joop Linthorst and OBR director Jan Doets were among those who joined Bakker in supporting the plan.[65] But Van der Have and company were advised not to rush things: they would do better to wait with setting up the hotel-restaurant until the area had begun attracting visitors on a more regular basis.[66] They waved this advice aside. They were convinced they would have their clientele, drawn there by the exceptional building and the exceptional location, which 'has everything Rotterdam stands for, its cosmopolitan air, its liberal outlook'.[67] Van der Have is of the opinion that people decide where they are going to eat or drink before they leave home, rather than en route. 'I hardly ever hear a decent analysis of people's behaviour when going out to eat or drink.'[68] He had had enough experience of that behaviour to be sure of what he was doing. Van der Have: 'You tell your friends: "We're off to a really special place, you have to go through a barrier and drive through the mud for a while." That makes it all the more interesting.'[69]

While Hotel New York was being refurbished, another famous Rotterdam caterer, Rob Baris, capitalized on the future arrival of the large restaurant by setting up an eating house close by in a former company canteen, Kantine Werklust. And indeed, it soon became obvious than people thought nothing of dining in an area with scant lighting and poor road surfaces and closed off with a barrier because of the stacks of aluminium ingots on site. A national daily reported on this phenomenon: 'Just imagine a restaurant in a large, bare, stridently lit space in a run-down dock area cordoned off with barriers. Imagine too, gigantic windows without curtains looking out either onto stacks of aluminium ingots or onto a barely illuminated wall with a mould-ridden rainwater pipe. Add to that a drab tiled floor, no-nonsense tables covered with flesh-coloured cloths sloppily ironed, and a menu card resembling a community centre bulletin sheet. Don't go there, you might think... But the reality is that in the eight months it has been around, Kantine Werklust has burgeoned into the most visited restaurant in Rotterdam. Even on a quiet weekday evening they can expect to welcome between 80 and 90 guests. At the weekend 200 is not unusual. The clientele consists of people who think they are somebody in Rotterdam public life – in other words, the in-crowd.'[70]

The magic of the place proved just as advantageous for Hotel New York, for since it opened on May 5, 1993 customers have been queuing up to get a table and the hotel has become an attraction in its own right where people stay to celebrate a special event.[71] But the lasting success of Hotel New York is not just because of its

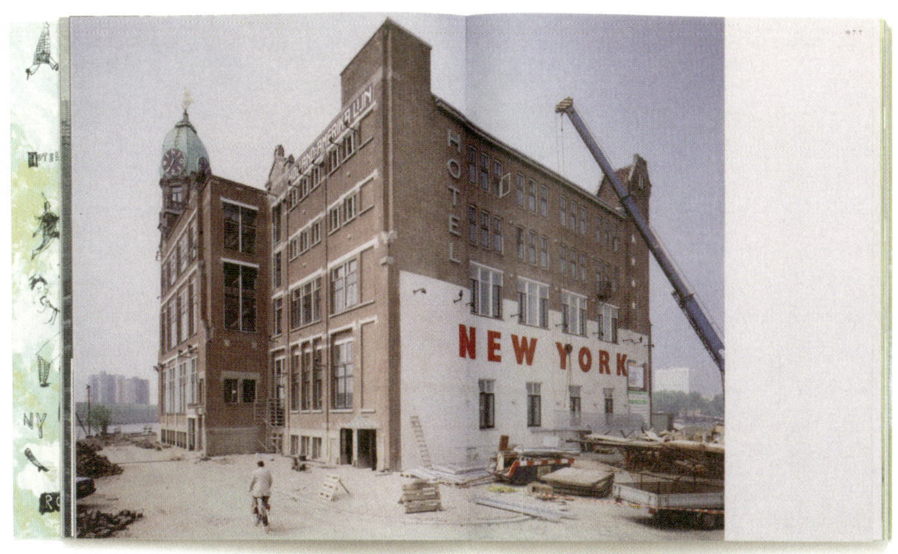

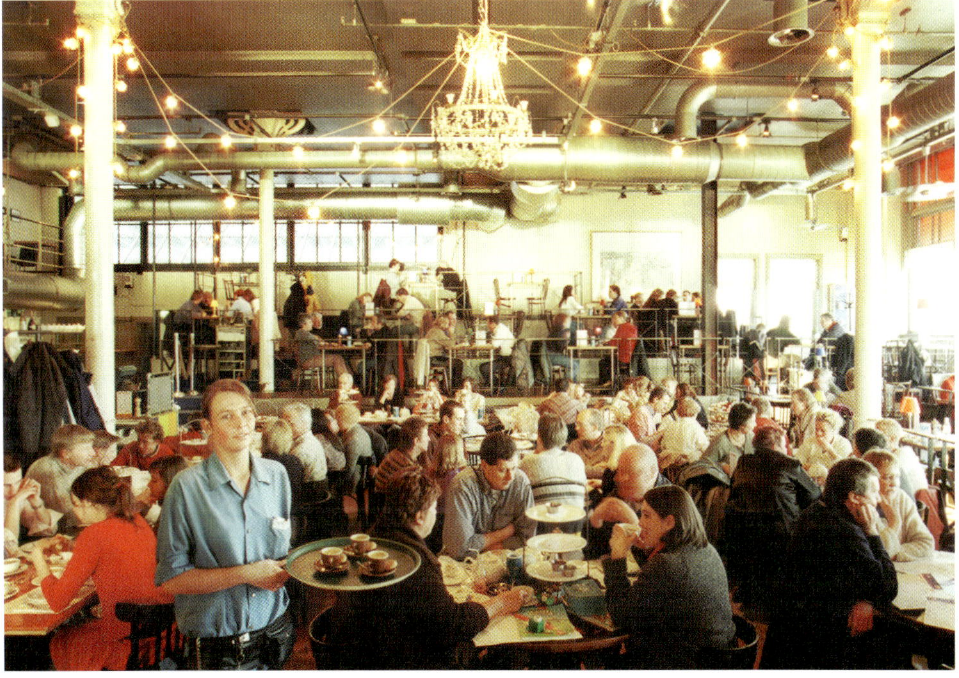

Top Hotel New York, photo from the anniversary book *Hotel New York: 10 jaar in Rotterdam*, Rotterdam 2003.

Bottom the café-restaurant at Hotel New York, photo by Rinie Bleeker.

setting. And not just because of the legendary quality of the beds, which some have even described as 'poor'.[72] More importantly, it is because every detail of the building is intended to engineer the fullest experience of Rotterdam and of 'everything Rotterdam stands for'. Hotel New York creates the ideal conditions for experiencing Rotterdam in accordance with the stereotyped image at centre stage in the foregoing chapters. Sitting at a table in the gigantic dining room or lying on a bed[73] in one of the hotel rooms overlooking the water, your perception of Rotterdam is being shaped for you. Seen from Hotel New York, Rotterdam is a city on the river, with a world-class port, in contact with the entire world, graced by an American-style skyline, with masses of space, where people behave in a worldly manner – having breakfast, lunch and dinner in public. Much more than a hotel cum restaurant, Hotel New York is nothing short of a spectacular stage set from which to experience Rotterdam. Indeed, Dorine de Vos compares her interior design for it to stage scenery.[74] And you can travel there by boat – a service that obtained from day one – which adds to the experience. This makes it a popular place to take foreign visitors.[75]

There are many who, looking back, attribute a share of the ambience and success of Wilhelminapier to Hotel New York and the other trailblazing activities. According to Riek Bakker, there are outsiders who even think that siting Hotel New York there was part of an ingenious strategy: 'Every new plan being made for somewhere in the Netherlands, or even far beyond our borders on occasion, names Hotel New York as a model. It often gets described as a sophisticated part of the overall planning of Kop van Zuid.'[76] It didn't happen that way, though. Like many other initiatives that have been key to Rotterdam's urban-cultural climate, Hotel New York was the result of a felicitous, more or less chance exchange between private plan-makers and council decision-makers. Just as Jan Riezenkamp stuck out his neck by giving Utopia the key to the former waterworks site, 'unorthodox methods'[77] (Bakker) clinched the deal to finance Hotel New York instead of an overall strategy. The idea that Hotel New York was part of the planning never ceases to amuse Riek Bakker, as witness an open letter to its three founders on the occasion of the enterprise's tenth anniversary: '(...) because I know better, if you hadn't been so industrious and creative and if we government officials of those days hadn't taken up your initiative solidly backed by the city authorities, Hotel New York would never have happened. Concept my eye. Human industriousness, I'd say!'[78]

Cultural cluster

Thanks to the pioneers and the pull of Hotel New York in particular, Wilhelminapier became a cool 'place to be'.[79] People went there to see and to be seen. These, according to the press, were the 'in-crowd' and later the 'jet set'; you only 'counted' if you had been there.[80] Inside, Hotel New York seems informal and unorganized, but in fact is embedded in cultural erudition: the furniture in the hotel rooms is old but made by famous designers, all original details of the building have been left intact,

reproductions of art works adorn the walls and even the tiniest details attest to
'good taste' as defined by a cultural elite. Hotel New York also hosts cultural events.
In the 1990s and on into the new century Wilhelminapier attracted many other cultural activities such as an institute of visual culture which remained in the pipeline,
Art Rotterdam (an international art fair held annually since 2000), a dance club,
the new Luxor Theatre (which opened in 2001 in a new building), exhibitions in the
former warehouse Las Palmas and the forthcoming Nederlands Fotomuseum (2007).
Yet although the original zoning plan for the pier referred to 'cultural and recreational
institutions at city and national level', the emphasis has always been squarely on
Wilhelminapier as a prime site for offices.[81] In Teun Koolhaas's scale model the pier
bristles with American-style skyscrapers. Some of these are already on site – the
World Port Centre and Toren op Zuid (KPN telecommunications) in 2000, Montevideo
in 2005 – and there are a few more tall ones to come. But it is the mix of culturally
tinged institutions and temporary events that sets the tone here. These are the result
of a knock-on effect, not a strategy outlined beforehand. Take the new Luxor Theatre.
It was originally projected for the city centre, next to the old Luxor. Those plans date
from 1993.[82] It was only in 1995 that the council decided to adopt alderman Kombrink's
proposal to site it at Kop van Zuid next to where Wilhelminapier begins.[83]

Wilhelminapier with its cluttered, piecemeal infill has proved more successful as a cultural cluster than the systematic approach taken at Entrepotgebied, also
part of Kop van Zuid. This last-named area was much more highly regarded as a
potential locality for culture than Wilhelminapier. For a start, the Entrepot Building,
a former bonded warehouse, was to house the Holland Art Line, an organization that
was to assemble art galleries and studios within that building. Even the surroundings
were to become an 'art district'.[84] The building was entrusted to property developers
though as yet these have failed to turn the area into a flourishing public precinct;
even the catering side has failed to take off. Waterstad is another example from
those years of a Rotterdam area earmarked by the council as a cultural cluster or, in
the words of the promotional campaign, as 'one of the key points in the city where
art, culture, recreation and science converge'. Projected in the city centre, Waterstad
has likewise failed to live up to expectations.[85] Its limits were poorly defined and it
failed to acquire a recognizable identity. An employee at Rotterdam City Development
Corporation recently admitted that Waterstad and indeed Entrepotgebied must be
regarded as failures, or partial failures. One possible reason for this, in his opinion, is
the fact that 'perhaps they were too much the brainchild of the council. This hasn't
worked. But a Hotel New York does work.'[86] Yet Wilhelminapier is driven in part by
the council and Hotel New York would never have existed were it not for the council's
cooperation. A much more essential difference with Waterstad and Entrepotgebied
is that in the case of Hotel New York the council was responding to the spontaneous
emergence of a cultural milieu on Wilhelminapier, whereas the other two areas
had been *planned* as cultural clusters. One simple ad-hoc decision can be more significant than a well-considered zoning plan, according to Daan van der Have of

Hotel New York, who cites the telling example of the permission the council gave for the Zenne restaurant terrace to be sited literally on the north bank of the Maas: 'It's so very simple sometimes, that a Turkish entrepreneur can arrange tables and chairs along the water and make that a permanent thing. This is so important.'[87]

Kop van Zuid has been developed thanks to 'the magic of images' (Riek Bakker). Bakker started with a future vision of Rotterdam imagined at her hotel window. She then succeeded in visualizing this image for others, as a councillor recalls: 'The intention was to win over our eyes and minds and so we were shown a dazzling array of slides of places all over the world where breath-taking buildings and boulevards were to be found.'[88] The founders of Hotel New York proceeded from a similar image of Rotterdam, one they had fostered since the beginning of the 1980s. Their Rotterdam was spacious, open, cosmopolitan, and after having created many places in the city where Rotterdam could be experienced in these terms, Hotel New York was their crowning achievement. By the same token, the Erasmus Bridge was chosen because of its expressive power.

The first to blaze a trail here were members of Rotterdam's creative class. In laying claim early on to Wilhelminapier in particular, they helped draw the area into urban life even before there was a bridge. Alderman Joop Linthorst was able to write back in 1994: 'We can already see the first signs that Rotterdammers don't just support the Kop van Zuid project but have literally "taken possession" of it, as shown by the success of Hotel New York and the accommodation campaign but also by the general interest taken in all the construction work.'[89]

With the development of Kop van Zuid, Rotterdam has come to resemble more than ever the image of it that emerged at the beginning of the 20th century: modern, spacious, big, with an American-style skyline, in contact with the world thanks to the river and the port. The city has never lent itself better to being photographed and filmed as a metropolis.

1 Bakker, R. (1994), *Ruimte voor verbeelding*, Rotterdam: 010 Publishers/Stichting Rotterdam-Maaskant, p. 29.

2 Zee, R. van der (2005), 'De brug als ansichtkaart', *HP/De Tijd*, September 23, 2005.

3 Planbureau Binnenhaven-Spoorweghaven-Wilhelminapier (1984), *Structuurschets 'DE KOP VAN ZUID'*, Rotterdam: DROS GB GW.

4 Planbureau Binnenhaven-Spoorweghaven-Wilhelminapier (1984), op. cit. (note 3), p. 8.

5 Bakker said this in an interview with the author on January 23, 2004. Joop Linthorst remembers it differently; according to him the expectations were indeed that Bakker would inject 'panache' into the city, as he put it in an interview with the author on January 12, 2004. Still, the fact that Bakker was originally confronted with the threatened axing of her department does lend credibility to her side of the story.

6 According to Bakker herself in an interview with the author, January 23, 2004.

7 Information from the author's interview with Riek Bakker, January 23, 2004 and Bakker (1994), op. cit. (note 1), unless stated otherwise.

8 Bakker (1994), op. cit. (note 1), p. 24.

9 Author's interview with Riek Bakker, January 23,

2004. For the results of the 'June project' see:
SO (Dienst Stadsontwikkeling) (1986), *SO Juniprojekt 1986*, Rotterdam: Dienst Stadsontwikkeling.
10 Bakker (1994), op. cit. (note 1), p. 25.
11 For more about these reports see chapter 4.
12 Author's interview with Riek Bakker, January 23, 2004.
13 idem.
14 idem.
15 Koolhaas, T. et al. (1987), *De Zuidkade van Rotterdam: Planbeschrijving behorend bij het stede-bouwkundig ontwerp De Kop van Zuid*, Almere: BV Ontwerpbureau ir Teun Koolhaas Associates, p. 1.
16 Bout, J. van den & E. Pasveer (eds) (1994), *Kop van Zuid*, Rotterdam: 010 Publishers, p. 22; Koolhaas et al. (1987), op. cit. (note 15); Stadsontwikkeling Rotterdam & Grondbedrijf Rotterdam ([1987]), *De Kop van Zuid: Een stedebouwkundig plan*, Rotterdam: Stadsontwikkeling Rotterdam/Grondbedrijf Rotterdam. Bestuursdienst Directie SOB (1994), *Kop van Zuid: Bijlagen bij overzicht van Raadsvoorstellen en -besluiten, Boek 2-A*, Rotterdam: Bestuursdienst, p. 235.
17 Koolhaas et al. (1987), op. cit. (note 15), p. 3.
18 Koolhaas et al. (1987), op. cit. (note 15), p. 4.
19 Stadsontwikkeling Rotterdam & Grondbedrijf Rotterdam ([1987]), op. cit. (note 16).
20 '"Manhattan" in Rotterdam-Zuid: Tweede brug nodig naar tweede stadscentrum', *Rotterdams Nieuwsblad*, June 3, 1987. To my knowledge, the expression 'Manhattan on the Maas' was first used in a themed sales campaign held in De Bijenkorf department store in October 1966. See *Bijenkorf. Personeelsorgaan van de Bijenkorf*, November 1966, 30 (327), [p. 5], archive of De Bijenkorf, Rotterdam.
21 Author's interview with Riek Bakker, January 23, 2004.
22 According to Riek Bakker in an interview with the author, January 23, 2004; publications make no reference to this 'hidden agenda'.
23 Bestuursdienst Directie SOB (1994), *Kop van Zuid: Overzicht van raadsvoorstellen en -besluiten, Boek 1*, Rotterdam: Bestuursdienst Rotterdam, p. 3.
24 Bakker (1994), op. cit. (note 1), p. 29.
25 Author's interview with Riek Bakker, January 23, 2004.
26 idem.
27 Bestuursdienst Directie SOB (1994), Bestuursdienst Directie SOB (1994), *Kop van Zuid: Bijlagen bij overzicht van Raadsvoorstellen en -besluiten, Boek 2-A*, Rotterdam: Bestuursdienst, p. 250.
28 Bestuursdienst Directie SOB (1994), op. cit. (note 27), p. 249.

29 Bestuursdienst Directie SOB (1994), op. cit. (note 27), p. 113.
30 Bestuursdienst Directie SOB (1994), op. cit. (note 27), p. 29.
31 The single-tower design was already being called the Swan in the council meeting of November 14, 1991. Bestuursdienst Directie SOB (1994), op. cit. (note 27), pp. 349-353.
32 See chapters 3, 4 and 5.
33 Bekaert, G., J. Beranová et al. (1996), *De brug: poëzie en kunst/The Erasmus Bridge: poetry and art*, Rotterdam: Gemeentewerken/NAi Uitgevers, p. 3.
34 Bekaert, Beranová et al. (1996), op. cit. (note 33), p. 10.
35 Bekaert, Beranová et al. (1996), op. cit. (note 33), p. 19.
36 Bekaert, Beranová et al. (1996), op. cit. (note 33), p. 8.
37 Heiden, M. & A. Piersma (eds) (2003), *Hotel New York: 10 jaar in Rotterdam*, Rotterdam: Hotel New York, pp. 7-8.
38 Acda, G.M.W. (1990), 'Het oude hoofdkantoor van de Holland Amerika Lijn in Rotterdam', *De Blauwe Wimpel*, 45 (9) September 1990, pp. 304-307 (p. 307).
39 Beek, G. van der (1988), 'Werkloze kunstenaars in "duurste kraakpand van de wereld"', *MUG, Maandblad voor uitkeringsgerechtigden Rotterdam*, (12) December 1988, p. 11.
40 P.P. ([1988]), '6000 m² geconfisceerd: Kunstenaars nemen het heft in eigen hand', *Town Magazine*, [1] ([3]), pp. 22-23 (p. 23).
41 Cornelissen, M. (1995), *Perspektief in Rotterdam 1980–1993*, Vakgroep Kunstgeschiedenis, Utrecht: Universiteit Utrecht, p. 75.
42 Cornelissen (1995), op. cit. (note 41), p. 69.
43 Neelissen, B. (1994), 'Bordello: dans- én kijklust: Tante Ted verheft party tot vorm van theaterkunst', *Rotterdams Dagblad*, July 7, 1994.
44 Perrée, R. (2000), 'Zien (1980–1986)', in: P. van Ulzen (ed.), *90 over 80: Tien jaar beeldende kunst in Rotterdam: de dingen, de mensen de plekken*, Rotterdam: Nai Uitgevers/Stichting Kunstpublicaties Rotterdam, pp. 198-199.
45 Groen, S. (2000), 'Alles moet multi', *Squeeze*, September 2000.
46 Vonk, R. (1988), 'Private Dance Party: Move your ass!', *Het Vrije Volk*, June 16, 1988.
47 According to Langenbach, quoted in Vonk (1988), op. cit. (note 46).
48 ibid..
49 Haas, M. ([1996]), 'Tien jaar Ted: Het aanhoudende succes van de MTC-party's', *Nieuwe Revue*, October 9-16,

pp. 52-57 (p. 54); Vinckx, Y. (2004), 'House is groot geworden in de Roxy', *NRC Handelsblad*, June 26/27, 2004. House broke through in the Netherlands in about 1988, to judge from the special the music magazine *Oor* devoted to it in September of that year; Smeele, N. (2006), *Dance als muziek en vrijetijdsproduct. Faculteit der Historische en Kunstwetenschappen*, Master's thesis, Rotterdam: Erasmus Universiteit, p. 8.

50 Author's interview with Beerend Lenstra, May 19, 2003.

51 Fons Burger quoted in Haas ([1996]), op. cit. (note 49), p. 54.

52 Ted (M.T.C.) ([1990]), 'Shake that Body Page', *Town Magazine*, [3] [July-August], pp. 20-21 (p. 21).

53 Haas ([1996]), op. cit. (note 49), pp. 52-57.

54 Neelissen (1994), op. cit. (note 43).

55 ibid.

56 Meijer, M. (1995), 'Mode aan de Maas: Voor Ted en Petra geen eenheidsworst maar punkglamour', *Rotterdams Dagblad*, January 12, 1995; Haas ([1996]), op. cit. (note 49), pp. 52-57.

57 Neelissen (1994), op. cit. (note 43).

58 Author's interview with Daan van der Have, January 14, 2003.

59 According to the Amsterdammer Henk Spaan in *Algemeen Dagblad* of April 18, 1994, quoted in: Heiden & Piersma (eds) (2003), op. cit. (note 37), p. 229.

60 Author's interview with Daan van der Have, January 14, 2003.

61 idem.

62 Author's interview with Riek Bakker, January 23, 2004.

63 idem.

64 Heiden & Piersma (eds) (2003), op. cit. (note 37), p. 99.

65 Heiden & Piersma (eds) (2003), op. cit. (note 37), p. 75.

66 Author's interview with Daan van der Have, January 14, 2003.

67 idem.

68 idem.

69 idem.

70 Stellweg, C. (1992), 'Een kantine voor de in-crowd', *Algemeen Dagblad*, November 6, 1992.

71 Heiden & Piersma (eds) (2003), op. cit. (note 37).

72 Richard Hutten in *Eigen Huis & Interieur*, 9, September 1999, p. 58.

73 The floors in the hotel rooms are raised 'so that you can see the ships from your bed'; Heiden & Piersma (eds) (2003), op. cit. (note 37), p. 105.

74 Heiden & Piersma (eds) (2003), op. cit. (note 37), p. 241.

75 See, for example, the remarks of designer Richard Hutten and museum curator Thimo te Duits in *Eigen Huis & Interieur*, 9, September 1999, pp. 58 and 59.

76 Heiden & Piersma (eds) (2003), op. cit. (note 37), p. 75.

77 ibid.

78 ibid.

79 Term derived from: Aalst, I. van & E. Hitters, *'The place 2B': explaining and exploring the logic of urban cultural clusters*, unpublished manuscript.

80 Stellweg (1994), op. cit. (note 70); Schulte, E. (1994), 'HAL-gebouw, Rotterdam', in: P. Nijhof & E. Schulte (eds), *Herbestemming industrieel erfgoed in Nederland*, Zutphen: Walburg Pers, pp. 130-131.

81 Gemeente Rotterdam (1991), *Bestemmingsplan Kop van Zuid*, Rotterdam: Gemeente Rotterdam.

82 Rozendaal, J. (1993), 'Miljoenen voor nieuwe Luxor en Feyenoordstadion', *Rotterdams Dagblad*, September 18, 1993.

83 'Nieuw Luxor naar de Kop van Zuid: Investering van zestig miljoen gulden', *Rotterdams Dagblad*, June 23, 1995.

84 Koolhaas et al. (1987), op. cit. (note 15), p. 9; Kuypers, K. (1989), 'Hier komt het nieuwe Manhattan', *Town Magazine*, 2 (5) June 1989, pp. 6-9.

85 Berg, L. van den, L.H. Klaassen & J. van der Meer (1990), *Strategische City-Marketing*, Schoonhoven: Academic Service, p. 126.

86 Jan Oosterman, leisure economy development manager at Rotterdam City Development Corporation, quoted in: Hemel, Z. (ed.) (2003), *Stedebouw & Ruimtelijke Ordening*, 84 (9), theme issue 'De Europese binnenstad', p. 31.

87 Author's interview with Daan van der Have, January 14, 2003.

88 From the minutes of the municipal council meeting of September 12, 1991; Bestuursdienst Directie SOB (1994), op. cit. (note 27), p. 235.

89 Van den Bout & Pasveer (eds) (1994), op. cit. (note 16), p. 5.

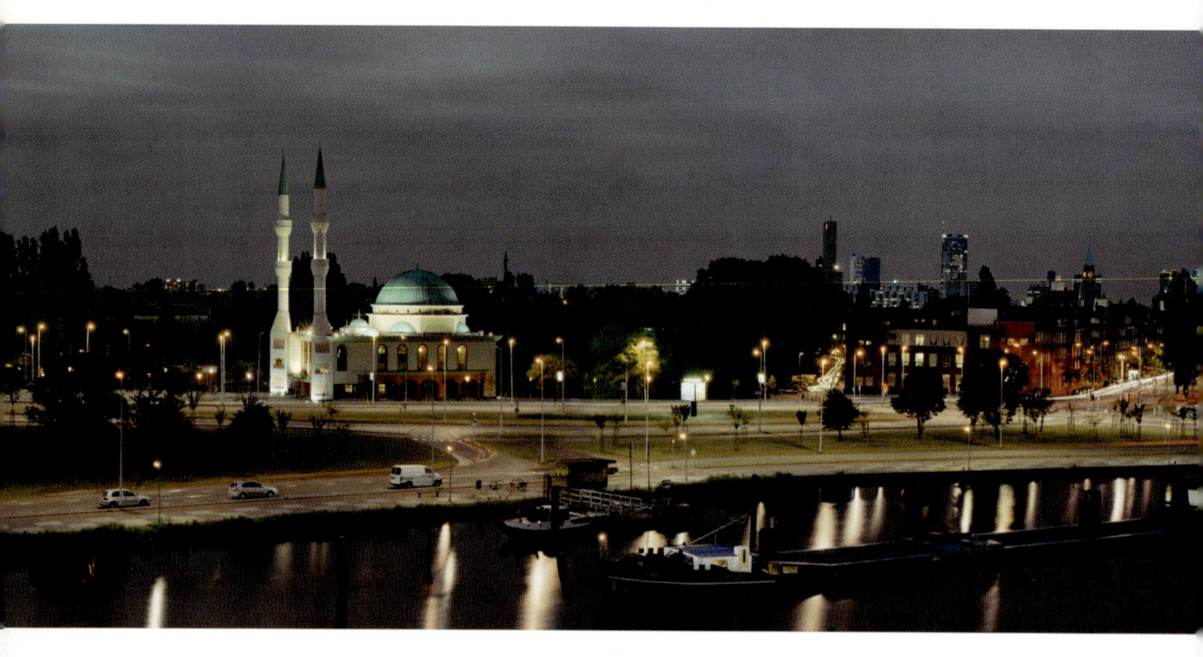

The Mevlana Mosque, from the series *Dutch Mosques*, 2004, photo by Hans Wilschut. In 2006 the Mevlana was voted the most attractive building in Rotterdam in a public survey organized by the City Information Centre.

Imagining a metropolis has done Rotterdam a lot of good. Anything ugly about the city looks beautiful when seen through metropolitan glasses. This first proved to be the case in the years separating the two world wars. And whatever is beautiful about Rotterdam looks ravishing in the metropolitan dream. The Rotterdam skyline these days is marvellous, but it is just plain breath-taking to those who believe it symbolizes a metropolitan ambience. The architect Birgitte Louise Hansen, who moved to Rotterdam in 1997, has described the symbolic power of the Rotterdam cityscape in a slim volume in which newcomers to Rotterdam talk about their favourite place in the city. The one Hansen chooses is the view of the city from the Erasmus Bridge. She got to know this place on her very first day in Rotterdam: 'It was almost dark when I ended up at the Erasmus Bridge. From the bridge, I looked out over the city neon lights, the buildings, the harbour and the cranes. Then I knew what I had come for.'[1] Although these are her words, obviously she had not come for the neon lights, the buildings, the harbour and the cranes. She was there for the thing these elements symbolize: a dynamic metropolis.

It is important for a city to have an image with a strong symbolic thrust such as that of a metropolis. To begin with, it steps up its capacity to attract tourists. Rotterdam's metropolitan aspects are indeed exploited to the full, as we saw in the introduction to this book. But it is just as important that the inhabitants have an image of their city too. The 'ordinary Rotterdammer', whom Daan van der Have calls 'Uncle Gerrit from Zuid', is attached to the stereotyped image of Rotterdam. It gives Rotterdammers something to go on, provides them with a collective identity. Jack Burgers, professor of urban studies at the Erasmus University in Rotterdam, had some interesting things to say about this in his inaugural lecture of 2002. He argues that at a time when urban communities are steadily fragmenting, people are becoming more attached to their city as something symbolic: 'Cities are what Benedict Anderson (1983) has called "imagined communities". People relate to a city intuitively, feel one with it – sometimes even without actually living there.'[2] The stronger a city's symbolic power, the more strongly people identify with it. Explaining Rotterdammers' objections to plans to make Rotterdam municipality part of a 'metropolitan province', Burgers puts it down to their devotion to 'the collective impression of Rotterdam as a symbol'.[3]

In recent decades the 'ordinary Rotterdammer' is more and more likely to originate from a country other than the Netherlands. 'Uncle Gerrit' is increasingly likely to be 'Uncle Wesley' or 'Aunt Fatima'. And for these Rotterdammers especially, the image of metropolitanism can be the place to start in securing an identity. One traditional characteristic of a metropolis, after all, is its international quality. The un-Dutch image of Rotterdam makes this city the ideal candidate – as the author

Ferdinand Bordewijk wrote back in 1938: 'Amsterdam is our national city, Rotterdam our international city.'[4] The image of the metropolis has gone global, it is more or less the same everywhere, from Africa to Asia. Many regret the fact that this uniformity is eroding cultural identity. The other, more positive side of the coin is that these cities can be understood symbolically by anyone anywhere. Rotterdam is a member, if a relatively minor one, of this family of world cities.

Attempts to make Rotterdam seem smaller than it really is, on the other hand, have done the city more harm than good. This was done most literally during the C70 event of 1970 and in the years that followed, small-scale structures of all kinds sprang up everywhere in a move to make the city where 'the wind blows the clothes from your body' more intimate. This fiddly, 'frumpish' architecture is now generally regarded as a temporary abberation. With hindsight, it seems unfair that the rational, large-scale architecture and urban design in Rotterdam should have been blamed for the city's lack of warmth and charm, as in Jan Schaper's film *Stad zonder hart* (City without a heart, 1966). Watching the film today – a film *designed* to show Rotterdam at its worst – we can only mourn the fact that in the 1970s so much visual clutter was allowed to disturb the consistent urban landscape of those days. The furious growth of vehicular traffic and years of inconvenience while the Rotterdam Metro was being built (1964–1968) were factors that encroached more on city life than the modernity of the architecture and urban design.

A much more recent attempt to belittle Rotterdam was metaphorical instead of literal. This was when the council published the so-called Rotterdam Citizens Code, one of the last measures taken by Rotterdam city council before the local elections of March 2006.[5] This curious document consists of seven rules of behaviour recommended by the College of Mayor and Aldermen plus an exhaustive explanation. The second recommendation of this 'Rotterdam Code' got the most media coverage and criticism. This runs as follows: 'We [Rotterdammers] use Dutch as our common language.' The accompanying explanation put it even more coercively: 'We speak Dutch in public – at school, at work, on the street and in the neighbour-hood centre.' Many saw this as an obligation to speak Dutch in public and therefore as a provincial, anti-cosmopolitan measure, an effrontery in a city like Rotterdam where more than 40 per cent of the inhabitants have a foreign background.[6] Paradoxically, the Rotterdam Code did uphold Rotterdam's metropolitan reputation: 'Working together to build a world city' is a slogan emblazoned on the first page. The Rotterdam Code was typical of the dismissive attitude of the city council of those days towards cultural differences in Rotterdam's urban society.

Two occurrences lead us to suspect that most Rotterdammers failed to appreciate such anti-cosmopolitan measures as making Dutch the one language to be spoken in public. One was the defeat suffered by the then incumbent coalition during the local elections of March 2006.[7] The other, less far-reaching but just as revealing, was the choice in April 2006 of the Mevlana Mosque as Rotterdam's most attractive building. Only in 2003, alderman Marco Pastors had spoken out against building mosques in the city. But now even the Erasmus Bridge had lost out to an Islamic house of prayer, described by those who voted for it as 'a symbol of warmth and hospitality'.[8]

Creation versus evolution

If one thing became certain during the research that led to this book, it is that cities follow an organic development of their own. The idea that they can be driven by long-term planning and city marketing can be compared to believing in the biblical creation. Against that faith in a creation from above, this book pits an urban theory of evolution. Cities develop gradually, and cannot be forced into a mould. Underground initiatives give rise to gradual shifts on the surface. Artists and creative people in general are able to engineer those shifts, as they are in a better position than others to feel where the power of a city lies. Hotel New York is an eloquent example. After decades of 'top-down' attempts to bring Rotterdam and the Maas closer together again, the arrival of Hotel New York and the water taxis that serve it reinstated Rotterdam as a city that coexists with the river.

The social implications of the city's image as outlined above were also a major spur for Rotterdam's creative class to launch such initiatives. Cultural entrepreneurs such as Rob Baris, Daan van der Have, Jacques van Heijningen, Ted Langenbach, Beerend Lenstra, Evan van der Most and Bob Visser have a strong sense of responsibility towards the city they live and work in. Rob Baris began a new restaurant in a disadvantaged area of Rotterdam not so long ago, with the intention of doing something positive for the community there. Ted Langenbach is enthusiastic about the youngsters from minority ethnic backgrounds who work for him and have dance culture as their common ground. Evan van der Most is currently housing in Hal 4 a funky theatrical troupe of young men and women from many cultural and ethnic backgrounds calling themselves Rotterdams Lef (roughly, 'Rotterdam grit'). All this belongs to the metropolitan dream.

So the imagined metropolis of Rotterdam is much more than a attractive stage set for flashy television commercials and hair-raising films. The importance of the city's image extends much further, influencing economic and social processes. This is why city marketing experts and council administrators are so eager to manipulate that image. Yet the most they can do is take processes that are already operative and point them in the right direction. And in Rotterdam during the years 1970–2000 there were times when they rose to the occasion.

1 Galema, W. (ed.) (2004), *Europe's Favourites: Architecture in Rotterdam*, Rotterdam: Stichting AIR, unpaged.
2 Burgers, J. (2002), *De gefragmenteerde stad*, Amsterdam: Boom, p. 23.
3 Burgers (2002), op. cit. (note 2), p. 24.
4 Bordewijk, F., *Karakter: Roman van zoon en vader*, Amsterdam 1998 (first edition 1938), p. 234. Amsterdam, 'a world city the size of a village' (according to Verbij, A. (1999), in 'Romsterdam', *De Groene Amsterdammer*, June 30, 1999), expressly manifests itself as a world-class city so as to make a success of its multicultural community. Karl Schlögel in his essays on the new Europe describes Rotterdam as a European capital city. Schlögel, K. (2005), *Marjampole oder Europas Wiederkehr aus dem Geist der Städte*, Munich/ Vienna: Carl Hanser Verlag, pp. 65-66.
5 http://www.rotterdam.nl/Rotterdam/Internet/ Collegesites/burgemeesteropstelten/015%20burger-schapscode-def-v4.pdf, site visited May 11, 2006.
6 For example Liukku, A., 'Nederlands op straat verplicht', *AD Rotterdam*, January 20, 2006 and in a column by Lower House Labour Party candidate Peter van Heemst on the website of Partij van de Arbeid Rotterdam, dated January 24, 2006, http://www.pvdarotterdam.nl/nieuwsbericht/2264, site visited May 11, 2006.
7 http://www.rotterdam.nl/Rotterdam/Openbaar/ Diensten/COS/Publicaties/PDF/gemeenteraadsver-kiezingen2006.pdf, site visited May 11, 2006.
8 'Moskee mooiste gebouw Rotterdam', *NRC Handelsblad*, April 3, 2006.

This book is the result of four years' research done at the Faculty of History and Arts of the Erasmus University in Rotterdam. My research was financed in large part by G.Ph. Verhagen-Stichting, a foundation devoted to supporting social and cultural enterprise in Rotterdam and to which I wish to extend my deepest thanks. Stichting Kunstpublicaties Rotterdam, on whose editorial board I sit, backed publication of this book from the very start, substantively as well as financially. To this foundation also I owe an enormous debt of gratitude.

Thanks too go to the many individuals who have helped me with the substance of my research during those four years. Top of the list is my thesis supervisor Prof. Dr. Marlite Halbertsma, without whose inspiring guidance I would never have embarked on this journey, let alone completed it. I am indebted also to the members of my inner doctoral committee, that is, Prof. Dr. Susanne Janssen, Prof. Dr. Jack Burgers and Prof. Dr. Paul van de Laar, for their support and their useful comments during the final stages. I am also most grateful to have had the opportunity to exchange ideas with Prof. Dr. Rolf Lindner who, I am delighted to say, was on my plenary doctoral committee.

The interviews I conducted with various people closely involved in Rotterdam's urban cultural life were essential and unique sources of material for this book. My thanks go to Carel Alons, Riek Bakker, Cees van der Geer, Daan van der Have, Beerend Lenstra, Ted Langenbach, Evan van der Most, Hans Oldewarris, Jacques van Heijningen, Hans Kombrink, Joop Linthorst, Paul Martens, Henk Molenaar, Paul Noorman, Bas van der Ree, Jan Riezenkamp, Adriaan van der Staay, Bob Visser and Bas Vroege for their patience and cooperation during these interviews and for giving me permission to quote from them. I could not have got as much out of these interviews without the rapid-fire typing of Janneke van Lisdonk. Hoos Blotkamp and Hans Oldewarris were gracious enough to let me browse through their personal archives.

To my fellow editors on the board of Stichting Kunstpublicaties Rotterdam, Frits Gierstberg, Marlite Halbertsma, Patricia Pulles, Wilma Sütö, Astrid Vorstermans and Kitty Zijlmans, I owe a special debt of thanks for their faith in me and for the rewarding conversations we had about my research.

Bettina Furnee and Louis Verschoor, who studied art history with me, must be named here for voicing their readiness to assist me as my paranimfen during the oral defence and presentation of my thesis, at a time when I had not yet typed a single letter of it. Louis Verschoor additionally passed on to me much useful information on pop music of the 1970s and '80s. My study of art history at Leiden University laid the spadework for the perspective I chose for my research. Although this book might seem to have taken me far away from art history in the strictest sense, the concern for representation and awareness of the need for interpretation reflected in it would be unthinkable had I not had a background in art history.

Thanks go also to my former colleagues at the Erasmus University for their interest and advice, particularly Ton Bevers, Nel van Dijk, Rick Dolphijn, Erik Hitters, Marijke Huisman, Miriam van de Kamp, Bernadette Kester, Wouter de Nooij, Julia Noordegraaf, Theresa Oostvogels, Marja Roholl and Valika Smeulders. Ian Horton has helped me on several occasions with conference papers I have presented in English. Herman van Ulzen transferred my audio material from minidisk to CD. Floris Paalman supplied me with information about the film-maker Andor von Barsy. I owe a further debt of gratitude to Bob Goedewaagen, Jeroen Grapendaal of Hotel New York, Jaap Jongert, Tom Kroeze, Petra Ligura, Paul Martens, Hajo Piebenga, Bas van der Ree, Matthijs Rorije of Dubbelklik, Peter Wilmer of Men at Work TV Produkties and Hans Wilschut for their help in acquiring photographic material. I also wish to acknowledge and thank the staff of Rotterdam Municipal Archives, Nederlands Film-museum, Rijksbureau voor Kunsthistorische Documentatie and Rotterdams Lees-kabinet for their friendly assistance in seeking out literature, sources and visual material.

Lastly, no-one can function without a stable home situation, least of all a doctoral candidate. For this I am indebted first and foremost to Ludo van Halem, with our childminder Trees van Hattem a close second. I thank Nina and Maria for the necessary distraction and for so much more. To them, my two boisterous muses, I dedicate this book.

Bibliography

Aalst, I. van (1997), *Cultuur in de stad: Over de rol van culturele voorzieningen in de ontwikkeling van stadscentra*, Utrecht: Van Arkel

Aarts, M. (ed.) (1987), *Leven in de stad: Rotterdam op weg naar het jaar 2000*, Rotterdam: 010 Publishers

Aarts, M. (ed.) (1995), *Vijftig jaar wederopbouw Rotterdam: Een geschiedenis van toekomstvisies*, Rotterdam: 010 Publishers

Aarts, M. & B. Maandag (eds) (2000), *Accelerating Rotterdam, Stad in versnelling*, Rotterdam: OntwikkelingsBedrijf gemeente Rotterdam

Achterberg, P., H.de Bruijn et al. (1986), *De Kop van Zuid... daar zit muziek in: uitgangspunten voor de ontwikkeling van nieuwe stedelijke funkties in de Kop van Zuid*, Rotterdam: Werkgroep ambtenaren van de dienst Stadsontwikkeling, projektgroep Bispo en projektgroep Katendrecht

Adrichem, J. van (1987), *Beeldende kunst en kunstbeleid in Rotterdam 1945–1985*, Rotterdam: Museum Boymans-van Beuningen

Albeda, W., W.S.P. Fortuyn et al. (1987), *Nieuw Rotterdam: een opdracht voor alle Rotterdammers*, Rotterdam: Adviescommissie Sociaal-Economische Vernieuwing Rotterdam, November 1987

Andela, G. & C. Wagenaar (eds) (1995), *Een stad voor het leven: Wederopbouw Rotterdam 1940–1965*, [Rotterdam], De Hef

Anscombe, I. (1978), *Not another PUNK! book*, London: Aurum Press Ltd.

Anscombe, I. & D. Blair (1978), *PUNK!*, New York: Urizen Books

Ashworth, G.J. & H. Voogd (1990), *Selling the City: Marketing Approaches in Public Sector Urban Planning*, London: Belhaven

Asscher, L. (2005), *Nieuw Amsterdam: De ideale stad in 2020*, Amsterdam: Bert Bakker

Backx, B., et al. (eds) ([1970]), *Rotterdam 25 jaar na dato*, Rotterdam: Stichting C70

Bailey, J.T. (1989), *Marketing Cities in the 1980s and Beyond*, Chicago: American Economic Development Council

Bakker, H. & T. van Hoorn (1977), 'Rotterdamse wethouder Mentink: ik wil over m'n graf heen regeren', *Plan*, (2) February, pp. 25-32

Bakker, R. (1999), 'Hoe kom ik aan de overkant?' in: P.O. Ostoja et al. (eds), *Kop van Zuid 2*, Rotterdam: 010 Publishers, pp. 8-17

Bakker, R. (1994), *Ruimte voor verbeelding*, Rotterdam: 010 Publishers/Stichting Rotterdam-Maaskant

Bakkes, J., et al. (eds) (1996), *De stad aan de man gebracht: Vijftig jaar gemeentevoorlichting in Rotterdam*, Rotterdam: Voorlichting Bestuursdienst Rotterdam

Balshaw, M. & L. Kennedy (eds) (2000), *Urban Space and Representation*, London/Sterling, Virginia, Pluto Press

Balzer, S. (1994), *Kop van Zuid, stad van morgen: Kwaliteit wordt realiteit*, Rotterdam: Communicatieteam Kop van Zuid, November 1994

Banham, R. (1980 (first print 1960)), *Theory and Design in the First Machine Age*, London: The Architectural Press

Barbieri, U., et al. (eds) (1982), *Architektuur- en Stedebouwkaart van Rotterdam*, Rotterdam: DROS/RKS/AIR

Barbieri, U., et al. (1982), *De Kop van Zuid: Ontwerp en Onderzoek*, Rotterdam: Rotterdamse Kunststichting

Beeren, W. (ed.) (1984), *Kunst uit Rotterdam*, Rotterdam: Museum Boymans-van Beuningen

Beeren, W., P.D. Duyvis, T. Schoon & C. Wiethoff (eds) (1982), *Het Nieuwe Bouwen in Rotterdam 1920–1960*, Delft: Delft University Press

Beijer, G., et al. (1994), *Over Rotterdam: Toekomstvisies aangeboden aan Joop Linthorst bij zijn afscheid als gemeenteraadslid en wethouder van de gemeente Rotterdam*, Rotterdam: 010 Publishers

Bekaert, G., et al. (1996), *De brug: poëzie en kunst/The Erasmus Bridge: poetry and art*, Rotterdam: Gemeentewerken/NAi Publishers

Berg, L. van den, J. van der Borg & J. van der Meer (1995), *Urban Tourism: Performance and strategies in eight European cities*, Aldershot (etc.), Avebury

Berg, L. van den, L.H. Klaassen & J. van der Meer (1990), *Strategische City-Marketing*, Schoonhoven: Academic Service

Berg, L. van den, J. van der Meer & A.H.J. Otgaar (1999), *De Aantrekkelijke Stad: Katalysator voor Economische Ontwikkeling en Socail Revitalisering: Een internationaal vergelijkend onderzoek naar de ervaringen van Birmingham, Lissabon en Rotterdam*, Rotterdam: European Institute for Comparative Urban Research (EURICUR) Erasmus Universiteit

RotterdamBestuursdienst Directie SOB (1994), *Kop van Zuid: Overzicht van raadsvoorstellen en -besluiten, Boek 1*, Rotterdam: Bestuursdienst Rotterdam, September 1994

Bestuursdienst Directie SOB (1994), *Kop van Zuid: Bijlagen bij overzicht van Raadsvoorstellen en -besluiten, Boek 2-A*, Rotterdam: Bestuursdienst, September 1994

Bianchini, F. & M. Parkinson (eds) (1993), *Cultural policy and urban regeneration: The West European experience*, Manchester /New York: Manchester University Press

Bienert, M. (1992), *Die eingebildete Metropole: Berlin im Feuilleton der Weimarer Republik*, Stuttgart: J.B. Metzlersche Verlagsbuchhandlung

Blazwick, I. (ed.) (2001), *Century City: Art and Culture in the Modern Metropolis*, London: Tate Publishing

Blijstra, R. (1965), *Rotterdam stad in beweging*, Amsterdam (etc.): De Arbeiderspers

Boehm, L.B.K. (1999), *Infamous City: Popular Culture and the Enduring Myth of Chicago*, Ph.D. Thesis Department of History, [Bloomington]: Indiana University

Boele, C. (1990), 'Rivaliteit Amsterdam-Rotterdam: De publiciteit rond de controverse Van Hall-Van Walsum (1957–1965)', *Geografisch Tijdschrift*, (XXV), pp. 252-261

Boele, C. & C. Helfferich (1986), *Amsterdam – Rotterdam: Drie eeuwen rivaliteit*, Rotterdam: Historisch Museum De Dubbelde Palmboom

Boer, J.W. de & C. Oorthuys (1959), *Rotterdam dynamische stad*, Amsterdam: Contact

Boode, A. de & P. van Oudheusden (1985), *De Hef. Biografie van een spoorbrug*, Rotterdam: De Hef

Boogaarts, I. (2001), 'Rotterdam is vele festivals', in: G. Engbersen & J. Burgers (eds), *De verborgen stad: De zeven gezichten van Rotterdam*, Amsterdam: Amsterdam University Press, pp. 215-227

Boomkens, R. (1998), *Een drempelwereld: Moderne ervaring en stedelijke openbaarheid*, Rotterdam: NAi Publishers

Boomkens, R. (2000), *Sign of the times: De popsong als volkslied van de globalisering*, Amsterdam: Vossiuspers AUP

Bordewijk, F. (1998 (first print 1938)), *Karakter: Roman van zoon en vader*, Amsterdam: BulkBoek

Borsay, P. (2000), *The Image of Georgian Bath, 1700–2000: Towns, Heritage and History*, Oxford, University Press

Borsay, P. (2002), 'Sounding the Town', *Urban History*, 29 (1), pp. 92-102

Bosma, K. & C. Wagenaar (2002), 'De macht van de makers: De planningseuforie bij de wederopbouw van Rotterdam en Warschau', in: M. de Keizer,

M.H. van Bruggen, E. Somers & A. van Son (eds), *Utopie: Utopisch denken, doen en bouwen in de twintigste eeuw eeuw* (Dertiende jaarboek van het Nederlands Instituut voor Oorlogsdocumentatie), Amsterdam: NIOD/Zutphen: Walburg Pers, pp. 184-208

Bout, J. van den & E. Pasveer (eds) (1994), *Kop van Zuid*, Rotterdam: 010 Publishers

Boyer, M.C. (1994), *The City of Collective Memory: Its Historical Imagery and Architectural Entertainments*, Cambridge, Massachusetts/London: The MIT Press

Brouwer, R. (1992), *Stedelijke revitalisering en kunstbeleid in Rotterdam*, Master's Thesis Vrijetijdswetenschappen, Tilburg: KUB

Brouwers, R. (1998), 'The NAI – the history of a design task', in: R. Brouwers (ed.), *The Netherlands Architecture Institute*, Rotterdam: NAi Publishers, pp. 64-83

Brusse, M.J., et al. (1938), *De schoonheid van ons land: Deel VI: Rotterdam*, Amsterdam: Uitgeverij Contact

Bureau Bakker en Bleeker B.V. (1987), *Toeristisch-recreatieve structuur Rotterdam*, Amsterdam: Bureau Bakker en Bleeker B.V., Tuin en Landschapsarchitecten, Adviseurs voor ruimtelijke ordening en planologie, January 1987

Bureau Voorlichting van Stadsontwikkeling & Bureau Voorlichting Stadhuis Rotterdam (1976), *Binnenstadsboek: 200 ideeën voor een betere binnenstad van Rotterdam*, Rotterdam

Burgers, J. (2002), *De gefragmenteerde stad*, Amsterdam: Boom

Burgers, J. (ed.) (1992), *De Uitstad: Over stedelijk vermaak*, Utrecht: Van Arkel

Burgers, J., A. Kreukels & M. Mentzel (eds) (1993), *Stedelijk Nederland in de jaren negentig*, Utrecht, Van Arkel

Buursink, J. (1991), *Steden in de markt: Het elan van citymarketing*, Muiderberg, Dick Coutinho

Cachet, E.A., M.K. Willems & G. Richards (2003), *Eindrapport Culturele Identiteit van Nederlandse Gemeenten*, Rotterdam: ERBS (Erasmus University Centre for Contract Research and Business Support BV/Rotterdams Instituut voor Sociaal-Weten-schappelijk Beleidsonderzoek BV), February 2003

Cammen, H. van der & L.A. de Klerk (1993 (first print 1986)), *Ruimtelijke Ordening: Van plannen komen plannen*, Utrecht, Het Spectrum

Centraal Planbureau (1999), *Randvoorwaarden voor een economische onderbouwing van een verbeterde zeetoegang voor het Noordzeekanaalgebied*, Centraal

Planbureau, 27 April 1999

Chambers, I. (1985), *Urban Rhythms: Pop Music and Popular Culture*, Hampshire, MacMillan

Colenbrander, B. (1995), *OMA: De sublieme start van een architectengeneratie*, Rotterdam: NAi Publishers

College van Burgemeesters en Wethouders Gemeente Rotterdam (1991), *Kop & Schouders: Strategische Visie en Plan van Aanpak tot wederzijds profijt voor de Kop van Zuid en de omliggende wijken*, Rotterdam, March 1991

Connell, J. & C. Gibson (eds) (2003), *Sound Tracks: Popular music, identity and place*, London/New York: Routledge

Coon, C. (1977), *1988: The new wave punk rock explosion*, London/New York: Orbach and Chambers Limited/ Hawthorn Books, Inc.

Cornelissen, M. (1995), *Perspektief in Rotterdam 1980–1993*, Master's Thesis Vakgroep Kunstgeschiedenis, Utrecht: Universiteit Utrecht

Crimson, P. Gadanho, B. Lootsma & R. van Toorn (eds) (2001), *Post. Rotterdam: Architecture and City after the tabula rasa/Arquitectura e Cidade após a tabula rasa*, Rotterdam: 010 Publishers

Cusveller, S. (1991), 'Recycling Rotterdam', in: H. Berens & D.L. Camp (eds), *DWL-terrein Rotterdam: Van water-fabriek tot woonwijk*, Rotterdam: 010 Publishers, pp. 56-63

Cusveller, S. (ed.) (1994), *Stad! De stad en haar identiteit*, Hoogezand: Molior

Deelder, J. (1994), *Renaissance: Gedichten '44-'94*, Amsterdam: De Bezige Bij

Deelder, J.A. & V. Mentzel (1984), *Stadslicht*, Rotterdam: Kreits

Devolder, A.-M. (ed.) ([1988]), *Trace Spoortunnel: Negen concepten/The Railway Tunnel Site: Nine Concepts*, Rotterdam: 010 Publishers

Dijk, H. van (1995), 'De gezelligheids-revolutie 1965–1985', in: M. Aarts (ed.), *Vijftig jaar wederop-bouw Rotterdam: Een geschiedenis van toekomstvisies*, Rotterdam: 010 Publishers, pp. 161-192

Donald, J. (1992), 'Metropolis: The City as Text', in: R. Bocock & K. Thompson (eds), *Social and Cultural Forms of Modernity*, Cambridge, Polity Press in Association with The Open University, pp. 417-461

DROS GB GW (1985), *Struktuurschets Kop van Zuid*, Rotterdam: DROS GB GW, January 1985

Duermeijer, E. (2000), *Booming Business: over de lucratieve stad en revitalisering: een analyse van twee waterfront projecten: de Docklands in Londen en de Kop van Zuid in Rotterdam*, Master's Thesis Faculteit der Historische en Kunstwetenschappen/Kunst en Cultuurwetenschappen, Rotterdam: Erasmus Universiteit

Elkins, J. (2003), *Visual Studies: A Skeptical Introduction*, New York/London: Routledge

Engbersen, G. & J. Burgers (eds) (2001), *De verborgen stad: De zeven gezichten van Rotterdam*, Amsterdam: Amsterdam University Press

d'Eramo, M. (2003 (first Italian print 1999)), *The Pig and the Skyscraper: Chicago: A History of our Future*, London/New York: Verso

Erve, I. van (ed.) (2004), *We Built Dreams: 25 jaar Hal 4*, Rotterdam: Hal 4

EUR (1999), *Het succes van de stad: De succesvolle stad van de 21ste eeuw – De stad als laboratorium: Lezingen uit het lustrumcongres 30 September 1998*, Rotterdam: Erasmus Universiteit Rotterdam Afdeling Interne & Externe Betrekkingen

Falkenburg, R.L. (1993), 'Iconologie en historische antropologie: een toenadering', in: M. Halbertsma & K. Zijlmans (eds), *Gezichtspunten: Een inleiding in de methoden van de kunstgeschiedenis*, Nijmegen: SUN, pp. 139-174

Featherstone, M. (1991), *Consumer Culture and Postmodernism*, London: Sage

Filmmuseum, Nationaal Fotorestauratie Atelier, Nederlands Fotoarchief, Nederlands Foto Instituut & V2_Organisatie (1999), *Las Palmas Het Plan: Internationaal Centrum voor Foto, Film & Mediatechnologie*, Rotterdam: Projectbureau Las Palmas/Communicatie-team Kop van Zuid, 30 September 1999

Fleming, J. (1995), *What kind of house party is this?* Slough, Berkshire, MIY Publishing

Florida, R. (2002), *The Rise of the Creative Class: And How It's Tranforming Work, Leisure, Community and Everyday Life*, New York: Basic Books

Frijhoff, W. (1989), 'De stad en haar geheugen', *Oase: Tijdschrift voor ontwerp, onderzoek en onderwijs*, (24), pp. 14-21

Frijhoff, W. (1993), 'Beelden, verhalen, daden: stads-cultuur', in: A.D. de Jonge & M.D. de Wolff (eds), *De Rotterdamse cultuur in elf spiegels*, Rotterdam: 010 Publishers, pp. 9-18

Gaemers, C. (1996), *Achter de schermen van de kunst: Rotterdamse Kunststichting 1945–1995*, Rotterdam: De Hef

Galema, W. (ed.) (2004), *Europe's Favourites:*

Architecture in Rotterdam, Rotterdam: AIR

Gehrels, C., et al. (Berenschot) ([2003]), *Choosing Amsterdam: Brand, concept and organisation of the city marketing*, Amsterdam: Gemeente Amsterdam

Gelder, K. & S. Thornton (eds) (1997), *The Subcultures Reader*, London/New York: Routledge

Gemeente Rotterdam (1991), *Bestemmingsplan Kop van Zuid*, Rotterdam: Gemeente Rotterdam, March 1991

Geurtsen, R., et al. (1990), 'Timmeren aan Rotterdam: Moderniteit als traditie', in: D.L. Camp & M. Provoost (eds), *Stadstimmeren: 650 jaar Rotterdam stad*, Rotterdam: Gemeente Rotterdam/Manifestatie Stadstimmeren, pp. 21-45

Gillett, C. (1983 (first print 1970)), *The Sound of the City: The Rise of Rock and Roll*, London: Souvenir Press

Goethem, M.P.F.A. van, et al. (eds) (1984), *Plannen in de vier grote steden: Inhoudelijke en procedurele ontwikkelingen met betrekking tot de structuurplanning in de vier grote steden*, Utrecht, Rijksuniversiteit Utrecht

Gold, J.R. & S.V. Ward (eds) (1994), *Place Promotion: The use of publicity and marketing to sell towns and regions*, Chichester (etc.): John Wiley & Sons

Goossens, J. & J. Vedder (1996), *Het gejuich was massaal: Punk in Nederland 1976–1982*, Amsterdam: Jan Mets

Gorkom, J.A. van, et al. (1979), *Tien jaar groei: Opmerkingen bij het vertrek van RKS-directeur A.J. van der Staay (sonde-special)*, Rotterdam: RKS

Green, N. (2005), 'Songs from the Wood and Sounds of the Suburbs: A Folk, Rock and Punk Portrait of England, 1965–1977', *Built Environment*, 31 (3), pp. 255-270

Groenendijk, A. (1991), *Het Produkt Rotterdam: Kan het beleid van de stad Rotterdam in de periode 1945–1990, gericht op bedrijvigheid en bevolking, een city-marketing beleid genoemd worden?* Master's Thesis Maatschappijgeschiedenis, Rotterdam: Erasmus Universiteit

Haan, H. de & I. Haagsma (1982), *Stadsbeeld Rotterdam 1965–1982*, Utrecht, Oosthoek's Uitgeversmaatschappij B.V

Haas, M. ([1996]), 'Tien jaar Ted: Het aanhoudende succes van de MTC-party's', *Nieuwe Revue*, 9 October – 16 October, pp. 52-57

Hagendijk, W. (1994), *10 jaar zomercarnaval Rotterdam*, Rotterdam: Museum van Volkenkunde/Van de Rhee

Hajer, M.A. (1993), 'Rotterdam: redesigning the public domain', in: F. Bianchini & M. Parkinson (eds), *Cultural policy and urban regeneration: The West European experience*, Manchester/New York: Manchester University Press, pp. 48-72

Halbertsma, M. (2000), 'Amsterdam, de eeuwige strijd met', in: P. van Ulzen (ed.), *90 over 80: Tien jaar beeldende kunst in Rotterdam: de dingen, de mensen, de plekken*, Rotterdam: NAi Publishers/Stichting Kunstpublicaties Rotterdam, pp. 22-23

Halbertsma, M. & P. van Ulzen (eds) (2001), *Interbellum Rotterdam: Kunst en cultuur 1918–1940*, Rotterdam: NAi Publishers

Hall, P. (1966), *The World Cities*, London: Weidenfeld and Nicholson

Hall, P. (1998), *Cities in Civilization*, New York: Pantheon Books

Happel, F. & P. Wilson ([1999]), *Het nieuwe Luxor/The new Luxor*, Rotterdam: Luxor Theater Rotterdam

Harding, V. (2002), 'Introduction: music and urban history', *Urban History*, 29 (1), pp. 5-7

Hazewinkel, H.C. & J.E. van der Pot (eds) (1942), *Vier eeuwen Rotterdam: Citaten uit reisbeschrijvingen, rapporten, redevoeringen, gedichten en romans*, Rotterdam: W.L. & J. Brusse's Uitgeversmaatschappij N.V.

Hebdige, D. (1979), *Subculture: The Meaning of Style*, London/New York: Methuen & Co

Hefting, P. & D. van Ginkel (1995), *Hard Werken Inizio*, Rotterdam: 010 Publishers

Heiden, M. & A. Piersma (eds) (2003), *Hotel New York: 10 jaar in Rotterdam*, Rotterdam: Hotel New York

Heijs, J. & F. Westra (1996), *Que le tigre Danse. Huub Bals een biografie*, Amsterdam: Otto Cramwinckel

Hemel, Z. (ed.) (2003), *Stedebouw & Ruimtelijke Ordening, themanummer de Europese binnenstad*, The Hague: Nederlands Instituut voor Ruimtelijke Ordening en Volkshuisvesting

Henry, T. (1989), *Break All Rules! Punk Rock and the Making of a Style*, Ann Arbor/London: U.M.I. Research Press

Hitters, E. (1996), *Patronen van patronage: Mecenaat, protectoraat en markt in de kunstwereld*, Utrecht, Jan van Arkel

Een hotel in Rotterdam aan de Maas (1991), Rotterdam: [Dizzy Holding]

Huijzer, D. & J.P. Schutten (eds) (1997), *Dat zijn nou typisch Rotterdammers: Gids voor xenofielen*, Leiden, Krikke c.s.

Hulscher, L. (1994), *De menselijke stem: 25 jaar Poetry International. Sphinx Cultuurprijs voor Martin Mooij*, Zutphen, Walburg Instituut

Jobse, R.B., H.M. Kruythoff & S. Musterd (1990),

Sladsgewesten in beweging: Migratie naar en uit de vier grote steden, Utrecht: Rijksuniversiteit Utrecht/ Delft: University of Technology/Amsterdam: Universiteit van Amsterdam

Jong, J. de, H. Meyer & M. Mooij (eds) (1984), *Die stad komt nooit af: Een collage van verhalen en foto's over stadsvernieuwing in Rotterdam*, Rotterdam: 010 Publishers

Kamp, M. van de (2003), *'One eye sees, the other feels': Het locatiekeuzeproces van kleine culturele onder-nemingen in Amsterdam en Rotterdam*, Master's Thesis Faculty of History and Arts, Department of Culture and the Arts, Rotterdam: Erasmus University

Kearns, G. & C. Philo (eds) (1993), *Selling Places: The City as Cultural Capital, Past and Present*, Oxford (etc.): Pergomon Press

Keunen, B. (2001), 'Artistic subcultures in the metropolis and the chaotic city experience: The case of the New York music scene of the 1980s', in: H. Krabbendam, M. Roholl & T. de Vries (eds), *The American Metropolis: Image and Inspiration*, Amsterdam: VU University Press, pp. 225-235

King, A.D. (ed.) (1996), *Re-Presenting the City*, Hampshire/London: Macmillan Press LTd.

King, A.D. (1995), 'Re-presenting world cities: cultural theory/social practice', in: P.L. Knox & P.J. Taylor (eds), *World cities in a world-system*, Cambridge, Cambridge University Press, pp. 215-231

Klamer, A. & D. Kombrink (2004), *Het verhaal van de Rotterdamse haven: Een narratieve analyse*, Rotterdam: Stichting Economie & Cultuur

Klein, A. & H. Besselaar ([1959]), *Amsterdam Rotterdam: Twee steden rapsodie*, Baarn: In den Toren

Klerk, L. de (1990), 'Hoe groot is Rotterdam?', *Geografisch Tijdschrift*, XXIV (3), pp. 200-211

Kloos, M. (ed.) (1988), *Amsterdam: An architectural lesson*, Amsterdam: THOTH

Kloosterman, R. (2002), 'De stad, de cultuur en het geld: Een eerste cijfermatige exercitie rond "cultural industries" in Nederland', *Stedebouw & Ruimtelijke Ordening*, 83 (2), pp. 26-29

Kloosterman, R. (2001), *Ruimte voor reflectie*, Amsterdam: Vossiuspers UvA

Kloosterman, R. & E. Stegmeijer (2004), 'Cultural Industries in the Netherlands – Path-Dependent Patterns and Institutional Contexts: The Case of Architecture in Rotterdam', *Petermanns Geographische Mitteilungen*, 148 (4), pp. 68-75

Kloosterman, R.C. (ed.) (2005), *Music and the City* (special issue of *Built Environment*), Volume 31, no. 3, Oxon: Alexandrine Press

Knaap, G.A. van der & G. Mik (1990), 'Internationalisering van de kantoren in het groot-stedelijk milieu: Rotterdam in een ruimere context', *Geografisch Tijdschrift*, XXIV (3), pp. 230-240

Knaap, G.A. van der & W.F. Sleegers (1990), 'Stedelijke vernieuwing en structuurverandering van de bevol-king in Rotterdam', *Geografisch Tijdschrift*, XXIV (3), pp. 212-223

Knippenberg, T. & P. Knippenberg (eds) [1971?], *Kralingen '70: 'n grote blijde bende*, Utrecht: Knippenbergs Uitgeverij

Koolhaas, R. (1996), *Conversations with Students*, Houston: Rice University School of Architecture/New York: Princeton Architectural Press

Koolhaas, R. (1988), 'Epilogue', in: M. Kloos (ed.), *Amsterdam: An Architectural Lesson*, Amsterdam: Thoth, pp. 108-118

Koolhaas, T., et al. (1987), *De Zuidkade van Rotterdam: Planbeschrijving behorend bij het stedebouwkundig ontwerp De Kop van Zuid*, Almere: BV Ontwerpbureau ir Teun Koolhaas Associates, 28 January 1987

Koot, R. (2001), 'De Hef en het imago van de modern-ste stad van Nederland: Een brug tussen haven en avant-garde', in: M. Halbertsma & P. van Ulzen (eds), *Interbellum Rotterdam: Kunst en cultuur 1918–1940*, Rotterdam: NAi Publishers, pp. 20-44

Kostelanetz, R. (2003), *SoHo: The Rise and Fall of an Artists' Colony*, New York/London: Routledge

Laar, P.T. van de (1998), *Veranderingen in het geschied-beeld van de koopstad Rotterdam*, Rotterdam: de auteur

Laar, P. van de (2000), *Stad van formaat: Geschiedenis van Rotterdam in de negentiende en twintigste eeuw*, Zwolle: Waanders

Laing, D. (1985), *One Chord Wonders: Power and Meaning in Punk Rock*, Milton Keynes/Philadelphia: Open University Press

Landry, C. (2000), *The Creative City: A Toolkit for Urban Innovators*, London: Comedia/Earthscan

Law, C.M. (1993), *Urban Tourism: Attracting Visitors to Large Cities*, London/New York: Mansell

Lee, M. (1997), 'Relocating Location: Cultural Geography, the Specificity of Place and the City Habitus', in: J. McGuigan (ed.), *Cultural Methodologies*, London: Thousand Oaks/New Delhi: Sage, pp. 126-141

Leeuw, K. de, S. Hoitsma, I. de Jager & P. Schonewille (eds) (2000), *Jong! Jongerencultuur en stijl in Nederland 1950–2000*, Zwolle: Waanders (etc.

Lewis, N. (1992), *Inner city regeneration: the demise of regional and local government*, Buckingham (etc.): Open University Press

Leyshon, A., D. Matless & G. Revill (eds) (1998), *The Place of Music*, New York/London: The Guildford Press

Lieftinck, M. (2003), *Appeltaart zonder appels? De beeldvorming van Rotterdam van 1945 tot 1975 in Nederlandse en buitenlandse architectuurtijdschriften*, Master's Thesis Faculteit der Historische en Kunst-wetenschappen, Kunst- en Cultuurwetenschappen, Rotterdam: Erasmus Universiteit

Lindner, R. (2002), 'Klänge der Stadt', in: C. Kaden & V. Kalisch (eds), *Musik und Urbanität*, Essen: Die blaue Eule, pp. 171-176

Lindner, R. (2003), 'Der Habitus der Stadt – ein kultur-geographischer Versuch', *Petermanns Geographische Mitteilungen*, 147 (2), pp. 46-53

Lindner, R. (2004), *Walks on the Wild Side: Eine Geschichte der Stadtforschung*, Frankfurt am Main: Campus

Lindner, R. (2005), 'Le grand récit des crottes de chien: De la mythographie de Berlin', *Sociologie et Sociétés*, 37 (1), pp. 217-229

Lindner, R. (2006), 'The Gestalt of the Urban Imaginary', *European Studies*, 23 (2006), p. 35-42

Linthorst, J. (1994), 'Over Rotterdam: Voordracht ter gelegenheid van het afscheid van Wim Crouwel als directeur van het Museum Boymans-van Beuningen op 27 november 1993 te Rotterdam', in: G. Beijer et al. (eds), *Over Rotterdam: Toekomstvisies aangeboden aan Joop Linthorst bij zijn afscheid als gemeente-raadslid en wethouder van de gemeente Rotterdam*, Rotterdam: 010 Publishers, pp. 14-25

Luxor Theater, F. Happel & LS Concept Design Management (eds) (2001), *Het nieuwe Luxor Theater Rotterdam*, Rotterdam: 010 Publishers

Lynch, K. (1960), *The Image of the City*, Cambridge, Massachusetts/London: The MIT Press

Maandag, B. (2001), *Rotterdam Hoogbouwstad*, Rotterdam: Dienst Stedebouw + Volkshuisvesting en OntwikkelingsBedrijf Rotterdam

Madsen, P. & R. Plunz (eds) (2002), *The Urban Lifeworld: Formation, Perception, Representation*, London/New York: Routledge

Manshanden, W., P. Rutten, P. de Bruijn & O. Koops (2005), *Creatieve industrie in Rotterdam*, Delft: TNO

Manshanden, W.J.J., O. Raspe & P. Rutten (2004), 'De waarde van creatieve industrie', *ESB*, 28 May 2004, pp. 252-254

Marlet, G. & C. van Woerkens (2006), *Atlas voor gemeenten 2006*, Utrecht: Stichting Atlas voor gemeenten

Marsman, E. (1995), 'Voltooid. De moeizame geschie-denis van het Nederlands Foto Instituut', in: H. van Dulken et al. (eds), *Stilstaande beelden: ondergang en opkomst van de fotografie (Jaarboek Kunst en beleid in Nederland*; dl. 7) Amsterdam: Boekmanstichting/Van Gennep, pp. 33-53

Marsman, E. (2005), 'Ieder voor zich en niks voor hen allen: Ontbrekend fotografiebeleid in Nederland', *Boekman*, 5 (63), pp. 11-31

Meer, J. van der (1989), *Wat beweegt de stad? Studie naar de stedelijke dynamiek in de Rotterdamse agglo-meratie*, Ph.D. thesis Rotterdam: Erasmus University

Metz, T. (2002), *Pret! Leisure en landschap*, Rotterdam: NAi Publishers

Meyer, H. (1999), *City and Port: Urban Planning as a Cultural Venture in London, Barcelona, New York, and Rotterdam: changing relations between public urban space and large-scale infrastructure*, Utrecht: International Books

Meyer, H. (1994), 'Monumentaal en informeel', in: J. van de Bout & E. Pasveer (eds), *Kop van Zuid*, Rotterdam: 010 Publishers, pp. 107-120

Meyer, H. (2002), 'Rotterdam: The promise of a new, modern society in a new, modern city 1940 to the present', in: J. Ockman (ed.), *Out of Ground Zero: Case Studies in Urban Reinvention*, Munich (etc.): Prestel, pp. 84-97

Micke, W. (1971), *Wat denkt U er eigenlijk van? Meningen van Rotterdammers over C'70*, Rotterdam: Universitaire Pers Rotterdam

Mik, G. (ed.) (1989), *Herstructurering in Rotterdam: Modernisering en internationalisering en de Kop van Zuid*, Amsterdam/Rotterdam, Koninklijk Nederlands Aardrijkskundig Genootschap/Economisch-geografisch Instituut Erasmus Universiteit Rotterdam

Miles, M., T. Hall & I. Borden (eds) (2000), *The City Cultures Reader*, London/New York: Routledge

Mitchell, W.J.T. (1994), *Picture Theory: Essays on Verbal and Visual Representation*, Chicago/London: The University of Chicago Press

Molotch, H. (1996), 'L.A. as Design Product: How Art Works in a Regional Economy', in: A. J. Scott & E. W. Soja (eds), *The City: Los Angeles and Urban Theory at the End of the Twentieth Century*, Berkeley/Los Angeles, pp. 225-227

Molotch, H., W. Freudenburg & K.E. Paulsen (2000),

'History Repeats Itself, But How? City Character, Urban Tradition, and the Accomplishment of Place', *American Sociological Review*, 65, December, pp. 791-823

Mommaas, H. (2002), 'City Branding: De noodzaak van sociaal-culturele doelen/The necessity of socio-cultural goals', in: Urban Affairs & V. Patteeuw (eds), *City Branding: Image Building & building images*, Rotterdam: NAi Publishers, pp. 35-47

Mommaas, H. (2003), 'De creatieve industrie: Korte introductie van een gedachtengang', in: H. le Blanc et al. (eds), *Het creatief DNA van de regio Eindhoven: Een inventarisatie*, Eindhoven: Stichting Alice, pp. 12-23

Nederlands Foto Instituut, Nederlands Fotoarchief & Nationaal Fotorestauratie Atelier (2001), *Blauwdruk voor het Nederlands fotomuseum*, Rotterdam: Nederlands Foto Instituut, Nederlands Fotoarchief, Nationaal Fotorestauratie Atelier, 1 December 2001

Neill, W.J.V., D.S. Fitzsimons & B. Murtagh (eds) (1995), *Reimaging the Pariah City: Urban development in Belfast & Detroit*, Aldershot (etc.): Avebury

Nelissen, N. (1989), *Stedenstrijd: Beschouwingen over inter- en intra-urbane rivaliteit*, Zeist: Kerckebosch

Noordman, T.B.J. (2004), *Cultuur in de citymarketing*, The Hague: Elsevier Overheid

Notenboom, E.W. & B. Maandag (2003), *Metamorfose Rotterdam 2*, Rotterdam: Rotterdams Dagblad/Eppo W. Notenboom

Nuchelmans, A. (2005), 'Een felomstreden erfenis: Het Wertheimer-legaat als splijtzwam', *Boekman*, 5 (63), pp. 68-77

O'Connor, J. (1999), 'Popular Culture, Reflexivity and Urban Change', in: J. Verwijnen & P. Lehtuvuori (eds), *Creative Cities: Cultural Industries, Urban Development and the Information Society*, Helsinki: University of Art and Design Helsinki, pp. 76-101

O'Connor, J. & D. Wynne (eds) (1996), *From the Margins to the Centre: Cultural production and consumption in the post-industrial city*, Aldershot: Arena

Oldewarris, H. & P. de Winter (eds) (2003), *20 jaar/years 010 1983–2003*, Rotterdam: 010 Publishers

OntwikkelingsBedrijf Rotterdam (2004), *Economische Verkenning Rotterdam 2004*, Rotterdam: OntwikkelingsBedrijf Rotterdam, November 2004

Oosterhout-Bos, R. van (ed.) (2002), *Generating Culture: Roots and Fruits*, z.pl. [The Hague], Deltametropool/Ministerie van VROM

Ostendorf, W. (1990), 'Het imago van Rotterdam', *Geografisch Tijdschrift*, XXIV (3), pp. 273-277

Ostendorf, W., J. Buursink & R. van Engelsdorp

Gastelaars (1988), *Atlas van Nederland: Deel 3: Steden*, The Hague, Staatsuitgeverij

Ostoja, P.O., et al. (eds) (1999), *Kop van Zuid 2*, Rotterdam: 010 Publishers

Oudheusden, P. van & H. Verhey (1986), *De Mensch Deelder*, Utrecht/Antwerp: Veen

Palmer, M. (1981), *New Wave Explosion: How punk became new wave became the 80's*, London/New York: Proteus Books

Panofsky, E. (1972 (first print 1939)), *Studies in Iconology: Humanistic Themes In the Art of the Renaissance*, New York: Icon Editions (etc.)

Park, R.E., E.W. Burgess & R.D. McKenzie (1976 (first print 1925)), *The City*, Chicago/London: The University of Chicago Press

Perrée, R. (2000), 'Zien (1980–1986)', in: P. van Ulzen (ed.), *90 over 80: Tien jaar beeldende kunst in Rotterdam: de dingen, de mensen de plekken*, Rotterdam: NAi Publishers/Stichting Kunstpublicaties Rotterdam, pp. 198-199

Pile, S. & N. Thrift (eds) (2000), *City A-Z*, London/New York: Routledge

Pinder, D. & K.E. Rosing (1988), 'Public policy and planning of the Rotterdam waterfront: a tale of two cities', in: B. S. Hoyle, D.A. Pinder & M.S. Husain (eds), *Revitalising the Waterfront: International Dimensions of Dockland Redevelopment*, London/New York: Belhaven Press, pp. 114-128

Planteam Binnenhaven-Spoorweghaven-Wilhelminapier (1984), *Structuurschets 'DE KOP VAN ZUID'*, Rotterdam: DROS GB GW, October 1984

Projectbureau Rotterdam Waterstad (1987), *Rotterdam 1990: Een inventarisatie van mogelijkheden (eerste concept)*, Rotterdam, Projectbureau 'Rotterdam Waterstad', July 1987

Provoost, M. (1991), 'Het DWL-terrein op de driesprong', in: H. Berens & D.L. Camp (eds), *DWL-terrein Rotterdam*, Rotterdam: 010 Publishers, pp. 32-39

Provoost, M. (1995), 'Massa en weerstand 1920–1945', in: M. Aarts (ed.), *Vijftig jaar wederopbouw Rotterdam: Een geschiedenis van toekomstvisies*, Rotterdam: 010 Publishers, pp. 65-96

Reijndorp, A. & H. Meijer (1987), 'Door de Maas zijn wij: Door niets anders', *Bouw*, (8) 17 April 1987, pp. 60-64

Reijndorp, A. & H. Meijer (eds) (1988), *Stedelijke identiteit en collectief geheugen* (reader bij symposium 2-3-4 November 1988 theater Lantaren/Venster Rotterdam), Rotterdam: Rotterdamse Kunststichting

Reuver, H. de (2000), *Hé de Hef. Een kranige brug*, Rotterdam: Duo Duo

Richards, G. (1996), 'Cultural Tourism in the Netherlands', in: G. Richards (ed.), *Cultural Tourism in Europe*, Oxon, UK, CAB International, pp. 233-247

Riezenkamp, J. (1978), *Kunstbeleid in Rotterdam deelnota: beeldende kunst*, Rotterdam: Gemeentedrukkerij Rotterdam

Riezenkamp, J. (1978), *Kunstbeleid in Rotterdam: Deel 1: persoonlijke beschouwingen*, Rotterdam: Gemeente

Riezenkamp, J. [1979], *Havennota*, [z.pl.]

Righart, H. (1995), *De eindeloze jaren zestig: Geschiedenis van een generatieconflict*, Amsterdam: Arbeiderspers

RKS (1982), *De Kop van Zuid: ontwerp en onderzoek*, Rotterdam: RKS

Rodwin, L. & R.M. Hollister (eds) (1984), *Cities of the Mind: Images and Themes of the City in the Social Sciences*, New York/London: Plenum Press

Roodenburg, L. (2004), Rotterdams Kookboek, Utrecht: Kosmos-Z&K

Rooijendijk, C. (2005), *That City is Mine! Urban Ideal Images in Public Debates and City Plans*, Amsterdam & Rotterdam 1945–1995, Ph.D. Thesis Faculteit der Maatschappij- en Gedragswetenschappen/Amsterdam Institute for Metropolitan and International Development Studies (AMIDSt), Amsterdam: Universiteit van Amsterdam

Rotterdamse Kunststichting sectie Architectuur (1984), *Rapportage betreffende de vestiging van een architectuurmuseum in Rotterdam*, Rotterdam: Rotterdamse Kunststichting, sectie Architectuur, January 1984

Ruarus, P. (1986), 'De permanente strijd van Hard Werken tegen eenvormigheid', *Graficus*, 68, 6 February, pp. 4-13

Rutten, P., W. Manshanden, J. Muskens & O. Koops (2004), *De creatieve industrie in Amsterdam en de regio*, Delft, TNO, 21 September 2004

Sabin, R. (ed.) (1999), *Punk Rock: So What? The cultural legacy of punk*, London/New York: Routledge

Savage, J. (1992), *England's Dreaming: Anarchy, Sex Pistols, Punk Rock and Beyond*, New York: St. Martin's Press

Schenke, M. (2005), *Vaan. Het bewogen bestaan van C.B. Vaandrager*, Amsterdam: De Bezige Bij

Scherpe, K.R. (ed.) (1988), *Die Unwirklichkeit der Städte: Großstadtdarstellungen zwischen Moderne und Postmoderne*, Hamburg: Rowohlt

Schlögel, K. (2005), *Marjampole oder Europas Wiederkehr aus dem Geist der Städte*, Munich/Wien: Carl Hanser Verlag

Schoot, H. (1993), 'De rechte lijn naar het paradijs: Rotterdams modernistische erfenis', in: W. Frijhoff (ed.), *De Rotterdamse cultuur in elf spiegels*, Rotterdam: 010 Publishers, pp. 115-123

Schulte, E. (1994), 'HAL-gebouw, Rotterdam', in: P. Nijhof & E. Schulte (eds), *Herbestemming industrieel erfgoed in Nederland*, Zutphen, Walburg Pers, pp. 130-131

Schwartz, V. (1998), *Spectacular Realities: Early Mass Culture in Fin-de-Siècle Paris*, Berkeley/Los Angeles/London: University of California Press

Scott, A.J. (2000), *The Cultural Economy of Cities*, London: Sage

Skai, H. (1982), *Punk: Versuch der künstlerischen Realisierung einer neuen Lebenshaltung*, [Hamburg]: Sounds

Smeele, N. (2006), *Dance als muziek en vrijetijdsproduct*, Master's Thesis Faculteit der Historische en Kunstwetenschappen, Rotterdam: Erasmus Universiteit

SO (Dienst Stadsontwikkeling) (1986), *SO Juniprojekt 1986*, Rotterdam: Dienst Stadsontwikkeling, June 1986

Staay, A.J. van der (1976), 'Rotterdam kunststad', *Magazijn*, February 1976, p. 16

Staay, A.J. van der (1993), 'Gelukkig één stad zonder culturele identiteit', in: W. Frijhoff (ed.), *De Rotterdamse cultuur in elf spiegels*, Rotterdam: 010 Publishers, pp. 79-91

Stadsontwikkeling, Grondbedrijf en Verkeersdienst Rotterdam (1984), *Binnenstadsplan Rotterdam 1985: Bijstelling van het Basisplan 1946: Concept Werkprogramma*, Rotterdam: Stadsontwikkeling, Grondbedrijf en Verkeersdienst Rotterdam, November 1984

Stadsontwikkeling Rotterdam (1981), *Stedebouw in Rotterdam: Plannen en opstellen 1940–1981*, Amsterdam: Van Gennep

Stadsontwikkeling Rotterdam (1985), *Discussienota Kop van Zuid (3e concept)*, Rotterdam: Stadsontwikkeling Rotterdam, 1 February 1985

Stadsontwikkeling Rotterdam (1987), *Leven in de stad: Rotterdam op weg naar het jaar 2000*, Rotterdam: 010 Publishers

Stadsontwikkeling Rotterdam & Grondbedrijf Rotterdam ([1987]), *De Kop van Zuid: Een stedebouwkundig plan*, Rotterdam: Stadsontwikkeling Rotterdam/

Grondbedrijf Rotterdam

Stevenson, D. (2003), *Cities and Urban Cultures*, Maidenhead/Philadelphia: Open University Press

Stichting C70 (ed.) (1970), *Internationale Gids C70: Rotterdam Communicatie C70 mei-september '70*, Rotterdam: Stichting C70

Stichting Communicatie 70 ([1970]), *C70: Feestelijke ontmoeting van mens en stad*, Rotterdam: Stichting Communicatie 70

Stieber, N. (1994), 'De representatie van de stad Groningen', in: S. Cusveller (ed.), *Stad! De stad en haar identiteit*, Hoogezand, Molior, pp. 59-80

Stokes, M. (ed.) (1994), *Ethnicity, Identity and Music: The Musical Construction of Place*, Oxford/New York: Berg

Straasheijm, W. & S. Buijs (1987), *Vernieuwing van Rotterdam*, Rotterdam: Gemeente Rotterdam, College van Burgemeester en Wethouders, October 1987

Strauss, A.L. (1968), 'Some Varieties of American Urban Symbolism', in: A. L. Strauss (ed.), *The American City: A Sourcebook of Urban Imagery*, London: Allen Lane The Penguin Press, pp. 19-35

Sutcliffe, A. (ed.) (1984), *Metropolis 1890–1940*, London: Mansell

Suttles, G.D. (1984), 'The Cumulative Texture of Local Urban Culture', *The American Journal of Sociology*, 90 (2) September 1984, pp. 283-304

Taverne, E. & C. Wagenaar (2003), '*Tussen elite en massa*: 010 en de opkomst van de architectuur-industrie in Nederland/Between elite and mass: 010 and the rise of the architecture industry in the Netherlands', in: H. Oldewarris & P. de Winter (eds), *20 jaar/years 010 1983–2003*, Rotterdam: 010 Publishers, pp. 29-68

Teaford, J.C. (1990), *The Rough Road to Renaissance: Urban Revitalization in America, 1940–1985*, Baltimore/London: The John Hopkins University Press

Teeffelen, J. van, et al. (eds) (1995), *Omzwervingen door het landschap van de toekomst – Rotterdam 2045, visies op de toekomst van stad, haven en regio*, [s.l.]

Thornton, S. (1995), *Club Cultures: Music, Media and Subcultural Capital*, Cambridge: Polity Press

Timm, T. (2003), *Hässliches Berlin: Berlin und sein negatives Image. Eine empirische Untersuchung*, Master's Thesis Institut für Europäische Ethnologie, Berlin, Humboldt Universität

Tio, S. (ed.) (2001), *30 jaar popfestivals in Nederland: Van Lochem tot Lowlands*, [s.l.], Koninklijke Theodorus Niemeyer B.V.

Ulzen, P. van (ed.) (2000), *90 over 80: Tien jaar beeldende kunst in Rotterdam: De dingen, de mensen, de plekken*, Rotterdam: NAi Publishers/Stichting Kunstpublicaties Rotterdam

Ulzen, P. van (2001), '1987. Nota Beeldende Kunst in Rotterdam', in: C. Boele et al. (eds), *Een eeuw Rotterdam. 101 fragmenten uit de 20ste eeuw*, Rotterdam/Zaltbommel, De Maze/Europese Bibliotheek, pp. 237-238

Vader, J.W.C. (1990), 'Het project Waterstad in de binnenstadontwikkeling van Rotterdam', *Geografisch Tijdschrift*, XXIV (3), pp. 266-272

Vanstiphout, W. (1995), 'Leegte: 1945–1965', in: M. Aarts (ed.), *Vijftig jaar wederopbouw Rotterdam: Een geschiedenis van toekomstvisies*, Rotterdam: 010 Publishers, pp. 113-144

Vanstiphout, W. (2005), *Maak een stad: Rotterdam en de architectuur van J.H. van den Broek*, Rotterdam: 010 Publishers

Vegt, C. van de & W.J.J. Manshanden (1996), *Steden en stadsgewesten: economische ontwikkelingen 1970–2015*, The Hague: SDU Uitgevers

Ven, C.J.M. van de (1977), 'De Rotterdamse bijdrage aan het Nieuwe Bouwen', *Plan: Maandblad voor ontwerp en omgeving*, (2), pp. 9-24

Verhelst, M., et al. (eds) (2001), *Agora: Tijdschrift voor sociaal-ruimtelijke vraagstukken: Themanummer over vrijplaatsen*, Utrecht: Stichting Tijdschrift Agora

Verwijnen, J. & P. Lehtuvuori (eds) (1999), *Creative Cities: Cultural Industries, Urban Development and the Information Society*, Helsinki, University of Art and Design Helsinki

Vijgen, J. & R. van Engelsdorp Gastelaars (1990), 'Hoe stedelijk is de Maasstad? Voorzieningen, bewoners en leefpatronen in Rotterdam en Amsterdam', *Geografisch Tijdschrift*, XXIV (3), pp. 241-251

Vletter, M. de (2004), *De kritiese jaren zeventig/The Critical Seventies: Architectuur en stedenbouw in Nederland 1968–1982/Architecture and Urban Planning in the Netherlands 1968–1982*, Rotterdam: NAi Publishers

Vries, F. de (2001), 'Vreemde stad: In Rotterdam zijn de nieuwe creatieven "lekker bezig"', *de Volkskrant*, 4 January 2001

Vries, J. de (1965), *Amsterdam Rotterdam: Rivaliteit in economisch-historisch perspectief*, Bussum: C.A.J. van Dishoeck

Wagenaar, C. (1992), *Welvaartsstad in wording: De wederopbouw van Rotterdam*, Rotterdam: NAi Publishers

Wagenaar, C. (ed.) (2005), *Happy: Cities and Public*

Happiness in Post-War Europe, Rotterdam:
NAi Publishers

Wagener, M. (1994), *Kunstgreep of toverkunst? Kunst en cultuur in het stedelijk beleid van zes Nederlandse gemeenten*, Master's Thesis Utrecht, Rijksuniversiteit Utrecht

Wagener, W.A. (1951), 'Rotterdam', in: C. Oorthuys et al., *Land en volk: Steden (De schoonheid van ons land;* 10), Amsterdam: Contact, pp. 68-73

Ward, S.V. (1998), *Selling Places: The Marketing and Promotion of Towns and Cities 1850–2000*, London: E & FN Spon

Wattjes, J.G. (1926), *Nieuw-Nederlandsche Bouwkunst*, Amsterdam: Uitgevers-Maatschappij 'Kosmos'

Wentholt, R. (1968), *De binnenstadsbeleving en Rotterdam*, Rotterdam: Ad. Donker

Werlemann, H. & A. David-Tu (1983), *Rotterdams kadeboek*, Rotterdam: 010 Publishers

Wiardi Beckman Stichting (1988), *De grote steden, hun stadsgewesten en het compacte-stadbeleid*, Amsterdam: Wiardi Beckman Stichting

Wigmans, G. (1998), *De facilitaire stad: Rotterdams grondbeleid en postmodernisering*, Delft, Delft University Press

Williams, R. (1985), 'The metropolis and the emergence of Modernism', in: E. Timms & D. Kelley (eds), *Unreal City: Urban experience in modern European literature and art*, Manchester, Manchester University Press, pp. 13-24

Wilschut, R. (1991), 'Tien jaar breken en bouwen', in: H. Berens & D.L. Camp (eds), *DWL-terrein Rotterdam: Van waterfabriek tot woonwijk*, Rotterdam: 010 Publishers, pp. 40-47

Winter, P. de (1988), *Evenementen in Rotterdam: Ahoy' E55 Floriade C70*, Rotterdam: 010 Publishers

Winter, P. de, J. de Jong et al. (eds) (1982), *Havenarchitectuur: Een inventarisatie van industriële gebouwen in het Rotterdamse havengebied*, Rotterdam: Rotterdamse Kunststichting Uitgeverij

Wohl, R.R. & A.L. Strauss (1957), 'Symbolic Representation and the Urban Milieu', *The American Journal of Sociology*, 63 (5) March 1958, pp. 523-532

Wynne, D. (ed.) (1992), *The Culture Industry: The Arts in Urban Regeneration*, Aldershot, Avebury

Zijderveld, A.C. (1991), *Rotterdam 1990: Analyse en evaluatie van de bestuurlijke gang van zaken*, Rotterdam, 31 January 1991

Zijderveld, A.C. (1994), *Van stedelijkheid en stedelijke festivals*, Rotterdam: Stichting Rotterdam Festivals

Zijderveld, A.C. (ed.) (1996), *Rotterdam naar 2005: Visies vanuit de wetenschap*, Kampen, Kok Agora

Zijderveld, A.C. (1998), *A Theory of Urbanity: The economic and civic culture of cities*, New Brunswick (USA)/London: Transaction Publishers

Zukin, S. (1995), *The Cultures of Cities*, Cambridge MA/Oxford: Blackwell

Zukin, S. (2001), 'How to Create a Culture Capital: Reflections on Urban Markets and Places', in: I. Blazwick (ed.), *Century City: Art and Culture in the Modern Metropolis*, London: Tate Publishing, pp. 258-264

Zukin, S. (1982), *Loft Living: Culture and Capital in Urban Change*, Baltimore/London: The Johns Hopkins University Press

Zundert, A. van (1988), *Wie verhuist er naar Rotterdam? Analyse van de binnenlandse vestiging*, Rotterdam: Gemeentelijk Bureau voor Onderzoek en Statistiek

List of interviewees

Carel Alons, Riek Bakker, Cees van der Geer,
Daan van der Have, Beerend Lenstra,
Ted Langenbach, Evan van der Most,
Hans Oldewarris, Jacques van Heijningen,
Hans Kombrink, Joop Linthorst, Paul Martens,
Henk Molenaar, Paul Noorman, Bas van der Ree,
Jan Riezenkamp, Adriaan van der Staay,
Bob Visser, Bas Vroege